3 GROUP BOMBER COMMAND
AN OPERATIONAL RECORD

To: John

"Remembering The Many"

All The Best

Steve Smith

3 GROUP BOMBER COMMAND
AN OPERATIONAL RECORD

Chris Ward
and
Steve Smith

Pen & Sword
AVIATION

First published in Great Britain in 2008 by
Pen and Sword Aviation
an imprint of
Pen & Sword Books Ltd
47 Church Street
Barnsley
South Yorkshire
S70 2AS

ISBN 978-1-84415-796-9

A CIP catalogue record for this book is
available from the British Library.

Typeset in 10/12 Times New Roman by
Concept, Huddersfield, West Yorkshire

Printed and bound in England by
CPI UK

Pen & Sword Books Ltd incorporates the Imprints of Pen & Sword Aviation,
Pen & Sword Maritime, Pen & Sword Military, Wharncliffe Local History,
Pen & Sword Select, Pen & Sword Military Classics, Leo Cooper,
Remember When, Seaforth Publishing and Frontline Publishing.

For a complete list of Pen & Sword titles please contact
PEN & SWORD BOOKS LIMITED
47 Church Street, Barnsley, South Yorkshire, S70 2AS, England
E-mail: enquiries@pen-and-sword.co.uk
Website: www.pen-and-sword.co.uk

Contents

Foreword

For some unfathomable reason hardly anything has been written about the exploits of Bomber Command's 3 Group during the Second World War. Numerous books have been written about the other Groups, recording their heroic involvement and sacrifices in Bomber Command's campaigns, but there is a conspicuous absence of a similar reference work on 3 Group. This sad omission is now rectified with this book. I have covered many 3 Group squadrons in my RAF Bomber Command Profile series, and have drawn heavily on those works.

I am fortunate to count Steve Smith as a good friend. He is the 218 Squadron archivist and a general authority on 3 Group as a whole. We often talked about a book, and now, at last, we have done something about it. Steve made available to me his massive store of Group, station and squadron records, and between us we decided what to include. When I write a book, I do so as if it were specifically for me. I like detail, facts and figures, dates, who did what and when. I like to bring everything about the subject under one cover, so that I don't have to delve and leaf through a library of books to find the snippet of information I want. I also like to think that I have included so much that there will be no point in another author covering the same subject. Of course, that is nonsense, as there is always something else to discover and to write. There is also not an infinite amount of space available, so much of what I would have put into a profile has had to be omitted. The narrative, therefore, reads very much like a diary of events, and is basically an account of Bomber Command's war, with the 3 Group involvement woven into it. Steve and I have tried to be even-handed with regard to the amount of information provided on each squadron, but obviously the longer serving units get the most mentions. One unique feature of 3 Group was its clandestine squadrons operating on behalf of SOE and SIS. They did not fit comfortably into wartime Bomber Command, but played a massively important role, and their story is a part of 3 Group's story. However, it is a story that requires a book in itself, and many fine works have been written on the subject providing a detailed operational history. We have recorded some events to give a flavour of the heroism of the crews of the 'moon' squadrons and to acknowledge their part in the 3 Group story. Conversely, although the Pathfinder Force came nominally under the control of 3 Group until being granted its own Group status, we have chosen to treat it as being outside of 3 Group for the purpose of this book.

Finally, the story of Bomber Command is one principally of people, not aircraft, targets and bombs, and we have tried to reflect this in the personal information included. Much of the information in the narrative is backed up in the appendices, and readers will thereby be able to make a speedy reference to any point of interest. Steve and I fervently hope that we have done justice to those who served 3 Group in WWII as that magnificent and now aged generation fades into history.

General Notes

This is a reference work on the activities of 3 Group and the squadrons serving with it in an operational capacity at some time during the Second World War. Bomber Command operated exclusively from stations in the UK, and used overseas bases purely for shuttle operations, or as advanced staging posts for specific purposes. For this reason, periods spent on detachment, or permanent postings to overseas Commands do not fall within the scope of this work.

This work is not intended to serve as a comprehensive history of the Group or squadrons, but to provide as much information as possible about them in a non-anecdotal form. The brief history narrative is basically an account of Bomber Command's war, with the Group's involvement interwoven into it. The publications listed in the Bibliography are not only recommended reading, but represent the best available sources of information for serious students of the subject. The operational record is based almost entirely on the figures provided in The Bomber Command War Diaries by Martin Middlebrook and Chris Everitt, and I am indebted to Martin Middlebrook for allowing me to use them.

An aircraft is included in aircraft history section if:

(a) it spent time on squadron charge, no matter how briefly, and irrespectively of whether or not it operated, and;
(b) the type was used operationally by the squadron.

Information is restricted in most cases to where from and where to, unless it completed its service with the squadron, in which case, some detail of its demise appears. Aircraft which failed to return have the date and target recorded. Where no information follows the serial number of a type still in use when the squadron departed Bomber Command, or at war's end, it can be assumed that the aircraft was still on squadron strength. However, where there is a blank space following the serial number of a type which has been withdrawn from service with Bomber Command, it signifies that I don't know its ultimate fate. An absence of information does not imply that the aircraft flew no operations during its time with the squadron.

In the narrative we have selected 149 Squadron to be representative of a 3 Group Wellington unit, 218 Squadron for Stirlings and 115 Squadron for Lancasters. This enables us to be more detailed with regard to incidents and losses in the limited space available. It can be assumed that what happened to these units was typical across the Group.

Finally, information has been drawn from a variety of sources, ranging from Records Branch to individuals with squadron connections, and I am grateful for their contributions. There will, however, inevitably be errors and omissions when dealing with a subject as vast as Bomber Command.

A special mention is due to Chris Salter of Midland Counties Publications, without whose generous assistance and encouragement at the outset, I would not have been able to compile a complete list of all operational aircraft on charge with Bomber Command squadrons during the war period, a list, incidentally, which comprises some 28,000 entries.

CHAPTER ONE

A Narrative History

Beginnings

3 Group takes shape. Pre-war organisation

On the 1st of May 1936 the Western Area Air Defence of Great Britain was renamed No. 3 (Bomber) Group under the command of Air Vice Marshall Patrick Henry Lyon Playfair CB, CVO, MC. The Group's initial head-quarters was located near Andover, Wiltshire, where it would remain for the rest of the year. When the Group relocated, its new headquarters would be at a station whose name was to become synonymous with the activities of the Group during the forthcoming world conflict. The arrival of the Group's HQ at Mildenhall in Suffolk would also establish a permanent association with East Anglia.

The move to Mildenhall in January 1937 was the result of the Air Ministry's decision to reorganise its existing Groups, which were 1 Group with it's single-engine light bombers, 2 Group equipped with twin-engine medium bombers and 3 Group, which operated twin-engine heavies. The majority of the squadrons within 3 Group were equipped with the ungainly all metal-structured, fabric-covered Vickers Virginia. This heavy night-bomber first entered service in 1924. The second type was to be the RAF's last biplane heavy bomber, the Handley Page Heyford. This aircraft entered service with 99 Squadron, then based at Upper Heyford, on the 14th of November 1933. Both aircraft had a good service record within the Group and were generally well liked by those who operated and maintained them. Two other types of heavy bomber serving with the Group in fewer numbers were the Fairey Hendon, which equipped 38 and 115 Squadrons for a brief spell and the Handley Page Harrow, which entered service with 214 Squadron in January 1937.

In 1937 the Group's strength stood at fourteen squadrons, 10, 78, 97 and 166 based at Boscombe Down, 58 and 215 at Driffield, 7 and 107 at Finningley and Leconfield respectively, 88 and 99 at Mildenhall, 9 and 214 at Scampton and finally 114 and 139 at Wyton. In February 1938 the first of a number of important changes took place within the Group. Air Vice-Marshall Playfair was appointed Air-Officer-Commanding (Bomber) Group with effect from the 21st of February, thus concluding, for the time being at least, an association with 3 Group. This association had begun in September

1933 when he was appointed AOC for the Wessex Bombing Area, the original name of the Western Area Air Defence of Great Britain. This highly respected officer would be called upon again by 3 Group half way through the war. He was succeeded at 3 Group with effect from the 14th of February by 43-year-old Air Commodore Arthur Ashford Benjamin Thompson, MC and Bar, AFC. Thompson had been commissioned as a Second Lieutenant on probation to the RFC in June 1913. He served in France with 14 Squadron RFC in August 1914, and by the end of the Great War he had risen to the rank of Temporary Lieutenant Colonel, having by then commanded 54, 56 and 33 Squadrons.

On the 10th of October 1938 3 Group introduced into service the revolutionary Vickers Wellington, the product of a design team led by the company's chief designer, Rex Pierson, and including Barnes Wallis, whose fame and impact on the war lay in the future. A revolutionary feature of the type was its geodetic construction, a fabric covered metal latticework, which enabled it to sustain and survive quite severe damage, and yet be easily repaired and quickly returned to service. The unit selected to introduce the Wellington to the RAF was 99 Squadron, based at the time at Mildenhall. Tragically, A/Cdr Thompson was killed on the 8th of August 1939 when he somehow came into contact with a revolving propeller while viewing the bombing up of a 115 Squadron Wellington at Marham. The loss of such a fine officer was a sad blow to the Group and Bomber Command.

His successor, Air Vice Marshal John Eustace Arthur Baldwin, DSO, OBE, a 47-year-old former WWI veteran, assumed command of the Group on the 29th of August 1939. A former officer in the 8th Royal Irish Hussars Regiment, Baldwin joined the RFC in 1914, and by October 1916 he was in command of 55 Squadron equipped with the DH4 bomber. Various appointments during the twenties kept Baldwin mostly in the Middle East, until he became Air Aide-de-Camp to the King in 1931, a role he relinquished in 1933. He was serving as Air-Officer-Commanding 21 (Training) Group when he answered the call to take over 3 Group.

In the final days of peace 3 Group consisted of six frontline squadrons, with a further two in reserve, each equipped with the Wellington. It could boast a force of more than 100 aircraft located at five East Anglian airfields. So successful would the Wellington prove to be, that it would remain the mainstay of bomber operations until well into the war, and still equip some squadrons in the second half of 1943.

1939

War again; cracks in the theory; the 'phoney' war; lessons learned

As September 1939 began, the disposition of 3 Group's frontline squadrons was as follows. 9 Squadron, commanded by W/C Lloyd, was based at

Honington, 37 Squadron at Feltwell with W/C Fogerty at the helm, 38 and 115 Squadrons resided at Marham under W/C Adams and W/C Rowe respectively, while Mildenhall was home to both W/C Walker's 99 Squadron and W/C Russell's 149 Squadron. Before September was over changes in leadership and station would affect a number of these units.

9 Squadron's history stretched back to December 1914, and it was, in fact, the second lowest numbered squadron to serve with Bomber Command during the second world war. As war broke out it was actually the lowest numbered squadron in the Command, as 7 Squadron would not be re-formed for a further eleven months. During its current incarnation the squadron operated successively Vimys, Virginias and Heyfords until converting to Wellingtons at Stradishall early in 1939.

37 Squadron first saw the light of day briefly in April 1916. The incarnation that is relevant to this narrative, however, began in April 1937, when 37 Squadron was reborn as a heavy bomber unit from B Flight of 214 Squadron, and in May 1939 the squadron traded its Harrows for Wellingtons. 38 Squadron's original formation predated that of 37 Squadron by two weeks. After spending years on the shelf it re-emerged when B Flight of 99 Squadron assumed the 38 Squadron designation in September 1935. In November 1938 Wellingtons arrived to replace the Hendons that had been operated solely by 38 Squadron.

99 Squadron dated from August 1917, and after its inevitable disbandment following the Great War it was reborn on the 1st of April 1924 as a bomber unit, operating a number of types until it became the first to receive the Wellington in October 1938. 115 Squadron came into existence on the 1st of December 1917, and then spent years on the shelf until June 1937, when it was re-formed at Marham from B Flight of 38 Squadron. Wellingtons replaced the Harrows in April 1939. 149 Squadron's Conversion from Heyfords to Wellingtons began on the 20th of January 1939, with the arrival on charge of L4252, L4253 and L4254. These were followed on the 24th by L4255, L4256, L4257 and L4258, and by L4249 and L4259 on the 6th of February, L4263 and L4264 on the 7th, L4265 and L4266 on the 10th, L4271 and L4272 on the 17th, and L4270 on the 9th of March. The squadron was thus the third in Bomber Command to receive the type after 99 and 38 Squadrons. W/C Russell had been in post since the 5th of January, and on the 1st of September, just two days before the declaration of war, he presided over a complement of twenty-four officers and 194 airmen, with twenty Mk I Wellingtons and three Mk Ias.

As war broke out each Group was required to hold one squadron in reserve to perform the function of a training unit to maintain a steady flow of operationally ready airmen to the front line. 214 Squadron was selected as the 3 Group reserve unit and was 'scattered' to Methwold on the 3rd of September under the command of W/C Sanderson. The original 214 Squadron was born on the same day as the Royal Air Force, the 1st of April 1918. Following disbandment it remained on the shelf until its re-forming on the

16th of September 1935. The squadron became the eighth in Bomber Command to equip with Wellingtons, when the first three examples were taken on charge on the 26th of May 1939. The squadron contained a sprinkling of men who would make a name for themselves as the war progressed, and the name 'Pick' Pickard will appear frequently in the story of 3 Group. One of his contemporaries at 214 squadron in 1939 was S/L Hugh Constantine, who would eventually become station commander at Elsham Wolds and see out the war as successor to Sir Ralph Cochrane as Air-Officer-Commanding 5 Group. Another future shining light was S/L Paul Harris, although he had been posted to 149 Squadron as a flight commander before the outbreak of war, and he flew his first operational sortie on the second day of the conflict. In August 1940, he would be given command of the newly re-forming 7 Squadron, and lead it through the troublesome introduction of the Stirling into operational service. A contemporary of Paul Harris, in fact, the other flight commander, was Denys Balsden, nicknamed 'God', who would go on to command 97 Squadron and lose his life in a blazing Manchester.

At 11 o'clock on the morning of Sunday the 3rd of September 1939 the mournful tones of Prime Minister Chamberlain announced over the airwaves that Britain was once more at war with Germany. 37 and 149 Squadrons had the honour of conducting 3 Group's first operation, which took place on that very day. Six Wellingtons from the former and three from the latter were dispatched to the Schillig Roads in search of enemy warships. The experiences of the 149 Squadron section reflected those of the others taking part. The A Flight commander, S/L Dabinett, took off from Mildenhall at 18.35 hours in L4254, with the crews of F/O Turner and Sgt Way in L4252 and L4264 respectively. In what was described as adverse weather conditions they were unable even to reach the search area, let alone locate any elements of the German fleet. Approaching darkness exacerbated the difficulties and they turned for home. As training to date had not dealt with the delicate subject of landing with bombs still on board, all the crews followed orders and jettisoned their four 500 lb bombs into the sea before touching down five minutes either side of 22.00 hours. 149 Squadron was fortunate in having two particularly fine officers as flight commanders, both of whom would achieve squadron commander status before long. S/L Dabinett would command 3 Group's 115 Squadron between July 1940 and January 1941, and 1 Group's 12 Squadron from the end of July 1942 until February 1943. The B Flight commander was the already mentioned S/L Paul Harris, formerly of 214 Squadron.

On the afternoon of the 4th 149 Squadron was directed to send formations on two separate operations to bomb elements of the German Navy in the Brunsbüttel area at the mouth of the Kiel Canal. The first, taking off at 14.46, consisted of six aircraft led by S/L Harris in L4302, although one of this section failed to get away. The force encountered bad weather during the outward flight, causing the formation to break up, and a number of aircraft returned to base. S/L Harris reached the target area, where he mistook the River Eider near Tönning for the mouth of the Kiel Canal, and dropped his bombs there. Only F/O Macrae claimed to have attacked the primary target in L4265, aiming his bombs at a warship in Brunsbüttel harbour. In the event the 500 pounders missed the ship and exploded on the quayside. In fact, he almost certainly attacked the Danish port of Esbjerg, where a house was destroyed and two people were killed. A court of enquiry failed to reach a definitive conclusion on the basis of insufficient evidence, and the squadron commander testified to the previously unblemished record of the pilot and the navigator involved. The second raid by three aircraft was led by F/L Duguid in L4272, but the weather conditions thwarted their attempt to reach the target area, and they made do with a low sweep across what they believed to be the German Frisian Islands to carry out reconnaissance. They reported no airfields or anti-aircraft activity, but Group suspected that they had actually overflown the more southerly Dutch Frisians by mistake. F/L Duguid was another 149 Squadron member who would attain higher command later in the war, when being appointed as the commanding officer of 196 Squadron in March 1943. At the time it was a 1 Group Wellington unit, and W/C Duguid vacated it at the time of its posting to 3 Group.

9 Squadron also dispatched two sections from Honington, at 15.39 and 16.04, led by F/L Grant and S/L Lamb respectively. The former attacked its target from 5,000 feet, but was so heavily engaged by AA that none of the crews hung around to observe the effect of their bombs. S/L Lamb pressed home his attack at Brunsbüttel from 300 feet, but he was also heavily engaged by flak and fighters and beat a hasty retreat without seeing the result of his gallant attack. He returned safely to base, but two other 9 Squadron Wellingtons failed to make it back having fallen victim to flak and fighters, and thus F/Ss Borley and Turner and their crews became 3 Group's first operational casualties of the war. The casualty list grew further on the 8th, when another 9 Squadron crew was lost to a training crash in Suffolk. That night 99 Squadron launched three aircraft to drop leaflets in the Hanover/Brunswick region. One returned early with technical problems, while the other two failed to locate the cities under what they described as a very effective blackout. They dispensed their pamphlets randomly over Germany, and reported on return that they found it impossible to distinguish between land and sea. It should be remembered, that only 4 Group had trained its crews in the art of night flying, and it was, therefore, a new experience for crews from other Groups to fly nocturnally. 99 Squadron was the first 3 Group operational squadron to change its address, when it moved to Newmarket on the 15th after almost five years at Mildenhall. The squadron had actually dispersed to Elmdon, now Birmingham Airport, on the 9th in accordance with Air Ministry instructions prepared before the war to keep the enemy guessing as to the disposition of the bomber fleet. It was a policy quickly abandoned, and Newmarket would remain home to 99 Squadron for the next eighteen months. A number of changes in

leadership took place towards the end of the month, when W/C Walker was posted from 99 Squadron to 8 Initial Training Wing on the 26th to be replaced by W/C Griffiths, and W/C Cole was promoted from within 9 Squadron on the following day on the departure of W/C Lloyd, who in 1941, having risen to the rank of AVM, would become Air-Officer-Commanding Malta.

What the Americans dubbed the 'Phoney War' restricted operational activity at this stage of the proceedings to daylight armed reconnaissance sweeps in search of enemy shipping. Following the flurry of activity immediately on the declaration of war, operations became sporadic. It was forbidden to drop bombs on enemy territory for fear of reprisals, and ships could only be attacked if at sea, in case a stray bomb damaged civilian property. As the Command was about to learn, ships were difficult to hit, and boasted a formidable defence in the form of their own batteries and an umbrella of fighters. The pre-war belief that the bomber formation would always get through to its target by daylight had not yet been tested, but when it was it would be found wanting. Even then it would prove to be a difficult idea to dislodge from the minds of its advocates. On the 29th of September 5 Group's 144 Squadron lost five Hampdens, but the warning bells did not sound. On the 30th of October three operations were mounted from Mildenhall involving eighteen aircraft, six each from 99 and 149 Squadrons on operations CA10 and CA11 respectively, and a further six aircraft drawn from the two squadrons on CA12. The objective was to attack enemy ships around the Frisian island of Terschelling, but nothing was found, and the aircraft returned safely to base, this time all but one with bombs still on board. Also on this day 9 Squadron sustained the loss of two more crews, and thus it continued to be the only 3 Group squadron to suffer fatal casualties since the outbreak of war. The previously mentioned S/L Lamb, a New Zealander, and F/O Chandler were involved in a mid-air collision at 800 feet over Honington village while training, and both Wellingtons plunged to earth killing all nine occupants.

115 Squadron, in the meantime, was not involved in these early forays, and enjoyed a gentle introduction to operations. The squadron did not operate for the first time until the 8th of October, when despatching six aircraft to Norwegian waters to ascertain the whereabouts of enemy shipping. All returned safely from what was an uneventful operational debut. While 2, 3 and 5 Groups were engaged in the fruitless activity of flying shipping sweeps and occasional propaganda leaflet drops, the Whitley crews of 4 Group undertook most of the long range leafleting sorties, or 'Nickels'. In so doing they gained invaluable experience in navigating over hostile territory in the dark, but also suffered unimaginable hardships, often spending ten hours and more aloft in their unheated aircraft, the pilots having to scratch ice from the inside of their windscreens in order to see outside.

149 Squadron installed a new commanding officer on the 6th of November on the departure to No. 6 School of Technical Training of W/C Russell.

W/C Kellett AFC had once been a member of the Long Range Development Unit, and had led the record breaking non-stop flight by the unit's Vickers Wellesleys from Ismalia in Egypt to Darwin Australia, a distance of 7,158.7 miles, which they covered in 48 hours between 5–7th of November 1938. On the 3rd of December twenty-four Wellingtons from 38, 115 and 149 Squadrons were sent to attack German warships in the Heligoland area. W/C Kellett led the 149 Squadron element of twelve aircraft in N2960, and despite the force being intercepted by fighters, no aircraft were lost. However, it was on this occasion that a 115 Squadron crew inadvertently dropped a hang-up onto Heligoland, the first RAF bomb to fall onto German soil in the war. On the 14th 99 Squadron lost five out of twelve Wellingtons during an attack on a convoy in the Schillig Roads. Three of them fell to fighters, and one of the victims collided with a fourth Wellington, causing it also to crash into the sea, while a fifth was shot down by flak. On return a further aircraft crashed killing three of the crew, and most of the surviving Wellingtons bore the scars of battle. Still the High Command failed to give credit to the enemy fighters, and blamed poor formation flying as the major contributory factor behind the disaster.

On the 18th another twenty-four Wellingtons drawn from 9, 37 and 149 Squadrons were sent in search of shipping off Wilhemshaven. Twenty-two aircraft reached the target area, and carried out an attack from 13,000 feet in clear conditions. As they turned for home enemy fighters fell upon them, and a running battle ensued in which twelve Wellingtons were shot down into the sea. 9 Squadron lost four aircraft without survivors, while a fifth ditched off the Norfolk coast and one man was lost. 37 Squadron likewise had four aircraft shot down and a fifth crash-landed in enemy territory. In all only five out of the twenty-six crewmen involved survived as prisoners of war. 149 Squadron got off relatively lightly in sustaining two losses without survivors. One of these, N2961, was successfully ditched by F/O Briden approximately 50 miles off the Norfolk coast, and S/L Harris attempted to drop a dinghy. On release it fouled the Wellington's tailplane, and made the rest of the return journey somewhat difficult. Harris eventually landed safely at Coltishall, where it was discovered that the Wellington had sustained a number of bullet holes. At least three of F/O Briden's crew were observed to climb out of the ditched Wellington, but no survivors were found by the Cromer lifeboat, and two bodies were washed ashore some time later. This disaster, and that of four days earlier, had a profound effect on attitudes to unescorted daylight operations. The 'Phoney War' and the arrival of a harsh winter restricted activity from this point, and allowed time for the policy makers to reconsider their options. The result of this would be effectively to commit Bomber Command, with the exception of 2 Group, to waging war by night, but it would be some time yet before the bombing war began in earnest. On the 27th of December W/C Mills was appointed as the new commanding officer of 115 Squadron in place of W/C Rowe DFC, who was posted to Maintenance Command.

1940

The 'phoney' war drags on; the Norwegian debacle; Vegetables and Nickels; nocturnal operations over Germany; the secret war; invasion fever; target London

The winter seemed to deepen as the year progressed, and it would be towards the end of February before it loosened its grip sufficiently to allow unrestricted operations. Because of this 3 Group dispatched only nine Wellington on Nickel sorties during mid January, starting with Hamburg on the 11/12th. On the 17th of January W/C Cole was posted from 9 Squadron to 75 Squadron at Harwell, and the 38 year-old New Zealander S/L McKee stepped up from his flight commander position to fill the breach. Bearing the nickname 'Square' because of his squat body, he had come to 9 Squadron from HQ 3 Group on the same day that W/C Cole was appointed commanding officer back in September. Thereafter, from February to April, the Wellington squadrons were only involved in isolated shipping searches in the North Sea, and a few further leafleting operations. A total of thirty Wellingtons were employed in daylight shipping searches on the 11th and 13th of February, but no targets were located. In between, on the 12th, 214 Squadron moved to Stradishall and welcomed W/C Nuttall as the new commanding officer. Between the 17–18th of February and the 6–7th of April 3 Group Wellingtons were responsible for 102 Nickel sorties. Night reconnaissance operations on the 20/21st, which were logged as training sweeps, cost the Group two 38 Squadron aircraft and another from 99 Squadron. One disappeared over the sea, a second was abandoned over Norfolk, and the last mentioned force-landed in Cambridgeshire. Three nights later 99 Squadron's N3004 force-landed in Belgium during a Nickel sortie, and the crew was interned for a short period before being returned to the squadron. Among a number of losses during this time of relative inactivity was that of the previously mentioned F/O Macrae DFC, who had been the subject of the court of enquiry concerning the accidental bombing of Esbjerg back in September. On the afternoon of the 8th of March he took off from the Vickers works at Weybridge to ferry N3017 back to Honington after it had undergone some modification work. It crashed immediately and burst into flames, and there were no survivors from among the five occupants.

214 Squadron added a third Flight on the 10th of March under F/L Wells, who was responsible for training and armaments, while the original A and B Flights had as their commanders two more officers who would go on to greater things. The already mentioned S/L Denys Balsdon led A Flight, while B Flight's commander was S/L Sellick, who would be in command of 7 Squadron at the time of its posting as a founder member to the Pathfinders in August 1942. Later, in 1944, he would command 576 Squadron, a 1 Group Lancaster unit.

Wellingtons were not involved in the first intentional bombing of enemy territory, which took place on the 19/20th of March. In retaliation for the inadvertent slaying by a stray bomb of a civilian on the island of Hoy during a *Luftwaffe* raid on elements of the Royal Navy at Scapa Flow, thirty Whitleys and twenty Hampdens carried out a two-phase attack on the seaplane base at Hörnum on the island of Sylt. Returning crews reported a highly successful outcome, which was enthusiastically reported by the press, but photographic reconnaissance on the 6th of April failed to detect any signs of damage. Such spurious claims would return to haunt the Command with the publication of the Butt Report in the summer of the following year.

A new squadron, one which would become among the most prolific in Bomber Command, took its first tentative operational steps at this time, unnoticed by all around. The seeds of 75 (NZ) Squadron were sown in 1937, when the New Zealand government placed an order for thirty Wellingtons, and sent New Zealand personnel to the UK for training and to ferry the aircraft home. On the 1st of June 1939 No. 1 New Zealand Flight was formed at Marham under the command of Squadron Leader Buckley RNZAF, and drew its personnel from among its countrymen serving in RAF units, and those arriving from home. At the outbreak of war these men expressed a wish to remain in the UK and participate in the conflict, and the New Zealand government magnanimously agreed to waive its entitlement to the Wellingtons ordered, and placed its personnel at the disposal of the RAF. Rather than distribute these airmen among existing units, it was decided to retain the New Zealand Flight in its present form, and raise it to full squadron status. In the meantime, however, it changed address a number of times to Harwell in September, Honington in January 1940, and Feltwell on the 16th of February. At the time a 75 Squadron already existed as a Group pool training unit based at Stradishall equipped with Ansons and Wellingtons. The declaration of war brought a move to Harwell, where it relinquished its Ansons. On the 4th of April 1940 75 Squadron was absorbed into 15 OTU, and on that day the number was passed to the New Zealand Flight, and the words New Zealand were added. S/L Buckley, who was already in his mid-forties, had come to England on an exchange arrangement in 1937, and prior to his posting to the NZ Flight he had been a flight commander at 38 Squadron. He was now promoted to Wing Commander and remained in command of the squadron. Although not officially coming into existence until the 4th of April 1940 at Feltwell, its formation was anticipated by the mounting of three leafleting sorties on the 27th of March to Brunswick, Ulzen and Lüneberg, led by the flight commander S/L Kay in P9206. The other aircraft and crew captains were F/O Collins in P9207 and F/O Adams in P9212, and all three returned safely. The same three Wellingtons plus P9210 took part in the squadron's second operation, which was a similar Nickeling trip to northern Germany on the 6/7th of April, and this too was completed without incident. As unfolding events in Skandinavia began to attract attention, 115 Squadron was detached to Coastal Command, and moved north to Kinloss on the 30th of March to fly reconnaissance patrols off Denmark. A patrol on the 7th of April cost the squadron its first failures to return from operations, when N2949 and P2524 were both shot down by BF110s off Denmark, and there were no survivors from the crews of P/Os Gayford and Wickencamp respectively.

April was the month in which the gloves finally came off, and the 'Phoney' war was consigned to history. At first light on the 9th German troops marched unopposed into Denmark, and began sea and airborne landings in southern Norway. Although Denmark was a lost cause from the outset, the British and French governments responded by despatching forces by sea, to attempt their own landings at Narvik in Norway. Prevented by the extreme range from directly supporting this operation, Bomber Command was ordered to direct its efforts against the southern airfields at Oslo, Stavangar and Trondheim, from which the enemy was launching its airborne troops into battle, and shipping on the main route from Germany. On the opening day of the campaign a 115 Squadron element attacked the German cruisers *Köln* and *Königsberg* at Bergen, and claimed damage to one of them. Six of the squadron's Wellingtons were sent to attack Sola airfield at Stavanger on the 11th, the first time a European mainland target had been intentionally bombed. P9284 failed to return after being shot down in flames in the target area, and there were no survivors from the crew of P/O Barber. F/S Powell and his crew narrowly escaped a similar fate, but the wounded pilot brought the damaged Wellington home to a belly landing, and in being awarded the DFM, became the first in 115 Squadron to be decorated for gallantry.

On the 12th eighty-three aircraft were involved in attacks on shipping at Stavanger, and this was the largest bombing operation of the war to date, and also the last major daylight effort by Wellingtons and Hampdens. In the face of a fierce fighter and flak defence nine aircraft were lost, including two from 149 Squadron. P9246 crashed into the sea in the target area, taking with it the crew of Sgt Wheller, and P9266 was believed to have fallen victim to a BF110, and also went into the sea, killing Sgt Goad and his crew. On the 18th 115 Squadron returned to Marham having concluded its period of detachment to Coastal Command, and W/C Mills talked about the squadron's Kinloss operations in a BBC broadcast. On the 21/22nd twelve Wellingtons attacked the airfields at Stavanger and Aalborg for the loss of one of their number. This was 149 Squadron's P9218, which crash-landed in Denmark, delivering F/O Knight and his crew into enemy hands, the first of many from the squadron to become PoWs. Operations against Norwegian airfields by the Wellington brigade continued for the remainder of the month, and that against Stavanger on the 25/26th involved 149 Squadron aircraft in an experiment. The ground crews attached small blue lights to the Wellingtons, to enable the crews to maintain visual contact with each other in cloud, but they proved impossible to see, and failed to prevent the formations from becoming dispersed. By the end of the first week of May the ill-fated Narvik expedition had already effectively failed gallantly. There was scarcely time to reflect on this, however, as events closer to home grabbed the attention of the world.

At dawn on the 10th of May German forces began their lightning advance through Luxembourg into Belgium and Holland, and this signalled the start of the massacre of the Battle and Blenheim squadrons of the Advanced Air Striking Force based in France, and the home-based Blenheim squadrons of 2 Group. It was on this day that W/C Whitley AFC assumed command of 149 Squadron in place of W/C Kellett. That night thirty-six Wellingtons were despatched to attack Waalhaven airfield at Rotterdam, and returning crews claimed hits on buildings and reported fires burning. A small number of Wellingtons and Whitleys attacked a road junction west of the Rhine on the 12/13th, and eighteen Wellingtons were involved in the Aachen area on the 14/15th. On the 15th the War Cabinet authorized the bombing of targets east of the Rhine, and this allowed the Command to strike for the first time at Germany's industrial Ruhr. That night sixteen targets were attacked in the Ruhr by a force of ninety-nine Wellingtons, Whitleys and Hampdens, the first occasion on which bombs were dropped east of the Rhine. This could be termed the true start of strategic bombing, and 115 Squadron was fated to suffer the first casualties of the strategic bombing campaign on this night. F/L Pringle and his crew took off in P9229, as part of a force briefed to attack oil refineries and marshalling yards at Duisburg, but the Wellington flew into high ground in France, and all five crew members were killed. In addition to these raids twelve Wellingtons and Whitleys targeted communications in Belgium, and consequently this was the first time that over 100 aircraft had been employed in a single night.

Although it was intended that 3, 4 and 5 Groups would concentrate solely on strategic targets, such was the speed of the enemy advance that it became necessary for them to lend tactical support to the retreating British Expeditionary Force. On the night of the 17/18th forty-six Wellingtons were sent to attack troops and communications in Belgium, and similar operations were mounted for the remainder of the month and through the Dunkerque evacuation. On the 19/20th 149 Squadron crews bombed a bridge at Courteilles in France, and another at Namur on the 21/22nd. A marshalling yard at Givet on the Franco–Belgian border was the target on the 23rd/24th, on return from which P9270 crashed in Suffolk, killing F/L Grant-Crawford and two of his crew. Two nights later bridges were attacked in the same region, and P9247 ran short of fuel. P/O Sherwood was forced to put down at Le Bourget, where he and his crew were not well received by their French hosts, and they returned home on the following day. An operation to St Omer on the 29/30th turned out to be expensive for 99 Squadron, as three of its Wellingtons had to be abandoned over East Anglia in very difficult weather conditions, and one pilot was killed.

On the same day that the evacuation from Dunkerque was completed, the 3rd of June, W/C Merton was posted from 215 Squadron to 37 Squadron to succeed W/C Fogarty as commanding officer. He had also spent a short period in command of 38 Squadron in 1937. W/C Fogarty, who had been awarded his DFC for action in Iraq in 1922, was posted to Mildenhall. That night the Command set a new record by dispatching 142 aircraft to mostly urban targets in Germany, while a few Wellingtons carried out the final attacks on enemy troop positions around Dunkerque. On the 6/7th further operations were mounted against enemy troops and communications in the Arras area, and on the 8/9th it was bridges at Abbeville. Italy entered the war on the 10th, an eventuality which had been anticipated, and for which provision had been made. A week earlier an order had been issued, ordering the formation of a special bombing force made up of six Wellingtons each from 99 and 149 Squadrons, the former to be based at Salon, and the latter at Le Vallon in southern France. The 'Haddock Force' was specifically intended for operations against Italy, and flew out to prepare for a raid. The permission of the French authorities had to be gained before the operation could take place, and as this was not forthcoming, the crews returned home. The French relented on the 14th, and the two squadrons flew out again for an operation on the following night, when eight Haddock Force Wellingtons set out for Genoa, but only one bombed. On the following night both Genoa and Milan were raided before the force returned to England on the 18th. In the meantime the first operational experience for 214 Squadron's personnel had come while it was still a reserve unit. S/L Sellick and P/O Sachs flew with 9 Squadron crews from Honington on the night of the 14/15th of June, when the incendiary device 'Razzle' was dropped into the Black Forest. This was one of a number of weapons tried out in the early stages of the war, and was intended to destroy by fire Germany's wooded areas and crop fields. The Command would persist with Razzle for a few months, but when it failed to persuade Hitler to sue for peace, it was consigned to the 'it was worth a try' file. Other 214 Squadron pilots accompanied 9 Squadron crews to Cologne and Essen on the 17/18th, Leverkusen on the 18/19th and Bremen on the 21/22nd, until finally, on the 25/26th, the squadron dispatched six aircraft from Stradishall on its first operation. This was a night on which twenty-one separate targets were earmarked for attention in Germany and Holland, and three 214 Squadron crews each were briefed for Monheim and Emmerich, from where they returned safely. 149 Squadron was also operating during this period, over the Ruhr on the 17/18th and 19/20th, and Bremen and Kamen on the 24/25th. Eleven aircraft were detailed for attacks on airfields in Holland on the 27/28th, but one of those bound for Ostheim burst a tyre on take-off, and was forced to abort.

Earlier on the 25th Sgt W D G Watkins had been presented with a DFM by AVM Baldwin, the 3 Group AOC. Watkins was destined to rise through the ranks, until being appointed to the command of XV Squadron in April 1944. This day also brought a change of leadership at 115 Squadron. W/C Mills was posted to 11 OTU at Bassingbourne and was succeeded by W/C Dabinett, who had been occupying the position of B Flight commander. He had joined the RAF in 1930, had served in Malta in 1932 and with 9 Squadron in 1935. It will be recalled that Dabinett had been in action on the very first day of the war, when, as the A Flight commander of 149 Squadron, he had led a section in search of enemy shipping in the Schillig Roads. He arrived at 115 Squadron during a loss-free period, which began in the early hours of the 21st of May, and would continue until the night of the 18/19th of July. On the 29th W/C Griffiths handed command of 99 Squadron to W/C Ford.

The father of the RAF, Viscount Trenchard, paid a visit to Mildenhall on the 3rd of July, and then it was back to the business of war on the 5th for its resident 149 Squadron. On this day the squadron dispatched seven Wellingtons to join fifty-three other aircraft in cloud-cover raids on German ports and airfields in Holland. The squadron contingent was assigned to Bremen, Wilhelmshaven and Emden, and all returned safely claiming a successful outing. Nine aircraft took off for night attacks on objectives at Bremen, Hamm and Osnabrück on the 9th, but were recalled because of worsening weather conditions. One crew failed to receive the recall, and pressed on to complete its sortie, before returning safely. Two nights later nine aircraft joined others to attack U-Boat yards and a naval base at Bremen. L7805 failed to return to Mildenhall, and there were no survivors from the crew of P/O Torgalson. The squadron sent off twelve Wellingtons on the 13/14th, three each to Hamm, Osnabrück, Hamborn and Duisburg, where port facilities and railway yards were the objectives. An aerodrome at Rottenburg was the target for nine of the squadron's aircraft on the 21/22nd, and two nights later ten carried out a raid on Gotha, and dropped leaflets. All aircraft returned safely, but one observer was killed by enemy action during the outward journey.

On the 24th of July W/C McKee was posted from 9 Squadron to 3 Group HQ. His successor, W/C Healy, was posted in from 40 Squadron, and it seems that he had previously commanded 107 Squadron between August 1936 and October 1937. The Duke of Gloucester visited Mildenhall on the 25th, and late that night 166 aircraft set off for the Ruhr and Holland, eight of them sent by 149 Squadron to attack aircraft factories at Dortmund. A new squadron joined 3 Group's ranks on the 29th in the form of 311 Squadron, which was formed at Honington and manned as far as possible by Czechoslovakians. The squadron had actually arrived at Liverpool on the 9th of July, and initial advice on RAF organisation and operations was provided by W/C Griffiths, the former 99 Squadron commanding officer. Once at Honington under the command of W/C Toman-Mares, Bomber Command sent W/C Percy 'Pick' Pickard, one of the RAF's great characters, to act as the British adviser and assist W/C Toman-Mares in the administration and training of the squadron. It was during this period that 'Pick' took part in the feature film *Target for Tonight*, in which fiction mirrored reality as he played the part of a Wellington pilot using genuine 149 Squadron aircraft. The final operations of the month for 149 Squadron took place on the 29/30th against industrial and railway targets at Monheim, Homberg and Cologne. As invasion fever began to mount and the Battle of Britain gained momentum overhead, each Group was required to have designated aircraft standing by at readiness to repel boarders, and this was the duty for six 149 Squadron crews on the 31st.

The 1st of August brought with it the re-forming of one of the RAF's oldest units. Originally formed on the 1st of May 1914, three months before the outbreak of the Great War, 7 Squadron would prove to be the lowest numbered squadron to serve with Bomber Command during the Second World War. Its First World War service began in April 1915 in France, but a year after the war ended it was disbanded. It was resurrected in June 1923 as a bomber unit, and frequent changes of equipment took place over the succeeding years. In April 1939 the squadron exchanged its recently acquired Whitleys for Hampdens, before two months later being designated a training squadron. Thus, when hostilities began in September 1939, 7 Squadron was nonoperational, and it would remain so until being absorbed into what became 16 OTU in April 1940, when it lost its identity. It was re-formed within weeks, but was just as quickly disbanded, and remained on the shelf until its latest rebirth at Leeming. The not inconsiderable task facing its commanding officer, W/C Paul Harris, was the introduction into operational service of the first of the new breed of heavy bombers, the Short Stirling. As already mentioned, Paul Harris had served before the war as a flight commander with 214 Squadron, before moving on to a similar post with 149 Squadron.

The procession of visiting dignitaries at Mildenhall continued on the 1st of August with the Duke of York, and that night ten 149 Squadron crews took part in a raid on industrial targets at Kamen, led by the commanding officer. All returned safely, and spent much of the next ten days on stand-by or stand-down. Ten crews were briefed on the 11th for an operation to Gelsenkirchen that night, and for Razzling and Nickeling. There were no losses to the defences, but P9244 collided with a radio mast on approach to Mildenhall on return, and crashed with fatal consequences for P/O Miller and his crew. 7 Squadron received its very first Stirling, N3640, on the 12th, and this allowed the training of crews to begin. Frankfurt, Soest and Hamm were the targets for eight 149 Squadron crews on the night of the 13/14th. On a busy night for the Command on the 16/17th the squadron dispatched two Wellingtons to attack the marshalling yards at Soest, and eight others to Koleda. R3174 failed to return from the latter with the crew of flight commander S/L Thwaites, and it was later learned that he and two others had lost their lives, and that the three survivors were in enemy hands. In the meantime, 75 (NZ) Squadron had moved to Mildenhall on the 15th, to share the facilities with 149 Squadron. Following a *Luftwaffe* raid on the 24th, in which some bombs were inadvertently dropped on central London, a retaliatory raid on Berlin was mounted by around fifty aircraft, mostly Wellingtons and Hampdens, on the night of the 25/26th. It was at best a token gesture, which succeeded only in destroying a wooden summer house in a resident's garden, but it did at least give lie to Goering's boast, that no enemy aircraft would penetrate deep into Reich territory. From this point on the capital would become a regular destination for small numbers of aircraft, although few would actually find the mark with their bombs. Two nights later, six 149 Squadron Wellingtons targeted the cruiser *Gneisenau* at Kiel, and lost one of their number in the process. P9272 contained the crew of F/L Vaillant, all of whom survived the experience to fall into enemy hands. 115 Squadron visited the capital for the first time on the night of the 28/29th to bomb a power station and Templehof airfield, and the crews were later to be seen on cinema screens in Movietone News. The month ended for 149 Squadron with a return by ten aircraft to Berlin on the 30/31st, and all got back safely.

The Battle of Britain would reach its peak in mid September, and much of the Command's effort over the coming weeks was to be directed at the build-up of marine craft in enemy occupied ports in preparation for Operation Sea Lion, the planned invasion of Britain. Such operations had been undertaken throughout the summer, but now they were to take precedence. The month began for 149 Squadron, however, with a return to the Black Forest by ten aircraft with Razzles on the night of the 2/3rd. The operation was repeated by seven aircraft on the 5/6th, while a single crew attacked barges at Delfzijl. R3163 was absent from Mildenhall on the following morning, and some time later news filtered through that F/O Burton and his crew were in captivity. Over 100 aircraft were committed to operations on the 8/9th, some against German ports containing U-Boat yards, and others to attack barges at Boulogne and Ostend. 149 Squadron contributed eight aircraft to the assault on barges at Boulogne, and two of them failed to return. P9245 crashed into the sea off the Essex coast, and flight commander S/L Andrews and all but one of his crew went down with the Wellington. The sole survivor was the second pilot, P/O Parish, who managed to swim ashore. He would enjoy a distinguished career with 75 (NZ) Squadron, before becoming a Pathfinder with 7 Squadron and losing his life in April 1943. R3175 was also lost in the sea, and there were no survivors from the crew of P/O Leeds. On the 11/12th nine crews were despatched to a variety of targets at Hamm, Ostend and Brussels, and this time all returned safely home. Two nights later nine crews carried out attacks on barges and other shipping at Antwerp, and again operated without loss. The 15/16th was a busy night, on which the main thrust was directed at the Channel ports. 149 Squadron put up nine aircraft for Calais, and a further three for Soest, and all returned safely having completed their assigned tasks. Later on the 16th 311 Squadron moved from Honington to East Wretham. It was similar fare for 149 Squadron on the 18/19th, when eleven crews were sent to Le Havre and Flushing, and one failed to arrive back with the rest. R3160 was lost in the Channel, and so was the crew of P/O Pay. Seven 149 Squadron aircraft participated in attacks on invasion craft at Dunkerque on the 21/22nd, before a major assault was mounted against Germany's capital on the 23rd/24th. The eighteen separate aiming points included railway yards, power stations, gas works and factories, to which 129 aircraft were despatched. A total of 112 crews claimed to have bombed within the Berlin area, although searchlight glare and ground mist made target identification almost impossible.

It was on this night that one of 75 (NZ) Squadron's originals, F/L 'Popeye' Lucas, completed his first tour of operations, having done thirty-seven, and he was posted to an OTU at Hampstead Norris. Lucas, from South Otago, was one of New Zealand's great characters and an inspiration to those around him. His facial resemblance to the cartoon character Popeye became even more pronounced when he removed his false teeth. His gumminess was the legacy of his determination to get into the air after being turned down by the RNZAF on the basis of his poor educational background. Undaunted he sailed to England as a deck hand, and the RAF accepted him on condition that he had his teeth fixed. It was back to barge concentrations at Calais for nine crews from 149 Squadron on the 25/26th, while two others were sent on the long journey to Mannheim in southern Germany to attack marshalling yards. The squadron's final operation of the month took place on the 28/29th, when six aircraft were sent to Hanau to attack industrial targets, while Le Havre and Soest were visited by one aircraft each. R3164 failed to return from the first mentioned, but P/O Petersen and four of his crew survived in enemy hands. The first incident of note involving 7 Squadron occurred on the 29th of September, when Flying Officer Bradley DFC was over the Isle of Man in N3640. Friendly flak caused damage to two engines, and in the ensuing forced-landing in Lancashire the aircraft was written off, becoming not only the first Stirling, but the first of the new four-engine generation of bombers to suffer destruction. Fortunately, on this occasion, there were no casualties.

The October account opened on the 1/2nd with almost 100 aircraft assigned to a variety of targets in Germany and on the Channel coast. This would set the pattern for the entire month, and characterize the ineffectiveness of the policy of small-scale operations. 149 Squadron briefed three crews for Berlin, five for Gelsenkirchen, and one each for Le Havre and Soest, and all returned safely home. From the 2nd to the 6th the squadron was required to have six aircraft on invasion alert stand-by at three hours readiness from dusk till dawn, and no operations were conducted during the period. The following night saw eighty aircraft abroad over Germany and the occupied countries, and it was similar fare on the 7/8th and the succeeding five nights. The 5th brought a change of leadership for the Command, with the departure of Sir Charles Portal to become Chief of the Air Staff, and the installation of Air Marshal Sir Richard Peirse as his successor. Ten 149 Squadron crews were airborne on the night of the 7/8th, four for the long slog to Berlin, and the remainder to continue the anti-invasion campaign at Boulogne. P/O Topham and his crew were 30 miles out over the sea in L7896, a Wellington borrowed from 99 Squadron, when they came under attack from an enemy nightfighter. The sortie was aborted, and with the undercarriage all but shot away a belly-landing was successfully carried out at Honington without injury to the crew, who scrambled clear before the wreckage was consumed by fire. They were more fortunate than their colleagues in P9273, which was lost without trace with the crew of P/O Furness during an operation to Herringhen on the 9/10th.

Earlier on the 9th of October a handful of Whitleys had turned up at Stradishall with a small and motley collection of men in RAF blue. It was the start of a war-long association between 3 Group and the highly secret Special Operations Executive, known in the most hushed tones as SOE. No. 419 Flight could also claim ownership of a couple of Lysanders, which they kept down at Tangmere in Sussex. On the night of the Flight's arrival at Stradishall, F/O Oettle delivered a French agent to the Fontainbleau area by Whitley and parachute, and on the 11th the unit sustained its first aircraft casualty. P/O Greenhill had been posted in as a Lysander pilot, apparently with no experience on Whitleys, and promptly wrote off P5025 in a landing crash on the 11th. No injuries were reported, but P/O Greenhill departed the Flight shortly afterwards. The first Lysander operation, to pick up the agent dropped on the 9th, was delayed by bad weather conditions until the 20/21st. The weather was still appallingly bad as F/L Farley, the Flight's commanding officer, departed Tangmere in R9027, but it had cleared by the time he reached the target area, and the pick-up was concluded successfully. Shortly after departing the French field, a rifle bullet smashed the compass, and this problem was compounded by the weather, which closed in again on the way home. Farley was forced to fly above it, and without compass or radio, set a rough course towards Tangmere, hoping for a break in the cloud to enable him to pinpoint his whereabouts. This was not forthcoming, and with fuel tanks almost dry, he put down at the first opportunity, wrecking the Lysander, but without injury to himself or his passenger. They had actually come down in Scotland, and had the fuel lasted much longer, they would almost certainly have been lost in the Atlantic. This was by no means an unusual experience for the remarkable men who would spend their war in the shadows, plying their trade under the most extreme conditions, relying on the highest standards of airmanship to see them through, and remaining silent about what they did.

It was during the dark days of summer 1940 that 419 Flight was born. Britain stood alone against the might of the all-conquering enemy, while the battle for air supremacy raged overhead and a few hundred brave young men in their Hurricanes and Spitfires were all that stood between survival for the time being and imminent invasion. Invasion fever gripped the nation like a vice, and Prime Minister Churchill already knew that a successful resistance now would condemn the country to a long war. He believed that every advantage must be found, no matter how small, to thwart the enemy until Britain and her allies had grown strong enough to take an offensive stance. Intelligence and armed resistance are vital constituents to a protracted war, and to these ends, a small group of people came together in a sparsely furnished block of offices in Baker Street, London. The existence of the Special Operations Executive was known only to those involved in its work, and other than to its directors, information was dispensed on a need to know basis only. Even the other services were kept in the dark, and knew it only as a set of initials at various addresses. To those who would carry out its orders, the organisation became known as the Firm. Its main objectives were as follows; to inspire in all of the occupied countries a belief in Britain and faith in victory; to organise sabotage of industrial plants and communications; to establish routes in and out of Fortress Europe; to encourage the afflicted; to harness the passion of zealots; to arm and train resistance groups; and to prepare a mighty army of patriots to rise up against the Nazis at the appointed hour. As a tiny but indispensable component of this enormous project, 419 Flight was formed on the 21st of August 1940 on the fighter station at North Weald. From here it would operate on behalf of the Special Operations Executive in support of resistance organisations in the occupied countries, and the Special Intelligence Service (MI6), delivering and collecting agents to and from fields in France. Operating under 11 Group Fighter Command, the new unit was commanded by F/L Farley, an experienced Hurricane pilot, who would find it difficult to restrict himself to his new role.

The Flight's initial equipment amounted to two Lysanders with a further two in reserve, and these were joined within days by two Whitleys. F/O Oettle was posted in as the official Whitley pilot, and was in action immediately, collecting an agent from Tangmere, and dropping him by parachute into the French countryside near Paris. On the night of the 28/29th of August he delivered a Dutch naval officer to Holland without the services of a reception committee, but this man soon fell into enemy hands and was executed the following summer. The *Luftwaffe*'s assault on Fighter Command airfields led to a number of attacks on North Weald, and 419 Flight was consequently relocated on the 3rd of September to Stapleford Tawney, a satellite field 5 miles to the south, where accommodation was initially of the canvas variety. Some people spent their days-off playing golf or generally relaxing, F/L Farley, on the other hand, reputedly spent his flying Hurricanes in the Battle of Britain on behalf of 46 and 151 Squadrons, the airfield's other resident units. F/L Keast was posted in from Hendon to train as the Flight's second Whitley pilot, but only two Whitley sorties were flown from the new home before the move to Stradishall. From this point until the end of the war, the clandestine units of Bomber Command, sometime known as the 'moon' squadrons, would remain under the control of 3 Group.

All of this passed unnoticed by those engaged in the bombing war. Over 100 aircraft were involved in operations to the Ruhr, Wilhelmshaven, Kiel and the Channel ports on the 13/14th, while more distant targets, Berlin, Stettin, Bohlen and Magdeburg featured on the following night. Kiel was again one of many targets on the 15/16th and 16/17th, and it was on the latter occasion that 311 Squadron sustained some casualties. One Wellington failed to return, a second iced up and crashed in Middlesex while outbound and a third was abandoned by its crew over Nottinghamshire on the way home. Another of its aircraft crashed during training on the following day, and this brought the death toll from the four incidents to twelve men, with two others falling into enemy hands. Eleven aircraft took off from Mildenhall for three destinations on the 21/22nd, Gelsenkirchen, Cologne and Hamburg, where the *Bismarck* was berthed. The importance of the German battleship was reflected in the fact that both 149 Squadron flight commanders, S/Ls Lynch-Blosse and Griffith-Jones took part, along with F/L Cookson, in R3206, T2737, and N2775 respectively. The battleship was not hit, but eight large fires were started within the city. On the 23/24th, the squadron contributed six aircraft to Berlin, and four to Emden, and it was on return from the latter that T2740 crashed while F/O Donaldson was trying to make an emergency landing near the Essex coast. He and his crew emerged unscathed, he and his second pilot, P/O Woollatt, ultimately to go on to better things. Woollatt was to play the role of second pilot to W/C 'Pick' Pickard in the already mentioned propaganda and morale boosting film, *Target for Tonight*, which was released in 1941, and featured Wellington F-Freddie. Later in the war Woollatt would be appointed flight commander with 12 Squadron in 1 Group. For his part, F/O Donaldson was not to be feted as a film star, but he would see out the final eleven months of the war as the commanding officer of 192 Squadron in 100 Group. There were just two more nights of operations for 149 Squadron before the turn of the month, starting with the 26/27th, when it contributed eleven aircraft divided between the oil refinery at Leuna, and industrial targets at Bremen. 7 Squadron moved to Oakington on the 29th of October, where it would remain throughout the war, and continued to work up on the Stirling, which was beset with technical problems. Slow production and constant modifications restricted the supply of aircraft, to the extent that only six of the type were on squadron charge by the start of 1941. The largest effort on the night of the 29/30th was reserved for Berlin, but only four of the thirty aircraft involved actually reached the target area in the face of bad weather. 149 Squadron contributed eleven Wellingtons to the capital, and two to Wilhelmshaven, and all returned safely. During the course of the month W/C Nuttall was posted away from 214 Squadron to take up a staff appointment at 3 Group, and he was replaced by W/C Loughnan.

Substantial changes to 3 Group were to take place during November involving the posting out of two squadrons and the posting in of four plus a station. The process began on the 1st with the arrival of three new recruits from 2 Group. Along with XV and 40 Squadrons came the station at Wyton, which had been their home since December 1939 following their somewhat premature withdrawal from France. Both had crossed the Channel with their Fairey Battles as part of the Advanced Air Striking Force on the day before war was declared, but returned to the UK to join 2 Group and re-equip with Blenheims. 57 Squadron had likewise operated with the Advance Air Striking Force (AASF) in France as a Blenheim unit from the start of hostilities, and joined 2 Group on its return to the UK. Its first 3 Group home would also be at Wyton, having arrived there on the 1st on posting from Elgin, and this was, in fact, the squadron's third period of residence at the Cambridgeshire station.

The history of XV Squadron, as it is traditionally depicted, stretches back to its original formation on the 1st of March 1915. On the last day of 1919 the squadron was disbanded, only to be resurrected on the 24th of March 1924 to test armaments for the A&AEE. When this body undertook its own testing from the 1st of June 1934, XV Squadron was re-formed in the day bomber role, exchanging its Hinds for Battles in June 1938.

40 Squadron was first formed on the 26th of February 1916. After eventual disbandment the re-forming took place on the 1st of April 1931, and after operating a number of types, Fairey Battles were taken on charge in July 1938. Like many units during the mid to late thirties 40 Squadron had among its ranks a number of officers who would enjoy distinguished careers during the impending conflict. In January 1936 B V Robinson was a Pilot Officer, and he would become a flight commander with 102 Squadron during the first year of war, before twice commanding 35 Squadron and becoming station commander at Graveley. Sadly, while in that post, he elected to take a 35 Squadron crew to Berlin in August 1943 and lost his life. A contemporary of Robinson's at 40 Squadron was P/O J R Maling, who was destined to be killed on an operation to Stuttgart in July 1944 while in command of 619 Squadron. Also from that era P/O Legood rose to the rank of Wing Commander, and was the incumbent commanding officer of 35 Squadron for the final months of the war. A 1937 photograph in the excellent book *Sweeping the Skies*, a history of 40 Squadron by David Gunby, depicts a young P/O L D Wilson who would progress to the command of 102 Squadron in 1944, and also P/O Partridge, a future commanding officer of 18 Squadron. Like the other Blenheim squadrons operating over France in May and June 1940, both XV and 40 suffered heavy casualties, and after the fall of France a switch to invasion barges and shipping targets mostly in daylight was no less daunting.

The history of 57 Squadron can be traced back to its original formation as a flying training unit on the 8th of June 1916. The squadron was disbanded on the last day of 1919, and remained on the shelf until being re-formed as a light bomber unit in October 1931. It would continue in this role, eventually taking delivery of Blenheims at the end of March 1938.

The swelling of 3 Group's ranks was not yet over, and by the time that 218 Squadron joined the fold on the 5th of November, it too had been tempered in the fierce fires of battle. First formed on the 24th of April 1918 as a light bomber unit, 218 Squadron was disbanded on the 24th of June 1919, and remained on the shelf until being re-formed from A Flight of 57 Squadron on the 16th of March 1936. In January 1938 its Hinds were replaced with Fairey Battles, and as the Second World War loomed, the squadron was based at Boscombe Down with 88 Squadron as part of 1 Group. On the 2nd of September 1939 1 Group ceased to exist, becoming part of the AASF earmarked for France, and on that afternoon 88 and 218 Squadrons departed

Boscombe Down for their new base at Auberive in France. 218 flew a number of reconnaissance sorties over the next three months, and then the winter set in to keep everyone on the ground. It was not until the German advance began in earnest on the 10th of May that matters began to heat up, and it was all over very quickly for 218 Squadron. On the afternoon of the 14th seven aircraft departed Auberive to bomb troop columns on the Bouillon–Givonne road, while four others were sent to target the Douzy bridge near Sedan, which was the alternative objective for the first section. Ten of the eleven failed to return, and the squadron was effectively knocked out of the battle at a single stroke. On the 19th the squadron contributed to attacks on enemy troop columns, and flew some sorties on the night of the 20/21st, before its remaining aircraft were deposited with 103 Squadron later on the 21st. All personnel proceeded to No. 2 Base area at Nantes, where they remained until evacuation to England.

The dismantling of the original squadron began on the 6th of June, when some of the senior NCOs, together with a number of wireless operators and air-gunners were posted to other squadrons. The ground crews proceeded to the UK at this time, settling in at Mildenhall, and by the 14th they had been joined by the rest of the squadron. A new era began for 218 Squadron on the 24th, when it was informed that it would convert to Blenheims and join 2 Group. Three days later the first four Mk IV Blenheims were taken on charge, and on the 28th W/C Combe was posted to the squadron to familiarize himself before assuming command two weeks hence. He would succeed W/C Duggan, who had led the squadron from the start of hostilities, and would now serve with 3 Group as the station commander at Oakington. The squadron's posting to 3 Group, with which it would now remain for the rest of the war, involved it in flying its third aircraft type in the space of six months. On the day after its posting, the 6th, a dual-control Wellington, L4293, was delivered, and that afternoon a brand new Mk Ic, R1009, arrived for flight testing by F/L Richmond. On the 7th Czech pilots flew in two more Wellingtons, R1008 and R1025, and these were followed by N2844 and T2801 on the 13th, along with another dual control Mk Ia, N2937, R1183 and T2885 on the 14th, and R1210 on the 15th. On the 23rd the squadron would again begin the upheaval of changing address, and completed its move to Marham on the 27th. W/C Combe was on ten days leave from the 20th, and the burden of overseeing the transfer fell upon the shoulders of S/L Gillam.

XV Squadron's first Wellington, N2781, came from 9 Squadron and arrived on the 7th of November. However, working up on the type under the watchful eye of W/C Cox would occupy the squadron for the next six weeks. There would also be no operational flying for nearly two months for 40 Squadron while they worked up on Wellingtons under the command of W/C Barnett. He had been commissioned way back in 1927 and had most recently commanded 84 Squadron in Iran. B Flight was already existing as an autonomous unit at Alconbury under S/L Little when the move to 3 Group took place, while A Flight remained at Wyton under S/L Springall. The Blenheim era had ended spectacularly on the 30th of September with the destruction of a JU88 by S/L Little, an officer who would later go on to command 623 Squadron. F/L Lynch-Blosse was the first to complete conversion, and it was he who collected the squadron's first Wellington on the 5th of November. In May 1942 he would assume command of 44 Squadron in 5 Group, and lose his life on his first operation two days later. In all, four Wellingtons were taken on charge that day, N3000, T2514, T2515 and T2718. S/L Arnold became the new A Flight commander, and was involved in the only mishap during the working up period, when T2718 crashed at Wyton on take-off on the 12th of December, and two of the crew were injured. It was actually on the 12th of November that 57 Squadron officially joined 3 Group, although it had received its first Wellington Ic T2804 on the 7th. A new home awaited the squadron at Feltwell, to where it would move on the 20th and share the facilities with 75 (NZ) Squadron. There would be no further operational activity for the squadron until the New Year, as it began to work up on the new type, and take on extra crew members. XV, 40 and 57 Squadrons had joined 3 Group as replacements for 37 and 38 Squadrons which had been ordered to prepare to depart for the Middle East. 37 Squadron left in two sections, the second of which headed for Malta on the 12th. By the end of the month 38 Squadron was established in Egypt and preparing for operations against targets in Libya. W/C Adams was posted to 3 Group HQ before departure, and S/L Bowles DFC was promoted to succeed him.

Now back to the operational front, where November would see the difficult weather conditions continuing, and a number of operations would be affected. 149 Squadron contributed eleven aircraft to the night's main activity at Berlin on the 1/2nd, and also sent three to Gelsenkirchen. Six aircraft were detailed for operations on the 4/5th, when Le Havre and Boulogne were the destinations, but one sortie was cancelled, and one aircraft was forced by the conditions to return early. Eighteen Wellingtons set out for Berlin on the 6/7th, seven of them from Mildenhall, but only one of the force reached its objective in the conditions. On the 8/9th nine 149 Squadron Wellingtons headed for the marshalling yards at distant Munich, and fared better than the two crews joining a raid on Gelsenkirchen, where bad weather intervened. It was a similar story on the 13/14th, and all three operations involving 149 Squadron crews, Berlin, Gelsenkirchen and Cologne, were ruined by adverse weather. It was, at least, a good month for the squadron in terms of losses, and, in fact, only one aircraft would fail to return. This was N2774, which crashed in Germany during an operation to Berlin on the 19/20th, and it was later learned that P/O Hide and his crew had been killed. On the 24th W/C Whitley was posted away from the squadron to be replaced temporarily by flight commander S/L Heather. In the rank of Group Captain Whitley would become station commander at Linton-on-Ouse in May 1941, a post which he retained until being shot down in a 76 Squadron Halifax in April 1943. Ever resourceful, he evaded capture and returned to resume his RAF career, ultimately seeing out the war as the

AOC 4 Group. On the 28th W/C Powell was appointed as 149 Squadron's new commanding officer, a position he would retain until the following summer. Among other postings towards the end of the month was that of W/C Buckley, who was declared tour expired at 75 (NZ) Squadron and posted to 214 Squadron Reserve Flight at Stradishall. In his place the Kiwis were pleased to welcome back their fellow countryman, the newly promoted W/C Kay, who had only departed the squadron in October at the end of his tour. W/C Kay was thirty-eight years old, and at the time of the award of his DFC on the 20th of June 1940 he had completed twenty-three operations.

December was to be a less demanding month operationally, particularly at the start, and it was the night of the 4/5th before 149 Squadron was first called into action. Five crews were briefed for Turin, while five others were to target Düsseldorf along with over seventy other aircraft. Less than half reached their respective objectives as the weather played its part, but no losses were incurred by the squadron. A number of operations were planned over the ensuing two weeks, but were subsequently cancelled because of the weather. A new commanding officer was installed at XV Squadron on the 14th in the shape of W/C 'Daddy' Dale, who succeeded W/C Cox DFC. 149 Squadron's R1294 crashed near the airfield during an air-test on the afternoon of the 16th, killing Sgt Lloyd, and the other six occupants. The flight had been in preparation for that night's major operation to Mannheim, which was intended as a retaliatory gesture after the recent heavy bombing of London, Coventry and Southampton. A forecast of poor weather at home reduced the numbers taking part to 134 aircraft, but this still represented the largest force yet sent to a single target. 149 Squadron put up a creditable fourteen aircraft for the operation, which was to be led by eight of the most experienced crews, whose bombs were intended to start fires in the city centre. This was not achieved and the attack was scattered, although a relatively large amount of damage for the period was inflicted on predominantly residential districts. During the remainder of the year, 149 Squadron took part in an operation to the Pirelli factory at Milan on the 18/19th, a raid on Berlin on the 20/21st, and Ludwigshaven on the 23/24th. 218 Squadron began its operational career on Wellingtons on the 20th, when two aircraft were despatched to bomb the docks at Ostend. The first Wellington sorties by XV Squadron were launched on the night of the 21/22nd with Bremen as the target, and there were no casualties. Bad weather delayed 40 Squadron's first operation, which had been planned for the 15th, and it too had to wait until the 21/22nd for its first three sorties to be launched by S/L Little, P/O Whitehead and Sgt Johnson with the docks at Antwerp as their objective. On the 23rd W/C Barnett handed command of 40 Squadron to W/C Davy. W/C Davy had joined the RAF back in 1930, having previously served as a 2nd Lieutenant in the Suffolk Regiment. The few days after Christmas were beset by inhospitable weather, and although aircraft took off for Lorient on the 28/29th, alternative targets were bombed.

As the year drew to a close life at 419 Flight was becoming a little complicated. F/O Hockey was posted in during the final week of November, and like F/L Keast, he came from 24 Communications Squadron at Hendon, where he had spent much of the war to date transporting VIPs. Shortly after his arrival he was hospitalized with exhaustion, and would play no further part in the Flight's activities until the following March. From then on, his contribution to SOE and SIS operations would be enormous, but for the time being, all Whitley sorties were conducted with F/O Oettle as captain and F/L Keast as second pilot. The manpower situation was further compromised during December by the loss of F/L Farley, who was shot down in a Hurricane while on leave, and broke a leg. He, too, would return in time, but for the present F/L Keast assumed command. By year's end 419 Flight had successfully completed ten Whitley operations to France, Belgium and Holland, delivering an agent on each occasion, and there had been just the one previously mentioned Lysander operation.

For the Command as a whole 1940 was a difficult year to categorize, having begun with the 'phoney' war and a rethink on the policy of unescorted daylight raids. Apart from 2 Group, Bomber Command had been largely untouched by the events in France, which had brought about the massacre of the AASF. The so-called heavy squadrons had gained experience in flying over hostile territory in the dark, but most of them did not have a clue where they were, to within ten to twenty miles, and many claims of success were born out of optimism. The best that could be said of Bomber Command in 1940 was that it was the only branch of the armed forces able to present a belligerent and defiant face to an as yet all-conquering enemy, and this it had done with enthusiasm.

1941

Disappointment, frustration, failure, disillusionment, the Butt Report, Bomber Command on the brink

A second successive harsh winter played its part in restricting operations during January, and most of those taking place were aimed at German and French ports. 75 (NZ) Squadron began the year by completing a move to Feltwell on New Year's Day. Bremen was the objective for the first three nights of January, although 149 Squadron only took part on the 2/3rd, when contributing twelve Wellingtons to a scattered and ineffective raid. Snow and bad visibility grounded the squadron from then until the 9/10th, when fourteen Wellingtons departed Mildenhall for Gelsenkirchen. Less than half of the 135 original starters claimed to have bombed as briefed, and many of these hit other Ruhr towns. Nine Wellingtons were sent across the Alps to Italy on the 12/13th, the 149 Squadron contingent led by W/C Powell. W/C Powell was awarded a DSO after this operation, and it was presented to him by His Majesty King George VI at Mildenhall on the 18th, when flight commander S/L Sawrey-Cookson also received an award. The latter was destined for higher office and a premature end, but this was to come with 75 (NZ) Squadron, which he would command from September, before losing his life in April 1942. 99 Squadron welcomed a new commanding officer on the 16th in the form of W/C Dixon-Wright.

Operations did not resume for 57 Squadron until the night of the 13/14th of January, when small-scale raids were launched by the Command against Wilhelmshaven and French ports. The single 57 Squadron sortie was flown by a freshman crew to Boulogne. On the 15th a new Air Ministry directive alluded to an approaching critical period for Germany's oil situation, and suggested that a concerted effort against this industry would have a material effect on the enemy's war effort. A list of seventeen targets was drawn up accordingly, the top nine of which represented 80% of Germany's production capacity, but it would be February before Peirse could attempt to carry out his orders. On the 16th W/C Arnold was posted from 40 Squadron on promotion to become the new commanding officer of 9 Squadron. He succeeded W/C Healy, who returned to 3 Group HQ. On the 20th W/C Dabinett concluded his tour as commanding officer of 115 Squadron, and swapped places with his successor, who was posted in from 11 OTU at Bassingbourne. Dabinett would return to the operational scene at the end of July 1942 as the commanding officer of 12 Squadron, a post in which he would remain until February 1943. His successor at 115 was the larger-than-life W/C 'Tiny' Evans-Evans, who would enjoy a colourful career until his untimely and entirely unnecessary death at the controls of a Lancaster early in 1945. Bad weather continued to keep 149 Squadron on the ground almost until the end of the month, when twelve aircraft were despatched to attack the *Tirpitz* at Wilhelmshaven on the 29/30th.

On the 1st of February 40 Squadron's A Flight left Wyton to join up with B Flight at Alconbury. February began for 218 Squadron with a change of commanding officer, as W/C Combe was posted to Bomber Command HQ on the 2nd, and was replaced by W/C Amison. The latter had been 'Mentioned in Dispatches' for distinguished services in Palestine in 1936, and was awarded the Czech Military Cross in 1939. His period of tenure would prove to be reasonably brief. It was not until the night of the 4/5th that 149 Squadron was next called into action. The target was an enemy warship at Brest, for which the squadron contributed nine of thirty-eight Wellingtons, and all returned safely. Peirse's monthly 'big night' for February fell on the 10/11th, when a new record number of 265 aircraft was despatched to various targets. The majority, 222, headed for Hanover, and 183 crews returned with claims of having bombed as briefed, while over thirty others attacked alternative targets. 7 Squadron was finally able to launch the first Stirling operation on this night, when three sorties were despatched to Rotterdam to bomb oil storage tanks near the docks in company with forty other aircraft, including three from 149 Squadron. 3 Group managed to put 119 aircraft into the air on this night, the first time that any Group had achieved 100. On the following night Bremen was the main target, while a small force returned to Hanover. 149 Squadron supported both operations with three and four aircraft respectively, and also sent four to Magdeburg. The weather on return meant diversions for some, and not all got down without incident. L7811 was abandoned by Sgt Turner and his crew on return from Bremen, but all made it safely down to terra firma. Having been to Hanover, P9247 crashed in Lincolnshire, killing one member of the crew of Sgt Warren, for whom this would be only a temporary reprieve. Three Marham-based Wellingtons had to be abandoned by their 115 Squadron occupants as fuel tanks ran dry. At least it wouldn't be necessary to explain themselves to the commanding officer, as W/C Evans-Evans was one of those hitting the silk. The oil directive was put into effect on the 14/15th at Gelsenkirchen and Homberg, while on the following night it was the turn of Sterkrade and Homberg, but the numbers of aircraft committed to these attacks precluded any chance of delivering a telling blow, even had all of the bombs found the mark, which they clearly did not. Nineteen Wellingtons bombed Wilhelmshaven on the 21/22nd for the loss of 149 Squadron's R1045, which disappeared without trace with the crew of F/O Henderson. W/C Garland's long spell in command of 57 Squadron ended on the 24th, and he was succeeded by W/C Bertram, who had served in 1940 as a flight commander with 99 Squadron.

Meanwhile at Stradishall, F/L Keast flew his first Whitley sortie as captain in mid February, a trip to France, and on the following night, the 14/15th, undertook the unit's longest flight yet, to deliver three Polish agents to their homeland. The operation lasted over eleven hours in difficult weather conditions, and was made possible only by the installation of additional fuel tanks inside the fuselage. Although probably somewhat weary, F/L Keast was called into action again on the night of the 17/18th to transport an SIS agent to Belgium. On the way home, and still over Belgium at low level, T4264 was hit by flak and lost an engine. The other engine failed shortly afterwards, and the Whitley was put down on its belly on the edge of a wood without serious injury to the occupants. Keast and his crew were soon in enemy hands, however, and they were the first to fail to return from SOE/ SIS operations. The manpower situation was now critical, with Farley and Hockey still in hospital, and Keast on extended leave in Germany, but the cavalry, in the form of S/L Knowles, rode over the crest of the hill to save the day. He was appointed as the new commanding officer, and would be joined over the ensuing weeks by an experienced new Lysander pilot, F/O Scotter, who was still only twenty-one years old. South African F/L Jackson was also added to the strength, while a replacement Whitley, T4165, was acquired from 4 Group's 78 Squadron. Gordon Scotter had been a Lysander pilot since joining 2 Army Co-operation Squadron back in January 1939, and he would prove to be a very valuable acquisition. He was to remain with 1419 Flight and its successor, 138 Squadron, until being posted briefly to the sister

'Moon' Squadron, 161, in May 1942. The nature of clandestine operations called for special characteristics among the pilots, and it seems that this was taken into consideration when selecting new recruits from the RAF generally. Another arrival in March was F/O Alan 'Sticky' Murphy, an outstanding athlete, who represented the Service in both track and field events before the war, and set a long-standing long jump record. He had spent most of the war to date training others, and he too would serve with both 'Moon' Squadrons. Sadly, having attained the rank of Wing Commander and while in command of 23 Squadron, one of 100 Group's Serrate Mosquito units, he would lose his life during an intruder operation in December 1944.

March began with an unusually effective attack on Cologne on the 1/2nd, which left around ninety houses destroyed, and many others seriously damaged, along with sundry river craft and commercial premises. Eleven 149 Squadron crews shared in the success, and then the squadron sat out the next week and a half on the ground. On the night of the 3/4th of March 7 Squadron suffered its first operational loss, when, with Brest as the target, N3653 crashed into the sea, killing S/L Griffith-Jones DFC and his crew. S/L Griffiths-Jones had come to 7 Squadron from 149 Squadron, where he had also served with distinction as a flight commander. On the 9th a new Air Ministry directive was issued in response to the continued and mounting losses of Allied shipping to U-Boats in the Atlantic. This menace, and its partner-in-crime, the Focke-Wulf Kondor long range maritime reconnaissance bomber, were to be hunted down and attacked wherever they could be found, at sea, in their bases, in the shipyards and assembly plants, and at the components factories. A new list of targets was drawn up headed by Kiel, Hamburg, Vegesack and Bremen, each of which had at least one U-Boat construction yard, while the last mentioned also contained a Focke-Wulf factory. On the 11/12th twenty-seven Wellingtons were despatched to Kiel, including twelve from Mildenhall. One returned early, but the others all bombed as briefed and came safely home. The 12/13th brought a busy night of operations, with Hamburg, Bremen and Berlin as the main targets for forces of eighty-eight, eighty-six and seventy-two aircraft respectively. The important Blohm & Voss U-Boat yards, and four other ship building concerns were hit in Hamburg, and twelve high explosive bombs landed in the Focke-Wulf factory at Bremen. Over 100 aircraft returned to Hamburg twenty-four hours later, and inflicted further damage on the Blohm & Voss yards, while starting over 100 fires elsewhere in the city.

The Gelsenkirchen authorities reported serious damage to an oil refinery after a raid by under 100 aircraft on the 14/15th, but one of the 149 Squadron participating crews was not able to attend debriefing. L7858 was shot down by a nightfighter over Holland, and there were no survivors from the crew of Sgt Hawley. This was the first of a number of aircraft and crew casualties for the squadron over a period of five nights, which continued on the 17/18th when R1474 was shot down by an intruder on final approach to Mildenhall when returning from Bremen. The crew was that of Sgt Warren, who, in the previous month it will be recalled, had survived the crash on return from Hanover. On this night only one of his original crew was on board, and sadly, there were no survivors. Two nights later, while returning from a disappointing all-Wellington effort against Cologne, R1159 clipped trees and crash-landed in Suffolk in the hands of Sgt Hall and his crew, who, happily, were able to walk away. 99 Squadron had moved from Newmarket to Waterbeach on the 18th, and there it would remain for the next twelve months. On the 19th W/C Toman-Mares stepped down at 311 Squadron, and S/L Schejbal stepped up from his role as A Flight commander. As home to a U-Boat base Lorient was one of a number of French ports to fall within the parameters of the recent directive, and was attacked on consecutive nights from the 20/21st. A force of Wellingtons and Whitleys targeted Berlin on the 23/24th, but complete cloud cover prevented an assessment of results. On the 29th, the German cruisers *Scharnhorst* and *Gneisenau* were reported to be off Brest, and by the following day, they had taken up residence. Thus began an eleven month saga, which would occupy much of the Command's attention, and cost it dearly in aircraft and crews for precious little return. That night fifty Wellingtons were among more than 100 aircraft sent to the port, but no hits were claimed on the warships. On the last night of the month 9 and 149 Squadrons sent six aircraft between them to Emden, for what, in its way, was a momentous occasion. Merlin-powered Mk II Wellingtons with superior lifting capacity were being fed in small numbers into the squadrons, and P/O Franks and crew took off in W5439 on this night to deliver the first ever 4,000 lb high capacity bomb, or 'cookie', on Germany. The aiming point was marked with incendiaries by 9 Squadron's S/L Wasse, a future commanding officer of both 9 and 149 Squadrons. No aircraft were lost to the defences, but 149 Squadron's R1229 crashed during the landing at Mildenhall, and although Sgt Morhen and his crew survived the incident, one man later succumbed to his injuries. 214 Squadron welcomed a new commanding officer in March in the shape of the New Zealander, W/C Jordan. He had begun the war in 5 Group as the commanding officer of 83 Squadron, where Guy Gibson was one of his junior officers, and then moved to the command of 144 Squadron in October 1939, where he remained until the following May. During the course of the month 419 Flight became 1419 Flight.

Brest provided the main focus of attention in April, while Kiel was the most frequently visited destination in Germany. Wellingtons made up more than half of the force bound for the former on the 3/4th, when the warships were difficult to locate. On the following night, a bomb landed in the dry dock occupied by the *Gneisenau*, but failed to explode. It was decided to move the ship out into the harbour while the bomb was dealt with, and it was while moored there on the next day, that a coastal command torpedo struck home and inflicted serious damage. The gallant crew of the Beaufort had known that they were embarking on what was tantamount to a suicide mission, and sadly, they all died in the withering hail of fire, ignorant of their success. The pilot, F/O Campbell, was posthumously awarded the Victoria Cross. The *Gneisenau* would require six months to repair, and in the meantime, she and *Scharnhorst* would continue to attract the attention of Bomber Command. Bad weather hampered a further tilt at the warships on the 6/7th, before two effective attacks were delivered on Kiel on consecutive nights. The first, on the 7/8th, employed over 200 aircraft, half of them Wellingtons, and inflicted useful damage in the docks area, and caused a two day loss of production at two U-Boat yards. The following night's raid was centred more on the town itself, and the casualty figure of 125 people killed and 300 injured was the highest of the war to date. 149 Squadron's X3167 failed to return to Mildenhall, having crashed into the sea, and there were no survivors from the crew of Sgt Jago.

On the 10th XV Squadron became the second in the Command to receive the Stirling, when N3644 arrived from 7 Squadron. While conversion and working-up went on alongside, operations continued with the trusty Wellington, which still represented the backbone of the Command, and would continue to do so for a further eighteen months. During the course of the 10th 149 Squadron's R1181 collided with trees while taking off for a training flight, and crashed near the airfield demolishing a cottage. The second pilot and another man were killed, and the pilot, P/O Fisher, and the other five occupants were injured. That night over fifty aircraft returned to Brest, 149 Squadron contributing nine aircraft led by S/L Cookson in R1593. Most crews carried out two bombing runs, dropping a stick on each occasion, and a number of near misses were claimed, although no hits. It was later established, however, that four bombs had struck the *Gneisenau* killing fifty men, and this further delayed the vessel's return to sea-going condition. While another raid on the port was in progress on the 12/13th, 149 Squadron participated in an attack on Merignac airfield at Bordeaux. T2897 failed to return home with the others, and news came through later that it had crashed in France, killing Sgt Morison and all but one of his crew. Later that day, and having fulfilled his commission to guide 7 Squadron through the trials and tribulations of bringing the troublesome Stirling to war, W/C Harris was posted away and replaced by W/C Graham, who would remain at the helm for a year. S/L Cookson again led the eleven strong 149 Squadron contingent when Kiel was the target on the 15/16th, and this time the sole 'cookie' was in the tender care of P/O Grimston in W5399. He was The Honourable Bruce Grimston, son of the 4th Earl of Verulam. His elder brother, The Honourable Brian Grimston DFC, or the Honourable Grimmy, as he was known, served with 156 Squadron of the Pathfinders, and lost his life in April 1943. Bruce Grimston would also be lost in July 1944, while serving with 524 Squadron of Coastal Command. On this night, however, it was Sgt Meynell and his crew who failed to return in R1439, which crashed in the target area with no survivors. Two nights later Berlin was the main target, for which 149 Squadron donated five aircraft, while among minor operations was one by ten Wellingtons against Cologne. Three failed to return, one of them 149

Squadron's P9248, which was lost without trace with the crew of Sgt Clifton. Two Merlin powered Mk II 'cookie'-carrying Wellingtons were delivered to 40 Squadron on the 20th, and one was assigned to each flight. W/C Amison was posted from 218 Squadron to 12 OTU at Benson on the 22nd, and was succeeded by W/C Kirkpatrick, who was posted in from his flight commander's post at 9 Squadron. He presided over his first operation and casualties that night, when the squadron contributed to the raid on Brest.

In remarkably quick time W/C Dale and his flight commanders at XV Squadron, S/Ls Menaul and Morris, both of whom would eventually gain commands of their own, the former with XV Squadron, and the latter with 218, brought enough crews to operational status to be able to launch the first Stirling sorties on the last night of the month. Four sorties were despatched to Berlin, captained by W/C Dale, S/Ls Menaul and Morris and F/L Raymond, along with six other Stirlings from 7 Squadron. W/C Dale's N3654 suffered engine trouble, and he settled for bombing near Hamburg, S/L Menaul turned back with similar problems when approaching the German coast, S/L Morris experienced excessive fuel consumption and bombed Kiel, and only F/L Raymond actually reached Berlin, but he too bombed Kiel, having been unable to identify the primary target. Only two of the 7 Squadron contingent reached the capital, and it was a poor reflection on the Stirling's reliability, something which would dog the type for a long time to come.

May began with a raid on Hamburg on the 2/3rd, where thirteen large fires were started, and this was followed by Cologne twenty-four hours later. Despite the commitment of 100 aircraft, no more than ten bomb loads fell within the city, and this outcome, which was typical for the period, was repeated at Mannheim on the 5/6th. A total of 141 aircraft set off for this southern city, but only twenty-five bomb loads found the mark, and damage was light and superficial. A similar story of inaccuracy blighted an attack on Hamburg on the 6/7th, before the Group joined in on another crack at the warships at Brest on the 7/8th. Hits were claimed on both of the resident German cruisers, which were not confirmed, but at least, no losses were incurred. On the 8th W/C Southwell become the new commanding officer of 57 Squadron on the posting out of W/C Bertram. It was back to Hamburg on the night of the 8/9th for over 180 aircraft, and this time, an effective attack developed, which resulted in over eighty fires, the destruction of ten apartment blocks, and a death toll of 185 people, the highest of the war to date from a Bomber Command operation. Four aircraft were missing, and 149 Squadron was represented by R1506, which fell victim to a nightfighter off Heligoland and crashed into the sea. F/S Burch and three of his crew were killed, while the two survivors were taken into captivity. The inauspicious introduction to Stirling operations for XV Squadron did not improve when returning to Berlin on the same night. Undaunted, two crews, those of W/C Dale and F/L Raymond, set off once more for the capital on the 10/11th. Again Raymond reached the target, and this time bombed, but was then hit by flak which caused an engine fire. Later the aircraft was attacked by a nightfighter, but the sturdy construction of the Stirling was ably demonstrated, and N6018 made it back home. Less fortunate was W/C Dale in N3654, which was attacked and shot down by a nightfighter, becoming the first Stirling to fall onto Dutch soil. Sadly, there were no survivors, and only the body of W/C Dale was recovered and buried. In 2004 the remains of the other crew members were recovered and in May were laid to rest in Bergen General Cemetery alongside their pilot in a moving ceremony conducted with full military honours before a large crowd of local people and representatives of the RAF and the fallen. Wing Commander Ogilvie was appointed as the new commanding officer on the 16th, and his first two months at the helm would produce only one night of loss, and that would not be until the end of June. A week before Ogilvie's appointment, W/C Powell had completed his tour as commanding officer of 149 Squadron, having been awarded the DSO in February. He would be 'mentioned in dispatches' later in the year and be awarded the OBE. Sadly, he was destined to lose his life with 19 Squadron, a fighter unit, on the 18th of September 1944. He was succeeded at 149 Squadron by W/C Beaman, formally of 15 OTU and 218 Squadron.

The twin cities of Mannheim and Ludwigshafen, sitting astride the Rhine in southern Germany, would feature prominently as Bomber Command targets throughout the war, and 146 aircraft set out to attack them on the 9/10th. In the context of the period the operation was moderately successful, and cost only two aircraft. On the following night 149 Squadron supported operations to Hamburg and Berlin, the former creating over 100 fires, while only twelve of twenty-three crews reported bombing in the Berlin area. 149 Squadron's Sgt Keymer and his crew failed to return from the main objective in R1512, and no clue to their fate was ever found. P/O Franks had been briefed for Berlin to deliver a cookie, but he was unable to reach that particular destination, and joined in at Hamburg instead. The 4,000 pounder was dropped from 14,000 feet, and the crew reported the largest explosion that they had ever witnessed. The third raid on Hamburg in four nights took place on the 11/12th, and this was also effective in leaving over eighty fires burning. A return to Mannheim and Ludwigshafen on the 12/13th was a dismal failure, and a raid on Hanover three nights later was inconclusive and almost certainly ineffective. Two attacks on Cologne on consecutive nights from the 16/17th were disappointing, the latter producing the better results, with the destruction of one industrial premises and thirty houses. Earlier on the 17th 149 Squadron's S/L Clark had taken R1587 for a training flight, and collided with a Hurricane of 1401 Met Flight over Cambridgeshire, with fatal consequences for all on board the Wellington.

On the 22nd 1419 Flight completed its move to Newmarket, an airfield on the racecourse site that boasted the longest grass runways in the RAF. It was around this time that another of the war's great characters joined the unit as a Whitley/Lysander pilot. F/L 'Whippy' Nesbitt-Dufort would become something of a legend, if, indeed, he had not already achieved that status. He acquired the 'Whippy' appellation before the war, while returning from the

Hendon Air Pageant, where he and others had thrilled the crowds with their aerobatic skill and daring. Sudden engine failure over Bedfordshire had him scouring the terrain below for a suitable landing ground, and an unbelievably flat and inviting area of green presented itself. He pulled off a perfect landing, and while congratulating himself on his deliverance, noticed a rhinoceros moving in his direction, head lowered. It was at this point, that a number of lions reputedly came to his attention, but he managed to beat all-comers to the fence. Here, he learned that he had landed in the grounds of Whipsnade Zoo, with which he would forever thereafter be associated. Posted in at the same time as 'Whippy' was another new Whitley pilot, Sgt Austin. W/C Pickard ended his association with 311 Squadron during the month, and W/C Batchelor took over as British advisor, a role he would perform until the end of July.

The first major operation in June for the bomber boys was mounted by a force of 150 aircraft against Düsseldorf on the 2/3rd. S/L 'Popeye' Lucas had recently returned to 75 (NZ) Squadron to begin his second tour, now as A Flight commander, and this was his first operation. He used it as an opportunity to check out a new crew captain, but having not ventured over Germany for six months or more, he went in too low and the Wellington was lucky to escape with just a severe beating. Despite the enthusiastic claims of returning crews, the city authorities reported only light, scattered damage. It was this kind of outcome, together with overly optimistic reports of damage, which would lead to calls for the dissolution of an independent bomber force a few months hence. It was at this time that the name Federated Malay States was added to the 214 Squadron number. This came by way of the squadron's adoption by the British Malaya Association, which raised funds for the purchase of a Wellington to bear the Association's insignia, and this, a tiger's head, was duly applied to W5442. Minor operations held sway for the next week, during which a daylight coastal reconnaissance foray on the 9th cost 9 Squadron two crews, including that of the commanding officer, W/C Arnold. Four Wellingtons, all from 9 Squadron with the crews of W/C Arnold, S/L Pickard, F/O Lamb and P/O Robinson, and twelve Blenheims were sent to patrol the French and Belgian coasts in search of shipping. When BF109s arrived on the scene R1758 and T2620 were shot down into the sea, while the other two Wellingtons fought them off and escaped into cloud. W/C Arnold's crew baled out from the former at low altitude to survive as PoWs, but he had insufficient time to do so and was killed. Only one gunner survived from the crew of F/O Lamb DFC, and he also fell into enemy hands. This was the first time 9 Squadron had lost a commanding officer on operations, but sadly, it would not be the last.

The first major operation for more than a week was mounted on the 10/11th, when 100 aircraft targeted the German cruisers at Brest, which now included the *Prinz Eugen.* Düsseldorf and Duisburg were the main targets on the 11/12th, but it seems that many of the bombs intended for them fell on Cologne. Briefed for the former, 149 Squadron's Sgt Harrison and his crew found themselves in captivity, after W5439 was hit by flak and had to be crash-landed in Holland. The night of the 12/13th was devoted largely to attacks on railway yards, those at Hamm and Osnabrück providing the objectives for all-Wellington forces. From mid month, Cologne and Düsseldorf dominated proceedings, and the two cities were targeted simultaneously on no fewer than eight occasions between the 15/16th and 26/27th without a single raid inflicting significant damage. On the 20th W/C Wasse was promoted from his flight commander post at 9 Squadron, and was installed as successor to the late W/C Arnold. During the course of the month W/C Wasse was awarded the DFC. A disappointing month ended with raids on Bremen on the 27/28th and 29/30th, the former resulting in the heaviest night loss of the war to date of fourteen aircraft. The latter cost 115 Squadron three Wellingtons, two of them missing and a third crashing on return.

The July account opened at Brest on the 1/2nd, and it was an inauspicious beginning to the month for 149 Squadron. R1343 crashed in the target area, killing P/O Vincent-Welch and his crew, and there were no survivors either from the crew of P/O Horsfield after R1408 crashed in France. The assault on Bremen continued on the 2/3rd and 3/4th, when good bombing was claimed, and Essen was also attacked by a predominantly Wellington force on the latter occasion. 311 Squadron welcomed a new commanding officer on the 3rd, when B Flight commander S/L Ocelka succeeded W/C Schejbal. Brest followed on the 4/5th and 6/7th, with Münster in between on the 5/6th and again on the 6/7th. On the 6th 101 Squadron was posted to Oakington to join 3 Group after serving with 2 Group since the start of the war, first as a training unit and then in the front line. Uniquely for a 2 Group squadron, 101 had already converted to the Wellington, and had eighteen on charge by the 22nd of May. Seven operations totalling fifty-five sorties had been flown, and these were the only ones by Wellingtons in 2 Group. W/C Biggs had been in command since the 16th of May following the departure of W/C McDougal DFC to 90 Squadron. The history of 101 Squadron dates back to its first formation in July 1917, when it was formed as a night bomber unit, carrying out operations from French bases. Following disbandment it remained on the shelf until March 1928, when it was re-formed as a day bomber squadron. June 1938 saw the arrival of Mk I Blenheims, and replacement of these with the Mk IV began in April 1939, at the same time that W/C Hargroves was appointed as the commanding officer. He was an experienced officer, who had held a similar post with 37 Squadron during 1938.

On the 7/8th an all-Wellington force of over 100 aircraft took off for Cologne, and those reaching the target delivered upon it its most effective raid of the year, while a smaller all-Wellington force also produced good results at Münster. 75 (NZ) Squadron's S/L Widdowson took L7818 to the latter with Sgt James Ward as second pilot, in order for him to gain experience before being given command of his own crew. A New Zealander born of English parents, Ward had arrived at Feltwell on the 13th of June, and undertaken a number of operations with experienced crews. On the return flight, and with the Dutch coast visible ahead, the Wellington was attacked by a BF110 nightfighter and raked with gunfire, which damaged hydraulics and caused a fire in the starboard engine. After a number of futile attempts to quell the flames Ward climbed out onto the wing, and tried to dampen them with a canvass bag stuffed into the seat of the fire. Eventually the bag was torn from his grasp by the slipstream, and unable to do more, he clambered, exhausted, back into the fuselage. His actions were sufficient to enable the aircraft to reach home, where a landing was made at Newmarket without flaps and brakes, the bomber eventually coming to rest against the boundary hedge. For his courage Ward was awarded the Victoria Cross, and was deemed ready to begin operations as a crew captain. On the following night Wellingtons returned to Münster to hit railway installations, and a smaller number of the type attacked a power station at Bielefeld. The former pre-empted a new Air Ministry directive issued on the 9th, which highlighted Germany's transportation system and the morale of its civilian population as its weakest points. The C-in-C was therefore urged to concentrate his efforts during the moon period against the major railway centres ringing the Ruhr. On moonless nights, however, the Rhine cities of Cologne, Düsseldorf and Duisburg would be easier to locate, while on dark nights with less favourable weather conditions more distant urban targets were to be attacked.

That night, the 9/10th, 101 Squadron opened its 3 Group account when sending out eleven aircraft. Aachen and Osnabrück were the main targets, and an unusually destructive raid fell on the former, with Wellingtons play-ing only a minor role, while the majority of the Wellingtons operating were failing dismally at Osnabrück. It was no better on the following night, when Wellingtons dominated in a raid on Cologne by over 100 aircraft, which achieved only slight superficial damage. 149 Squadron had sustained no losses since the first night of the month, but T2737 failed to return from what was claimed as a highly successful raid on Bremen on the 14/15th, and the entire crew of P/O Dixon was later reported to be in captivity. Three nights later a flak damaged N2853 crashed in Suffolk on return from Cologne after Sgt Stewart was blinded by a searchlight. He and four of his crew suffered injuries, and one man was killed.

2 Group had begun mounting 'Circus' operations in January, in an attempt to draw enemy fighters into a war of attrition with escorting squadrons of RAF fighters. It was decided to use these occasions to send small numbers of heavy bombers against targets in daylight under cover of cloud. Targets were generally airfields, power stations and industrial plants, and XV Squadron's experiences were no doubt typical of those involved. The first such operation for XV came on the 5th of July. Three Stirlings captained by S/L Menaul, F/L Gilmour and F/O Thompson went to the Fives-Lille steel works, picking up their escort over the Essex coast and returning safely. S/L Piper had now replaced S/L Morris as a flight commander, and he and

S/L Menaul each led a section back to Fives-Lille on the afternoon of the 6th, and for the second day running, encountered BF109s, which inflicted damage to F/L Gilmour's aircraft, but again, all returned. On the 7th it was a chemical works at Chocques which was attacked by three of the squadron's Stirlings, while three more failed to hit a power station at Lille on the following day. Ground haze forced a squadron element to attack a secondary target at Lebuisiere on the 9th, and similar conditions thwarted an attack on Fives-Lille on the 11th, when Hazebrouck marshalling yards were bombed instead. On the 18th clear skies forced the abandonment of a raid on Wesel, and N6030 crashed into the sea, killing F/O Marshall and his crew, the first to be lost to a Circus operation. On the following day, S/L Piper, in N6018, led a section to bomb a factory at Lille. Crossing the enemy coast at Dunkerque, the formation was met by predicted flak, and the leader's aircraft went down in flames, S/L Piper and one other alone surviving by parachute to fall into enemy hands.

The remaining attempts to operate under the Circus arrangement failed in the face of unfavourable weather conditions, and XV Squadron's involvement was terminated. This did not, however, mean an end to daylight operations. After ineffective operations against Cologne, Frankfurt and Mannheim over the next few nights, a major daylight attempt on the cruisers at Brest was planned for the 24th. However, when the *Scharnhorst* slipped out of port and headed south to La Pallice on the 23rd, it forced a change of the plan that had originally involved around 150 aircraft. 7 and XV Squadrons despatched three Stirlings each to attack the *Scharnhorst* at sea, but the XV Squadron effort became an expensive fiasco. P/O Needham was forced to abandon his sortie with the undercarriage jammed down, Sgt Jones attacked the wrong target, and although F/O Campbell is believed to have delivered an attack, he and his crew failed to return in N6038 after it crashed fifty miles out from the Welsh coast with no survivors.

The new plan for Operation Veracity called for an attack on the *Scharnhorst* at its new location by Halifaxes, while Wellingtons from 1 and 3 Groups concentrated on the *Gneisenau* and *Prinz Eugen* at Brest. Three Fortresses of 2 Group's 90 Squadron were to carry out high-level bombing runs to draw up some of the enemy fighters, while Hampdens of 5 Group did likewise at a less rarified altitude under the umbrella of a Spitfire escort. The seventy-nine Wellingtons were to take advantage of the distractions to make their attack without cover, and would hopefully fight their way through to the target. In the event, the fighter opposition was far stronger than expected, and ten Wellingtons were shot down. Among 40 Squadron's participants was a Wellington flown by Sgt Joe Lancaster. His gunners fired on a BF109, as did gunners from other aircraft, and the enemy pilot was seen to bale out as the fighter spiralled down towards the sea. Sgt Lancaster would survive his time with 40 Squadron, and eventually serve a second tour with 12 Squadron on Lancasters. After the war he enjoyed a successful career as a test pilot. Six hits were claimed on the *Gneisenau*, although they were unconfirmed, but the

Halifaxes severely damaged the *Scharnhorst*, at great cost to themselves, and she was forced to return to Brest, where better repair facilities existed. The month ended with another ineffective raid on Cologne on the 30/31st, for which the continuing period of bad weather was blamed. During the course of the month, a representative of the government of the Gold Coast visited 218 Squadron with a view to adopting it, and henceforth, it became officially titled 218 (Gold Coast) Squadron.

August's operations for the Wellington brigade began at Hamburg and Berlin on the 2/3rd, 149 Squadron providing eleven aircraft for the former, two of which brought their bombs home while two others attacked alternatives. The month continued with a useful raid on Mannheim on the 5/6th, for which the squadron again put up eleven aircraft. R1524 was absent from Mildenhall after this operation, having crashed in Belgium, and there were no survivors from the crew of Sgt Fowler. The same target claimed X9633 on the following night also over Belgium, and took to their deaths the crew of Sgt Farmer. Essen escaped with light damage on the 7/8th, despite the commitment of over 100 aircraft, including thirty-two Wellingtons, while forty-five others were sent to bomb railway yards at Hamm. On the 10th of August the previously mentioned S/L 'Pick' Pickard, who is often credited with the famous phrase, 'there's always bloody something', was posted from 9 Squadron to 3 Group HQ at the conclusion of his tour, with over sixty operations to his credit. Hamburg was the target for Wellingtons on the 8/9th, and Hanover and Berlin on the 12/13th. 149 Squadron's P/O Beamer and his crew were briefed for Hanover, and they all died, when R1024 was shot down into the sea off Sylt. T2716 was hit by flak, which killed one member of the crew, and was further damaged by the attentions of a nightfighter. P/O Fox crash-landed the Wellington in Suffolk, and another member of the crew subsequently succumbed to his injuries.

On the 14th W/C Freeman DFC was posted to 115 Squadron from 57 Squadron to succeed W/C Evans-Evans as commanding officer. Evans-Evans would eventually gain the rank of Group Captain, and in 1944 become the station commander at Coningsby, the home of 83 and 97 Squadrons. They would be posted back to 5 Group from the Pathfinders in April 1944 to act as the heavy element in 5 Group's own marker force. 'Tiny' Evans-Evans never lost his desire to be 'one of the boys', and he occasionally took a Lancaster on operations with a scratch crew, despite his immense bulk fitting somewhat uncomfortably into the confined space of the cockpit. There was some suggestion that his flying skills left something to be desired, but he was a popular figure, and was a buffer between the crews, who were disgruntled at being posted from 8 Group, and the abrasive and unpopular 54 Base commander, Air-Commodore 'Bobby' Sharpe. On the night of the 21/22nd of February 1945, G/C Evans-Evans would climb into an 83 Squadron Lancaster with a 97 Squadron crew, and set off to attack the Mittelland Canal at Gravenhorst. He would not return, and would lose his life with all but one of those on board.

Twenty-five year old W/C Freeman was a New Zealander, who, before the war, had flown Gauntlets and Spitfires with 74 Squadron. He had also been an original member of the New Zealand Flight, which became the nucleus of 75 (NZ) Squadron in April 1940. He completed a tour with that squadron, and was awarded a DFC. He presided over his first operation and casualty on the night of his appointment, when Hanover and Magdeburg were the main targets for 3 Group's Wellington and Stirling brigades. It turned out to be quite an expensive night for 7 and XV Squadrons, the former writing off three Stirlings in landing crashes, while the latter had two go down shortly after taking off and a third ditched in the North Sea, from where its crew was picked up by the enemy. Most of the Wellingtons operating on the 16/17th were sent to Cologne and Duisburg, the 149 Squadron contingent of seven targeting the latter. It was on the 18th that civil servant Mr D M Butt completed his analysis of recent Bomber Command operations, and its disclosures were to send shock waves reverberating around the Cabinet Room and the Air Ministry. Having studied around 4,000 photographs taken during 100 night operations in June and July, he concluded that only a tiny fraction of bombs were falling within miles of their intended targets. This swept away at a stroke any notion that the Command was having an effect on the enemy's war effort, and demonstrated its claims of success to be little more than propaganda. It also provided ammunition for the detractors, who were calling for bomber aircraft to be redistributed to other Commands, to help in the battle against the U-Boat, and to redress reversals in the Middle East. These damning revelations would forever unjustly blight the period of tenure as C-in-C of Sir Richard Peirse, and would ultimately lead to his departure.

On the night of the report's release forty-one Wellingtons, including seven from Mildenhall, were sent to attack railway installations at Duisburg. 149 Squadron's X9704 failed to return having been shot down by a nightfighter over Holland. P/O Lynn and one of his crew were killed, and a further man succumbed to his injuries while in captivity. X9746 was also engaged by a nightfighter and severely damaged, but P/O Gregory was able to nurse it back home to a safe landing, where it was declared to be beyond economical repair. It was this exploit which sealed the award to P/O Gregory of the DFC, while his co-pilot, Sgt Billington, received the DFM. The final third of the month was dogged by bad weather, and operations to Kiel on the 19/20th, Mannheim on the 22nd/23rd, Karlsruhe on the 25/26th, Cologne on the 26/27th, Mannheim again on the 27/28th, Duisburg on the 28/29th, Frankfurt and Mannheim on the 29/30th and Cologne and Essen on the night of the 31st were generally ineffective, and at not one location was damage significant. The earlier of the Cologne raids resulted in an eventful time for S/L Hal Bufton, a 9 Squadron flight commander. W5703's engines started to play up just before the target was reached, but the bombs were delivered in accordance with the briefing. Shortly afterwards one engine caught fire and the other seized, forcing the crew to bale out near Catillon.

Bufton landed in a field, where he immediately destroyed his papers and set about finding his crew. Despite walking until dawn he was unable to locate his crew, and made contact instead with the curator of the local church, who directed him to the Mayor. He was then taken to a farm where he met up with a member of his crew, Sgt Crampton. Bufton spent the next few weeks travelling between villages using various modes of transport, until the resistance organised transport via Abbeville to Tours and Marseilles. On the 4th of November he travelled by train to Perpignan, before continuing on foot across the Pyrenees to reach the British Embassy in Madrid on the 11th of November. It was the 8th of December before he reached Gibraltar, and he finally arrived back in the UK on the 20th of December. As matters turned out, his safe deliverance was something of a fortuitous event for Bomber Command. We will meet up with Bufton again shortly.

In the midst of the flurry of ineffective operations, W/C Davy was posted from 40 Squadron on the 23rd for a period of duty at the Air Ministry, but he would return to the operational scene in March 1942 to take command of 214 Squadron for a short spell. S/L Stickley was promoted from flight commander to assume command of the squadron on the same day. Another change in leadership during the course of the month involved 75 (NZ) Squadron, to which W/C Sawrey-Cookson DSO, DFC, a former member of the Royal Artillery, and unlike his predecessors, an Englishman, was posted from his flight commander post at 149 Squadron to replace W/C Kay as commanding officer.

On the 25th 1419 Flight became 138 Squadron, the number it would carry proudly until the end of the war. The original 138 Squadron was formed on the 1st of May 1918, but it was still only a nucleus when the process was suspended on the 4th of July to provide crews for front line units. Re-formation took place at Chingford on the 30th of September, but the squadron failed to achieve operational status as a fighter/reconnaissance unit before hostilities ended, and it was eventually disbanded on the 1st of February 1919. The squadron boasted a complement of six Whitleys and four Lysanders, and S/L Knowles remained in command, but was promoted to Wing Commander with the now Squadron Leaders Jackson and Nesbitt-Dufort as A Flight (Whitleys) and B Flight (Lysanders) commanders respectively. The newly commissioned P/O Austin had earlier been officially re-posted to the squadron along with P/O Smith, but the hand written entries in the ORB suggest that these movements predate the formation of the squadron. P/O Widdup arrived from 10 OTU on the 31st, by which time 138 Squadron had carried out its first operation. At 20.35 on the 29th, Z6473 took off on Operation Trombone, with F/O Hockey at the controls, and S/L 'Pick' Pickard as second pilot.

Percy Pickard, as we have learned, was already a legend. His reputation within Bomber Command did not, of course, rely on his acting ability, but rather on his outstanding record of operational service, which, we can remind ourselves, had begun with 99 Squadron at Newmarket at the outbreak of war. From there he moved on to act as British advisor to the newly formed Czechoslovakian unit, 311 Squadron between July 1940 and May 1941. After that he was appointed as a flight commander with 9 Squadron, and it was at the conclusion of this tour in early August, that 'Pick' was posted to 3 Group HQ at Exning. Apparently taking advantage of a spot of leave he called in at Newmarket to visit his friend F/O Hockey. Never one to turn down a spot of excitement, Pickard talked his way into the right-hand seat, and he and Hockey successfully delivered their cargo from 500 feet to a location near Châteauroux, before returning safely after almost eight hours in the air. On the last night of the month, 'Pick' flew as second pilot to F/L McGilivary on a most unusual operation, which is not recorded in the ORB. The aircraft was a Wellington borrowed from 214 Squadron based at Stradishall, presumably because of a shortage of serviceable Whitleys, and its cargo was six 250 lb bombs and half a million cigarettes, the latter for the benefit of the unfortunate Dutch people under occupation. This concluded Pickard's involvement with special duties for the time being, but he would return in October 1942 to command 138's sister squadron, 161, which would be formed early in the coming year. In the meantime, he was posted to the command of 4 Group's 51 Squadron, and would lead the famous Bruneval operation, in which commandos were successfully parachuted onto an enemy radar station on the French coast. They dismantled the equipment, captured an operator, and returned safely home, enabling British scientists to examine a working example of German radar technology.

Another change in leadership during the month took place at 214 Squadron, where W/C Jordan's tour of duty came to an end. His successor was W/C Cruikshanks, whose period of tenure would be brought to a premature conclusion.

Cologne hosted a small raid by Wellingtons and Hampdens to open the September account on the 1/2nd, and this was followed by Frankfurt and Berlin twenty-four hours later. 1, 4 and 5 Groups were recalled while outbound for Brest on the 3/4th, but the 3 Group crews pressed on to bomb on estimated positions through a smoke screen. The first large-scale operation in September was directed at Berlin on the 7/8th, when almost 200 aircraft were despatched. Less than 140 crews claimed to have bombed in the target area, and they inflicted a modest degree of damage on housing, transport and public utilities and a handful of war industry factories. It was achieved at a cost of fifteen aircraft, plus three others from a simultaneous raid on Kiel, and this made it the heaviest night loss of the war to date. XV Squadron's N6045 crashed in Holland after being hit by flak, but the eight man crew of F/L Wallace-Terry all survived. After the war the crew's navigator, Sgt Richard Pape, wrote an inspiring and sometimes harrowing account of his time in German hands entitled, *Boldness Be My Friend*. Another failure to return was 214 Squadron's R1784, which was bearing the crew of W/C Cruikshanks, all of whom died. W/C MacFadden was appointed as his successor, but he too would be lost on operations towards the end of his tour. The weather relented in time for the first major attack of the war on

Kassel on the 8/9th, and clear skies provided an opportunity for the crews to inflict some useful damage on two important industrial premises, some public buildings and a railway station.

The night of the 10/11th brought the first Stirling operation to Italy, a difficult destination for the type because of its inability to attain sufficient altitude to clear the Alps with room to spare. The target on this night was the Royal Arsenal at Turin, and while all seven Stirlings from 7 Squadron rose literally to the challenge, only three of XV Squadron's contingent of six made it all the way. Fifty-five Wellingtons were despatched to bomb shipyards at Kiel on the 11/12th, and two of them failed to return. Of these, X9879 was one of seven aircraft from 149 Squadron, and it crashed in the target area killing Sgt Bennett and his crew. On a brighter note, there would now follow almost six weeks of loss-free operations for 149 Squadron. Frankfurt was the main target on the 12/13th, when 130 assorted types were dispatched, but bombing was scattered over a wide area and the bulk of the damage was to housing. Almost 150 aircraft were detailed for Brest on the 13/14th, but most crews bombed on approximate positions through a smokescreen. More encouraging results were achieved at Hamburg on the 15/16th, when over 100 aircraft delivered a telling blow, which caused damage to various districts. This was a bad night for 75 (NZ) Squadron, however, after X3205 was hit by flak and crashed in the target area. Sgt Jimmy Ward, recently awarded the Victoria Cross for his courage two months earlier, was killed along with two of his crew, the remainder escaping by parachute to fall into captivity. 9 Squadron's X3222 became the first Mk III Wellington to be written off in Bomber Command service when it crashed in Norfolk late on the 26th after being recalled from an intended raid on Emden. 99 Squadron suffered a wounding night on the 28/29th when Frankfurt was the target. Two of its Wellingtons failed to make it back and two others crashed on return leaving a death toll of fifteen men, with three in captivity and three more on the run, who would eventually get back home.

Convertees to the Stirling soon discovered that operating efficiency would be restricted by the constant technical failures afflicting the type, particularly failures associated with the undercarriage. Rarely would operational strength rise above 50% of actual strength during this first year of operations. On the 10th of October a ceremony was held at XV Squadron to bestow upon Stirling N6086 the name 'MacRobert's Reply', and the aircraft was then assigned as the personal chariot of F/O Boggis. Lady MacRobert, a widow, had lost three sons to flying, one in an accident before the war, and two in RAF service, and she donated money for the purchase of four Hurricanes and one Stirling. There was nothing special about the particular Stirling selected, and sadly, it would be badly damaged in a take-off accident during a detachment to Lossiemouth early in 1942, and the name passed on to another aircraft. On the 12th Stirlings N6093 and W7448 arrived at Mildenhall in preparation for 149 Squadron's conversion to the type, following in the footsteps of 7 and XV Squadrons. The first major night of activity of the month, and indeed, the first large-scale operation of the war against Nuremberg, the birth place of Nazism, took place on the 12/13th, which coincidentally, was MacRobert's Reply's first operational sortie. Some 152 assorted aircraft took off for southern Germany, while ninety-nine, mostly Wellingtons and Hampdens, went north to Bremen, and ninety Hampdens and Manchesters targeted a chemicals factory at Hüls near the Ruhr. The 373 sorties represented a new record in one night, but this massive effort was not rewarded with success, and few bombs found the mark at any of the targets. Matters did not improve much, if at all, at Düsseldorf on the 13/14th, Nuremberg again on the 14/15th, Duisburg on the 16/17th and Bremen once more on the 20/21st.

The latter Nuremberg operation cost 40 Squadron three missing crews, and then the Duisburg raid of two nights later proved to be the Squadron's final operation in its present form. It resulted in the failure to return of the B Flight commander, S/L Kirby-Green, who alone of his crew survived to be taken prisoner. Sadly, he was one of those murdered by the Gestapo following the Great Escape in 1944. Earlier in the day notification had been received, that the squadron was to prepare for a move to Malta for a two month tour of duty on special operations. Following the recent heavy losses aircrew strength was now down to eight trained crews and two freshmen, and six new crews were posted in to fill the gaps.

Haze was blamed for difficulties at Bremen again on 21/22nd, an operation that brought the attentions of the Grim Reaper back upon 149 Squadron. Z8795 crashed into the River Scheldt on the Belgian bank, and there were no survivors from the crew of P/O Hodge. Cloud and icing conditions hampered an attempt on Mannheim on the 22/23rd, but some hits were scored on the Deutsche Werke U-Boat yards at Kiel on the 23/24th. Unfavourable weather persuaded most crews to abandon their efforts to reach Frankfurt on the 24/25th, but at last, two nights later, some useful damage was caused at Hamburg, although this could not be repeated when fifty-six crews returned there on the last night of the month.

Now back to 40 Squadron's departure from 3 Group and Bomber Command. Shortly after 21.00 hours on the 23rd W/C Stickley and the new flight commander, S/L Greer, led B Flight on a direct route to Malta. On the 25th S/L Craigen took A Flight to Hampstead Norris as a forward staging point, with a view to a departure for Gibraltar in the early hours of the 26th. S/L Craigen's aircraft became unserviceable, and it was planned for the other seven aircraft to take off without him, and for him to follow on. Accordingly, the first two aircraft got away at 03.00 hours, and were followed by X9974 with P/O Saunders at the controls. Keeping the Wellington very low to gain maximum flying speed, P/O Saunders misjudged the height, and tore off the pitot head on the boundary fence. Robbed of all indication of speed, the pilot attempted to complete a circuit before landing, but the heavily laden Wellington clipped trees, crashed, exploded and killed all ten men on board. The five remaining take-offs were scrubbed, and it was decided to despatch these from Portreath, a more suitable airfield for fully laden aircraft. After a spell of bad weather, they finally got away on the 30th, and all arrived safely at their destination. What remained of 40 Squadron at Alconbury was little more than a skeleton, the entire operational and most of the technical and administrative staff having departed for warmer climes.

As November began 149 Squadron had eight Stirlings on charge, and conversion training was well under way. Thick cloud over Kiel on the 1/2nd allowed the residents to hear the bomber force above, but prevented the crews from locating the target, and no bombs fell within the town. On the 6th 40 Squadron began a rebuilding process under S/L Spence, who was posted in from his flight commander post with 218 Squadron. No doubt frustrated by the recent spell of bad weather, and eager to erase the memory of the Butt Report, Peirse planned a major night of operations for the 7/8th. The original plan was to raid Berlin with over 200 aircraft, but a discouraging weather forecast prompted the 5 Group AOC, AVM Slessor, to object, and he was allowed to withdraw his aircraft and send them instead to Cologne. A third operation was also to be mounted, involving Wellingtons and Stirlings of 1 and 3 Groups, whose destination would be Mannheim. Together with the night's support and minor operations, the 392 sorties despatched represented a new record high. A total of 169 aircraft ultimately took off for the capital, including five 149 Squadron Wellingtons as follows; X9832 F/L Fox, X9758 P/O Barnes, X9878 Sgt Dane, X9824 Sgt Parker and Z8837 Sgt Swain. Sixty-one Hampdens and fourteen Manchesters headed for Cologne, and fifty-three Wellingtons and two Stirlings took on Mannheim. The night's largest contribution was provided by 218 Squadron, whose thirteen Wellingtons were assigned to Berlin, and in the light of the unfolding events, it would prove to be a magnificent effort indeed. Among the squadron's crew captains on this night were S/L Spence, S/L Price and F/L Dunham, all of whom we will meet again as they step up to positions of command. The night degenerated into a disaster, partly as a result of the weather, and less than half of the Berlin force reached the target area. A massive twenty-one aircraft failed to return from what was a dismal failure, which had succeeded in destroying only fourteen houses and damaging a few dozen other buildings. 149 Squadron was represented among the missing by X9878, in which Sgt Dane and all but one of his crew lost their lives, but 99 Squadron was the hardest-hit among the 3 Group representatives, losing three aircraft. 214 Squadron's flak-damaged X3206 had to be ditched in the Channel by P/O Ercolani, who arrived with his crew on the Isle of Wight three days later, apparently none the worse for the experience. After the war P/O Ercolani would be a founder of the Ercol furniture company, which was well known in the fifties and sixties. The Cologne contingent fared much better and came through unscathed, but so did the intended target. No bombs at all fell on Mannheim, and seven Wellingtons were lost in the process. Together with the missing from all other activity, the Command registered the loss of thirty-seven aircraft, more than twice the previous highest, and this was the final straw for the War Cabinet and the Air Ministry. Peirse was summoned to a meeting with Churchill to make his explanations, and on the 13th he was instructed to restrict further operations, while the future of Bomber Command was considered at the highest level.

There were no operations of any description for the main force from the 10th until the night of the 15/16th, when small-scale raids were mounted against Emden and Kiel. 99 Squadron sent some aircraft to the former, and two failed to come back, while a third crashed on return, and 149 Squadron's R1627 was also lost on the same operation, disappearing without trace with the crew of Sgt Bramhall. Meanwhile, new crews and aircraft had begun to assemble at Alconbury, where 40 Squadron was rebuilding, and the first training flights were conducted by the crews of S/L Spence, P/O Bain and Sgt Griffith on the night of the 22nd. Earlier that day 149 Squadron registered its first Stirling casualty. W7456's starboard outer caught fire on take-off from Oakington for a training flight in the hands of P/O Lofthouse, who carried out a successful crash-landing in Cambridgeshire, without injury to the crew. P/O Lofthouse would go on to a distinguished career as a Pathfinder with 7 Squadron, which would be brought to an abrupt end by an enemy nightfighter on approach to Berlin in August 1943. On board the Lancaster was the Oakington station commander, G/C Willetts, and happily all eight men survived to be taken prisoner.

Three XV Squadron Stirlings were sent to the Ruhr by daylight on the 25th, but all turned back short of the target area, W7450 as a result of engine problems. At the controls was Sgt Fraser Barron, a young New Zealander on his first tour. Barron had ahead of him a distinguished career, which would take him to 7 Squadron as a Pathfinder. Rising through the ranks to squadron leader he began his second tour with 7 Squadron, his third tour in all, in December 1943 as a flight commander, and was promoted to wing commander in February 1944, ultimately to assume command of 7 Squadron at the end of April. Three weeks later, while acting as Master Bomber for an operation against marshalling yards at Le Mans, his seventy-ninth sortie, he and his Lancaster were lost, possibly having collided in the air with his deputy master bomber. Also on the 25th, 138 Squadron bade farewell to W/C Knowles DFC and S/L Jackson. The former was appointed station commander at Jurby on the Isle of Man, where, sadly, his tenure and his life would be brought to an untimely end. Taking advantage of the presence on his station of a Whitley in transit to Belfast, he borrowed it to take some friends for a jaunt, and died when it crashed on take-off. He was replaced at 138 Squadron by the familiar form of W/C Farley DFC, the original commander of 419 Flight, now fully recovered from his broken leg. W/C Heath was posted in as 40 Squadron's new commanding officer on the 26th, and S/L Spence was posted to the command of 149 Squadron on promotion to succeed W/C Beaman. That night W/C Spence presided over his first operation, which also brought the operational debut of 149 Squadron's Stirlings. N6099 went to Ostend in company with seventeen Wellingtons, and returned safely. It was on this night also that 'Popeye' Lucas concluded his second tour of operations with 75 (NZ) Squadron. After a training course he would go on to command 1519 Beam Approach Training (BAT) Flight, before returning to New Zealand in March 1942. In November 1943 he would set sail again for England, and serve as a flight commander with 487 (NZ) Squadron of the 2nd Tactical Air Force, completing his third tour of operations on the 11th of July 1944. Limited operations began for 40 Squadron on the night of the 27/28th, when Sgts Swain and Griffith made up the numbers in a tiny force of seven aircraft to attack Ostend. Düsseldorf was actually the main target on that night, but Cologne received many of the bombs intended for it. The month ended with 181 aircraft heading for Hamburg to attack the city and its shipyards. During the course of the month 149 Squadron's A Flight commander, S/L James, was screened, but he would return to the operational scene in the following May as the commanding officer of 9 Squadron.

December would be dominated by the port of Brest and its lodgers, and no fewer than thirteen operations of varying sizes were sent against it. A daylight operation was launched on the 18th under the codename Operation Veracity, undertaken by eighteen Halifaxes, eighteen Stirlings, nine each from 7 and XV Squadrons, and eleven Manchesters. Having joined forces over Land's End, the formation, minus the Manchesters which were late, headed for Brest, and it was the Stirlings which were first into the attack. They were met by a fierce flak barrage and BF109s, which shot down two 7 Squadron aircraft. The XV Squadron crews bombed from 17,000 feet, while beating off persistent fighter attacks, and a number of BF109s were claimed as destroyed. The fighters, however, were able to shoot down two XV Squadron Stirlings, and there were no survivors from either crew. On the credit side, a number of XV Squadron crews claimed hits on the *Gneisenau*, and smoke was seen to be issuing from her.

Targets in Germany during the month included Aachen on the 7/8th, Cologne on the 11/12th, Wilhelmshaven on the 16/17th, Cologne again on the 23/24th, Düsseldorf on the 27/28th, and Wilhelmshaven, Hüls and Emden on the 28/29th, and only the latter Wilhelmshaven raid produced any significant damage. One of the minor operations on the 11/12th was to Le Havre, and this was P/O Lofthouse's first in a Stirling. Sadly, complete cloud cover forced him to return with the bombs still aboard N6103, but he took the same aircraft to Dunkerque on the following night, and delivered his payload across the docks from 12,500 feet. W/C Dixon-Wright DFC was posted from 99 Squadron to 3 Group HQ on the 12th, but he would resume his operational career in the summer. His replacement at 99 Squadron was W/C Peter Heath (Not to be confused with the W/C Peter George Roland Heath at 40 Sqn). On the 16th Stirling N6127 arrived at Marham to begin a new era for 218 Squadron, which thus became the fourth 3 Group unit to receive the type after 7, XV and 149 Squadrons. N6126 was taken on charge on the following day, and N6128 on the 23rd, but it would be February before the crews were fully converted and the working up period was completed. In the meantime, operations would continue with the Wellington.

Article XV of the British Commonwealth Air Training Plan (BCATP) Agreement, which was signed on the 7th of January 1941, called for the formation of twenty-five Canadian squadrons by May 1942. All such units were to be numbered in the 400 series, and 419 Squadron (not to be confused with 419 Flight) was the third to be formed in Bomber Command after 405 and 408 Squadrons. The former found its first home in 4 Group, and the latter in 5 Group, while 419 Squadron became the first from Canada to enter 3 Group. The squadron came into existence on paper on the 15th of December 1941, and took up actual residence at Mildenhall on the 21st under the command of W/C John 'Moose' Fulton, a Canadian with seven years RAF service and a tour of operations behind him. Another Canadian, S/L Turner, was appointed as A Flight commander, and B Flight came under a British officer, S/L Reid, both men also having extensive operational experience.

During the stand-down moonless period 138 Squadron changed address by moving to Stradishall, one of the former homes of both 419 and 1419 Flights. It would prove to be a temporary arrangement, however, and when the next move came, it would be to an airfield dedicated to secret operations. In the meantime, W/C Farley and F/L Hockey brought down the curtain on the year's operations with sorties on the night of the 28/29th. In a case of extremes, Farleys turned out to be perhaps the shortest on record, while Hockey's was among the longest. Shortly after Farley became airborne in Whitley Z6728, the airspeed indicator failed along with the radio, and the sortie was immediately abandoned. Farley's prudence was made manifest when both engines failed on touchdown. Hockey's task was to transport an assassination team to Czechoslovakia, at the request of the Czech government in exile. Their brief was to kill the SS chief Reinhardt Heydrich, a ruthless, ambitious high-ranking officer and one of Hitler's inner-circle, who had been installed as the governor, and was the embodiment of Nazi evil. Two other teams were to be dropped at other locations to set up communications and a training function. It was, therefore, a fully laden Halifax L9613 which lifted into the air from Tangmere at 22.00 hours, and headed for the French coast, before turning towards Darmstadt in southern Germany. The deeper the penetration into enemy territory, the thicker the cloud became, and the heavier the snow lay on the ground, blotting out useful features needed for navigation. Nevertheless, shortly before 02.15, Pilsen was identified by the flak it threw up, and this provided the pinpoint for the next stage of the flight to the first drop zone. There were to be no reception committees, and it was entirely Hockey's responsibility to select the terrain within the briefed area. The two assassins parachuted at 02.24, after which, the visibility deteriorated in low cloud, making it almost impossible to recognize the landscape. Within twenty minutes of the first drop, however, the remaining two teams, one of three men and the other of two, got away, and it was estimated that each landed within a dozen miles of the planned landing grounds. The return flight was reasonably uneventful, and the exhausted crew touched down at Tangmere at 08.19 after ten hours and nineteen minutes in the air.

Many accounts have been written about the assassination attempt, which was not carried out until the end of May. It was carefully planned to take place at a sharp bend in the road, where Heydrich's open-top limousine was forced to slow down *en route* to his Prague office. On the appointed day one assassin carried a submachine gun, and the other a hand grenade, but the gun jammed at the vital moment, and the grenade exploded in the gutter beside the car. Heydrich had risen to his feet to draw his pistol, and sustained shrapnel wounds, which, while quite serious, were not believed to be life-threatening. He had, in fact, even been able to give chase to the fleeing assassins before collapsing. Fortunately, a piece of horsehair from the car seat had penetrated his body, and this caused blood poisoning, which ultimately resulted in Hydrich's death on the 5th of June. Sgts Jan Kubic and Josef Gabcik were eventually betrayed, and died after a gun battle with German soldiers while they were trapped in the basement of a church.

It had been a bad year for the Command, despite the promise of three new aircraft types entering operational service during the spring. The Stirling, Halifax and Manchester had all failed to match expectations, and each had undergone long and frustrating periods of grounding, while essential modifications were put in hand. The inability of the crews to locate and hit targets at night had come to a head with the damning Butt Report in August, and a dark shadow had been cast over the Command and its C-in-C Peirse. In truth, he and his crews had done their level best with the equipment available to them, but there was never a chance of fulfilling the often unrealistic demands placed upon them by the decision makers. It stemmed from a naïve pre-war belief that dead reckoning and astro-navigation would take crews unerringly to precision targets, and as a result, insufficient priority had been given to the development of navigation aids. Only now was the Gee device in the trials stage, and it would be March before it became available for general use in the hands of selected squadrons. As the New Year dawned, the future of the Command was still hanging in the balance, the one bright spot emanating from 44 Squadron, to which the first production Lancasters had just been delivered.

1942

A new hand on the tiller; fresh tactics; the shining sword; Millennium; Pathfinders; the turning of the corner

419 Squadron's progress to operational status was hampered somewhat by an initial lack of aircraft, and it was not until the 2nd of January that the first Wellington Ic was taken on charge. X9748 was joined on the following day by Z1145, while X9757, Z1077 and Z1083 arrived on the 8th, and X3201,

X9874 and Z1053 on the 9th. Just two days later 419 Squadron launched its first sorties in anger, when W/C Fulton and P/O Cottier and their crews took off for Brest in X9748 and Z1145 respectively. This reflected the fact that January was beginning as December had ended with the continuing obsession with the port. It was just one of eleven raids of varying sizes sent against the target during the month, and these came at the tail end of the saga which had been running since March 1941. The somewhat tortured reign of Sir Richard Pierse came to an end on the 9th as he relinquished the hot seat at the head of Bomber Command. He left under a cloud, but in truth he was a fine officer, much admired and respected by the man who would ultimately step into his shoes in six weeks time. In March he would become Commander-in-Chief of Air Forces India, and in November 1943 Commander-in-Chief Air Command South-East Asia. As a temporary measure 3 Group's AVM Baldwin filled the breach as C-in-C Bomber Command until the greatest Bomber baron of them all, Sir Arthur Harris, arrived at the helm on the 22nd of February.

218 Squadron began 1942 with a new commanding officer, W/C Kirkpatrick DFC having been posted to 3 Group HQ on New Year's Eve. Later in the year he would be appointed station commander at Wyton, and would serve as senior-air-staff-officer 3 Group HQ between 1943 and 1945. He was succeeded at 218 Squadron by W/C Holder, a thirty-year old South African who had been awarded the DFC in October. XV Squadron also underwent a change in leadership, when W/C Macdonald DFC, AFC was appointed on the 5th of January. He was a very experienced officer, who had previously served as a flight commander with 4 Group's 102 Squadron, before commanding 77 Squadron between June and August 1940, and 2 Group's 82 Squadron from then until December. Also on this day 57 Squadron moved to Methwold, where it would stay for the remainder of its time with 3 Group. On the 10th W/C Inness was promoted from flight commander to succeed W/C Wasse at 9 Squadron. The latter would return to the operational scene in September to take command of 149 Squadron. The first trip of the year to Germany by the Command involved 124 aircraft, whose crews were briefed for Wilhelmshaven later that night. Returning crews claimed a successful outcome, but this was not confirmed by the local authorities. 101 Squadron appointed a new commanding officer in the shape of W/C Nicholls on the 14th. Hamburg was attacked on the night of the 14/15th and 15/16th, for which ninety-five and ninety-six aircraft respectively were dispatched. Fires were started on both occasions, but no significant damage was inflicted. Hamburg also found itself designated as an alternative target for Bremen on the 17/18th, when only eight of eighty-three aircraft attacked the primary in what might have been poor weather conditions. 99 Squadron's time with 3 Group and Bomber Command effectively ended on the 19th, when it conducted its final sorties during a sea-search. It would remain at Waterbeach until mid March, when it would take passage in stages to India to resume its war, this time against the Japanese.

Meanwhile, back at Alconbury, W/C Heath was finding the rebuilding process of 40 Squadron a somewhat trying business as a result of the posting out of its Canadian and New Zealand aircrew to 419 and 75 (NZ) squadrons respectively, while others were sent to 215 Squadron serving in the Far East. There was also another matter on his mind as the month drew to a close, and although it was of a more political nature, it impinged upon the very fundamentals of British military life, i.e. pride in and loyalty to one's unit. On the last day of 1941 an Air Ministry communiqué was received, to the effect that the Malta echelon would be renumbered 156 Squadron, and proceed to Egypt rather than return to Bomber Command, while the Alconbury echelon would retain the coveted original 40 Squadron identity. This news was not well received by W/C Stickley in Malta, who had as an ally W/C Beare, whose own 104 Squadron had also been posted to the Middle East from Bomber Command, and was now to be renumbered 158 Squadron. Following strong representations by both men over the succeeding weeks, the decision was reversed, and the home based squadrons would undergo renumbering instead.

On the 21st 149 Squadron Conversion Flight was established at Lakenheath, where detachments from the squadron proper were in residence from time to time. The Conversion Flight would remain here until being absorbed into 1657 CU on the 2nd of October. There were no major calls on Stirlings during this period, but a number of squadrons detached aircraft and crews to Lossiemouth as part of a force intended to attack the *Tirpitz* at its Norwegian mooring. Operation Oiled was mounted in the early hours of the 30th, when nine Halifaxes and seven Stirlings took off for Aa Fjord, but bad weather forced most of them to turn back when still 100 miles short of their objective. The crews remained at Lossiemouth awaiting a change in the weather, but as this was not forthcoming a return was made to Wyton on the 7th of February. It was at the end of the Lossiemouth detachment that N6086, the original MacRobert's Reply, came to grief. The last few of the XV Squadron element returning to Wyton were diverted to Peterhead for an overnight stay, and it was here that it crashed on take-off on the following morning, and was seriously damaged. It was eventually repaired, however, and found its way to 1651 Conversion unit, where it gave good service until crashing in March 1943. The MacRobert's badge and the name were applied to another aircraft, W7531, but this too would have an unhappy fate.

There was little activity at the start of February, and the obligatory raid on Brest was delivered inconclusively on the 6/7th. Another small-scale operation was mounted to the port on the 10/11th, and later that day 101 Squadron completed its move from Oakington to Bourn. Within hours of yet another raid on Brest, this time by eighteen Wellingtons on the evening of the 11th, the three warships slipped anchor in atrocious weather conditions, and, under a heavy escort of destroyers and *Schnell*-Boats, headed into the English Channel in an audacious bid for freedom. A British plan had been prepared for this precise eventuality under the code name Operation Fuller, but it seems that not all charged with its implementation were fully appraised of its requirements. In the event, it was already 10.30 hours on the 12th, when the enemy fleet was first spotted, and only 5 Group was standing by at four hours readiness. The first sorties were launched at 13.30 hours, by which time the warships had almost run the gauntlet of the Channel, and in the inhospitable weather conditions of squalls and low cloud, it proved almost impossible to establish and maintain contact. It was quite late before 3 Group was able to respond, and few if any of its aircraft located their quarry. Despite the commitment of a record number of 242 daylight sorties, few attacks were carried out, and no hits were scored. The flotilla made good its escape through the Straits of Dover and into open sea, and although *Scharnhorst* and *Gneisenau* struck mines recently laid by 5 Group, all the ships arrived in home port on the following morning.

218 Squadron's contribution to Operation Fuller was six aircraft in what was a landmark occasion, the closure of the old era and the opening of a new one. Three Wellingtons carried out the final sorties by the type in 218 Squadron service, although two returned early, leaving Sgt Griggs and his crew in R1448 to have the honour of completing the very last one. This operation also brought the first 218 Squadron Stirling sorties, flown by S/L Kerr in N3700, F/O Allen in N6127 and Sgt Tompkins in N6089, who took off between 14.30 and 15.15 hours. F/O Allen sighted two destroyers through a break in the cloud, but it was only after circling for thirty-six minutes that the cruisers were spotted from 1,500 feet. An attack was carried out against one of them, but the bombs fell harmlessly into the sea 100 yards off the starboard quarter. The Stirling was hit in the bomb bay by flak, and was then engaged by three BF110s, one attacking from dead astern, and later from the starboard quarter. After a spirited riposte from the Stirling's gunners, the assailant was seen to break away in a vertical dive, and was lost from sight. N6089 was also attacked by a BF110, but arrived home safely with its bombs, having been unable to locate the ships. S/L Kerr was the last back at 19.00 hours, having caught the briefest glimpse of his quarry before cloud obscured the aiming point. His Stirling was engaged by a Do 217, and sustained slight damage, but both aircraft dived into cloud, and that was the end of the encounter. Fifteen Bomber Command aircraft were lost, including one of the twelve contributed by 214 Squadron. W/C MacFadden ditched somewhere off the Dutch coast, and only one of the seven men on board the Wellington survived to fall into enemy hands. The 'Channel Dash' episode was a major embarrassment to the government and the nation, but on the credit side, this annoying itch had been scratched for the last time, and the Command could now concentrate on more suitable strategic targets. W/C Davy was appointed as 214 Squadron's new commanding officer, and although his stay would be brief, it would be so as the result of a posting. He had previously commanded 40 Squadron between December 1940 and August 1941, where he was respected but considered to be somewhat aloof.

As we used 149 Squadron as representative of a 3 Group Wellington unit, so we now see life as a Stirling unit through the eyes of 218 Squadron. On the day after the Channel Dash, the squadron gained its first experience of the Stirling malaise, when N3713's undercarriage collapsed on landing at Lakenheath at the end of a training flight in the hands of Sgt Lamason and his crew. This crew took part in the squadron's second Stirling operation, when two were dispatched on the 18th to bomb Le Havre and drop leaflets over Paris. Sgt Lamason completed the operation in N3700, but Sgt Gregg and crew returned short of fuel having bombed Le Havre, and as N6089 touched down at Oakington, a 500 lb bomb fell off onto the runway without detonating.

The debacle of the 12th was the final operation for W/C Heath and his men under the 40 Squadron number. On the 14th it became 156 Squadron, and as a result it would be 156 Squadron rather than 40 which went on to fame as a founder member of the Pathfinder Force, and 158 Squadron, not 104, which became one of the mainstays of 4 Group's offensives for the remainder of the war. Also on the 14th a new Air Ministry directive was issued, which opened the way for the blatant area bombing of urban Germany, and an assault on the morale of the civilian population, particularly its workers. This had, of course, been in progress for a long time, but it could now be prosecuted in the open, without the pretence of aiming for industrial and military targets. Waiting in the wings, or rather, rolling in the Atlantic swell, was a new leader, who would pursue this policy with a will, and who had the force of character to fight the Command's corner against all-comers. A few days earlier, on the 10th, the armed merchant ship *Alcantara* had departed Boston on America's eastern seaboard, and set course for England, carrying among its passengers Air-Chief-Marshal Sir Arthur Harris. He had spent the previous eight months as part of a diplomatic and military mission to the United States, and had played a major role in cementing relations between the two nations. He was coming home to assume the post of Commander-in-Chief Bomber Command, having spent the war up to November 1940 as Air-Officer-Commanding 5 Group. From then until the American interlude he had been a Deputy Chief-of-the-Air-Staff to Sir Charles Portal, and was a bomber baron to the core. He had been a squadron commander in the twenties in the Middle East, and spent much of his time developing the theory and practice of bombing by both day and night.

The 14th also brought an expansion to the 'secret war' programme with the formation of 161 Squadron at Newmarket around a nucleus of 138 Squadron personnel. The commanding officer was W/C 'Mouse' Fielden, who had formerly commanded the King's Flight, and he was able to call upon the services of 'Sticky' Murphy and Guy Lockhart, as these and 138 Squadron's Lysanders were posted in. Guy Lockhart was another remarkable young man, and although considered eccentric by some, he would shine brightly and inspirationally, both in his present role and later as a Pathfinder. After serving with 161 Squadron he would join 627 Squadron as a flight commander, before being given command of 692 Squadron, both Mosquito units of the Light Night Striking Force. When 7 Squadron lost its commanding officer on operations Lockhart was posted over as his successor, and it was in one of its Lancasters that his light became extinguished at the end of April 1944. 161 Squadron was originally formed as a day bomber unit in June 1918, but was disbanded five weeks later without becoming operational. It was originally intended to use the squadron for SIS operations and all pick-ups, and its initial complement of aircraft consisted of five Lysanders from 41 Group in A Flight and five Whitleys and a Wellington in B Flight plus a Hudson from Benson. Elsewhere, 156 Squadron began its operational career by sending three Wellingtons on a roving commission to Essen on the 16/17th, from which all returned safely.

Harris took up his appointment on the 22nd, and immediately set about the massive task of turning Bomber Command into a war-winning weapon. He arrived at the helm with firm ideas already in place on how to win the war by bombing alone, a pre-war theory, which had never been put to the test. He recognized, that to destroy an urban target with acceptable losses, it was necessary to overwhelm the defences and emergency services, by condensing the raid into the shortest possible time. He also knew, that to deliver a knock-out blow, he must concentrate his forces at a single target, rather than deliver ineffective pin-prick attacks at multiple targets simultaneously. He was aware too, that built-up areas are most efficiently destroyed by fire rather than blast, and it would not be long before the bomb loads carried by his aircraft reflected this thinking. This all signalled the birth of the bomber stream, and an end to the former practice, whereby crews determined for themselves the details of their sorties. It would be March before the first signs of a new hand on the tiller were made manifest, and in the meantime, he continued with the small-scale attacks on German ports. It was during such an operation on the 26/27th, that the war threw up one of its great ironies. In an attack on the floating dock at Kiel, a high explosive bomb entered the bows of the *Gneisenau*, now supposedly at safe haven after enduring eleven months of almost constant bombardment at Brest. A total of 116 of her crew lost their lives and her sea-going career was ended for good. Later on the 27th a second undercarriage collapse, this time at Marham, wrote off 218 Squadron's N3715 after a training sortie, but Sgt Tompkins and his crew emerged unscathed. On the last day of the month a 218 Squadron Conversion Flight was established at Marham, where it would remain until being absorbed into 1657 HCU at Stradishall in October.

The 1st of March was a busy day for the moon squadrons, firstly for 161 Squadron as it moved from Newmarket to Graveley, and secondly for both units in preparing for a heavy night of operations. 138 Squadron put five Whitleys into the air over France in an attempt to clear up some outstanding operations, which had been abandoned over the past month through weather or technical problems. W/C Farley delivered one agent and stores, and S/L Davies two agents on behalf of SIS. A further five agents were dropped by

Whitleys captained by F/S Peterson and Sgt Thompson, and only Sgt Wilde was unable to complete all his assigned tasks. After circling his first drop zone for an age awaiting a signal from the ground, he gave up and proceeded to his second location, where he successfully disgorged two agents, and on the way home dispensed leaflets over Douai.

The first unmistakable sign of a new hand on the tiller came at the start of March, when Harris selected the Renault lorry factory at Billancourt in Paris for his first major operation. A meticulous plan was prepared, which would exploit his tactics and set a pattern for future operations. Mounted on the night of the 3/4th it was a three wave attack, led by experienced crews, and with extensive use of flares to provide illumination. A total of 235 aircraft took off, the largest force yet to a single target, and 223 crews claimed to have bombed as briefed. 218 Squadron contributed four Stirlings led by S/L Kerr, and all completed their part in the operation. In the face of a weak flak defence most of them delivered their attack from low level, both to aid accuracy, and to avoid civilian casualties in adjacent residential districts. The operation was an outstanding success, which destroyed 40% of the factory's buildings, halting production for a month, and was achieved for the loss of just one Wellington. The satisfaction was marred only by the deaths of 367 French civilians, more than twice the previous highest death toll from a Bomber Command attack even on a German target, and collateral damage was a problem that would never satisfactorily be addressed. On return to Marham at 22.55 hours a bomb fell from F/O Allen's N3712 and exploded, and the Stirling was consumed in the ensuing fire. Sgt Laidlaw and P/O Gales, respectively the flight engineer and bomb-aimer, re-entered the blazing bomber to rescue their colleagues, but all seven men sustained injury, to which the wireless operator and a gunner later succumbed.

It was somewhat paradoxical, that Harris, as a champion of area bombing, should gain his first victory by way of a precision target. Essen was to feature prominently in Harris's future plans, and the first of three raids on consecutive nights, and five during the month, took place on the 8/9th. Over 200 aircraft were involved on this night, including twenty-seven Stirlings, and the leading aircraft were equipped with the Gee navigation device for the first time. While it helped with general orientation, it could not pinpoint Essen, which remained concealed beneath its ever-present blanket of industrial haze, and damage was only slight. On the following night 187 aircraft set off, and those reaching Essen succeeded in destroying just two houses, while scattering bombs over a score of other Ruhr towns. It was a similar story on the 10/11th, when 149 Squadron registered its first failure-to-return of a Stirling. Another of its aircraft crashed while trying to land, and F/O Pilkington and six of the eight men on board were killed. Flying as second pilot on board R9295/G, a presentation aircraft called East India III, was S/L Coleman DFC*, a New Zealander, who had completed a tour with the squadron in 1940 before serving with 148 Squadron in the Middle East. He began his third tour with 115 Squadron at Marham in September 1941, where he took part in some of the flying sequences for the feature film, *Target for Tonight*. He was posted back to 149 Squadron part way through his tour, and at the time of his death he had fifty-three operational sorties to his credit. The night of the 12/13th brought a successful attack on the port area of Kiel, where the Deutsche Werke U-Boat yards was the specific target. Five of sixty-eight Wellingtons failed to return, and three of them belonged to 75 (NZ) Squadron. The first successful Gee-led raid fell on Cologne on the 13/14th, when some useful industrial damage was inflicted, and 1,500 houses were damaged to some extent.

During the monthly stand-down on the 14th 138 Squadron moved to a new and permanent home, where it would remain until a matter of weeks before the end of hostilities. Tempsford lay nine miles to the east of Bedford, and was built on what might be termed a reclaimed bog. As time was to prove, this was a fact that would be difficult to ignore for pilots who put a wheel off the concrete taxi ways. Built by John Laing and Sons between late 1940 and the last days of summer 1941, it spread across Gibraltar Farm, a name that would persist throughout its occupation by the RAF. A few of its original farm buildings were retained and used as offices and stores, and they acted as a natural camouflage to casual onlookers from the air. To these were added the necessary hangers, a control tower and nissen hut accommodation, and a standard triangulation of runways, two of which terminated just short of the main LNER railway line from London to Edinburgh.

On the 19th W/C Southwell was posted from 57 Squadron, and at the end of June he would commence a nine month period in command of 9 Squadron. In August 1943 he would be posted to the Middle East to command 150 Squadron, and remain in that post until the middle of October. The new commanding officer of 57 Squadron was W/C Peters-Smith DFC, who presided over a period of relative activity, during which three Stirlings carried out the first mine-laying, or 'gardening' sorties by the type off Lorient on the night of the 23/24th. It was on the 25/26th that a new record force of 254 aircraft was dispatched for another tilt at Essen. A decoy fire site at Rheinberg drew off a proportion of the bombing, and the remainder was wasted elsewhere, leaving the intended target almost entirely unscathed. There was no improvement on the following night, when a smaller force tried again, but Harris would not give up, and the campaign would resume in April. The problem, as Harris well knew, was how to navigate at night over a blacked out country, which was often concealed under cloud. He believed, however, that if he could provide his crews with pinpoints on the ground, they would do the rest. Coastlines provided the best reference points, and this was a major factor in his selection of the Baltic port of Lübeck as the target for an area attack on the 28/29th. Other factors were the half-timbered construction of the buildings in the narrow streets of its old centre, which would aid the spread of fire, and the paucity of its defences. 218 Squadron contributed nine of the twenty-six Stirlings among the 234 aircraft taking off over a two-hour period during the mid evening, for an operation to be conducted along similar lines to those employed so successfully at Billancourt at the start of the month. The predominantly incendiary bomb loads reflected the fire-raising intention, and this was duly achieved in the first major success for the area bombing policy. Many crews came down to as low as 2,000 feet to make their attacks, and 400 tons of bombs rained down onto the historic city, destroying over 1,400 buildings and seriously damaging a further 1,900. Later photographic evidence suggested that 30% of the city's built-up area had been reduced to rubble, mostly as a result of fire. The operation cost twelve aircraft, three of them Stirlings, all from 7 Squadron. 218 Squadron's W7507 was almost the fourth Stirling to be lost after sustaining severe damage through flak and later a nightfighter. The Stirling was nursed back to base by F/L Humphreys and his crew, and was subsequently declared to be beyond economical repair. For their part in bringing the aircraft home, F/L Humphreys received the immediate award of the DFC, and the wireless operator, Sgt Wheeler, the DFM. It had been a good first full month of Stirling operations for 218 Squadron, in which forty-six sorties were dispatched for the loss of two aircraft at home.

By the end of the war many squadrons would be able to look back on at least one occasion, when their world collapsed around them. For 214 Squadron it was the night of the 1/2nd of April 1942, when fourteen aircraft were despatched as part of a force of forty-nine Wellingtons and Hampdens to attack railway targets at Hanau and Lohr. Carried out from low level they proved to be very costly operations, which deprived the Command of thirteen aircraft and crews. All but one of the missing aircraft were Wellingtons, whose crews were briefed to attack the former, and they were shared between just 214 and 57 Squadrons. 57 Squadron from Feltwell posted missing five crews, and 214 Squadron seven, from which only one man survived as a PoW. The Stradishall station commander, G/C Boyle, had chosen to fly on this operation, and he was in one of the seven aircraft to arrive home safely. Disasters of this magnitude were not allowed to disrupt operational con- siderations, and four nights later a new record force of 263 aircraft went to Cologne to deliver another disappointing raid. Among the five Wellingtons lost was X3489, which belonged to 75 (NZ) Squadron and contained the squadron commander, W/C Sawrey-Cookson. In contrast to his predecessors he had failed to endear himself to his men, and morale had suffered as a consequence. He and his crew were killed, and he was the first 75 (NZ) Squadron commanding officer to be lost on operations. A new commanding officer was appointed in the shape of W/C Olsen, who had apparently been 'Popeye' Lucas's initial flying instructor. Like the unit's first two commanders, W/C Olsen was comparatively advanced in years, and he used his maturity to lead a revival in morale at a time of frequent losses. The 5th was also the day on which Stirling N6092 arrived at Stradishall in preparation for 214 Squadron's conversion onto the type, for which a Conversion Flight had already been set up. N3751 would follow on the 13th, N3729, R9317, W7526 and W7527 on the 19th, R9316 on the 21st, W7532 on the 27th and R9319 on the 28th. By the middle of May the squadron would have a full complement of the type, and be declared operational, but in the meantime, operations continued with Wellingtons. A new commanding officer was appointed at 214 Squadron in April to replace W/C Davy, who was posted out. W/C Knocker would be in place to oversee 214 Squadron's conversion to the Stirling, but like some others before him, his period of command would be brought to a premature conclusion.

Stradishall also saw the arrival of C Flight and HQ Flight of 109 Squadron on the 6th. It had been born out of the Wireless Intelligence Development Unit, which was redesignated 109 Squadron at Boscombe Down in December 1940 and tasked to identify the enemy's use of radio beams and to develop radar aids for the RAF. In January 1942 parts of the squadron were dispersed to Tempsford and Upper Heyford, but came together again at Stradishall with the main purpose of developing Oboe, a blind bombing device which would revolutionise bombing from March 1943 in the hands of 105 and 109 Mosquito Squadrons of the Pathfinder Force. During its brief time with 3 Group 109 Squadron boasted a variety of aircraft including Ansons, Wellingtons and Mosquitos, but it would be in the last-mentioned type that it would carry out its finest work. W/C McMullen was in command, and among his senior pilots was the previously mentioned S/L Hal Bufton, who had been with the unit at the start back in 1940, initially as temporary CO, and had been posted back in January 1942 after serving as a flight commander with 9 Squadron and evading capture. He would undertake much of the trials flying himself, and ultimately become the squadron commander. Bufton was the brother of Sid Bufton, a former squadron commander in 4 Group and now Deputy Director of Operations at the Air Ministry. Also on the 6th, and after spending five years at Mildenhall, 149 Squadron moved out and took up residence at Lakenheath, which it had been using as a satellite station for some time.

The next tilt at Essen came on the night of the 6/7th of April, but severe storms and icing conditions persuaded many crews to bomb elsewhere, and this most important centre of war production again escaped serious damage. Yet another new record was set on the 8/9th, when 272 aircraft took off for Hamburg to encounter icing conditions and electrical storms. A little short of 200 crews reported bombing in the target area, but the local authorities reported only a few bomb loads within the city. A new commanding officer took over at 7 Squadron on the 10th, when W/C Sellick DFC, who it will be recalled had served as a flight commander with 214 Squadron earlier in the war, succeeded W/C Graham. On the 11th 161 Squadron moved out of Graveley and joined 138 Squadron at Tempsford, thus centralizing on one station the business of servicing the 'secret war'. That said, the Lysander Flight remained at Tangmere, where also stood the famous cottage in which agents spent their remaining hours before departure to the unknown. Essen was raided ineffectively twice more, on the 10/11th and 12/13th, bringing the number of major operations against it during the Harris era to eight.

Over this period, 1,555 sorties had been launched at a cost of sixty-four aircraft, in return for which damage had been slight and insignificant. Harris turned his attention to Dortmund on the 14/15th and 15/16th, but despite a combined total of 360 sorties, only a handful of houses were destroyed, and bombs were again distributed over a wide area of the Ruhr. A moderately successful operation started seventy-five fires in Hamburg on the 17/18th, and this was followed on the 22/23rd by an experiment to gauge the efficacy of Gee as a blind bombing device. Cologne was selected as the target for a force of sixty-four Wellingtons and five Stirlings, every one of which was equipped with Gee. Around fifteen bomb loads fell within the city, thus demonstrating the limitations of the device for precision bombing.

After a number of abortive attempts to deliver a pair of Russian agents into Austria, 138 Squadron tried again on the night of the 20/21st. W/C Farley decided to name himself among the crew to fulfil the role of dispatcher, and it proved to be a fateful decision. Flying in dense fog Halifax V9976 smacked into the side of a Bavarian hill, killing all eight crewmen and their NKVD passengers. The loss of W/C Farley was clearly a blow to 138 Squadron, but at least in S/L Hockey, it would find the perfect replacement, and he was promoted to Wing Commander to fill the breach. At the same time, F/L Outram was promoted to Squadron Leader to take over the Halifax flight.

In an attempt to repeat the success at Lübeck at the end of March, Harris chose another Baltic port, Rostock, for a series of raids during the final week of the month. The presence nearby of a Heinkel aircraft factory was an added attraction, and a proportion of the force would be directed specifically at this. There were many similarities with Lübeck, its coastal location, narrow streets and light defences, and the first of four operations on consecutive nights was mounted on the 23/24th. 218 Squadron put up six of the thirty-one Stirlings in an overall force of 161 for what was a disappointing start to the campaign. The squadron's W7473 suffered engine failure and crashed in Norfolk twenty-three minutes after take-off, killing Sgt Davidge and his entire crew. The centre of the town was heavily bombed on the following night, although the Heinkel factory again escaped damage. The third raid, on the 25/26th, was also accurate, and this time, W/C Guy Gibson led a 106 Squadron contingent against the Heinkel works, and at last scored some hits. Also on this night six Stirlings undertook the long trek to Pilsen in Czechoslovakia, to attack the Skoda armaments factory. At least five of them arrived and bombed, but whether 218 Squadron's W7506 was shot down over Germany before or after reaching the target is uncertain. What is known, is that there were no survivors from the eight man crew, and that P/O Millichamp was an experienced pilot on his seventeenth operation. This was the first 218 Squadron Stirling to fail to return from an operation. The final attack on Rostock was perhaps the most concentrated, and the combined tally of destruction amounted to over 1,700 buildings destroyed, and 60% of the main town area was deemed to be in ruins. A remarkable feature of the series was the loss of just eight aircraft from a total of 520 sorties, and the only missing Stirling was a 149 Squadron aircraft from the final operation.

The success was followed up at Cologne on the 27/28th, when 1,500 houses and nine industrial premises were damaged to some extent, and all three shipyards in Kiel sustained damage on the 28/29th. 419 Squadron almost lost its commanding officer during this operation. On the way home over the North Sea W/C Fulton's Wellington was attacked and severely damaged by a BF110, which wounded the rear gunner and trapped him in his turret. The hydraulics system was punctured, causing the wheels and bomb doors to lower, many of the instruments were smashed, and a blade on the port propeller was splintered, causing massive vibration and the need to shut down the engine. A dramatic loss of height persuaded Fulton to restart the engine, and a shaky return was eventually made to Mildenhall, where the shattered Wellington was belly-landed without further distress to the crew. For his superb airmanship and coolness in a crisis, Fulton was awarded the DSO, and his observer's gallantry in releasing the trapped gunner from his turret, tending his injuries when he himself was wounded, and then assisting his captain in bringing the crippled aircraft home, was recognised by the award of the DFM. The month ended with a failed attempt to hit the Gnome & Rhone aero-engine factory at Gennevilliers in Paris on the following night. 218 Squadron managed a creditable 112 sorties during the month, the highest by any of the four Stirling units, and this was achieved for the loss of just one aircraft and crew. By this time 311 Squadron had ceased operations with Bomber Command, and on the 28th departed East Wretham to begin a new career with Coastal Command.

Hamburg opened the May account on the 3/4th, when over 100 fires were started, and eleven blocks of flats were demolished by a cookie. The first of three raids on consecutive nights against the southern city of Stuttgart and its Bosch factory began twenty-four hours later, and was a disappointing failure brought about by a decoy fire site and ground haze. 218 Squadron's W7521 was severely damaged by flak, but made it back to a crash-landing in Norfolk, from which Sgt McAuley and the other seven occupants were able to walk away. Also on this night five Stirlings returned to the Skoda works at Pilsen, and the single loss was 218 Squadron's N6070, which crashed in Germany, killing F/S Gregg and all but one of the other seven men on board. Among the dead was the previously mentioned Sgt Wheeler, who had been awarded the DFM when flying with F/L Humphreys. Forty year-old S/L Ashworth took a freshman crew on a Nickeling trip to France in R9313, and this was shot down over Essex on return by two RAF fighters, a Turbinlight Havoc and a Hurricane from 1445 Flight at Tangmere, although none of the eight occupants was seriously hurt. The two succeeding attacks on Stuttgart failed to land a single bomb within the city despite the combined commitment of more than 170 aircraft.

Recent raids on Baltic coastal targets had been a great success, and perhaps this was why Warnemünde and its nearby Heinkel factory were selected for attention on the 8/9th. In the event, the attack was at best only modestly effective, and cost a hefty nineteen aircraft. Thereafter, minor operations occupied the Command for ten nights, and it was during this period, on the 17/18th, that 3 Group mounted a large mining effort in northern waters and around the Frisians. 218 Squadron's N6071 was shot down by a night fighter flown by Leutnant Rudolf Schonert over Denmark, and had to be abandoned to its fate by F/L Humphreys DFC and his crew. Three of them were hit by shrapnel as they descended, and the Australian bomb-aimer failed to survive, while the rest of the crew fell into enemy hands. It was Humphreys' twenty-seventh operation with 218 Squadron. A 3 Group mining effort involving sixty Stirlings and Wellingtons took place on the 17/18th around the northern Frisians and Heligoland. 214 Squadron launched its first Stirling sorties on this night, when five aircraft went gardening, and another carried out a leaflet drop over Vichy France. Nightfighters arrived to harass the 'gardeners', and seven aircraft failed to return, although none from 214 Squadron. An attempt to hit Mannheim on the 19/20th resulted in most of the bombs finding open country at a cost of eleven aircraft, three of which were 7 Squadron Stirlings. Two of them produced thirteen survivors, all falling into enemy hands, but those in the third aircraft were killed after it collided with a BF110 nightfighter over Belgium. 218 Squadron's DJ977 failed to return to Marham, and was lost without trace with the eight man crew of F/S Coggin. Thereafter a period of operational inactivity descended upon the Command, and during this spell, on the 27th, W/C James DFC returned to the operational scene to succeed W/C Inness at the helm of 9 Squadron, having served in 1941 as a flight commander with 149 Squadron. W/C Inness was posted to Air Staff HQ Bomber Command, and would become Group Captain Plans HQ Bomber Command in 1944.

On taking up his appointment as C-in-C, Harris had asked for 4,000 bombers with which to win the war. While there was never the slightest chance of this being granted, he needed to ensure at least, that those earmarked for him were not spirited away to what he considered to be less deserving causes. Bomber Command had not yet done enough to rescue its tarnished reputation, and the vultures were still perched in high places ready and waiting to pick over its carcass should the opportunity arise. Harris was determined that it should not, and to guarantee the Command's future he had to nullify the calls, principally from the Admiralty, for bomber aircraft to be diverted to the war against the U-Boat in the Atlantic. Others pointed to the need to compensate for reverses in the Middle-East. What Harris required was a major success, and perhaps, a dose of symbolism, to silence the critics and help his cause. Out of this was born the Thousand Plan, Operation Millennium, the commitment of 1,000 aircraft in one night against an important German city, for which Hamburg was pencilled in. Harris did not have 1,000 front-line aircraft, and in order to achieve the magic figure, he would need the support of other Commands, most notably Coastal. This was forthcoming in a letter on the 22nd, but following an intervention by the

Admiralty, Coastal Command withdrew its offer of help. Undaunted, Harris, or more likely his able deputy, AM Sir Robert Saundby, scraped together every airframe capable of controlled flight, or something resembling it, and pulled in the screened crews from their instructional duties. Come the night, not only would the magic figure be achieved, it would be comfortably surpassed. Over the last week of May, a collection of aircraft from the training units took up residence at bomber stations from Yorkshire to East Anglia, giving rise to much speculation, but as usual, it was only the civilians in the local towns and villages who knew what was actually afoot. All that remained in question was the weather, and as the days ticked inexorably by towards the end of the month, this seemed in no mood to comply.

During this tense build-up period a second attempt was made against the Gnome & Rhone factory at Gennevilliers on the 29/30th following the failure to hit it exactly a month earlier. Sadly, the mixed force of seventy-seven aircraft again failed to find the mark, and among the five missing aircraft was the Wellington containing 156 Squadron's commanding officer, W/C Heath. He and his crew were killed when X3706 crashed near Paris. He was succeeded by W/C Price DFC, who was posted in from 218 Squadron, where he had been A Flight commander with eighteen operations to his credit. Like his predecessor, his own period in command would be brought to a premature conclusion. 218 Squadron also lost the eight man crew of F/L Jones on this night, who were all killed when W7535 crashed in the target area.

Harris, meanwhile, was acutely aware of the very real danger that the giant force might draw attention to itself and compromise security, and the point was fast being reached, when the operation would have to take place or be scrubbed for the present. It was in this atmosphere of frustration that 'morning prayers' began at Harris's HQ at High Wycombe on the 30th, when all eyes were turned upon the chief meteorological adviser, Magnus Spence. He was finally able to give a qualified assurance of clear skies over the Rhineland after midnight, with a strong possibility of moonlight, while north-western Germany and Hamburg would be swathed under buckets of cloud. Thus did the fickle finger of fate turn away from Germany's Second City, and point unerringly at Cologne as the host for the first 1,000 bomber raid in history.

That night, 1,047 aircraft lined up for take-off either side of 23.00 hours, for the now familiar three-wave attack, with the four engine heavies bringing up the rear. Marham produced 3 Group's best effort of the night, in despatching eighteen 115 Squadron Wellingtons, and nineteen Stirlings from 218 Squadron, all but two of which would complete the operation and return safely home. W/C Holder led 218 Squadron in W7530, which was carrying as a passenger the most senior officer flying that night. Harris had slapped a ban on A-O-Cs taking part in this momentous operation, but 3 Group's AVM Baldwin chose to ignore it, and worry about the consequences when he got back. Some of the older training hacks pressed into the operation took somewhat reluctantly to the air, and were probably lifted more by the enthusiasm of their crews than by the power of their engines. Unable to climb to a respectable height, a number of these would fall easy prey to the defences, or would simply drop from the sky through mechanical failure. The conditions over the target were as forecast, and the operation was, by any standards, an outstanding success, which left over 3,300 buildings destroyed, and serious damage to many industrial premises, where loss of production resulted. W/C Fulton was reluctant to deprive one of his 419 Squadron pilots of a Mk III Wellington, and in a typically selfless act took to the air in an old Mk Ic hack used by the squadron for training, and completed the trip at a sedate pace without the assistance of Gee.

The loss of forty-one aircraft was a new record high, but in conditions favourable to attackers and defenders alike, it was an acceptable figure, particularly in the context of the scale of the success. 218 Squadron's W7521 was badly damaged by flak, and was ultimately abandoned by three of the crew, two of whom attempted to use a single parachute. The navigator, F/S Borrowdale, clung to Sgt Tate, one of the gunners, but was unable to maintain his hold when the parachute jerked open, and he fell to his death. Sgt Tate and one other survived to be taken prisoner, but P/O Davis and the rest of his crew perished in the crash in Germany. The eight men on board R9311 had known almost from the outset that they faced a belly landing on return, after damaging the undercarriage on take-off. Having successfully completed their part in the operation, Sgt Falconer put the Stirling down safely, and all eight men walked away. May had been an expensive month for 218 Squadron, which lost eight aircraft and five crews from seventy-nine sorties. During the course of the month, W/C Spence concluded his tour as commanding officer of 149 Squadron, and he was replaced by W/C Charlton-Jones.

Plans had been afoot since the 5th of May to convert 101 Squadron to Stirlings in line with the rest of 3 Group, and a Conversion Flight was established under S/L Crompton on the 1st of June at Oakington. Fortunately for the squadron, the Stirling's technical problems and slow rate of pro-duction meant that there was insufficient of the type for full conversion to go ahead. This would ultimately lead to an entirely new direction for 101 Squadron with another Group in five month's time, and the new command-ing officer appointed on this day, W/C Eaton, would oversee the change. Harris was anxious to use the thousand force again as soon as possible, and after a night's rest, he ordered it to be prepared for a raid on Essen on the night of the 1st/2nd. Only 956 aircraft were available to answer the call to arms for the attack, when the crews, as usual, found the target difficult to identify, and the Ruhr Valley was showered with bombs. Fifteen 218 Squadron Stirlings were led by the flight commanders, S/Ls Kerr and Ashworth, although Sgt McAuley and his crew were forced to return early with engine problems, and they walked away from the crash-landing. The remainder of the squadron's crews completed their sorties, delivering over 112,000 lb of bombs. Other towns suffered far greater damage and casualties than the intended target, where only eleven houses were destroyed in return for the loss of thirty-one aircraft.

Later that day W/C Lay, who had completed a tour with 7 Squadron in 1941, during which he rose to the rank of Squadron Leader and flight commander, was appointed as the new commanding officer of XV Squadron. The outgoing W/C Macdonald was promoted to Group Captain, and was posted to Horsham-St-Faith as station commander. This was the home of 2 Group's 105 and 139 Squadrons, the former the first Bomber Command unit to receive the Mosquito. 139 Squadron had not yet acquired its own Mosquitos, and borrowed from 105 Squadron to carry out occasional operational sorties. A follow-up raid on Essen on the 2/3rd by under 200 aircraft was equally unconvincing, but some compensation was gained on the following night, when Bremen reported its heaviest raid to date. Among eleven aircraft missing from the operation was 218 Squadron's W7474, which fell victim to a nightfighter over Holland, and only one man survived as a PoW from the eight man crew of P/O Webber. Harris couldn't leave Essen alone, and he sent another 180 aircraft back there on the 5/6th to produce another dismal failure. It was an eventful night for 149 Squadron's F/S Whitney and his crew, who were on their way home over Belgium, when R9314 collided with a nightfighter. The rear turret fell away from the aircraft, and took with it to his death Sgt Roderick, but the Stirling remained airborne until being ditched, from where the crew were picked up by an air-sea rescue launch. The nightfighter crew apparently also survived, having parachuted to safety. ACM Harris turned away from the Ruhr for a night, and sent over 200 aircraft to the port of Emden on the 6/7th, the first of four attacks during the month. This was the only successful one, and it left 300 houses in ruins, and a further 200 seriously damaged. Harris tried a final fling at Essen, with raids on the 8/9th and 16/17th, but there was no improvement, and thus this five raid series during the month had cost the Command eighty-four aircraft from 1,607 sorties, with nothing to show for it but a few broken houses.

The return to Emden on the 19/20th, 20/21st and 22/23rd did not build on the earlier success, and left a combined total of fifty houses destroyed, with a few hundred damaged. The raid of the 20/21st was the first on which W/C James led 9 Squadron into battle, and it was his twenty-eighth sortie in all. Intercepted by a nightfighter, his aircraft, X3713 was shot down, and W/C James and his crew were killed. 218 Squadron lost flight commander S/L Ashworth DFC, who died with two of his crew when W7530 was shot down by a nightfighter over Holland. The last of the series also cost the squadron a crew, when N6078 was lost without trace with the crew of P/O Medus. It was during this time, on the 20th, that W/C Freeman was posted away from 115 Squadron to be replaced by W/C Dixon-Wright. He had spent almost the entire year of 1941 as the commanding officer of 99 Squadron, before being posted in December to 3 Group HQ. Sadly, his period of tenure at 115

Squadron would be brief. W/C Freeman would go on to other things, ultimately securing an overseas posting and a return to fighters, his pre-war role. On the 17th of December 1943 he would lose his life in a Curtis Kittyhawk while attacking a Japanese airfield.

The Thousand force was reassembled for the final time for an operation to Bremen on the 25/26th. A total of 960 aircraft were made ready, including twenty Manchesters, which were operating for the very last time before being retired to training duties. Ordered by Churchill himself to participate, Coastal Command also put up 102 aircraft, in what was classed as a separate raid. This meant that the numbers converging on the target actually exceeded those going to Cologne at the end of May, and while a similar level of success was not achieved, the results far surpassed the debacle at Essen. A fraction under 700 Bomber Command crews claimed to have bombed the city, leaving 572 houses in ruins, and damage to war industry factories, in return for a new record loss of forty-eight aircraft. 218 Squadron contributed fourteen Stirlings and lost W7503, which was shot down by a nightfighter onto the banks of the Ijsselmeer in northern Holland, killing the entire crew. P/O Ball was on his fifteenth operation, and had flown on all of the 'thousand' raids, and his wireless operator, Sgt Rogers, had completed twenty-four sorties. On the 27th W/C Southwell arrived to assume command of 9 Squadron, having relinquished that position at 57 Squadron on the 16th of March. Two follow-up raids on Bremen on the 27/28th and 29/30th achieved significant levels of damage to industry, port facilities, shipping and housing, but 218 Squadron lost DJ974 to flak over Germany during the former, and there were no survivors from the crew of Sgt Waters. The squadron registered a record 113 sorties during the month, but lost six aircraft and five crews in the process.

The 2nd of July brought varying fortunes for two former stalwarts of 3 Group in general and XV Squadron in particular. The 139 Squadron commanding officer, W/C Oakeshott, a XV Squadron veteran of the Battle of France, borrowed a Mosquito for a daylight raid on Flensburg, and ever the warrior, G/C Macdonald, the recently departed XV Squadron commander, did likewise. The two aircraft took off shortly before noon, and both were shot down. W/C Oakeshott's aircraft crashed into the sea without survivors, but G/C Macdonald and his navigator were able to abandon their's, and both spent the remainder of the war as guests of the Reich. That night Bremen received its third follow-up raid, and it was another effective attack, which damaged over 1,000 buildings. It was, however, a bad start to the month for 214 Squadron. W/C Knocker and his crew failed to return in BF313, having been shot down by a nightfighter over Holland, and all eight men were killed. N7318 also went missing with the crew of P/O Jeary, and this proved to be 218 Squadron's final casualty at Marham, which it vacated on the 7th to take up residence at Downham Market. Despite the move the squadron contributed to almost 300 aircraft sent to Wilhelmshaven on the night of the 8/9th. Most of the bombs fell into open country, however, and damage in the town was fairly modest. W/C Hal Bufton succeeded W/C McMullen at 109 Squadron on the 10th, and he would oversee trials of a new radar countermeasures device called 'Window'. However, it would be a full year before it was employed against the enemy with devastating effect for the first time. A five raid series of operations against Duisburg began on the 13/14th, and unfavourable weather conditions did little to assist the crews to locate and hit the target. Damage was light, and the series would mirror the Command's experiences at Essen.

On the 15th W/C Smythe DFC was posted to 214 Squadron to fill the breach left by the failure to return of W/C Knocker at the start of the month. Twenty-one Stirlings set off shortly before 19.00 hours on the 16th for an ambitious dusk attack on a U-Boat yard near Lübeck, using cloud-cover to mask their approach across the North Sea and Denmark. All the Stirling squadrons provided aircraft, but only eight crews reported bombing as briefed, and two failed to return, while 218 Squadron's W7475 was fortunate to survive an attack by five fighters. On the 19/20th Halifaxes, Stirlings and Lancasters attempted to bomb the Vulkan U-Boat yards at Vegesack through cloud on Gee, but no bombs found the mark. The Duisburg campaign continued on the 21/22nd, 23/24th and 25/26th, and resulted in very modest housing damage. In total 819 sorties had been launched for the loss of thirty-one aircraft. Three of these came from 115 Squadron during the first raid. The largest non-1,000 force to date of 403 aircraft took off for Hamburg on the evening of the 26th, and those arriving over the city delivered the most effective assault of the war after Cologne. Over 800 fires were started, more than 500 of them classed as large, and 823 houses were destroyed. On the debit side twenty-nine aircraft failed to return, a massive number for the period, and this time 115 Squadron posted missing four crews. Among them was that of the commanding officer, W/C Dixon-Wright in BJ615, which crashed into the sea without survivors.

On the 27th eight Wellingtons flew daylight cloud-cover sorties to northern Germany, and lost two of their number. One of them was X3653, which was carrying the crew of the 57 Squadron commanding officer, W/C Peters-Smith DFC, and there were no survivors. A repeat effort against Hamburg was planned for the 28/29th, but bad weather kept 1, 4 and 5 Groups on the ground, and it was left to 3 Group and the Training Units to carry on. In the event, the Training Unit aircraft were recalled, and many 3 Group crews turned back as the weather worsened. The seventy-one Stirlings despatched represented the best effort yet by the type, but only sixty-eight aircraft reached the target area to bomb, and fifteen large fires were started. It was a bad night for 3 Group in general and for 75 (NZ) Squadron in particular, which suffered the loss of six Wellingtons, in which twenty-five crewmen lost their lives. 9 Squadron posted missing three crews, and there were three empty dispersals also at Alconbury on the morning of the 29th to tell the story of 156 Squadron's fortunes. One of them should have been occupied by Wellington BJ603, which crashed in the sea, taking with it W/C Price DFC and his crew. 218 Squadron had one Stirling missing with the crew of the recently appointed flight commander, S/L Powell DFM. BF309 was shot down by flak into the sea off the German coast, and S/L Powell died with two of his crew, while the five survivors were marched off into captivity. S/L Powell's DFM had been awarded for a low-level attack on Stavangar aerodrome in a Blenheim in 1940. Two Stirlings were also missing from the 218 Squadron's Conversion Flight. It was a particularly tragic night for the men of 419 Squadron, who lost their highly popular and respected commanding officer, W/C Fulton. A message was received from X3488 suggesting that it had been attacked by a nightfighter, wounding some of the crew, and it is presumed to have crashed into the North Sea. It was a bitter blow to the squadron, and shortly afterwards, as a token of the high esteem in which W/C Fulton was held, his nickname, 'Moose', was added to the squadron title, and its permanent place would be confirmed when His Majesty the King authorized the squadron's official crest in June 1944. Flight commander, S/L Wolfe, stepped into the breach at 419 Squadron until the appointment of a permanent successor to Fulton. W/C Cook became the new commanding officer of 156 Squadron in time to preside over a new era for the unit, which would begin in a little over two weeks. The 30th brought W/C Laine to the helm of 57 Squadron on promotion from flight commander.

Saarbrücken hosted its first large-scale raid of the war on the 29/30th, and bombing from medium level, 248 aircraft destroyed almost 400 buildings. The last night of the month saw over 600 aircraft, again including some from the training units, winging their way towards Düsseldorf, and 484 arrived in the target area to bomb. As would always happen from this point when large forces attacked this city, some of the bombing spilled over into nearby Neuss, and 453 buildings were destroyed at the two locations. The success was gained at the high cost again of twenty-nine aircraft, but not one of the sixty-one participating Stirlings fell to the defences. This was the first operation presided over by 115 Squadron's new commanding officer, W/C Cousens, who was promoted from within on the 30th. Towards the end of the month W/C Olson completed his tour as commanding officer of 75 (NZ) Squadron, and passed the reigns to W/C Mitchell, who would continue the good work.

There would be a gentle start to August for most crews, during which spell, on the 5th, W/C Walsh was appointed as the new commanding officer of 419 Squadron. He had earned the DFC while serving with 9 Squadron in 1940, and had more recently been awarded the Czech Military Cross, but sadly, his period of tenure was destined to be brief. 109 Squadron moved to Wyton on the 6th, and effectively left 3 Group. The move anticipated the formation of a new organisation which would be known as the Pathfinder Force, or PFF. That night the first major operation of the month was mounted. This was the final raid of the series on Duisburg, and it went the way of the others, with very modest damage, and most of the bombs finding open country. The tally of destruction over the five raids made gloomy reading. Just 212 houses had been destroyed for the loss of forty-three aircraft from 1,229 sorties. Five aircraft failed to return from this final effort, and among them was 218 Squadron's N6072, which was despatched by a nightfighter over Holland, killing four of the crew, while Sgt Laidlaw and two others survived as PoWs. On the 7th 3 Group bade farewell to one of its premier units, as 9 Squadron moved to Waddington to join 5 Group and convert to Lancasters. Two nights after Duisburg forty Stirlings took part in a raid by a mixed force on Osnabrück. A number of industrial buildings were hit, 200 houses were destroyed, and all of the Stirlings returned home. The first major raids of the war on Mainz inflicted heavy damage on the 11/12th and 12/13th, for a combined loss of nineteen aircraft. Six of the Wellingtons missing from the earlier raid came in equal numbers from 75 (NZ) and 156 Squadrons. Shortly after take-off on the same night 218 Squadron's W7568 developed an engine fire and crashed in Suffolk, killing the pilot, P/O Abberton, and his navigator, the other five members of the crew having baled out in time. In the middle of this activity 101 Squadron moved from Bourn to Stradishall on the 11th, while 419 Squadron departed Mildenhall and 3 Group on the 12th to take up temporary residence at Leeming, before moving into its new home at Topcliffe on the 18th as 4 Group's latest recruit. Having been at Wyton since December 1939 XV Squadron moved out on the 14th to make way for a new set of residents, and set up home a few miles to the south-east at Bourn.

A disappointing attack on Düsseldorf on the 15/16th came at the end of a day that had seen the start of a new era in Bomber Command, with the arrival on 3 Group stations of the founder squadrons of the Pathfinder Force. For the purpose of administration this new organisation came technically under the control of 3 Group, and Wyton was selected as the initial HQ for the Air-Officer-Commanding, Group Captain Don Bennett, and the 5 Group representative, 83 Squadron. 7 Squadron was posted in as the 3 Group representative, bringing with it the station of Oakington, 35 Squadron from 4 Group moved into Graveley, while 156 Squadron was posted from 3 Group to Warboys as 1 Group's representative, despite never having actually served with 1 Group. Harris had been opposed in principle to the idea of a separate and elitist-sounding target marking force, a view which was shared by all but one of his Group commanders, 4 Group's Roddy Carr, but typically of the man, and to his eternal credit, having been overruled by higher authority, he gave it his full support. His choice of the then Group Captain Don Bennett as its leader was both controversial and inspired, and more than a few feathers were ruffled by the appointment of such a relatively junior officer. 3 Group's AVM Baldwin was among the most fiercely opposed to the PFF, and he offered a number of equally elitist alternatives in his desperation to sabotage its formation. This would lead to an uneasy existence between the PFF and 3 Group HQ through which orders would be channelled. Harris was eager to send the new force into battle at the earliest opportunity, but in the meantime, over 100 aircraft returned to Osnabrück on the night of the 17/18th, and inflicted moderate damage on northern and north-western districts.

The first Pathfinder-led operation took place on the 18/19th, with the port of Flensburg as the objective. Situated in the eastern side of the narrow neck of land where Germany and Denmark meet, it should have been a relatively easy target to find. In the event, in an inauspicious beginning to what would become an illustrious career, the fledgling force ended up over Denmark, where a number of towns reported being bombed. A major night of gardening on the 20/21st resulted in mines being laid at many points on the enemy coast. 218 Squadron crews were briefed for the Kiel and Baltic areas, and four failed to return. W7573 went down near Schleswig in the same region as Flensburg, and F/O Sanderson and his crew were all killed. W7615 was lost in the Baltic taking with it the crew of the previously mentioned P/O McAuley DFC. F/O Bullock and crew all lost their lives in BF319, which crashed south-west of Kiel, while the single survivor from the night's 218 Squadron casualties was the rear gunner in F/S Hartley's BF338, which also crashed near Schleswig. The second Pathfinder-led operation was to Frankfurt on the 24/25th, and its crews again found difficulty in identifying the target. Most of the bombs fell into open country north and west of the city, although there was moderate property damage, and seventeen large fires were started. The Pathfinders achieved success for the first time at Kassel on the 27/28th, when good illumination allowed the main force crews to destroy over 140 buildings, and seriously damage over 300 more. The Command paid a price of thirty-one aircraft, and a further twenty-three were missing from a raid on Nuremberg twenty-four hours later. On this occasion the aiming point was marked with great accuracy, the Pathfinder crews employing target indicators for the first time, but the main force crews did not fully exploit the opportunity, and damage was only moderate. 115 Squadron sustained the highest casualties among 3 Group squadrons with four Wellingtons failing to return, while a fifth crash-landed. 149 Squadron's N6081 was shot down by a nightfighter over Germany, and the commanding officer, W/C Charlton-Jones, was killed with five others of the eight men on board. He was the first of the squadron's commanders to be lost in action, and he was replaced by W/C Wasse, who had completed a six month tour in command of 9 Squadron in January.

218 Squadron began September with a new commanding officer. It is not clear exactly when W/C Holder DSO, DFC officially departed the squadron, but in the Operations Record Book (ORB) the monthly summaries for August, September and October were signed by S/L Samson, and for November by S/L Hiles. W/C Montague Francis Baldwin Read, a Canadian, was appointed on the 1st. He apparently possessed great athletic prowess, and had once served as a sergeant with the Cameron Highlanders of Ottawa. He had also spent time on 99 and 83 Squadrons during the 1930s, having been commissioned in 1933. He was posted to RAF HQ Cairo in April 1939 on promotion to Squadron Leader, where he was eventually seconded to the American Legation. He rose to Wing Commander rank on the 1st of June

1941, and returned to England a year later. Presumably he would learn the practicalities of night bombing over Germany 'on the job'. It was not unique for a long standing Wing Commander without operational experience to be given command of a squadron.

Operationally, September began with the pathfinders posting a 'black' on the night of the 1/2nd. Briefed to mark Saarbrücken, its crews identified the non-industrial town of Saarlouis in error, and much to the chagrin of its inhabitants, the main force delivered an accurate attack. This might have been an ill-omen for the month, but, in fact, from this point, the Command embarked on an unprecedented series of effective operations, which took it through to mid month. It began at Karlsruhe on the 2/3rd, where photographic reconnaissance revealed much damage to housing and industry, and continued at Bremen on the 4/5th, when 480 buildings were destroyed. Earlier on the 4th 57 Squadron completed its move from Methwold to Scampton to begin a new career with 5 Group and Lancasters. In March 1943 its C Flight would become the nucleus of 617 Squadron, which would become known throughout the world as the Dambusters. A total of 114 buildings were reduced to rubble at Duisburg on the 6/7th, and while this was a modest return, it still represented something of a victory at this notoriously difficult target. The run of successes was halted temporarily at Frankfurt on the 8/9th, but an attack on Düsseldorf on the 10/11th signalled a return to winning ways, and produced perhaps the most damaging raid of the war thus far after Cologne. The Pathfinders employed 'pink pansies' as target indicators for the first time, and over 900 houses were destroyed, and fifty-two industrial premises in the city and in Neuss were so severely damaged, that production was halted for varying periods. It was a raid in which the training units participated, and they shared in the heavy loss of thirty-three aircraft. 75 (NZ) Squadron was the hardest-hit 3 Group unit with three failures to return. 218 Squadron's R9357 had to be ditched in the middle of the North Sea after an explosion shattered the starboard inner engine, ripped away part of the fuselage, and caused a loss of power in both outer engines. F/S Cozens and four of his crew were rescued and returned to the squadron, but the navigator and bomb-aimer lost their lives. BF351 was shot down by a nightfighter over Holland, and there were no survivors from the crew of F/S Milligan. Bremen received its second raid of the month on the 13/14th, and the damage sustained by the city exceeded that inflicted by the Thousand force in June. Some 848 houses lay in ruins, and a number of important war industry factories were hit, thereby losing production.

The 14th brought a change at the top for 3 Group with the appointment of AVM the Hon. Sir Ralph Cochrane as Air-Officer-Commanding in place of AVM Baldwin. Baldwin would soon be off to join his former boss, Sir Richard Pierse, as Deputy A-O-C-in-C Air Forces India, an appointment he would take up on the 9th of October. Born in 1895 as the youngest son of the 1st Baron Cochrane of Cults, the Honourable Ralph joined the Royal Navy in 1912, and transferred to the RAF in 1918. He served extensively in the

Middle-East during the early twenties, for a period as a flight commander under Harris, and it was at this time that the two men forged a respect for and understanding of each other that would prove fruitful during the current conflict. Among his appointments in the thirties were spells as the first Chief of the Air Staff Royal New Zealand Air Force from the 1st of April 1937, and Air Aide-de-Camp to King George VI from September to December 1939. In October 1940 he became Director of Flying Training, a position he held until taking the reins at 3 Group.

Wilhelmshaven reported its heaviest raid to date on the 14/15th, a night on which 218 Squadron's N3725 was forced to return early with only three good engines, and crashed in Norfolk, killing F/O Frankcombe and five of his crew. Even Essen was hit harder than ever before on the 16/17th, with damage to the giant Krupp armaments producing complex, on top of the more familiar catalogue of destruction to residential and public property. It was by no means a precision operation, however, and many other Ruhr towns reported bombs falling within them. As far as losses were concerned, though, this was a bad night for the Command, the Thousand bomber raids aside, its worst to date from a single operation. Thirty-nine aircraft were missing, more than half of them Wellingtons, including some from the training units.

It can be no coincidence, that this remarkable run of successes came at a time, when the Pathfinder Force was emerging from its shaky start, and the crews were coming to terms with the complexities of their demanding role. There would be no overnight transformation, however, and failures would continue to outnumber successes for some time to come, but the encouraging signs were there, and it boded ill for Germany in the coming years. Two operations were mounted on the 19/20th, the larger one to Saarbrücken, while sixty-eight Lancasters and twenty-one Stirlings targeted Munich. Less than half the crews at the latter found the mark, and most of the bombs fell into the suburbs. Among small-scale operations on the 23/24th was one by twenty-four Stirlings against shipyards at Vegesack. Only one failed to return, R9187 of 218 Squadron, which contained the crew of flight commander S/L Raymond DFC, a New Zealander on his eighth operation with the squadron. They were brought down off the Frisian Islands by the night fighter of Feldwebel Pfeiffer of IV/NJG/I. S/L Raymond had previously flown thirty-five operations with XV Squadron on Blenheims, Wellingtons and Stirlings, and had taken part in all three One Thousand Bomber raids while serving with 1651 Conversion Unit. 100 sorties during this month cost the squadron a more tolerable five aircraft, but this still involved the loss of four complete crews. After more than five years at Marham 115 Squadron completed its move to Mildenhall on the 24th for what would be a short-term residence. On the 29th 101 Squadron left 3 Group to begin a new life at Holme-on-Spalding-Moor in 1 Group, with which it would remain until war's end. From October 1943 its Lancasters would carry radio jamming equipment as well as a full bomb load and provide a presence in almost all major Bomber Command operations until the end of hostilities. By the end of the war, as a result of this additional duty, it would have suffered the highest personnel casualty figures in the entire Command.

October began for 3 Group with another small-scale Stirling raid, this time against the U-Boat yards near Lübeck on the night of the 1/2nd. Three aircraft were lost, and two of them were from 218 Squadron. N3763 crashed in Germany, killing Sgt Griffiths and his crew, and W7613 was brought down over Denmark with the crew of the recently promoted, F/L Du Toit, a South African on his seventeenth operation. All eight occupants were killed, and flying as second pilot on just his third operation was W/C Read, who had been in command of the squadron for exactly one month. W/C Morris became the new commanding officer of 218 Squadron, taking up his appointment during the first week of the month. He had previously served as a flight commander with XV Squadron in 1941.

Elsewhere, the 1st of October brought with it the return to a 3 Group operational role for W/C 'Pick' Pickard. On this day he was installed as the new commanding officer of the clandestine 161 Squadron at Tempsford on the posting out of W/C Fielden. 'Pick' knew only how to lead from the front, and he would carry out numerous daring single-handed flights in Lysanders to drop and pick up agents in France on behalf of the SOE and SIS organisations. This day also brought a change of surroundings for 214 Squadron with a move to Chedburgh. The month's operations continued with a disappointing raid on Krefeld in the Ruhr by 188 aircraft in unhelpful weather conditions on the night of the 2/3rd. This number quickly diminished by one, when 218 Squadron's W7636 swung on take-off and came to grief, although without injury to Sgt Hill and his crew. Within days Sgt Hill would become F/S Hill, and a few days later, after just nineteen days on the Squadron and four operations, he and his crew would go missing. The weather helped Aachen to escape with only slight damage three nights later, in another operation that began badly for 218 Squadron, when severe local thunderstorms probably caused BF322 to crash in Suffolk twenty minutes after take-off, killing F/S Hall and his crew. A moderately successful attack on Osnabrück destroyed 149 houses and six industrial premises on the 6/7th, and this was the last bombing operation for a week. Mining continued, however, and W/C Morris undertook his first operation as 218 Squadron's commanding officer with a 'mining' sortie on the night of the 10/11th. On the following night, eighty aircraft took part in wide-ranging mining, when the single missing Stirling was 218 Squadron's R9190. The previously mentioned F/S Hill and his crew had been briefed to lay their mines in the Baltic, and were shot down into the sea off Denmark by a nightfighter. It seems that the pilot had managed to maintain some control as the aircraft went down, and all were apparently still on board on impact. Those in the front section sustained quite serious injury, and the bomb-aimer succumbed to his two days later while in captivity. A decoy fire site drew away half of the bomb loads intended for Kiel on the 13/14th, but the remainder inflicted a reasonable degree of damage. A similar decoy attracted most of the bombs at Cologne on the 15/16th, rendering the operation a failure. Earlier on the 15th 75 (NZ) Squadron began to detach crews to Oakington for conversion training on Stirlings. The first of the type, N3704, was taken on charge on the 16th, while R9243 and R9247 arrived on the 21st and BF396 and BF397 two days later.

A new campaign began on the 22/23rd in support of Operation Torch, the Allied landings in North Africa, which would ultimately lead to Montgomery's victory over Rommel at El Alamein. It involved the Command in attacks on the major Italian cities, and would occupy much of its resources until well into December. Proceedings were opened by 5 Group at Genoa on the 22/23rd, and 3 and 4 Groups followed up at the same target on the next night. Unfortunately, cloud cover confounded the crews, and it was later discovered that the raid had fallen on the town of Savona, some thirty miles away. The missing Stirling was from 218 Squadron, and crashed into the sea off the French coast, taking with it the eight man crew of P/O Studd. 5 Group again had the first crack at Milan by daylight on the 24th, and it was 1 and 3 Groups which followed up that night in a raid spoiled by the weather. Crossing the Alps was never a picnic for the lower-ceilinged Stirlings, and on this night the crews encountered storms during the outward flight, which prevented almost half of them from reaching the target to bomb. 218 Squadron's R9241 was still over Suffolk outbound when an engine caught fire, and soon afterwards the Stirling broke up. It plunged to earth taking F/S Higgott and six of his crew to their deaths, while one of the gunners just managed to escape by parachute at the last second, and was injured in the heavy landing. This effectively concluded a month, which had seen the squadron despatch ninety-four sorties, the highest by any Stirling squadron, for the loss of seven aircraft and six crews. On the 29th a small force of Wellingtons was sent roving over the Ruhr by daylight searching for targets of opportunity. In hindsight it would seem to have been a misguided move, and this was confirmed by the loss of three 115 Squadron Wellingtons.

The first week of November brought little activity for the Wellington squadrons of 3 Group. 75 (NZ) Squadron moved to Newmarket on the 1st to begin working up to operational status with the Stirling, but would continue to detach aircraft and crews to Oakington until the end of the year. It was also a low-key start to the month for the Stirling squadrons as they continued with their mining activities. The area chosen for the night of the 6/7th stretched from Lorient to the Frisians, and it was from the Gironde Estuary that 218 Squadron's R9185 failed to return with the crew of Sgt Hyde. The Stirling crashed in France, delivering the pilot and four others into enemy hands, but sadly, the navigator and bomb-aimer, who were both Canadians, lost their lives.

When 90 Squadron was re-formed on the 7th of November in temporary lodgings at Bottesford on the Leicestershire/Nottinghamshire border, it was its fifth incarnation since its original founding on the 8th of October 1917 as a fighter unit. It began the Second World War as a Blenheim training unit, and was absorbed into 17 OTU on the 4th of April 1940. On the 7th of May 1941 the squadron was once more taken off the shelf to be re-formed, this time at Watton under the command of Wing Commander J MacDougall DFC, who was posted in from his command of 101 Squadron at Oakington. The squadron became part of 2 Group, and was tasked with introducing the B17C to RAF service under the designation Fortress I. The first hand-picked crew arrived from Marham on the 5th, the requirement being for young, fit, experienced men, who were thought to be best able to cope with the rigours of high altitude flying. The first of the type, AN521, had been flown into Watton by Major Walsh of the USAAC on the 30th of April, but this was sent for modification on the 7th, and AN534 arrived as the first of twenty of the type to be taken on charge. Two days later more crews were posted in, and they were briefed on the squadron's intended role. In the event the Fortress turned out to be beset with technical problems and totally unsuitable for the job required of it. The serviceability rate was abysmal, there were unanticipated losses, and in September 1941 it ceased to operate. 90 Squadron remained intact as a functional unit, and training continued for another five months, but it was clear that operations with the Fortress in winter were not feasible. In October a detachment was sent to the Middle East, where it became absorbed into 220 Squadron. From then until disbandment on the 14th of February 1942 the home echelon used Blenheims, although not operation-ally. Now, under the command of W/C J C Claydon, the intention was to install 90 Squadron with 3 Group and equip it with Stirlings.

The first bombing operation in November to involve Stirlings came on the 7/8th, when Genoa was the target for a mixed force of 175 aircraft. The attack was successfully concluded for the loss of six aircraft to the defences, while the 218 Squadron casualty occurred in England. BK606 arrived back with empty fuel tanks, and crashed in Cambridgeshire as Sgt Richards was trying to reach Oakington, fortunately with only one crew member sustaining injury. After a short period of residence at Mildenhall 115 Squadron changed address again with a move to East Wretham on the 8th. That night W/C Morris took what was presumably a freshman crew, to deliver 'toilet paper' to the residents of the Toulon area of France. On return, and running short of fuel, W7612 clipped trees on final approach to Tangmere and crashed, although all of the occupants were able to walk away. The spate of losses and accidents continued twenty-four hours later, when W7475 failed to return from Hamburg with the crew of B Flight commander S/L Hickling, who had been awarded a DFM while serving with 10 Squadron in 1941. Some time later it was established, that the Stirling had crashed in Germany with total loss of life. BK626 was the first Stirling to arrive on 90 Squadron charge on the 15th, and W7570, W7627, BF324, BK598, BK625, BK627 and BK628 were delivered by Air Transport Auxiliary pilots on the 16th and 17th. One of these was the well-known aviation pioneer, Jim Mollinson, whose even more famous wife, Amy Johnson, had been lost ferrying an Airspeed Oxford for the ATA during the previous year.

The Italian campaign went on, with main force Stirling involvement at Genoa on the 15/16th and Turin on the 18/19th and 20/21st. XV Squadron's S/L Wyatt and crew were in BK595 for the latter, which was afflicted by engine trouble on the way to the target. Wyatt elected to continue with the operation and bombed as planned, before force-landing in Spain on the way home. A period of internment followed, but the crew would return home in January, and Wyatt would later go on to command 75 (NZ) Squadron and 514 Squadron. A force of over 200 aircraft delivered a disappointing attack on Stuttgart on the 22/23rd, when a layer of thin cloud and ground haze concealed the city centre. The month's final major effort was against Turin on the 28/29th, which developed into an accurate and destructive attack. 218 Squadron's S/L Hiles and crew were forced to return early, when BK607 suffered engine failure. The Stirling came to grief on landing, but the eight occupants were able to walk away from the scene. This was the night and the operation that brought the first award of a Victoria Cross to a member of a Stirling crew. F/S Middleton was an Australian, who had joined 149 Squadron in February 1942, and been involved in a crash on landing at Oakington in April, while flying as second pilot to F/L Evans. This had led to a meeting on a train with the previously mentioned W/C 'Hamish' Mahaddie, who at the time, was a flight commander with 7 Squadron of the Pathfinders. Mahaddie was impressed with Middleton, and invited him to apply for a posting to 7 Squadron to join his flight. Middleton eventually took up the offer in August, but it soon became clear that his navigator was not up to the required standard. W/C Mahaddie offered him the chance to remain at 7 Squadron with a new crew, or return to 149 Squadron. A fierce crew loyalty persuaded him to take the latter option, and as he and his crew took off at 18.14 hours on that fateful evening, one of seven from 149 Squadron, they were embarking on the twenty-ninth operation of their first tour. Once in the target area, Middleton came down to 2,000 feet to establish his position, and made three runs across the city, sustaining damage from light flak. A shell exploded in the cockpit, severely wounding both pilots and the wireless operator, but the second pilot was able to deliver the bombs while his captain was unconscious, before turning for home. Further flak damage was sustained on the return flight, and on arrival at the Kent coast short of fuel, and doubtful of his ability safely to attempt a landing, Middleton selected a parallel course and baled out five members of his crew. They all survived, but sadly, Middleton and two others were still on board when BF372 crashed into the sea, and the subsequent VC was awarded to him posthumously. Eighty sorties by 218 Squadron during the month had seen five aircraft lost, but only two crews.

The December account opened at Frankfurt on the 2/3rd, a relatively small-scale affair, which, in keeping with past raids on this city, failed to produce a telling blow, and most of the bombs were wasted in open country.

218 Squadron's BF401 experienced a torrid time at the hands of flak and nightfighters, but eventually made it back to base, where the undercarriage collapsed on landing. Perhaps the crew's deliverance was due in part to the efforts of Sgt Holland in the rear turret, a native of Lutterworth, a small town on Leicestershire's border with Warwickshire, where John Wycliffe, the man responsible for translating the Bible from Latin into English, was the vicar for many years in the 14th century. In the 1930s Lutterworth became the location of the then Squadron Leader Frank Whittle's Power-Jet company. Sgt Holland would become a member of the legendary 617 Squadron in 1944, and bear the distinction of being one of a very select band of men to be classed as Master Gunners.

Cloud cover over Mannheim forced crews to bomb on dead reckoning on the 6/7th, after the Pathfinders withheld their flares, and damage was scant. W/C Lay DSO, DFC concluded his tour as commanding officer of XV Squadron and S/L Menaul was promoted from his flight commander position on the 7th to fill the breach. While 5 and 8 Groups continued the assault on Turin on the 8/9th, elements of 1, 3 and 4 Groups went mining off the German and Danish coasts. Stirlings operated against Italy for the last time during the current campaign on the 9/10th, when Turin was the target, and the same city brought the offensive to an end, when attacked by 1, 4 and 5 Groups on the following night. On the 16th W/C Cousens DFC was posted to 8 Group HQ from 115 Squadron at the conclusion of his tour. In March 1944 he would be appointed to the command of 635 Pathfinder Squadron, and a month later lose his life while operating as a Master Bomber against railway yards at Laon. The new 115 Squadron commander was W/C Sisley, an Australian whose destiny also lay in death while leading from the front, although that would come with another squadron, in another Group and in another year. Disaster attended a night of minor operations over Germany on the 17/18th, when 5 Group lost nine of twenty-seven Lancasters, while six Stirlings and two Wellingtons also failed to return from an unsuccessful attempt to destroy the Opel works at Fallersleben. Of five Stirlings dispatched by 75 (NZ) Squadron, four went missing, including BF396, containing the commanding officer, W/C Mitchell DFC, MiD. Just as many good commanders often did, he was flying with a new crew, and they disappeared without trace. 218 Squadron also posted missing two crews with Kiwi pilots, those of F/O Marshall in W7614, and F/L Shepherd in BF403. The former crashed in Germany, killing three of the crew, while the pilot and three others were taken prisoner. The latter was shot down by flak to crash into the sea between Texel and the Dutch mainland, and there were no survivors. S/L Fowler stepped into the breach at 75 (NZ) Squadron until a new commanding officer could be appointed in the New Year.

Minor operations saw the Command through to the 20/21st, a night on which a highly significant operation took place almost unnoticed. While over 200 aircraft carried out an attack on Duisburg, six Mosquitos of 109 Squadron set off for a power station at Lutterade in Holland, led by their commanding officer, W/C Hal Bufton. Since becoming a founder member of the Pathfinder Force in August, 109 Squadron had been engaged in magnificent pioneering work with the Oboe blind-bombing device, marrying it to the Mosquito, and ironing out the teething troubles. This night's operation involved the first Oboe-aimed bombs as a calibration test to gauge the margin of error. Three aircraft experienced equipment malfunctions, and bombed Duisburg instead, but W/C Bufton and two others successfully released their bombs. Sadly, a mass of craters from a recent misdirected raid on Aachen invalidated the calibration aspect of the operation, but further trials would take place, leading to a revolution in bombing accuracy in the coming year. Working up to operational status was by this time well under way for 90 Squadron, but the Stirling malaise of collapsing undercarriages brought about the death of the experienced ground crew member, F/S McGavin, on the 18th, when he was crushed while trying to shore up a unit which was about to give way. On the 29th the squadron attempted a move to its first operational home at Ridgewell, a satellite of Stradishall, whereupon F/S Freeman crashed on landing in BK625, happily without crew casualties, but allegedly forcing the others to return to Bottesford for the night. 218 Squadron despatched fifty-four sorties during December, losing three aircraft and two crews. It had been a testing year for the squadron, and one in which it had lost fifty-two Stirlings on operations, more than any other operator of the type. The coming year would be a little more expensive, but a number of other Stirling units would suffer greater casualties, as the type became the bottom layer in the ever-increasing volume of Bomber Command aircraft over the targets. It had been a much better year for the Command after the tribulations of 1941, and the advent of Oboe promised much for the future.

1943

Expansion; Oboe; the Ruhr succumbs; Hamburg burns; Peenemünde and Berlin round 1; the winter campaign begins; the Stirling is found wanting; a war of attrition

The year began with the formation of 6 Group on New Year's Day, and most of the Royal Canadian Air Force squadrons transferred immediately. On New Year's Eve the first production example of a Mk III Stirling, BK648, had arrived at Bourn, for XV Squadron to carry out trials, having been selected as the unit to receive the first batch. Re-equipping with the type would take time, but began early in the New Year when a further six were taken on charge, BK652 on the 3rd, BK654 on the 20th, BK658 and BK667 on the 21st, BK657 on the 25th, and BK656 on the 26th. Another ten would arrive in February, and a full complement would be on charge when the final six were delivered in early March. On the operational front a continuation of the Oboe trials programme saw 109 Squadron marking for small forces of Lancasters from 1 and 5 Groups. During the first two weeks of January no less than seven of these operations were directed at Essen, and one at Duisburg. A new squadron joined 3 Group's ranks on the 4th, when 1474 Flight was redesignated 192 Squadron at Gransden Lodge. The number had first been used between September 1917 and December 1918 by a night-flying training unit. It was now to be a special duties unit engaged in identifying enemy radar wavelengths and patterns to assist in the development of counter-measures. The first aircraft to arrive on the 5th were a collection of Mk 1c, III and X Wellingtons, along with a Mosquito and a Tiger Moth. The first Halifax would arrive on the 9th. W/C Willis was the commanding officer, and he oversaw the initial working up period, which would culminate in the squadron's first operation later in the month. The Pathfinder Force was finally granted Group status as 8 Group on the 8th, and it took with it the 3 Group stations upon which it had been lodging. That night 90 Squadron opened its 3 Group account with mining sorties.

75 (NZ) Squadron appointed a new commanding officer in the shape of W/C Lane, who was a Londoner, and formerly chief flying instructor at 22 OTU. He had been awarded a DFC for service with 51 Squadron in 1940. On the 14th of January a new Air Ministry directive was issued, authorizing the area bombing of those French ports which were home to U-Boat bases and support facilities. A target list was drawn up accordingly, which was headed by Lorient, and that night, over 100 aircraft, mostly Halifaxes and Wellingtons with twenty Stirlings in support, carried out the first of nine raids on the port over the next month. It was not a very satisfactory attack, but a better performance by the crews on the following night led to the destruction of 800 buildings. Stirlings were excluded from two disappointing raids on Berlin on the 16/17th and 17/18th, when custom designed target indicators were employed by the Pathfinders for the first time. Stirlings were back in action on the 23/24th and 26/27th, however, for the third and fourth raids of the series on Lorient. Düsseldorf was left to the Lancasters and Halifaxes on the 27/28th, when Oboe ground marking was employed for the first time. Fifty-four aircraft were mining around the Frisians and the Baltic on this night, and the single casualty was 218 Squadron's N6077, which crashed into high ground in Germany on the way home, leaving just one survivor from the eight man crew of P/O Gough. That survivor was Sgt Bill Jackson, who went on to write *Three stripes and four Brownings*. Wellingtons and Halifaxes returned to Lorient on the 29/30th, while a predominantly Lancaster force wrapped up the month's activity at Hamburg on the 30/31st, for the first H2s raid of the war. A few days earlier on the 26th F/L Fernbank undertook 192 Squadron's first operation with a successful sortie along the Dutch and Belgian coasts. By the end of the month four operations had been completed by the squadron, and the Tiger Moth was almost destroyed in a gale on the 30th. 218 Squadron was required to launch forty-nine sorties during the month, and suffered only the loss of the aircraft and crew just mentioned.

February began for 138 Squadron with the departure on the 2nd of W/C Hockey, who, having concluded his highly successful tour as commanding officer, was posted to the Air Ministry. It would be the end of the month before his replacement arrived, and in the meantime, the burden of responsibility doubtless fell upon the shoulders of S/Ls Boxer and Gibson. For the main force the month began with an operation to Cologne on the night of the 2/3rd involving a modest, mixed force of 160 aircraft, and various methods of target marking. The attack resulted in scattered damage, but nothing of a serious nature. On the following night 263 aircraft, including sixty-six Stirlings, set out for Hamburg in weather conditions that persuaded many crews to return early. Those who persevered started over forty large fires, but the damage was commensurate with the capacity of a much smaller force. Half of the sixteen failures to return were Stirlings, and it was not a good night for 218 Squadron. BF406 was shot down by a nightfighter over Holland with the crew of Sgt Dodd, which contained two Americans, and all on board lost their lives. BF408 took the eight man crew of F/S Treves to a watery grave in the Straits of Dover. Stirlings were also well represented at Turin on the 4/5th, and they contributed to the creation of widespread damage. The sixth operation against Lorient took place on the same night, without a Stirling presence, and the seventh was delivered by 300 aircraft in a two phase attack on the 7/8th, for which sixty-two Stirlings were despatched. The main force Stirlings sat out a highly destructive raid on Wilhelmshaven on the 11/12th, when a naval ammunition depot went up in spectacular fashion, and laid waste to 120 acres of the town and dockland. The heaviest attack of the series on Lorient took place on the 13/14th at the hands of over 400 aircraft, which included the first sorties by 218 Squadron Mk III Stirlings, and more than 1,000 tons of bombs added to the previous destruction. A force of Halifaxes, Wellingtons and Stirlings raided Cologne on the 14/15th, when H2s based skymarking was used in the face of cloud cover, and around 100 buildings were destroyed. Lorient's ordeal ended on the night of the 16/17th, by which time it was little more than a deserted ruin.

Three raids on Wilhelmshaven, on the 18/19th, 19/20th and 24/25th, all failed to find the mark, and most of the bombing was wasted in open country. Nuremberg escaped a telling blow on the 25/26th, when the bombing caught only the northern rim of the city, but even so, 300 buildings sustained damage, and nine aircraft were lost. BF450 failed to return home with the rest of 218 Squadron's participants, and was by that time a wreck on German soil containing the remains of Sgt White and his crew. The run of disappointing operations continued, when 400 aircraft returned to Cologne on the 26/27th and again wasted many bombs, but those which hit the city produced the familiar catalogue of damage to housing and public buildings. Having dealt with Lorient, the Command now turned its attention upon St Nazaire, and on the last night of the month, laid waste to 60% of the town's built-up area. 218 Squadron's R9189 was unable to contribute, after crashing on take-off in the hands of P/O Cozens, who walked away from the wreckage with his crew. It was a record month for 218 Squadron, with a tally of 124 sorties, the highest among Stirling squadrons, at a cost of four aircraft and three crews.

138 Squadron's new commanding officer, W/C Batchelor, took up his appointment on the 28th, having thus far enjoyed a wartime career remarkably similar to that of W/C Pickard, the current 161 Squadron commander. Firstly, both had served as flight commanders with 9 Squadron, although in the case of Ken Batchelor, this was his first operational unit, which he joined in the final quarter of 1940. When Pickard departed 311 Squadron in May 1941, he was succeeded as British advisor by Batchelor, and now both were at Tempsford running a squadron engaged in special duties. 3 Group welcomed a new A-O-C on the 28th, as AVM Cochrane moved to 5 Group and 49-year-old AVM Harrison stepped into his shoes. Among his former appointments was a period in command of 78 Squadron in 1937, a spell as Senior Air Staff Officer at 1 Group HQ from December 1940 and another as Deputy Senior Air Staff Officer HQ Bomber Command from January 1942.

A new era began for 115 Squadron on the 1st of March, with the arrival from 5 Group's 61 Squadron of Lancaster Mk II, DS612. 61 Squadron had formed a third flight to conduct operational trials, but now reverted to standard Mk Is and IIIs, leaving 115 Squadron to become the first unit to be fully equipped with the Hercules powered version. The power plant would offer a higher rate of climb over the Merlin, but above 18,000 feet the performance dropped off, and this ensured that 115 Squadron crews would generally bomb from below their Merlin-powered Lancaster cousins, although well above their 3 Group brothers-in-arms of the Stirling fraternity. Conversion began immediately, but until operational status was achieved the squadron would continue with the trusty Wellington.

March would bring with it the first major campaign of the war for which the Command was adequately equipped and prepared. All the previous campaigns had been forced upon it by the War Cabinet in response to situations brought about by the enemy. The battles for Norway, the low countries and France were lost before they began, and the Command was constantly in the position of having to play catch-up. The anti-invasion operations and the first oil and transportation campaigns called upon the crews to operate against targets requiring a level of precision which was beyond them with the aircraft and aids available. The U-Boat offensive was in support of the navy, the attacks on Italian cities were in support of the army, while the obsession with the enemy warships at Brest was a costly distraction against unsuitable targets. Although the crews performed magnificently in whatever was demanded of them, it was only when Harris persisted with his strategic offensive against Germany that any telling blow was struck against her war effort. Now Harris had a predominantly four-engine bomber force with an unprecedented bomb carrying capacity, and the Oboe device to negate the ever-present industrial haze blanketing and protecting the Ruhr.

Bombers, particularly Lancasters, were rolling out of the factories in large numbers, while the Empire Training Scheme guaranteed an endless supply of new crews, and all of this meant that the time was right to demonstrate just what the Command could achieve.

First, however, there were operations to Berlin and Hamburg for the crews to negotiate. The former took place on the 1/2nd, and involved a force of 300 aircraft, sixty of which were Stirlings, including ten from 218 Squadron. The massive urban sprawl of the capital made it difficult for the Pathfinder crews to pick out the city centre aiming point, and the subsequent bombing was scattered over a very wide area, with the main emphasis in south-western districts. Despite the lack of concentration, Berlin underwent its most damaging attack of the war thus far, registering the destruction of almost 900 buildings, while many of its factories were hit. 218 Squadron's BK666 crashed in Norfolk on return, although F/O Berridge and his crew escaped injury. Two nights later a further misinterpretation of H2s returns led to the town of Wedel receiving many of the bombs intended for Hamburg, although 100 fires had to be dealt with by the city's fire brigades. Harris now felt ready to set his hand against Germany's industrial heartland, the Ruhr, a region which had thus far proved elusive and had never experienced a decisive blow. As one of the most important industrial cities in Germany, Essen was selected to open proceedings, and a plan was prepared for over 400 aircraft to deliver a three-wave attack.

The Stirlings were assigned to the second wave, along with Wellingtons, and 218 Squadron put up twelve aircraft in a total of 442. They took off either side of 19.00 hours and headed towards the Ruhr, but an unusually high number of early returns and the bombing of alternative targets reduced the numbers arriving over Essen to 362. These produced a highly successful outcome, and it was, in fact, the first telling blow of the war on this city. The bombing devastated 160 acres of built-up area between the city centre and the Krupp works, which sustained damage to fifty-three of its buildings, and over 3,000 houses were destroyed. All this was in return for the loss of a fairly modest fourteen aircraft. Eight 218 Squadron Stirlings reached the Essen area, and of these R9333 was shot down by flak in the target area killing P/O Ratcliffe and his crew, and it is not known whether this occurred before or after they had bombed. Before round two of the Ruhr campaign took place Harris turned his attention upon southern Germany, attacking Nuremberg on the 8/9th, Munich on the 9/10th and Stuttgart on the 11/12th. These were all beyond the range of Oboe, and consequently relied upon visual and H2s Pathfinder marking. The first mentioned suffered from an extensive creep-back, a feature of many heavy raids, and much of the bombing under-shot the target by some distance. Even so, the attack achieved the destruction of 600 buildings, and a number of important war industry factories were hit. At Munich the wind pushed the attack into the city's western half, where almost 300 buildings were destroyed, and part of the BMW aero-engine factory was put out of action for more than a month. The Stuttgart raid was less effective, possibly as a result of the first recorded use of dummy target indicators, which drew many bomb loads away from the city into open country. BF343 was missing from its Downham Market dispersal on the following morning, having crashed in France with no survivors from the crew of F/S Parkinson, a New Zealander with twenty-three operations to his credit.

Keen to capitalize on his success at Essen, Harris returned there on the 12/13th with over 400 aircraft, and delivered another effective assault. The Oboe marking went according to plan, and this time the Krupps works found itself in the centre of the bombing area, sustaining 30% more damage than a week earlier. Although substantially less buildings were destroyed on this night, the total amounting to around 500 houses, the degree of concentration was greater, and it was another successful operation. Among the twenty-three missing aircraft was 115 Squadron's BJ756, which was sent crashing into the Ijsselmeer by a nightfighter, killing Sgt Fallon and his crew. As events were to prove, this was to be the final one of 114 Wellingtons lost by the squadron as a result of operations, ninety-eight of them having fallen on foreign soil or into the sea. No squadron suffered higher casualties of this type, but then, no squadron flew as many Wellington operations and sorties. There were no major operations during the middle part of the month, the 'moon' period, but this was when the Tempsford squadrons were ranging far and wide over occupied Europe. The night of the 14/15th brought operations to Czechoslovakia and Poland, from which two 138 Squadron Halifaxes and one from 161 Squadron failed to return. A second 161 Squadron Halifax crashed while outbound for France as a result of engine trouble. It was during this period also that 115 Squadron ventured forth in Lancasters for the first time in the only operational activity on the night of the 20/21st. Twelve Wellingtons and four 115 Squadron Lancasters were detailed for a mining effort off the Biscay ports. The Wellingtons were recalled, but the Lancasters, DS612, DS622, DS623 and DS625, carried out their assigned tasks before returning safely home.

As we continue to use 218 Squadron to reflect life in a Stirling unit, now we will also observe operations in Lancasters through the eyes of 115 Squadron. An attack on the port of St Nazaire signalled a resumption of major activity on the 22/23rd, although 3 Group issued a recall to its Stirlings, and all but eight crews complied. This was the first bombing operation for 115 Squadron Lancasters, and those taking part were DS612, DS613, DS614, DS615, DS621, DS623 and DS624, all of which returned without mishap. The Ruhr offensive moved on to Duisburg on the 26/27th, but equipment failure among a high proportion of the Oboe Mosquito force led to inaccurate skymarking, and the bombing was scattered and ineffective. The month ended with two raids on Berlin, sandwiching another tilt at St Nazaire. The first attack on the capital was mounted by almost 400 aircraft on the 27/28th, and it fell well short of the city centre. Bombs fell over a wide area in the southern half of the city, but only a handful of houses were completely destroyed, although many other buildings sustained superficial damage. W/C Morris DSO concluded his tour as commanding officer of 218 Squadron on the 28th, and the highly experienced and somewhat mature W/C Saville DFC was posted in as his successor. Born in 1903 at Portland in New South Wales, Donald Saville transferred from the RAAF to the RAF on a short service commission in 1928, and by the end of 1941 he was an acting Squadron Leader and flight commander with 458 Squadron RAAF, having previously served, it is believed, with 12 Squadron earlier in the year. Between August and December 1942 he commanded 104 Squadron in Malta, and this was his last operational post before arriving at 218 Squadron.

The weather intervened for the second Berlin raid on the 29/30th, and most of the bombs fell into open country south-east of the city. It was not a good night for 218 Squadron, which posted missing two of its crews. There were no survivors from the crew of Sgt Hoar after flak accounted for BK702 over Germany, and BK716 was lost without trace with the crew of F/O Harris. Thus, five aircraft had been lost during the month with four crews, and this was from 122 sorties, the second highest number in the Group. This was the first time that 115 Squadron operated Mk II Lancasters in numbers, and the inevitable first loss occurred on this night. DS625 was also the first Mk II Lancaster to be lost in Bomber Command service, and it disappeared without trace with the crew of Sgt Ross. Piloting DS621 and returning safely was F/L Ian Bazalgette. After completing his tour in August, and being threatened with the prospect of becoming a flight commander at an OTU, he wrote to the former 7 Squadron and 3 Group stalwart, W/C 'Hamish' Mahaddie, who was now in charge of recruiting for the Pathfinders under the unofficial appellation of the 'Pathfinder Horse Thief'. He begged Mahaddie to rescue him from this posting, pointing out, that he would be far more useful to the war effort in an operational capacity with 8 Group. He got his wish, but sadly, lost his life during a daylight attack on a flying bomb store at Trossy-St-Maxim on the 4th of August 1944, while a member of 635 Squadron. While performing the function of Master Bomber for the operation, his aircraft was severely damaged, lost both starboard engines and was on fire. Despite this inconvenience he pressed on to mark the target, knowing that the success of the attack depended upon his so doing. Having fulfilled his duty as far as the operation was concerned, he did likewise with regard to his crew, and most took to their parachutes. Two men remained on board, and Bazalgette attempted a forced-landing in France. On touch-down the Lancaster exploded, killing the occupants, one of whom had already been mortally wounded. For his outstanding gallantry and devotion to duty, Bazalgette was posthumously awarded the Victoria Cross.

W/C Sisley concluded his tour as commanding officer of 115 Squadron on the 30th, and was packed off to Mildenhall pending a posting. He would return to the sharp end in mid July 1944, to assume command of 1 Group's 550 Squadron on the death in action of its incumbent, W/C Connolly. Sadly, W/C Sisley's end would follow on the last day of August during an attack on a V-2 site at Agenville in France. The new commander of 115 Squadron was

W/C Sims MiD, who was posted in from 1657 Conversion Unit for what would be a relatively short term of office. W/C Smythe DSO, DFC, MiD was promoted to Group Captain, and was posted from 214 Squadron to become the station commander at Methwold. He was succeeded at 214 Squadron by W/C Clube.

April would prove to be the least rewarding month of the Ruhr offensive, but this was largely because of the number of operations conducted away from the region and beyond the range of Oboe. On the 1st 75 (NZ) Squadron added a C Flight, and with the improved serviceability of the Stirling and the efficiency of the ground crews, this enabled it to achieve a consistently high sortie rate. S/L Broadbent would arrive on the 17th as C Flight commander, having spent nineteen months at an OTU after completing a full tour with 40 Squadron. The other flight commanders, S/Ls Fowler and Allcock, remained in post to continue providing quality leadership under W/C Lane. 192 Squadron began to pull out of Gransden Lodge on the 3rd, in preparation for the station's transfer to 8 Group, and was fully resident at Feltwell by the 7th.

The month's operations began in encouraging manner with another successful assault on Essen on the 3/4th, in which over 600 buildings were destroyed in mostly central and western districts. On the following night the largest non-1,000 force to date, comprising 577 aircraft, set off for Kiel, where strong winds and decoy fire sites were blamed for a dismal failure. Two further attempts were made on Duisburg, first on the 8/9th by a mixed main force, and twenty-four hours later by Lancasters, but neither succeeded in inflicting more than very modest damage. Among the nineteen missing aircraft from the former was 218 Squadron's BF502, which was lost without trace with the crew of Sgt Tomkins. All previous efforts against Frankfurt had failed to bring the hoped-for significant blow, and a force of 500 aircraft, including ninety-eight Stirlings, proved no more able on the 10/11th, when only a few bombs fell into southern districts. 115 Squadron's DS604 crashed in France, and there were no survivors from the crew of Sgt Thomas. In the midst of all the activity XV Squadron changed address for the final time on the 14th when moving to Mildenhall. The creep-back phenomenon, a feature of most Bomber Command heavy raids, rescued an attack on Stuttgart on the 14/15th, by falling across one industrial and a number of residential suburbs, destroying almost 400 buildings. Unusually, Wellingtons represented almost a third of the 462 strong force, while the Stirling was the least populous type, but each lost eight in an overall loss of twenty-three aircraft, and this represented an unhealthy 9.6% for the Stirling.

Harris divided his forces on the 16/17th, sending the Lancasters and Halifaxes to attack the Skoda armaments works at Pilsen in Czechoslovakia, while a predominantly Stirling and Wellington force carried out a diversionary raid on Mannheim. The former was a failure, caused by Pathfinder route markers being confused for target indicators, and the disappointment was compounded by the loss of thirty-six aircraft, split evenly between the two types. The latter operation was moderately effective, but also cost eighteen aircraft, and this brought the night's total casualty figure to a new record of fifty-four. 218 Squadron's BF514 was brought down over France, killing P/O Howlett and four of his crew, but the flight engineer and wireless operator escaped with their lives to evade capture. 75 (NZ) Squadron sustained the highest 3 Group casualties with two aircraft missing and another written-off in a crash on return. While Lancasters and Halifaxes carried out a highly destructive raid on Stettin on the Baltic coast on the 20/21st, eighty-six Stirlings peeled off to attack the Heinkel aircraft factory at Rostock. An effective smoke-screen thwarted the crews, leading to scattered bombing, and eight aircraft, a hefty 9.3%, failed to return. 218 Squadron's BK596 crashed in Denmark killing Sgt Jopling and three of his crew, while the three survivors were taken into captivity.

The most effective raid on Duisburg thus far took place at the hands of 500 aircraft on the 26/27th, when 300 buildings were destroyed. This moderate success came despite the fact, that many of the bombs missed the city altogether. However, as events were soon to prove, this city's charmed life was about to come to an end. 115 Squadron registered its third missing Lancaster as a result of this operation, when DS609 went down in the target area, and there was total loss of life among the crew of P/O Minnis. Two large mining operations were mounted on the 27/28th and 28/29th, the latter, by 207 aircraft sowing 593 mines, proving particularly expensive for 3 Group, which lost seven of thirty-two Stirlings dispatched, a massive 21.9%. 75 (NZ) Squadron was hardest-hit with four missing crews, but 218 Squadron also lost three. EF356 and BF515 both fell to nightfighters over Denmark with the crews of Sgt Hailey and F/L Berridge respectively, with just one survivor from the former. These were experienced pilots on their fifteenth and twenty-second sorties, and men that the squadron and the Command could ill afford to lose. BF447 also crashed on Danish soil, and two men survived to be taken prisoner from the crew of P/O Brown, who was on his eleventh operation with the squadron, having previously served with the secret 138 Squadron at Tempsford. The month was brought to an end by a modestly successful attack on Essen without the assistance of Stirlings on the night of the 30th. 218 Squadron put up a record 127 sorties during the month, and lost six aircraft and crews. During the course of the month W/C Wasse was posted away from 149 Squadron to be replaced by W/C Harrison, a twenty-eight year old Canadian.

May would bring a return to winning ways, with a number of spectacular successes. On the 3rd W/C Wyatt became the new commanding officer of 75 (NZ) Squadron. He was posted in from XV Squadron, having recently returned to Bourn from Spain, where, as previously mentioned, he had crash-landed his Stirling during an operation to Turin. A new record non-1,000 force of 596 aircraft took off for Dortmund on the 4/5th, and despite the presence of a decoy fire site, which inevitably attracted a proportion of the bombs, over 1,200 buildings were destroyed. War industry factories, dock facilities, public buildings and housing all featured in the catalogue of damage, but the success was achieved at a cost of thirty-one bombers, the highest loss of the campaign to date. XV Squadron was the hardest hit among the 3 Group participants with three missing Stirlings, and 218 Squadron posted missing the eight-man crew of F/L Turner DFC, only three of whom survived the destruction of BF505 by a nightfighter over Holland. W/C Menaul relinquished command of XV Squadron around this time, and was succeeded on the 7th by W/C Stephens, who was posted in from 149 Squadron, where he had served as a flight commander. W/C Sims concluded his short term of office at 115 Squadron on this day, and was posted to HQ Mildenhall for duties at East Wretham. After more than two years of dodging most of the bombs intended for it, there was no escape for Duisburg on the 12/13th, after the Pathfinders were finally able to mark the city accurately. Over 500 aircraft destroyed almost 1,600 buildings, and inflicted damage on some important war industry factories, while 60,000 tons of shipping was either sunk or seriously damaged in Germany's largest inland port. Bomber Command losses were again high at thirty-four aircraft, another new record for the campaign, and 218 Squadron was again represented. BK705 was shot down by flak into the North Sea, and there were no survivors from the crew of P/O Bryans.

138 Squadron mounted eight sorties to France on this night, half of them cargo drops, one of them flown by S/L Robinson and his crew in Halifax BB313. S/L Robinson was one of those remarkable men who couldn't be kept away from the operational scene, and were prepared to drop a rank to remain at the sharp end. Having concluded a five month tour of duty as commanding officer of 4 Group's 158 Squadron in March, he volunteered his skills in the cause of secret operations and joined 138 Squadron. On this night, while at low level and still over France on the way home, BB313 was hit by light flak from an airfield, and fire took hold. S/L Robinson gave the order to bale out, and the flight engineer and one gunner managed to do so before the Halifax crash-landed in a field. Robinson and other members of the crew sustained injuries in the process, but all the crew survived, and having assisted his colleagues as best he could, the second pilot, Sgt Tweed, made good his escape, and ultimately evaded capture. He returned to the UK in September, the month following the arrival home of the gunner and flight engineer. S/L Robinson and the other members of the crew fell into enemy hands, the navigator and bomb-aimer suffering injury serious enough to bring about their repatriation in February 1945.

On the following night, Bochum suffered the destruction of almost 400 buildings at the hands of a mixed force, while a predominantly Lancaster effort failed to rectify the recent disappointment at the Pilsen Skoda works. For the third raid running, 218 Squadron sustained casualties, although both incidents occurred at home. BF480 crashed on landing on return, without injury to Sgt Carney and his crew, but when EF367 crashed at Chedburgh, five of the occupants were killed, while the pilot, Sgt Nicholls, and his navigator were hurt. There would be no major operations by the heavy brigade thereafter for nine nights, which allowed much needed time for rest and replenishment. It was during this period that 617 Squadron booked its place in history with its epic attack on the Dams on the night of the 16/17th. After their long lay-off the main force and Pathfinder crews returned refreshed to the fray on the 23/24th. For the second time in the month Dortmund was selected to host a raid by a new record non-1,000 force, this time amounting to a massive 826 aircraft, of which the Stirling squadrons managed to put up a creditable 120 aircraft, seventeen of them from 218 Squadron. Clear weather conditions allowed the Pathfinders to mark the centre of the city, and 2,000 buildings were reduced to ruins, including many industrial premises. The defenders fought back to claim thirty-eight aircraft, yet another record casualty figure for the campaign, and this time 214 Squadron sustained the Group's worst casualties with three missing Stirlings. 218 Squadron's BK706 also failed to return, having crashed in the target area, and there were no survivors from the crew of F/O Phillips, who was on his sixth operation.

On the 24th W/C Batchelor concluded his short term of office as 138 Squadron's commanding officer, and was posted to Chedburgh as a Group Captain and station commander. Later in the war he would move to a similar post at Mildenhall, and remain in the RAF until his retirement in 1964. In 1987 he became the chairman of the Bomber Command Association, and passed away at the age of 79 in 1994. Had S/L Robinson not failed to return from operations earlier in the month, he may, perhaps, with his previous experience as a squadron commander, have succeeded W/C Batchelor. In the event, the position passed to W/C 'Dickie' Speare DFC*, another seasoned campaigner, who had served as a flight commander with 7 Squadron back in the spring of 1941, and until recently, had held a similar post with 1 Group's 460 Squadron RAAF.

Over 700 aircraft tried to repeat the recent successes at Düsseldorf on the 25/26th, but this time cloud and decoy fire sites contributed to an expensive failure. The disappointment was compounded by the loss of twenty-seven aircraft, which included 218 Squadron's EH887. This Stirling contained the eight-man crew of Sgt Collins, and he was one of seven who died, when it was shot down by a nightfighter over Germany. The Stirling brigade sat out a raid by 500 aircraft on Essen on the 27/28th, when almost 500 buildings were destroyed. A thus far loss-free month for 115 Squadron came to an end two nights later, as 500 aircraft delivered the fifth raid of the campaign on Essen. Almost 500 buildings were destroyed at a cost of twenty-three aircraft, one of which was the squadron's DS655. The Lancaster blew up over the target, flinging clear the pilot, F/O Cammell, who alone of his crew survived, albeit in enemy hands. 218 Squadron took the opportunity to send a freshman crew on a mining sortie to the Frisians to gain their first taste of operations, but F/S Mills and his crew were never seen again, and the cause of BF405's demise remains a mystery. The month ended with an operation to Barmen on the 29/30th, this one of the twin towns known jointly as

Wuppertal. Over 700 aircraft were involved, and accurate Pathfinder marking was exploited by the main force crews to leave an estimated 80% of the town's built-up area in ruins. Some 4,000 houses were destroyed, along with most of the large factories, and 3,400 people lost their lives. It was rarely a one-sided contest, however, and thirty-three bombers were brought down by the defenders. Another bad night for 75 (NZ) Squadron saw four of its Stirlings fail to return, and 218 Squadron also had two empty dispersals. BF565 and BK688 both fell victim to the nightfighter of Heinz Wolfgang Schnaufer over Belgium, and neither produced a survivor from among the crews of P/O Allan and F/S Davis respectively, both of whom were Australians. It was also an eventful night for 115 Squadron, which ended in the failure to return of one aircraft, and the wrecking of two others. DS627 was shot down by a nightfighter over Belgium, killing Sgt Fleming and his crew, while DS616 barely survived a similar encounter. Badly damaged, and with the rear gunner fatally wounded, the Lancaster was crash-landed at East Wretham by F/O Andrews without further injury to the occupants. Before coming to rest the aircraft collided with DS616, and this was also declared a write-off. This was the final operation undertaken by 90 Squadron from Ridgewell. On the 31st a move was made to West Wickham, which would be renamed Wratting Common on the 21st of August. It had already been a very expensive month for 218 Squadron by the time P/O Rich took EF365 for an air-test on the 31st, and the flight ended with a crash-landing in Norfolk after engine failure, although without injury to the occupants. It is remarkable how frequently a crew involved in such an incident would go missing soon afterwards, and although P/O Rich couldn't know it, he had but three weeks left to live. This brought the month's tally to ten aircraft and eight crews lost from 113 sorties.

Elsewhere, 'Pick' Pickard was posted from 161 Squadron during the month on promotion to Group Captain and a station commander's job at Lissett, home to 4 Group's 158 Squadron. By this time Pickard had been awarded a second bar to his DSO, making him at the time the only holder of three DSOs won during a single war, each of them coincidentally won during the month of February. The first was for service with 311 Squadron in 1941, the second for the Bruneval raid in 1942, and the third for a remarkable operation carried out on behalf of 161 Squadron on the night of the 24/25th of February 1943. It was a typical winter's night of sleet and snow as Pickard took off from Tempsford in Hudson 'O' Orange to pick up seven agents in the Tournais/Cuisery region of France. They were being pursued by the Gestapo, and it was essential to get them out without delay. The target area was reached after three hours flying, but in appalling conditions it took another two hours of abortive attempts before a heavy landing was accomplished. After taxiing the Hudson became bogged down and had to be dug out, which occupied another half hour. By this time many locals had gathered at the landing site, alerted by the sound of aircraft engines droning over their rooftops for two hours. The Hudson became bogged down for a second time as 'Pick' taxied to take-off position, and it took another ninety minutes of digging, pushing and pulling by the villagers before he was at last ready to go. There was absolutely no guarantee that the aircraft would attain flying speed before running out of field, but somehow it did, although the leading edge of a wing scraped through a treetop while the Hudson was already on the point of stalling. By a miracle and Pick's incredible airmanship they remained airborne and arrived back at Tempsford at 08.00 after a trip lasting nine and a half hours. Pickard would be appointed to command 140 Wing of the 2nd Tactical Air Force in December. Sadly, he and his long time navigator, Bill Broadly, were to lose their lives in a 464 Squadron Mosquito during the famous raid on the walls of Amiens prison in February 1944.

His successor at 161 Squadron was W/C Bob Hodges, who was promoted from flight commander. He had enjoyed an eventful war to date, even escaping from the clutches of his German captors in 1940 while serving with 5 Group's 49 Squadron. It was dawn on the 5th of September, and he was on his way home from Stettin after nine hours aloft. His Hampden was desperately short of fuel as he began an approach to what he believed was St Eval in Cornwall. However, a burst of light flak had him scrambling for height and the fuel lasted long enough for two of his crew to bale out. With insufficient height to do likewise, Hodges crash-landed, whereupon he and his crewman discovered they were in Brittany. They were captured and moved to a camp at Toulouse in southern France, from where they escaped and returned home via Gibraltar.

W/C Rainsford MiD arrived at 115 Squadron from 1657 Conversion Unit on the 1st of June to assume command at the departure of W/C Sims. Born in 1909 he had been raised in Ireland, and joined 502 (Ulster) Squadron in 1936, before becoming navigation officer of 215 Squadron, and then progressing to flight commander at 11 OTU, flight commander and then commanding officer of 148 Squadron, Officer Commanding RAF Molesworth in 1942, and then Chief Flying Instructor at 29 OTU. 192 Squadron flew its first Halifax sortie on the 2nd with a sweep along the Dutch coast, and its first Mosquito operation would follow on the 11th. There was a ten-night rest for the main force at the start of the month, which allowed the crews another welcome opportunity to draw breathe and the squadrons to replenish after an intensive and expensive round of major operations. The bombing campaign resumed at Düsseldorf on the 11/12th, when almost 800 aircraft departed their stations. Despite an errant Oboe marker attracting a proportion of the effort, massive damage was inflicted on the city, and almost 9,000 separate fire incidents were recorded. Production was brought to a complete halt at forty-two war industry factories, and many others were at reduced capacity for a period, while eight ships were sunk or damaged in the port. The losses equalled the campaign's previous highest at thirty-eight, and while 218 Squadron was not represented among them, 115 Squadron lost DS647 to a nightfighter over Holland, and flight commander, S/L Fox, died with his crew. A successful attack on Bochum was delivered on the following night without the assistance of Stirlings, A nightfighter accounted for 115 Squadron's DS652 off the Dutch coast, and there were no survivors from the crew of F/S Ruff. Later on the 13th thirty-three year old W/C Giles assumed command of 90 Squadron on the posting out of W/C Claydon to the Bombing and Gunnery School at Sutton Bridge. Lancasters went alone to Oberhausen on the 14/15th, and were joined by a few Pathfinder Halifaxes on the 16/17th for an experimental raid on Cologne, for which the marking was by H2s rather than Oboe. Problems with H2s sets led to late and scattered marking, which was reflected in the inaccuracy of the bombing, but 400 houses were never the less destroyed, along with nine railway stations, and many industrial premises were damaged. Elements of 3, 4, 6 and 8 Groups went to the Schneider armaments factory at Le Creusot on the 19/20th, the scene of a 5 Group daylight raid in the previous October. It was a difficult target, which had to be identified by the crews individually in the light shed by Pathfinder flares, and only 20% of the bombs fell within the factory complex. 3 Group also dispatched twelve Lancasters on this night to lay mines in the River Gironde. Only one did not make it back, and this was DS668 of 115 Squadron. The Lancaster failed to survive an encounter with a nightfighter while on the way home over France, and the crew was forced to abandon it to its fate. Sadly, the pilot, F/O Brown, landed in the River Loire and drowned, but his flight engineer and wireless operator managed to evade capture, while the remaining four members of the crew were rounded up.

Three squadrons had been formed or re-formed on the 7th of November 1942, 90 Squadron, which has already been dealt with, 196 Squadron, which is covered in the July account, and 199 Squadron. The last mentioned was originally formed as a training unit in June 1917 to provide pilots for night bomber squadrons in France. A period of disbandment lasted from June 1919 until November 1942, when it was reborn at Blyton as a 1 Group bomber squadron operating Wellingtons. Its final operation with 1 Group took place on the 13th of June, and on the 20th it was posted to 3 Group to operate Stirlings out of Lakenheath. It would take until the final week of July before working up was complete, a process overseen by the commanding officer, W/C Howard DFC. He had been commissioned in 1927 and served with 99 Squadron in 1931. His DFC had been awarded for service while a flight commander with 77 Squadron. A brand new squadron, 620, was formed in 3 Group at Chedburgh on the 20th to operate Stirlings under the command of W/C Lee, who was posted in from 1651 CU. The squadron would be ready to go to war for the first time just two nights later.

A hectic round of four operations in five nights began at Krefeld on the 21/22nd. The attack at the hands of 700 aircraft, including more than 100 Stirlings, became a perfect example of the Command at its most destructive. A record number of 5,500 houses were reduced to rubble, while over 1,000 people lost their lives. Bomber Command's losses were also a record for the campaign, however, and the 72,000 people rendered homeless would have been cheered to know that forty-four of their tormentors would not be returning home. Two of these were from Downham Market, BK712, which was shot down by a nightfighter over Belgium with no survivors from the eight-man crew of P/O Shillinglaw, and BK722, a victim of flak over Holland. The previously mentioned P/O Rich died alongside his bomb-aimer and one of the gunners, while the four survivors were taken into captivity. On the following night over 500 aircraft attacked Mülheim, and destroyed more than 1,100 houses there and in neighbouring Oberhausen, while causing serious damage to the towns' public buildings and industry. It was another night of heavy losses for the Command, however, amounting to thirty-five aircraft, and 75 (NZ) Squadron was again 3 Group's worst-hit unit with three missing Stirlings. 218 Squadron did not come through unscathed, and lost BF572, which crashed into the North Sea and took with it F/S Smith and five of his crew. The sole survivor was one of the gunners, who presumably baled out while the stricken aircraft was still over land, and he became a PoW. The euphemism for the Ruhr was 'Happy Valley', and its fearful reputation was being justifiably earned.

After a night's rest 630 aircraft took off for the Elberfeld half of Wuppertal, and visited upon it an ordeal even greater than that suffered by its twin Barmen at the end of May. Some 3,000 houses and 170 industrial premises were destroyed, and an estimated 94% of the town's built-up area was deemed to be in ruins. Thirty-four aircraft failed to return, and there were two more empty dispersals at Downham Market which should have been occupied by 218 Squadron's BF501 and EH892. The former was accounted for by a night-fighter over Belgium, and it took the eight-man crew of Sgt Hoey to their deaths. The latter contained the crew of flight commander S/L Beck, who was one of four men killed when it became a victim of flak over Germany, while the three survivors joined the growing roll-call of 218 Squadron airmen in PoW camps. Despite the losses, it was a highly effective series of operations, which was halted at the notoriously elusive oil town of Gelsenkirchen on the 25/26th. Complete cloud cover and equipment failure afflicting a number of the Oboe Mosquitos led to a disappointing raid, and in an echo of the past, bombs were sprayed over a wide area of the Ruhr, and the target escaped lightly. Not so the bomber force, which lost a further thirty aircraft, and for the third time in four operations 218 Squadron had to post missing two crews. Nightfighters over Holland were responsible for the demise of both EF430 and EH898, the former containing the crew of flight commander S/L Maw, who all baled out into the arms of their captors. The latter was the chariot of Sgt Hughes and his crew, and was shot down from 13,000 feet while outbound, with only the navigator escaping by parachute to become a PoW. 115 Squadron's DS666 was absent from its dispersal following this operation, and the fate of the crew of Sgt Rashley has never been established. Also missing from a simultaneous mining operation off Lorient was DS663, in which Sgt Whitehead and his crew lost their lives. The combined total of the Command's losses for the four operations in five nights was a staggering 143, or the equivalent of six three-flight squadrons.

75 (NZ) Squadron changed address for the final time during the war with a move to Mepal on the 28th, and that night came the first of a series of three operations against Cologne, which would span the turn of the month. Over 600 aircraft took part on this night, and those reaching the target produced the most outstanding raid of the war to date. Over 6,400 buildings were destroyed, including dozens of an industrial nature, and 4,377 people lost their lives, a new record number, while 230,000 others were rendered homeless. The twenty-five missing aircraft included five of the seventy-five Stirlings despatched, three of them belonging to 149 Squadron, but 218 Squadron came through unscathed. Having closed the June account, it fell to Cologne to open that of July, and on the night of the 3/4th it underwent another ordeal at the hands of 600 aircraft. The attack was aimed at the more heavily industrialized districts on the east bank of the Rhine, and was carried out with stunning accuracy, which led to the destruction of twenty industrial premises and 2,200 houses. Thirty aircraft failed to make it home, two of them from 90 Squadron, which lost another to a crash on return. 115 Squadron's DS662 went down somewhere between the Dutch/German border and the target, and Sgt Stokes-Roberts and five of his crew lost their lives, with only the bomb-aimer surviving to fall into enemy hands. The series against Cologne was brought to a conclusion by an all-Lancaster heavy force on the 8/9th, after which, the city authorities were able to assess the extent of the damage and casualties arising out of the three raids. It was the most extensive catalogue of misery of the war thus far, and included 11,000 buildings destroyed, 5,500 people killed, and a further 350,000 without homes. Some 110 sorties during the month made June marginally the least active for 218 Squadron since January, and it had cost seven aircraft and crews.

A disappointing failure took place at Gelsenkirchen on the 9/10th, which the Stirlings sat out at home, and this effectively brought an end to the Ruhr offensive, even though two further operations to the region would take place at the end of the month. It had been a bruising contest, but Harris could look back over the past four months with genuine satisfaction at the performance of his squadrons. Losses had been grievously high, but much of Germany's industrial heart lay in ruins, and the aircraft factories at home had more than kept pace with the rate of attrition. The training schools, too, continued to pour eager new crews into the fray to fill the gaps, and a gradual expansion was taking place, which had enabled all Stirling squadrons to add a C Flight during May. Perhaps Harris derived his greatest satisfaction from the success of Oboe, which had been the crucial factor in the battle, the difference between success and failure, by providing, at last, the means to 'see' through the previously impenetrable barrier of haze and cloud. With confidence high Harris now sought an opportunity to rock the very foundations of Nazi morale, by consigning to oblivion a major German city in a short, sharp series of attacks until the job was done. In the meantime, Lancasters were sent to Turin on the 12/13th, while a mixed force including over fifty Stirlings raided Aachen on the following night. The latter was an outstanding success, which left almost 3,000 buildings in ruins, while many large industrial premises and public buildings sustained heavy damage. It was, however, a costly night for 115 Squadron, which posted missing two of its crews. F/O Larson, the pilot of DS660, was the sole survivor of his crew after an encounter with a nightfighter over the Pas-de-Calais, while DS690 succumbed to a similar cause over the Luxembourg/Belgian frontier, and only the flight engineer from the crew of S/L The Hon R A G Baird escaped with his life.

3 Group welcomed a new recruit on the 19th as 196 Squadron was posted in from 4 Group. It had formed in November of the previous year, and conducted operations with the Wellington Mk X. Having settled in at Witchford the crews were sent to 1651 Heavy Conversion Unit to learn the ways of the Stirling. Mostly brand new aircraft began to arrive during what remained of the month, and working up to operational status was overseen by W/C Alexander, who had been appointed commanding officer on the 26th of June. As events turned out 196 Squadron's time with 3 Group would be relatively brief.

It was the last week of the month before Harris was ready to launch Operation Gomorrah, the appropriately, as it turned out, code-named series of raids for which Hamburg was selected. Bomber Command had gone to Hamburg during the final week of July in each year of the war to date, and this tradition would be continued in 1944. Having been spared by the weather from hosting the first 1,000 bomber raid in history more than a year earlier, Hamburg suited Harris's criteria now in a number of respects. As Germany's Second City, its political status was undeniable, as was its importance as a centre of war production, particularly with regard to U-Boat construction. It was also accessible to the Command without the need to traverse large tracts of hostile territory, and its location near a coastline would both aid navigation, and allow the aircraft to approach and retreat during the few hours of total darkness afforded by mid summer. Finally, lying beyond the range of Oboe, Hamburg boasted the wide River Elbe to provide a strong H2s signature for the navigators flying high above.

Operation Gomorrah began on the night of the 24/25th, and was attended by the first operational use of 'Window'. This was the tinfoil-backed strips of paper, which, when dispensed into the slip stream in great clouds, would flutter slowly to earth, and swamp the enemy's nightfighter control, searchlight and gun-laying radar with false returns. It will be recalled that 109 Squadron had carried out trials of the device a year earlier, but its use had been vetoed in case the enemy copied it. The enemy had, in fact, already developed a similar system of its own under the code name Düppel, which had also been withheld for the same reason. 791 aircraft took off after 22.00 hours, including 114 Stirlings from 3 Group, twenty of them provided by 218 Squadron with W/C Saville in the lead on his ninth operation since taking command. EF352 returned early with intercom problems, but the remainder pressed on, encountering little contact with enemy night-fighters during the outward flight as they headed for the rendezvous point over the North Sea. Those few aircraft shot down at this stage were invariably off course and outside of the protection of the bomber stream. At the appointed position the designated crew member in each aircraft began to dispense the bundles of Window into the night sky, and its effect became apparent once they arrived in the target area. Here they found the usually efficient co-ordination between the searchlight and flak batteries absent. Defence was sporadic and random, and the opportunity was there to mark the target almost unhindered. In the event, the markers were slightly misplaced, but over a period of fifty minutes almost 2,300 tons of bombs cut a swathe of destruction from the city centre, back across the north-western districts along the line of approach, and out into open country, where a proportion of the bombing was wasted. It was, never the less, a highly encouraging start to the campaign, and was achieved for the modest loss of twelve aircraft, for which much of the credit belonged to Window. At a stroke the device had rendered the entire enemy defensive system impotent, but an advantage was rarely held for long before a counter-measure was found, and this would eventually see the balance swing back in Germany's favour.

It was a sad night for 218 Squadron, however, whose crews awaited in vain the return of their commanding officer. BF567 was shot down by a night-fighter over Germany, and the bomb-aimer alone of the eight men on board escaped with his life to spend the rest of the war in a prison camp. Shortly before his death W/C Saville had been awarded the DSO, the citation for which is quoted from A.M.B.10952, dated July 1943. 'This officer has completed a large number of sorties, and has displayed outstanding deter-mination to achieve success. He is a fearless commander, who invariably chooses to participate in the more difficult sorties which have to be undertaken. Whatever the opposition, W/C Saville endeavours to press home his attacks with accuracy and resolution. By his personal example and high qualities of leadership, this officer has contributed materially to the operational efficiency of the squadron'.

On the following night Harris switched his force to Essen, to take advantage of the chaos dealt to the enemy's defensive system by Window, and another massive blow was delivered upon the city. Over 2,800 houses were destroyed, and the Krupp works sustained its heaviest damage of the war in return for the loss of twenty-six aircraft, among which were three Stirlings from 620 Squadron. It was on this night that the Mk I Stirling operated with 218 Squadron for the final time.

218 Squadron's new commanding officer was W/C Oldbury, who had been posted from 1651 CU to 620 Squadron as a flight commander as recently as the 9th of July, and had completed one operation with that unit before his posting to 218 Squadron on the 27th. That night, having enjoyed the previous night on the ground, 787 aircraft took off for round two of Operation Gomorrah, and what followed their arrival over the city was both unprecedented and unforeseeable, and the product of a conspiracy of circumstances. A period of unusually hot and dry weather had left parts of

the city a tinderbox, and the initial spark to ignite it came with the pathfinder markers. These fell two miles east of the planned city centre aiming point, but with unaccustomed concentration into the densely populated working class residential districts of Hamm, Hammerbrook and Borgfeld. The main force crews followed up with uncharacteristic accuracy and scarcely any creep-back, and delivered the bulk of their 2,300 tons of bombs into this relatively compact area. The individual fires joined together to form one giant con-flagration, which sucked in oxygen from surrounding areas at hurricane velocity to feed its voracious appetite. Such was the ferocity of this meteoro-logical phenomenon, the first recorded bombing-induced firestorm in history, that trees were uprooted and flung bodily into the flames, along with debris and people, and the temperatures at the heart of the inferno exceeded 1,000 degrees Celsius. The flames only subsided once all the combustible material had been consumed, by which time it was already too late for the 40,000 people who had perished. On the following morning the first of an eventual 1.2 million people began to file out of the city, and did so under strict instructions not to talk about what they had witnessed. Seventeen aircraft failed to return, but 218 Squadron welcomed all eighteen of its participants home.

Two nights later eighteen more 218 Squadron Stirlings contributed to a force of 777 aircraft sent back to the tortured city. By the time the early returns had dropped out 707 aircraft were left approaching from the north. The Pathfinders again dropped their markers two miles to the east of the centre, and a little south of the firestorm area. This time a creep-back spread across the devastation of two nights earlier, before falling onto other residential districts further north, where a new area of fire was created, although of lesser proportions, and extensive damage and casualties resulted. The city's fire service was already exhausted, while access to the freshly afflicted districts was denied by rubble strewn and cratered streets, and there was little to be done other than to allow the fires to burn themselves out. As the enemy defences began to recover from the shock of Window, so the bomber losses crept up, and twenty-eight aircraft were missing. Two of these were the 218 Squadron Stirlings, BF578 and EE895. The former's demise came at the hands of a combination of flak and a nightfighter over Germany, and Sgt Pickard was killed with one of his crew. The latter was a victim of flak in the target area, and there were no survivors from the crew of Sgt Clark. Both crews were just emerging from their freshman status, and were on their third and fifth operations respectively. July ended with a devastating attack on Remscheid by roughly equal numbers of Halifaxes, Lancasters and Stirlings on the 30/31st, and this brought down the final curtain on the Ruhr offensive. A fairly modest force of around 250 aircraft destroyed over 80% of the town's built-up area, including most of its industry and 3,100 houses, and 1,100 people lost their lives. The Stirling brigade sustained the highest numerical casualties at eight aircraft, and also the highest percentage losses at nearly 10%, and alarm bells were beginning to ring at Bomber

Command HQ. One of the missing Stirlings was 218 Squadron's BF519, which was dispatched by a nighfighter over Holland killing Sgt Taylor and his crew. BF440 crash-landed on return, but Sgt Knight and his crew were unhurt. The squadron launched a new record of 130 sorties during the month, losing five aircraft and four crews, including that of the commanding officer. W/C McGlinn, a superb pilot, who had served previously as an instructor in Canada, succeeded W/C Clube at 214 Squadron. However, he had no operational experience, and it would take time for him to gain the respect of battle-hardened crews.

Operation Gomorrah was concluded on the night of the 2/3rd of August, when violent electrical storms and icing conditions during the outward flight persuaded many crews to jettison their bombs, or to attack alternative targets. Thirty aircraft were lost, some of them to the conditions, and little fresh damage was created within the city. Not one of 115 Squadron's ten participants reached Hamburg, and it sustained the Group's highest casualties with three missing Lancasters without a single survivor. F/S Button and his crew disappeared without trace in DS685, DS715 was sent crashing into the target area by a lightning strike, taking with it the crew of P/O Mosen, and Sgt Bennett and crew fell victim to a nightfighter off the north-western coast of Germany in DS673. 218 Squadron dispatched fifteen crews, one of which returned soon after take-off, nine jettisoned their loads, two brought their bombs home, and just three attacked the target as briefed. This undoubtedly saved lives in Hamburg, but the damage to the city and German morale had already been done. 218 Squadron's overall contribution to the campaign amounted to seventy-one sorties, fifty-seven of which bombed as briefed, and three aircraft failed to return. 115 Squadron launched sixty-two sorties, of which fifty-one were completed as briefed, and it too suffered three losses. Before the next phase in Bomber Command operations 115 Squadron changed address yet again with a move on the 6th to Little Snoring.

Italy was by now teetering on the brink of capitulation, and Bomber Command was invited to help nudge it over the edge with a series of raids on its major cities during the second week of August. 1, 5 and 8 Groups began the assault, with all-Lancaster attacks on Genoa, Milan and Turin on the 7/8th. Before the Alps were crossed again, Mannheim suffered the destruction of 1,300 buildings on the 9/10th in the absence of a Stirling contingent. Later on the 10th 218 Squadron donated one of its flights to form the nucleus of a new unit, 623 Squadron, with which it would share Downham Market until the latter was disbanded in December. W/C Oldbury supervised the squadron initially until the appointment of W/C Little DFC and 3 times MiD, who, it will be recalled, had served as a flight commander with 40 Squadron at the time of its transfer from 2 to 3 Group in late 1940. Jack Little was a devoted and fervent Christian, who regularly preached in the church at Fakenham. On the same day XV Squadron gave birth to 622 Squadron at Mildenhall by hiving off its C Flight. 622 Squadron's initial complement of seven Stirlings was inherited from XV Squadron and constituted A Flight. The numbers would be made up over the succeeding days to sixteen with four in reserve. The original crews posted in on the 10th were those of S/L Martin, who would be nominally in command until the appointment of a permanent commanding officer, F/L Bould, F/Ss Batson, Clarke, Marsh and Rollett, and Sgt Jackson, with aircraft, BF521, BK652, BK766, BK816, EF391, EH897 and MZ264, to be followed by EF490 on the 12th and EF461 on the 14th. Additional aircrew were posted in from training units to bring the squadron up to full strength, but the presence of experienced crews enabled it to be declared operational on the day of its formation. S/L Martin conducted his first briefing on the afternoon of the 10th for an operation that night to Nuremberg. 622 Squadron would contribute seven Stirlings among 119 of the type taking part in an overall force of over 600. After a late evening take-off the crews found the target concealed by cloud, but were still able to deliver an effective raid, which destroyed some historic buildings and left one district engulfed in flames. It was, in fact, the first time that a telling blow had been struck at this significant city. This was achieved at a cost of sixteen aircraft, of which three were Stirlings. 218 Squadron's EE885 crashed in southern Germany after being hit by incendiaries over the target. Seven of the crew abandoned the stricken aircraft safely and fell into enemy hands, but the pilot, F/L Fillmore, was killed, possibly through sacrificing his chance of survival to save his crew. 115 Squadron's DS665 almost made it home, but broke up in the air near Huntingdon at 04.30 on the 11th, and F/O Erwin and crew died in its wreckage. All of the 622 Squadron aircraft came through their operational debut unscathed, although two were forced to return early with technical problems.

The night of the 12/13th was devoted to Italy, the Lancasters and Halifaxes targeting Milan, while 112 Stirlings, with thirty-four Halifaxes and a handful of Pathfinder Lancasters raided Turin. On approaching the target 218 Squadron's EF452 was hit by fire from another bomber, killing the navigator instantly, and wounding other members of the crew, including the pilot, F/S Aaron DFM. He was hit in the face and chest, and was unable to use his right arm. The flight engineer and bomb-aimer took control of the Stirling, which now had only three good engines, and pointed its nose towards North Africa, while the pilot was given morphine and made as comfortable as possible. As the North African coast was reached, Aaron, whose jaw was shattered, and who consequently was unable to speak, insisted on trying to take control. It proved impossible for him to do so, but he remained conscious and wrote instructions with his left hand to help his colleagues with the landing. Finally, at the fifth attempt, the Stirling was successfully belly-landed at Bone airfield in Algeria, where F/S Aaron succumbed nine hours later to his injuries. Had he rested quietly during the flight from Turin, the likelihood is that he could have survived, but instead, he became the second and last Stirling crewman to be awarded the Victoria Cross. It will be recalled that Ron Middleton's VC had also been awarded posthumously for actions during an operation to Turin in November 1942. Lancasters continued the assault on Milan on the 14/15th and 15/16th, before the Command's interest in Italy was concluded with a raid on Turin on the 16/17th, conducted by a predominantly Stirling force. 115 Squadron awaited in vain the return of DS684 and its crew of S/L Watson, and it was later established that they had all perished in a crash in France. It was on this operation that W/C Wyatt led 75 (NZ) Squadron into battle for the last time. On return many of the 3 Group stations were fog-bound, and extensive diversions were necessary. A proportion of the aircraft involved in those would not get back to their home stations until the following day was well advanced, and consequently, they could not be made ready in time to participate in the night's supremely important operation. One 218 Squadron Stirling, EH884, did not return at all, having been shot down by a night-fighter over France while outbound. P/O Chudzik and four of his crew were killed, but two men did survive, a gunner, who fell into enemy hands, and the navigator, who didn't, and managed to retain his freedom. This was P/O Chudzik's tenth operation as crew captain, and his parents were destined to lose another son, when his brother was killed with 420 Squadron RCAF in June 1944.

Since the start of hostilities, intelligence had been filtering through concerning German advances in rocket technology. As secret codes were broken, and signals traffic intercepted and deciphered, it became clear that such activity centred upon a research centre at Peenemünde on the island of Usedom off the Baltic coast. Through this means, it became possible for the brilliant scientist, Dr R V Jones, to monitor the V-1 trials taking place over the Baltic, and reconnaissance flights were made to the general area to gather further information. Churchill's chief scientific adviser, Professor Lindemann, or Lord Cherwell as he became, steadfastly refused to give credence to rocket weapons, and even when confronted with a photograph of a V-2 on a trailer at Peenemünde, taken by a PRU Mosquito as recently as June 1943, he remained unmoved. It required the combined urgings of Dr Jones and the later well-known political figure Duncan Sandys to convince Churchill of the need to act, and an operation was planned for the first available opportunity. This arose on the night of the 17/18th of August, for which a meticulous plan had been prepared. An innovation was the employment of a Master of Ceremonies to control all aspects of the raid by VHF, in the manner so successfully employed by Gibson at the Dams. The officer selected for the role was G/C Searby, the commanding officer of 83 Squadron, and successor to Gibson at 106 Squadron. He would be required to remain in the target area throughout the raid, within range of the defences, directing the marking and bombing, and exhorting the crews to press home their attacks. There were to be three aiming points, the housing estate where the scientists and technical staff lived, the assembly buildings and the experimental site, each of which was assigned to a specific wave of bombers. A spoof raid on Berlin by eight Mosquitos of 139 Squadron was designed to keep the enemy night-fighters away from the scene, and this would be led by the former 49 Squadron commander, G/C Slee.

A total of 597 aircraft answered the call for a maximum effort, the numbers somewhat depleted by the absence of a proportion of the Stirling brigade for the reasons already mentioned. Fifty-four Stirlings were available, and 90 Squadron provided fifteen of them, the largest contribution to the operation by a 3 Group squadron. 218 Squadron managed only five aircraft, led by W/C Oldbury in BF522, but he was forced to return early with a faulty intercom. This left S/L Ryall in EE888, F/L Kingsbury in EH923, W/O Grant in BK700 and F/S Adams in BK650, all of whom would reach the target area without incident. Twelve 115 Squadron Lancasters lined up for take-off at Little Snoring at around 21.30 hours, and they were as follows; DS653, F/L Christianson, DS626, F/L Eggleston, DS720, F/L Starkey, DS659, F/O Barnes, DS630, F/O Pusey, DS691, F/O Seddon, DS722, P/O Cade, DS683, W/O Boutillier, DS678, W/O Hicks, DS667, F/S Tinn, DS631, F/S Townsend and DS664, F/S Wolfson. All got away safely, and headed for the narrow neck of southern Denmark, before turning south for the target at the final turning point at Rügen, an island to the north of Usedom.

After last minute alterations to the plan, 3 and 4 Groups were assigned to the first aiming point, 1 Group the second, and 5 and 6 Groups the third. Thus, 115 Squadron, operators of Mk II Lancasters, would be the odd man out in a wave of Stirlings and Halifaxes. The initial marking over the residential area went awry, and the target indicators fell around the forced workers camp at Trassenheide more than a mile beyond, where heavy casualties were inflicted on the friendly foreign national inmates, who were trapped inside their wooden barracks. Once rectified, the operation proceeded more or less according to plan, and a number of important members of the technical team were killed. 1 Group's attack on the assembly buildings was hampered by a strong cross-wind, but substantial damage was inflicted, and this left only 5 and 6 Groups to complete the operation by bombing the experimental site. It was as they approached the target area, that the nightfighters belatedly arrived from Berlin, and once on the scene, they proceeded to take a heavy toll of bombers, both in the skies above Peenemünde, and on the route westwards towards Denmark. Forty aircraft were shot down, twenty-nine of them from the final wave, while only two Stirlings were lost. 3 Group posted missing just three crews in all, after a relatively quiet time at the head of the raid. All twelve 115 crews bombed the target as briefed, but only eleven made it home, after DS630 was brought down by a nightfighter over Denmark without survivors among the crew of P/O Pusey on only the third operation of their tour.

The Pathfinders were generally the first to get back after an operation, but the honour on this night fell to the 115 Squadron crew of F/L Eggleston. It was the final operation of their tour, and they had opened the taps on the powerful Hercules engines for the return flight, landing well ahead of the first

8 Group Lancaster. The operation was deemed a success, and it certainly delayed the V-2 development programme by a number of weeks, and forced the manufacture of secret weapons underground. A few days after Peenemünde W/C Wyatt left 75 (NZ) Squadron on posting to 3 Group HQ, but he would return to the operational scene as the commanding officer of 514 Squadron at Waterbeach in 1944. He was replaced at 75 (NZ) Squadron by W/C Max DFC, a battle-hardened officer who had been in at the start, flying Fairey Battles in France and later Wellingtons with 103 Squadron. On completion of his first tour he became an Atlantic Ferry pilot, bringing Hudsons over from the United States. 622 Squadron appointed its first commanding officer on the 20th in the shape of W/C Gibson, who had previously commanded 104 squadron in North Africa from December 1942 until the end of February 1943.

Harris maintained his view that bombing could win the war on its own, without the need for the kind of bloody and protracted land campaigns, which he had personally witnessed during the Great War. He had long believed that Berlin held the key to ultimate victory, and that, as the seat and symbol of Nazi power, its destruction would demoralize the nation to the point where it would demand peace. On the night of the 23/24th Harris embarked on the first phase of what would be the longest and most bitter campaign of the war, when sending over 700 aircraft to the capital, among them 124 Stirlings. Past experience at the 'Big City' had demonstrated the difficulty of identifying a specific aiming point by H2s, and on this night it was the southern suburbs which were marked. Many bomb loads fell onto outlying communities and open country, something which would become a feature of all Berlin raids, but those hitting the city destroyed or seriously damaged over 2,600 buildings, most of them houses, and over 800 people were killed. The defences were very active, both in terms of flak and night-fighters, and a new record fifty-six aircraft were lost, of which three were from 75 (NZ) Squadron. It was a bad night for the Stirlings generally, which registered a 12.9% loss rate, compared with 9.2% for the Halifaxes and 5.1% for the Lancasters. Three Downham Market dispersals lay empty next morning, two belonging to 218 Squadron and one to 623 Squadron. The 623 Squadron loss was the unit's first, and it was keenly felt also across the tarmac at 218 Squadron. S/L Hiles DSO, DFC had completed two tours with 218 before being posted as a staff officer to 3 Group HQ. He had put together something of a scratch crew for this operation, mostly made up of 218 Squadron airmen, and all were killed when they were shot down by a nightfighter a little south of Berlin. The rear gunner was New Yorker W/O De Silva DFM, who had been S/L Hiles regular rear gunner, and was kicking his heels waiting to be posted when he volunteered to join his former skipper.

One of the missing 218 Squadron aircraft was BF522, which contained the recently commissioned P/O Martin and his crew, and was ditched in the North Sea. A Stirling of 149 Squadron containing F/Sgt Bower and his crew took of from Lakenheath at 09.30 to carry out a sea search in the North Sea.

During the course of the flight they and another Stirling located a dinghy containing five personnel from BF552 some 160 miles north-west of Heligoland. Both Stirlings circled the area and transmitted a request for assistance. Two Hudsons of 279 Squadron flown by F/L Fitchew and F/S Neil left Bircham Newton at 14.15, arriving in the search area two hours later. One of the Hudson dropped its lifeboat at 16.00, and all five survivors were observed to have successfully climbed aboard at 16.25, by which time both Stirlings had turned for home. At 16.30 two Me110s joined the circuit and immediately began to attack the lifeboat. The Hudsons closed in for mutual protection while keeping a westerly course, but in the ensuing action F/S Neil and his crew were shot down and killed. F/L Fitchew made it back to base with severe damage and having fired between 600–700 rounds. It is thought that an engine of one of the Me110's was set on fire. The other missing 218 Squadron Stirling was EH986, which contained the crew of F/S Williams, and went down in the target area with just two escaping death to become PoWs. 115 Squadron's single missing aircraft was DS722, which had to be ditched off the Frisians four hours after take-off. Whether or not the entire crew survived the impact is unclear, but only the pilot, Sgt Townsend, and two others were found in the dinghy after a six day ordeal afloat, and they were taken into captivity.

The high Stirling loss rate continued at Nuremberg on the 27/28th, when 104 of them joined 570 Lancasters and Halifaxes for an attack that fell mainly outside the city limits after a major creep-back developed. Eleven of each type failed to return, and three of the Stirlings were from 620 Squadron. 218 Squadron's EF448 crashed in Germany, killing F/S Davis and four of his crew, while the two survivors joined their recently captured colleagues. The Stirling casualty rate represented a whopping 10.6%, and later in the year this unacceptable vulnerability would lead to the withdrawal of the type from operations over Germany. 115 Squadron's DS659 failed to survive an encounter with a nightfighter in the target area, and F/L Mott and his wireless operator died in the ensuing crash, while their five colleagues were taken prisoner. The Command was due a success, and the twin towns of Mönchengladbach and Rheydt obliged in a two-phase attack on the night of the 30/31st, for which 660 aircraft took off. Unlike the two-phase operations of 1944/45, which would allow a two or three hour gap between waves, this was a two minute pause, while the Pathfinders transferred the marking from the former to the latter. The main force crews exploited accurate marking in what was the first major raid on these targets, and over 2,300 buildings were destroyed for the loss of twenty-five aircraft. 218 Squadron posted missing two crews, those of F/S Clague in BK650, and Sgt Bennett in EF903. The former was shot down by a nightfighter over Holland on the way home, and it was later learned that the pilot and three others had been killed, while the navigator and a gunner were in enemy hands, and the bomb-aimer was on the run, ultimately to evade capture. There was no good news concerning the latter, however, which crashed in the target area with total loss of life. It was back to Berlin for over 600 aircraft on the last night of the month for a dismal failure caused by undershooting. Bombs fell up to thirty miles back along the line of approach, and forty-seven aircraft failed to return, seventeen of them Stirlings, a massive 16%. 75 (NZ) Squadron lost four aircraft, with another crashing on return, and 214 Squadron lost three. 623 Squadron lost its commanding officer, W/C Little, who was killed along with the other seven occupants of their Stirling after it was brought down by flak over Germany. Remarkably, 218 Squadron came through unscathed to post a monthly tally of 107 sorties for the loss of eight aircraft and seven complete crews.

A brand new squadron formed in 3 Group on the 1st of September on the station at Foulsham. 514 Squadron began life under the command of W/C Sampson DFC with a mixture of new and previously owned Mk II Lancasters. On the same day 623 Squadron welcomed W/C Wynne-Powell as its new commanding officer. He was a flamboyant twenty-eight year old Canadian known for the red silk lining of his tunic, and arrived from 199 Squadron. Like his predecessor he would not remain long with the squadron, but he would at least survive his tenure. Finally in this round of musical chairs W/C Elliott was appointed to command XV Squadron on the departure of W/C Stephens on the 3rd.

Berlin was left to the Lancaster squadrons on the night of the 3/4th of September and this was a modestly effective raid in which some of the bombing hit the Siemensstadt district, where a number of important war industry factories suffered a serious loss of production. 115 Squadron's only casualty was DS658, which was damaged beyond repair in a landing accident, although P/O Barnes and his crew were able to walk away. The twin cities of Mannheim and Ludwigshafen sit on opposite banks of the Rhine in southern Germany. Their relative positions provided an ideal opportunity to capitalize on the creep-back phenomenon, and build it into the plan of attack. The aiming point on the night of the 5/6th was in the eastern half of Mannheim, with an approach from the west, and the plan worked perfectly to inflict severe damage on both cities. Eight Stirlings were among the thirty-four missing bombers, 7% of those dispatched, and the alarm bells continued to ring at Bomber Command HQ. 149 Squadron was hardest-hit with three failures to return. The Stirlings were rested on the 6/7th, when Lancasters and Halifaxes raided Munich, but they were out in numbers two nights later to take part in Operation Starkey. This was an attempt to mislead the enemy into believing that an invasion was imminent, and had begun in mid August with highly visible troop movements, and the assembling of landing craft and gliders, which any self-respecting enemy reconnaissance crew could not fail to notice. Harris was not amused at being ordered to participate in what he considered to be play-acting, but in the event, bad weather prevented the planned Bomber Command involvement during the final week of the month. It was not until the night of the 8/9th of September that the opportunity arose to carry out his orders to bomb heavy gun emplacements at either end of the small resort town of Le Portel near Boulogne. Perhaps in a gesture of his attitude towards the whole Starkey affair, he committed only his two Oboe Mosquito squadrons and two heavy Pathfinder units, along with the Stirlings of 3 Group and Wellingtons from the training units. Phase I was aimed at the northern site, code-named Religion, and phase II at the southern site, Andante. Four 218 Squadron Stirlings took part in the attack on the Andante site, and all returned without mishap. Neither attack was successful, and Le Portel sustained heavy damage and civilian casualties. Training and flight testing could be almost as dangerous as operations, as 115 Squadron's F/S Bradford and his seven-man crew discovered when they took DS780 for an air-test and bombing practice on the 14th. The Lancaster crashed in Norfolk, killing the pilot and five others.

A bad six-night period for 138 Squadron began on the night of the 14/15th when SOE operations were mounted to Poland. Four Halifaxes failed to return, and two more went missing on the following night and yet two more on the 19/20th. In the meantime, on the 15th, a new unit, 513 Squadron, was formed at Witchford to operate Stirlings, but remarkably, no personnel or aircraft would be posted in for more than a month. That night an operation was scheduled against the Dunlop Rubber factory at Montlucon in central France, for which 369 aircraft of 3, 4, 6 and 8 Groups were detailed. 218 Squadron's P/O Adams took EF425 for an air-test in preparation for the operation, but it crashed on take-off and was written off, although without injury to the crew. W/C Deane of the Pathfinder's 35 Squadron acted as the Master Bomber for the night's operation, and he oversaw a successful outcome, which hit every building within the factory complex for the loss of just three aircraft. 218 Squadron sent out fourteen aircraft, and all returned safely having carried out their assigned tasks. On the following night the same Groups went to Modane in southern France to attack the main railway line to Italy, but the awkward location of the target in a steep valley thwarted the crews' best endeavours, and the operation failed. This time 218 Squadron dispatched fifteen crews, and for the second night running there were no early returns, and all got back safely after delivering 54,480 lb of bombs.

A series of four raids on Hanover over a four week period began on the 22/23rd, and involved over 700 aircraft, including 137 Stirlings. Stronger than forecast winds hampered the marking and bombing, and damage was believed to be modest, a poor return for the loss of twenty-six aircraft. Two 218 Squadron Stirlings were among the missing aircraft, and a third crashed in England after struggling home with severe flak damage. The flight engineer and both gunners had abandoned EJ105 over Germany, but one of the gunners failed to survive the descent, while his colleagues were taken prisoner. F/S Duffy managed to regain the Suffolk coast despite an engine fire, but the Stirling crashed soon afterwards, killing those left on board. EF139 was hit by bombs from above, an ever-present risk for the lower flying Stirlings, and crashed in the target area, killing Sgt Spencer and four of his crew. Finally,

BK700 also crashed in Germany, and there were no survivors from the crew of P/O Colquhoun. 115 Squadron's DS675 fell victim to a nightfighter in the general target area, and F/O O'Farrell died with five others, and two survivors were taken into captivity. Also in the wars literally was 90 Squadron, one of whose Stirling's developed an engine fire and was torn apart by an explosion at 500 feet some twenty-five minutes after take-off. A second aircraft from the squadron failed to return, and another was written off in a crash-landing on return. Mannheim hosted its second raid of the month again by more than 600 aircraft on the 23/24th, when over 900 houses and twenty industrial premises were destroyed, and an important I G Farben chemicals factory in the northern part of Ludwigshafen was seriously damaged. 218 Squadron's EJ104 was brought down over Germany, one of thirty-two failures to return, and only the wireless operator from the crew of F/O Brace was able to save himself. 678 aircraft departed their stations to return to Hanover on the 27/28th, and most of them wasted their bombs on open country north of the city, after wrongly forecast winds misled the Pathfinders. Some 9% of the 111 Stirlings failed to return, and 218 Squadron registered the loss of two more. Both BF472 and EE937 crashed in Germany, the former in the target area, and neither produced a survivor from among the crews of F/L Balding and P/O Knight respectively. Another testing month saw 218 Squadron launch ninety-four sorties, for the loss of seven aircraft and six crews.

October began in hectic fashion for the Lancaster squadrons, which were required to operate on six of the first eight nights. Hagen and Munich were their first two targets, on the 1/2nd and 2/3rd respectively, and it was on the following night that the Stirlings were called into action for the first time for activity other than mining. The target was Kassel, the first major raid on this city, where the main weight of the attack fell onto western suburbs and outlying communities, although the north-eastern district of Wolfshanger was also devastated. A total of 113 Stirlings took part, and six of these were among the twenty-four missing aircraft. 218 Squadron's EH984 was hit by flak over Germany, but the entire crew of F/S Riley managed to escape by parachute before the crash, and all were taken into captivity. At first light 115 Squadron despatched F/O Newcomb and his crew to carry out a search over the North Sea for crews reported to have ditched. DS721 did not return to Little Snoring, and no trace of it or its crew has ever been found. Seventy Stirlings were part of a 400 strong force targeting Frankfurt on the 4/5th, a city which had always escaped serious damage at the hands of the Command despite many attempts in the past. Its apparently charmed life ended on this night, when the eastern half and the inland docks were engulfed in flames, and many public and administrative buildings in the centre were damaged in exchange for the modest loss of ten aircraft. W/C Howard concluded his tour as commanding officer of 199 Squadron on the 6th, and was posted to Witchford as station commander. He was succeeded by W/C Bray, who arrived from 1657 CU. 101 Squadron operated its radio-countermeasures ABC Lancasters in numbers for the first time in a raid on Stuttgart on the 7/8th, and they might well have been responsible for the remarkably low loss of just four Lancasters. On the following night 500 aircraft were detailed for the third raid of the series on Hanover. Matters finally proceeded according to plan, and only the western districts escaped severe damage. Almost 4,000 buildings were completely destroyed, while 30,000 others sustained varying degrees of damage, and 1,200 people were killed. A diversionary raid on Bremen by ninety-five Stirlings failed to prevent twenty-seven aircraft being lost on the main operation, among them 115 Squadron's DS691, which was damaged by flak and finished off by a nightfighter somewhere fairly close to the target. F/O Cade and four of his crew escaped with their lives to become PoWs. 218 Squadron posted missing the crew of F/S Rogers, who all died when BK687 crashed in Germany. This aircraft had completed fifty-four operations, more than any other Stirling III.

A welcome lull in main force operations kept most of the Pathfinder and main force crews on the ground for the next nine nights, and even mining operations were suspended until the 17/18th. During this period 90 Squadron made its final wartime change of address on the 13th, when taking up residence at Tuddenham. The Hanover series was concluded by an all-Lancaster force on the 18/19th, and was another disappointment, which cost eighteen aircraft. Among them was 115 Squadron's DS769, in which Sgt Whitehead and his crew lost their lives. W/O Boutilier and his crew almost became another missing in action statistic, when DS683 was attacked and severely damaged by a nightfighter over the target. The rear gunner was killed in the engagement, and the flight engineer and wireless operator wounded, while the Lancaster sustained damage to two engines and control surfaces. Only the outstanding airmanship of the crew enabled them to return home, where the pilot and wireless operator received immediate awards of the DFC and DFM respectively. Only one of the Hanover operations had been a success, and perhaps this was sufficient compensation for the loss of 110 aircraft from a massive 2,253 sorties. The Lancaster crews suffered a bad time at the hands of the weather when attacking Leipzig on the 20/21st, and the city escaped serious damage. 115 Squadron's DS769 was one of sixteen missing aircraft, and contained the eight man crew of F/L Anderson, who all died on German soil. The second raid of the month on Kassel took place on the 22/23rd, without a contribution from the Stirling squadrons. It was an outstandingly successful operation, which reduced over 4,300 apartment blocks to ruins, and destroyed or seriously damaged over 150 industrial buildings and dozens of others of a public nature. A firestorm developed, and although it was not as extensive as that which had devastated parts of Hamburg three months earlier, it never the less played its part in the deaths of around 6,000 people.

The inactivity at 513 Squadron, which, it will be recalled, had been formed in mid September, had finally come to an end on the 21st of October with the arrival from 75 (NZ) Squadron of Stirlings EE958 and EF465. These were quickly followed on the 24th by a further five aircraft again transferred from 75 (NZ) Squadron at Mepal, and three more from 196 Squadron on the 25th. This was the day also that W/C G E Harrison was posted in from 149 Squadron to assume command. He was succeeded at 149 Squadron by W/C Wigfall. Crews started to arrive on the 26th, the first three, those of F/O Clarke, F/O Sanders and New Zealander F/Sgt P Keogh via 1651 and 1657 Conversion Units. By the 7th of November the squadron strength would stand at sixteen Stirlings plus four in reserve. On the 14th of November one of 75 (NZ) Squadron's most experienced captains, 23-year-old S/L Jack Joll DFC, DFM, would be posted in to assume command of 'A' Flight. Jack Joll was on his second tour with 75 (NZ) Squadron, his first on Wellingtons resulting in the award of the DFM in 1941 in recognition of an attack on Essen and Duisburg, where his flair for new methods of evasive tactics proved especially successful. The citation for the award of his DFC in October 1943, again with 75 (NZ) Squadron, described him as an exceptional captain and flight commander. Within twenty-four hours of S/L Joll's arrival instructions would be received from 3 Group HQ to disband the squadron with effect from the 21st of November. Crews would continued to arrive, however, only to be posted immediately to other Stirling units within 3 and 38 Groups. W/C Harrison would depart for 1665 CU on November 25th to be joined there by S/L Joll on the 28th. All remaining personnel would proceed to 1663 CU.

The final entry in the Squadron ORB records ... 'It has been said that No. 513 squadron by reason of the 13 in the number was fated never to take its place amongst the operational units of Bomber command. Unlucky it certainly was, because the officers (particular the section leaders) airman and women were very keen to make 513 one of the leading squadrons within the group. The majority of the personnel came from the famous 3 Group squadron No. 75 (NZ) Squadron, and although they were loathe to leave that unit, they soon settled down and gave their best. By the middle of November training was fully organised and specialist officers gave lectures in all manner of subjects. Day flying was carried out when weather was favourable and progress was being made rapidly. Everyone was looking forward to the day when the first 513 aircraft would take off for operations, and a bitter disappointment was felt when the news was received that 513 was to be disbanded. Immediately interests waned and overnight the squadron became merely a collection of individuals awaiting disposal.'

November began as October had ended, with the Stirling squadrons sitting out the few bombing operations mounted. November would bring a resumption of the Berlin offensive, but the first operation took a large force to Düsseldorf on the 3/4th. While 500 aircraft were delivering a destructive blow against this Ruhr city, thirty-eight Mk II Lancaster crews were briefed to attack the Mannesmann tubular steel works on its northern outskirts employing the G-H blind bombing device. This was the first large-scale live trial of G-H, for which 115 Squadron provided eleven aircraft, and 3 Group's newest addition, 514 Squadron, the only other squadron in the Group to be equipped with Mk II Lancasters, made its operational debut with two aircraft. The remaining twenty-five Mk IIs were from 6 Group, but equipment failure reduced the numbers bombing on G-H to fifteen, although these left a number of assembly halls burnt out. The Stirlings were absent from this successful raid, but a few of them went mining around the Frisians without loss. On the following night three 75 (NZ) Squadron Stirlings failed to return from another mining effort. Bound for French coastal waters shortly after midnight on the 8th, 115 Squadron's DS825 came to grief when an engine failed on take-off. The Lancaster careered off the runway, but F/L Mackie and his crew climbed out without any injuries to report. Lancasters alone rectified the September failure at the Modane railway yards in southern France on the 10/11th, but a Halifax main force failed in an attempt to bomb a similar target at nearby Cannes on the following night, and hit the town instead. This was the last major activity, as Harris cleared the decks for the resumption of the Berlin offensive.

196 Squadron departed 3 Group and Bomber Command on the 18th for airborne support duties with 38 Group. The long and rocky road to Berlin was rejoined by an all-Lancaster force on the night of the 18/19th, thirteen of which were from 115 Squadron. They became airborne without mishap either side of 18.00 hours and set course, while a predominantly Halifax and Stirling force made their way towards southern Germany for a diversionary raid against Mannheim and Ludwigshafen. The main raid was scattered and only moderately effective, but the loss of just nine aircraft may have been due to the diversion. 115 Squadron would come through completely unscathed from only two of the sixteen Berlin raids during this main phase of the battle, and suffered its first casualty on this night. DS680 was shot down by a nightfighter over Belgium, and there were no survivors from the eight man crew of P/O Peate. The diversionary operation was a more productive affair, which destroyed over 300 buildings, including four of an industrial nature, and others sustained damage for the loss of twenty-three aircraft. 218 Squadron's EE884 crashed in Germany, killing P/O Hine and all but one of his crew. It was the Lancasters' turn to sit out the night at home as elements of 3, 4, 6 and 8 Groups went to Leverkusen on the 19/20th, the home of an important I G Farben chemicals factory. It turned out to be a night to forget after many of the Oboe aircraft suffered equipment failure, and only one high explosive bomb landed in the town.

A maximum effort was demanded on the 22/23rd, and 764 aircraft answered the call to raid Berlin. It developed into the most devastating attack of the war on the capital, with 3,000 houses and twenty-three industrial premises reduced to rubble, while a number of firestorms erupted, 2,000 people were killed and a further 175,000 were rendered homeless. Twenty-six aircraft were lost, including five of the fifty Stirlings, and 218 Squadron posted missing one of its flight commanders, S/L Prior DFC, who died with his crew when EF180 crashed in the target area. S/L Prior was well into his second tour, and had completed thirty-nine operations at the time of his death. 115 Squadron posted missing two crews from this operation, that of Sgt Harris in DS782 without trace, while six of Sgt Smith's crew parachuted into captivity from DS764, and the pilot alone lost his life. The 10% loss rate among the Stirling brigade proved to be the final straw for Harris. From this point on the type would be withdrawn from operations over Germany, and assigned to other important if secondary duties. This effectively removed 3 Group from the front line, and left only its Lancaster Mk II equipped 115 and 514 Squadrons to represent it over Germany until XV and 622 Squadrons completed their conversion to the Lancaster I and III in December. This can not have been a happy state of affairs for a Group used to being in the vanguard of operations since the very start of hostilities. From now on Stirlings were to play an even greater role in mining operations, and, in fact, had already been responsible for around 50% of such sorties during 1943. A new role also beckoned at this time, as support increased for the resistance organisations in the occupied countries. The restrictions placed on Stirling operations applied only to Germany, and this still left the way clear for bombing operations over France, where a new menace was being prepared for use against Britain. V-1 launching sites were being set up, and these would become targets for 3 Group's Stirling contingent during December and January.

The 23rd of November brought the formation of a new Group to Bomber Command. 100 Group was created to support the heavy bomber fleet and reduce the increasingly prohibitive losses being inflicted nightly by German nightfighters employing the 'Tame Boar' running commentary system. This had been born out of the success of Window, which, at a stroke, had rendered ineffective the previous 'Himmelbett' nightfighter control system based on defined boxes. Radio Countermeasures (RCM) was one of the answers to the nightfighter scourge, and involved powerful jamming devices carried by heavy bombers dispersed throughout the bomber stream to interfere with enemy fighter communications. 1 Group's 101 Squadron, it will be recalled, had been operating in this role since October, and would continue to do so independently of 100 Group. 100 Group would also employ squadrons of Mosquitos to hunt down the Luftwaffe nightfighters with the aid of the Serrate radar device. 3 Group surrendered Foulsham to the new Group, which meant that 514 Squadron had to move out and take up residence at Waterbeach, where it would remain until after the war. 3 Group also bade farewell to two of its squadrons on this day. 192 Squadron was posted to 100 Group as a founder member and moved from Feltwell to Foulsham, and 620 Squadron was posted to 38 Group for airborne support duties and moved to Stoughton airfield near Leicester.

The Lancasters and Halifaxes would press on with the Berlin campaign, and it was an all-Lancaster main force that delivered a highly destructive follow-up on the 23/24th. Guided by the glow of fires still burning and visible through the cloud cover, the attack laid waste to a further 2,000 houses and eight industrial premises, and killed around 1,500 people. A predominately Halifax force from 4 and 6 Groups achieved only moderate results at Frankfurt on the 25/26th, before over 400 Lancasters returned to the 'Big City' on the 26/27th, and more by luck than judgement, destroyed thirty-eight war industry factories in a north-western suburb. 115 Squadron's DS793 was brought down over Germany, and there were no survivors from the crew of F/O Woolhouse. The squadron had mounted this operation from its new home at Witchford, having completed the move from Little Snoring earlier in the day, an upheaval, which of course, was not allowed to interfere with operational requirements. W/C Wynne-Powell relinquished command of 623 Squadron on the 29th, and was succeeded by W/C Milligan AFC. Born in 1915 W/C Milligan was a former personal assistant to the AOC Middle East in 1938. He had been awarded his AFC in June 1942 in recognition of his time as commanding officer of No. 32 Service Flying Training School, Moose Jaw, Saskatchewan, Canada. 218 Squadron flew a modest forty-four sorties during the month for the loss of two aircraft and crews, and December would make even fewer demands.

Mining became the staple diet for the Stirling squadrons during December, while the Lancasters, in particular, and the Halifaxes kept up the pressure on Berlin. A tragic event involving a 75 (NZ) Squadron Stirling occurred on the night of the 1/2nd, when EH880 crashed into a farmhouse while trying to land at Acklington in Northumberland on return from a mining sortie in Danish waters. W/O Kerr and five of his crew died in the wreckage of the aircraft, and five children were killed in the farmhouse. Berlin was the destination for over 400 Lancasters in company with some Pathfinder Halifaxes and Mosquitos on the 2/3rd, and forty aircraft failed to return, all but three of them Lancasters. The raid was scattered across southern districts from west to east, and some useful damage was inflicted, but many bomb loads were wasted. Exploiting the enemy expectation that Berlin would be the target again, over 500 aircraft flew directly towards it twenty-four hours later, before turning off for Leipzig. Halifaxes shared the load in this highly successful raid, which resulted in the deaths of over 1,100 people. Twenty-four aircraft were shot down, many on the homeward journey, and 115 Squadron's DS765 was missing from its Witchford dispersal. It was later learned that the Lancaster had crashed in Germany, killing F/S Clark and his crew, who had recently been posted in from 620 Squadron. W/C Giles departed 90 Squadron on the 6th to attend No. 11 course RAF Staff College, and W/C Wynne-Powell was posted in from 623 Squadron as his successor. His time with 90 Squadron would be brief, lasting only into the first week of January. 623 Squadron ceased to exist from this day as a result of the previously mentioned expansion of conversion units. Its crews were dispersed to other units, principally 90, 218 and 514 Squadrons, while W/C Milligan went to 31 Base until something else came up. During an eleven night rest period for 214 Squadron a move was completed from Chedburgh to Downham Market on the 10th.

Minor operations then held sway until the night of the 16/17th, when an all-Lancaster heavy force of almost 500 aircraft became airborne between 16.00 and 17.00 hours and headed for Germany's capital. 115 Squadron's contribution was fourteen aircraft, one of which returned early, while the remainder pressed on to contribute to a moderately successful attack. The main weight of bombs fell into central and eastern districts, where housing was the principal victim. Twenty-five aircraft were shot down, many of them accounted for by nightfighters over Holland and Germany while outbound, and this was the fate of 115 Squadron's DS835, which went down over the former, killing P/O Newton and his entire crew. The greatest difficulties, however, were encountered by 1, 6 and 8 Group crews as they arrived home to find their airfields covered by a blanket of dense fog. With little reserves of fuel available for diversions, the tired crews began a frantic search to find somewhere to land, stumbling blindly through the murk to catch a glimpse of the ground. For many this proved fatal, while other crews gave up any hope of landing, and took to their parachutes. Twenty-nine Lancasters either crashed or were abandoned by their crews during what became known as 'Black Thursday', and around 150 airmen lost their lives in these most tragic of circumstances. Also on this night twenty-six Stirlings, including four from 218 Squadron, joined in the first of a series of attacks on flying bomb sites at Tilley-le-Haut near Abbeville. The attack failed, despite being marked by Oboe Mosquitos, and this highlighted the limitations of Oboe as an aid to precision bombing. Although ideal for urban areas, where a margin of error of a few hundred yards was immaterial, a small target required pinpoint accuracy. A simultaneous attack on a site at Flixecourt by 617 Squadron under W/C Cheshire had also failed for the same reason, but the difference here was that 617 Squadron and Cheshire had the influence to do something about it. The frustrations born out of this and a later failure would lead to 617 Squadron developing its own low-level visual marking technique using Mosquitos, and this would ultimately result in 5 Group becoming an independent force from April 1944. While these operations were in progress other Stirlings carried out mining sorties around the Frisians and in French coastal waters. 218 Squadron's EE888 failed to return, and was lost without trace somewhere in the Bay of Biscay with the crew of F/S Williams. MZ263 arrived back over Cornwall short of fuel in the kind of bad weather conditions that had caused so much distress to the crews of 1, 6 and 8 Groups. F/O Locke managed to pull off a crash-landing at St Eval, and he and his crew all sustained injuries.

There were also SOE operations on this night, and the conditions played their part in the outcomes. 138 Squadron lost one aircraft in the sea off Harwich while outbound for France, a second was abandoned on return and a third crashed while attempting to land. Two 161 Squadron Lysanders also crashed on return, while three Halifaxes were lost in similar circumstances, either abandoned or crashing.

Most of 3 Group could only stand by as over 600 aircraft attacked Frankfurt with moderate success on the 20/21st for the loss of forty-one of their number. W/C Rainsford DFC was officially posted from 115 Squadron to 33 Base on the 21st. He had already departed the squadron, however, having been admitted to Ely hospital with tonsillitis. W/C Annan was promoted from flight commander to succeed him. A small Stirling contingent and 617 Squadron returned to the flying bomb sites on the 22/23rd, 218 Squadron providing one aircraft for the Abbeville site and six for one in the Cherbourg area. This was the final occasion on which XV Squadron went to war in Stirlings, and on the 28th it took delivery of its first Lancasters in preparation for a new era. There is no question that it had been a very tough year for XV Squadron, always at the forefront of operations, and suffering the high casualty rate to which all the Stirling units had grown accustomed. It had been spared from all but one of the Berlin operations before the turn of the year, but once the crews had completed their conversion programme, the capital would become for them a major focus. The 'Big City' was the objective for a predominantly Lancaster main force on the 23/24th, when cloud cover led to scattered marking, and only the south-eastern suburbs suffered significant damage. 115 Squadron's DS773 was one of sixteen failures to return, and P/O Pirie and his crew lost their lives. The fifth wartime Christmas came and went in relative peace, and a couple of days afterwards 622 Squadron welcomed its first Lancaster, W4163, which was something of a veteran, and an aircraft which would not enjoy a long career with its new owner. The year 1943 ended with another tilt at Berlin on the 29/30th, which would turn out to be the first of three raids against the capital in the space of five nights spanning the turn of the year. More than 700 Lancasters and Halifaxes took off, and those reaching the target produced only modest damage in the face of cloud cover and skymarking. 115 Squadron's DS834 was dispatched by a nightfighter over Holland on the way home, killing four of the crew, but the pilot, F/S Lee, and his navigator survived as PoWs, while the flight engineer retained his freedom.

218 was the least employed of the Stirling units during the month, and launched only twenty-five sorties for the loss of two aircraft and one crew. It had been a year of steady and persistent losses for 218 Squadron, with a few bad nights, but unlike many other units, there had been no catastrophes, and the coming year would bring a drastic reduction in missing aircraft and crews. It had been a rewarding year for the Command, despite the heavy losses, but it had also signalled the decline of the Stirling, which was a first generation four-engine bomber, and was unsuitable for development. Its time in Bomber Command was not yet over, however, and it would remain in 3 Group hands, albeit in reducing numbers, for the bulk of the coming year.

1944

The winter campaign; the Phoenix rises; interdiction; invasion; parallel campaigns; Hurricane

The New Year promised nothing other than more of the same for both the hard-pressed crews of Bomber Command and the beleaguered residents of Germany's capital city. Proud of their status as Berliners first and Germans second they were a hardy breed of people, and equally as capable as their counterparts in London during the Blitz of 1940 of withstanding any amount of bombing. They bore their trials just as resolutely and cheerfully, they developed their own black humour, and carried banners through the streets which proclaimed 'you may break our walls, but not our hearts.' They also sang along with the most popular song of the day, *Nach jedem Dezember kommt immer ein Mai* (after every December there's always a May), a sentiment which hinted at a change of fortunes with the onset of spring. To some extent this would come true for the Berliners at the conclusion of Bomber Command's winter campaign at the end of March, from which point RAF heavy bombers would pay the capital no further attention. In the meantime, though, both they and the bomber crews were praying that Berlin would cease to be the main object of Harris's attention. It was not to be, and before New Year's day was done over 400 Lancasters were winging their way across Holland on an almost direct route to the capital. Complete cloud cover and the use of skymarking caused most of the bombs to fall beyond the city boundaries into wooded and open country, and the loss of twenty-eight aircraft was a poor return for the destruction of around twenty buildings. The 115 Squadron casualty was, fortunately, only a Lancaster, DS769, which F/S Chantler force-landed in Cambridgeshire on return, before he and his crew walked away uninjured. On the following night 383 aircraft, most of them Lancasters, took off for the capital, arriving overhead in the early hours of the 3rd after two distinct changes of course to throw off the nightfighter controller. Most of the engagements took place in the target area, and twenty-seven Lancasters failed to return from another hugely disappointing raid. 115 Squadron's DS667 was one of those to go down in the Berlin defence zone, and although all of the crew survived to be taken prisoner, the pilot, F/S Hayes, succumbed to his severe injuries three weeks later.

It must have been strange for the Stirling crews to be somewhat sidelined from the main offensive, although the obvious benefit was a reduction in the formerly prohibitive rate of attrition. Mining operations would involve the Group on ten nights during January and keep elements of the Stirling contingent active. The last of 622 Squadron's Stirlings was flown off on New Year's Day, and the crews got on with the business of working up to operational status on the Lancaster. W/C Wynne-Powell was posted from 90 Squadron to 31 Base on the 6th, from whence came his successor, W/C Milligan on the 9th, the second time the latter had stepped into the former's shoes. W/C Wynne-Powell would return to operations with 620 Squadron in 38 Group in October. Fifty-seven Stirlings continued the war against flying bomb sites on the 4/5th, twelve of them from 218 Squadron, whose target was at Hazebrouck. 617 Squadron was assigned to a similar target elsewhere, and both sites were plastered without loss. It was also on this night that Bomber Command made mention for the first time of flights on behalf of the Special Operations Executive (SOE). The delivery and collection of agents from French fields, and the dropping of arms and supplies to resistance organisations had, as previously mentioned, been in progress for two years under a cloak of secrecy. The secrecy would remain in place, but such was the demand for these flights, that 3 Group detached elements of its Stirling squadrons to Tempsford on a rota basis.

After a bruising start to the year's operations the heavy brigade redressed the balance to some extent with a very destructive assault on Stettin on the Baltic coast on the 5/6th. 218 Squadron put up eight aircraft for a flying bomb related target in the Pas-de-Calais on the 10/11th. The first major attack of the war on Brunswick by an all-Lancaster force of almost 500 aircraft cost 115 Squadron two eight man crews on the 14/15th. DS720 and LL673 crashed on German soil without survivors from the crews of P/O Blackwell and F/L Christiansen respectively. Thirty-six other aircraft failed to return on this bad night for the Command, without even the compensation of a successful attack. The Pathfinders in particular were suffering unsustainable casualties, and 156 Squadron alone had lost fourteen aircraft in the four major operations since the start of the year. While the Brunswick raid was in progress fifty-nine Stirlings contributed to further attacks on V-weapon sites, 218 Squadron sending nine crews to a site at Cherbourg, and a further ten to the same area on the 20/21st. The main operation on this night was by over 700 Lancasters and Halifaxes, which answered the call for the first maximum effort of the year and took off in the late afternoon for Berlin. They headed for a point on the German coast opposite Kiel, where the nightfighters were again able to infiltrate the bomber stream early on and inflict heavy casualties throughout the approach and much of the withdrawal stages. Complete cloud cover prevented an assessment of the results, and it was some time later before it was established that the hitherto less severely damaged eastern districts had been hardest hit. The Command paid the heavy price of thirty-five aircraft, one of which was 115 Squadron's LL650, shot down by a nightfighter near the target. P/O Canning and all but one of his crew lost their lives, the rear gunner alone surviving in enemy hands.

Eighty-nine Stirlings were sent to five flying bomb related targets on the 21/22nd, 218 Squadron dispatching ten to Hazebrouck and two to Cherbourg, while 617 Squadron attended to a sixth, and again there were no losses. This was the night of the ill-fated Magdeburg raid, of which the crews themselves unwittingly gave notice to the enemy, as they always did during the preparations for a major operation. German radar was able to detect H2s transmissions during night flying tests and equipment checks, and the nightfighter controller was thereby always aware of an imminent heavy raid. On this night the nightfighters were able to infiltrate the bomber stream even before the German coast was crossed, and the two forces remained in contact all the way to the target. Some aircraft were driven to the target early by stronger than forecast winds, and bombed ahead of the Pathfinders. The resultant fires and some decoy markers attracted other crews, and the Path-finders were unable to centralize the attack. In return for a disappointing effort, a new record of fifty-seven aircraft failed to return, the bulk of them falling victim to nightfighters. In the absence of Stirlings the Halifax con-tingent suffered particularly heavy casualties amounting to thirty-five aircraft or almost 16%, while 115 Squadron registered the loss of one aircraft. The squadron had expanded at the end of 1943 to become a three flight unit, and it was a C Flight Lancaster, DS777, which was missing from its dispersal. It had been shot down by a nightfighter in the target area, killing F/S Moncrieff and three of his crew. Twenty-two other Lancasters also failed to return, and among them were four from 3 Group's 514 Squadron.

214 Squadron's long association with 3 Group was now about to end. On the 16th of January the squadron concluded its short stay at Downham Market and took up residence at Sculthorpe. Just two more operations would be flown from here on behalf of 3 Group, four aircraft for the flying bomb operation mentioned above on the 21/22nd, and a single mining sortie on the 23/24th. 214 Squadron's future now lay with 100 Group in a bomber support role jamming enemy communications, and it was stood down to convert to the B17 Fortress. Flying bomb sites remained the fare for 3 Group's Stirling brigade on the 25/26th, for which 218 Squadron put up seven aircraft for a target at Cherbourg. The main force stayed at home on this night, and prepared for a major push on Berlin a few days hence. It would require of the Lancaster crews three trips to the 'Big City' in the space of an unprecedented four nights from the 27/28th, while the Stirling fraternity carried out diversionary mining operations. An all Lancaster heavy force of over 500 aircraft took off in the early evening of the 27th, the 115 Squadron contingent becoming airborne without mishap either side of 18.00 hours. A complex route took the bomber stream towards the north German coast, before it swung to the south-east over the Frisians and northern Holland. Having feinted towards central Germany, the force turned north-east to a point west of Berlin, from where the final run-in commenced. Dummy fighter flares and route markers were partially successful in reducing the numbers of enemy nightfighters making contact, but thirty-three Lancasters were lost in return for a scattered but moderately effective raid, which afflicted many outlying communities. 115 Squadron's LL668 crashed in Germany, while LL682 went into the North Sea on the way home, and neither produced a survivor from among the crews of F/O Ryder and F/S Morris respectively.

Halifaxes joined the Lancasters on the following night to make up a force of over 670 aircraft, which approached the capital this time from the north-west having overflown southern Denmark. Western and southern districts of the city sustained the greatest damage, but more than seventy hamlets beyond its boundaries also reported bombs. Nightfighters were very active over the target, and many of the missing forty-six aircraft fell victim here. 115 Squadron again posted missing two crews, those of P/O Tinn, who went down over Germany in LL649 with only the bomb-aimer surviving to tell the tale, and F/L Harris in DS833, the fate of which has never been established. In return for these grievous losses sufficient damage was inflicted to destroy the houses of 180,000 people. The final operation of this concerted effort against Berlin was mounted on the 30/31st by a predominantly Lancaster heavy force of over 500 aircraft. Following a route similar to that adopted two nights earlier, the bomber stream remained relatively free of harass-ment until approaching the target, where central and south-western districts suffered heavy damage and serious fires erupted. Many bomb loads were again scattered liberally around other parts of the city, or were wasted on outlying communities, and at least 1,000 people were killed in Berlin. Thirty-three bombers failed to return, among them 115 Squadron's LL648, which crashed in Germany with no survivors from the crew of F/L Hicks.

On the 1st of February W/C Gibson DFC concluded his tour as com-manding officer of 622 Squadron, and was posted to 1665 HCU. He was replaced by W/C Swales, otherwise known as 'Blondie', another highly experienced officer, whose operational career had begun as a sergeant pilot at 38 Squadron in 1940. His award of the DFM was gazetted in October of that year, and in mid 1941 he joined XV Squadron to undertake a second tour, still in the rank of sergeant. He was eventually commissioned, and was awarded the DFC in March 1942, before being promoted to acting Flight Lieutenant in April. A week or so later he was posted to XV Squadron's Conversion Flight for instructional duties, and spent most of the next twenty-two months officially away from the operational scene. However, like many instructors, he was able to take part in the first 1,000 bomber raid on Cologne at the end of May 1942.

In December 214 Squadron had detached crews to Tempsford to assist in the dropping of supplies to the armed resistance groups in France. In January it was the turn of 75 (NZ) Squadron, and now in February it fell to 149 Squadron. While the crews remaining at Lakenheath had little to do during the month, launching a modest eighteen mining sorties, forty-four special duties flights were carried out by the squadron's crews at Tempsford. It was dangerous work, calling for low flying in difficult winter conditions, and many deliveries failed to take place through an inability to identify the dropping zone. The squadron suffered its first casualty from this line of work on the 5/6th, when EF187 crashed in France without survivors. Earlier in the evening of the 5th F/S Bishop had taken his 115 Squadron DS827 for bombing practice with seven other occupants, and all were killed when the Lancaster crashed in Essex.

The main force had no doubt benefited from being kept on the ground by the weather for the first two weeks of the month. It was clear from the rate of early returns during the previous month's series against Berlin that nerves were frayed and morale was beginning to crack. Crews embarking on their first tour during the winter campaign can have seen little prospect of surviving. It was on the night of 15/16th that the Command 'got back on the horse' in numbers to return to the fray with a record-breaking operation to Berlin. The 891 aircraft taking part represented the largest non-1,000 force to date, and it was the first time that 500 Lancasters and 300 Halifaxes had operated together. A massive seventy-five early returns reduced the force, but those reaching the target delivered a record 2,600 tons of bombs into Berlin and its surrounds, and inflicted extensive damage for the loss of forty-three aircraft. Two of the Lancasters were from 115 Squadron, LL651, which crashed in Germany, killing F/S Whyte and all but one of his crew, and LL689, which had almost run the gauntlet of the defences on the way home, and was over the Ijsselmeer when it was intercepted by the already mentioned Oblt Schnaufer, one of the *Luftwaffe*'s foremost nightfighter pilots. The Lancaster went down into the water, breaking up on the way, and throwing the navigator and bomb-aimer into space, where they were able to deploy their parachutes. F/S Ralph and the remainder of the crew perished, but the two survivors were rescued from the water and taken prisoner. Although the crews of Bomber Command couldn't know, they had just taken part in the penultimate raid of the war by RAF heavy bombers on Berlin, and it would be more than five weeks before they carried out the final one.

After another three nights on the ground 823 aircraft took off for Leipzig, and headed into the greatest disaster yet to befall the Command. Enemy night-fighters were waiting at the Dutch coast, and a running battle ensued all the way into eastern Germany. Inaccurately forecast winds caused some aircraft to arrive at the target early, and they were forced to orbit while they waited for the target indicators to go down. The local flak batteries accounted for around twenty of these, while four other aircraft were lost through collisions. The operation was inconclusive in the face of complete cloud cover and sky-marking, but what was not in question was the enormity of the Command's losses. When all the returning aircraft had been accounted for, there was a massive shortfall of seventy-eight, the heaviest loss of the war by a clear twenty-one aircraft. 514 Squadron sustained the highest casualties in 3 Group with three Lancasters failing to return. The Halifaxes suffered a loss rate of 13.3%, and like the Stirlings before them, the less efficient Mark II and V variants were immediately withdrawn from operations over Germany. The Stirlings had conducted a diversionary mining operation on this night, but this was obviously in vain, and did not fool the nightfighter controllers.

The main force enjoyed a better time at Stuttgart on the 20/21st, inflicting extensive damage for the loss of just nine aircraft. 115 Squadron had avoided the carnage at Leipzig, and all of its aircraft returned to home airspace on this night also, but sadly, LL729 crashed near Bedford, and there was total loss of life among the crew of F/S Wood. A new tactic was introduced for the next two operations in an attempt to reduce the prohibitive losses.

The force of 734 aircraft bound for Schweinfurt on the evening of the 24th was split into two waves, the first of 392 and the second of 342. They were separated by two hours, in the hope of catching the nightfighters on the ground refuelling and rearming as the second wave passed through. 115 Squadron contributed aircraft to each phase of the operation, which suffered from undershooting by much of the main force, after some Pathfinder backers-up failed to press on to the aiming point. In that regard it was a disappointing night, but an interesting feature was the loss of 50% fewer aircraft from the second wave in comparison with the first, in an overall casualty figure of thirty-three. 115 Squadron's LL701 took the early shift, and was lost without trace with the crew of F/L Hornby, while LL644 crashed in Germany during the second phase, without survivors from the crew of F/O Nice. On the following night, almost 600 aircraft were involved in a similar two-phase assault on the beautiful south-German city of Augsburg. It was one of those relatively rare occasions, when all facets of the operational plan came together in near perfect harmony, and it spelled disaster for this lightly defended treasure trove of culture. The heart of the city was torn out by blast and fire, and almost 3,000 houses were destroyed, along with buildings of outstanding historical significance. Twenty-one aircraft failed to return, but 115 Squadron came through unscathed.

Apart from 149 Squadron's detachment at Tempsford, the Stirling squadrons' efforts during the month were devoted entirely to mining. On each of the nights when main force operations were laid on, the Stirlings were out in numbers to provide a diversion. When Berlin was attacked, and on the night of the Leipzig debacle, they were mining in Kiel Bay, for Stuttgart they operated in French coastal waters, and then it was back to Kiel Bay and the Kattegat during the Schweinfurt and Augsburg raids. Mining also took place on nights when the main force stayed at home, and 218 Squadron registered its first loss of the year during one of these. EJ125 crashed into the sea after being hit by flak while sowing its vegetables near Borkum, and F/L Wiseman and his crew lost their lives. The squadron despatched a total of fifty-nine mining sorties during the month, and then on the 28th detached twelve aircraft to Tempsford under the A Flight commander, S/L Overton, to begin its stint on behalf of SOE.

The main force went back to Stuttgart on the night of the 1/2nd of March, and despite cloud cover, inflicted widespread damage on central, western and northern districts for the remarkably low loss of just four aircraft. Thereafter, the main force remained at home until mid month, while minor operations took place. During the lull SOE operations continued from Tempsford, and the night of the 3/4th cost 138, 161 and 199 Squadrons one aircraft each. Seventy-six aircraft were involved in SOE sorties on the 4/5th, and on return from one of them 218 Squadron's EE944 lost its port outer engine during final approach to Tempsford. The pilot tried to overshoot, but was unable to prevent the port wing from dropping, and the Stirling side-slipped into the ground. P/O Edwards and four of his crew died in the wreckage, while the two gunners sustained injuries. Some good news for 3 Group on the 6th was the arrival at Mepal of 75 (NZ) Squadron's first Lancaster, and by the end of the month nineteen of them would be on charge. Working up on the type was conducted at No. 3 Lancaster Finishing School at Feltwell, while Stirling operations continued from Mepal.

It was during this period of minor operations that the first salvoes were fired in the pre-invasion campaign. This was in support of the Transportation Plan, the systematic dismantling by bombing of the French and Belgian railway networks, to inhibit the movement of enemy forces before and after D-Day. Initially, it was the Halifax squadrons that provided the bulk of the aircraft for attacks on railway yards at Trappes on the 6/7th and Le Mans on the following night, while the Stirlings continued with mining and SOE sorties. 218 Squadron had completed its move from Downham Market to Woolfox Lodge on the 7th, and on the 9th W/C Oldbury concluded his tour as commanding officer, and was posted to Bomber Command HQ to attend a course at the Army Staff College. He was replaced by the experienced W/C Fenwick-Wilson, who had previously commanded 405 Squadron RCAF between August 1941 and February 1942. Fenwick-Wilson was another Canadian, and he had been in temporary command of Downham Market when appointed to 218 Squadron.

It was around the 13th when W/C Alan Boxer, a New Zealander, was posted back to 161 Squadron at Tempsford for another tour, this time as commanding officer. He succeeded W/C Bob Hodges, who was posted to RAF Staff College, and later became commanding officer of 357 special duties Squadron in India. Boxer had been a Flight Lieutenant during his first tour with 161 Squadron beginning in April 1942, and, as an experienced Whitley pilot, had been assigned to parachute drops on the departure to Fighter Command HQ of S/L Nesbitt-Dufort. Since the completion of that tour he had been at A12(c), a branch of the Air Ministry Intelligence service, where he had taken over from the previously mentioned Guy Lockhart. Tempsford had been temporarily posted from Bomber Command to 38 Group, which was expanding to provide air transport support for airborne forces during the invasion period. (For the purposes of this book 138 and 161 Squadrons will be treated as still part of Bomber Command.)

Le Mans was raided again by Halifaxes on the 13/14th, but thirty-eight Stirlings joined in to bomb railway yards at Amiens on the 15/16th, the night on which over 800 aircraft of the Pathfinders and main force returned to Stuttgart for the third time in three weeks. The nightfighters made contact as the bomber stream was approaching the target, and began to score heavily. Some of the early bombing was accurate, but thereafter the bulk of it under-shot and fell into open country. In return for this disappointing outcome thirty-seven aircraft failed to return, and after two loss-free operations, 115 Squadron was forced to post missing the crew of P/O Rodger. He was killed with four of his crew, when LL693 was shot down over Germany, and only the wireless operator and rear gunner survived as PoWs. On the 16th the 218

Squadron detachment concluded it period of duty at Tempsford, having flown forty-four sorties. Halifaxes and Stirlings returned to Amiens that night, and delivered a successful attack without loss. Two utterly devastating operations against Frankfurt were delivered by forces numbering over 800 aircraft on the 18/19th and 22/23rd, the former alone leaving over 6,000 buildings destroyed or seriously damaged. The latter was even more destructive, and condemned half of the city to life without electricity, gas and water for an extended period. Each of these operations cost 115 Squadron aircraft and aircrew lives, although only one instance was a failure to return. The missing Lancaster was LL640, which crashed in Germany during the first raid, killing P/O Frampton and all but his flight engineer, who was captured. DS629 almost became a similar statistic following a brush with a nightfighter, during which the rear gunner was wounded. F/S Williams brought the aircraft home to a landing at Coltishall, however, where it was declared to be beyond economical repair. DS766 was severely damaged by the Frankfurt flak on the latter occasion, and crashed on approach to the emergency landing strip at Woodbridge, killing F/S Pope and three of his crew, while another succumbed to his injuries three days later. An attempt by elements of 3, 4, 6 and 8 Groups to destroy the railway yards at Laon on the 23/24th was halted by the Master Bomber half way through, when civilian housing was hit.

The stage was now set for the nineteenth and final operation of the campaign against Berlin, which had begun back in August. It was more than five weeks since the main force had last visited the capital, and on this night, the 24/25th, over 800 aircraft took off, timed to open the attack shortly before 22.30 hours. 115 Squadron put up eighteen Mk II Lancasters, led by the highly experienced S/L Mackie DSO, who was, in fact, a bomb-aimer, but because of his standing held the status of crew captain. He was in LL622, while the other aircraft and crews were; LL726 F/L Seddon, LL704 P/O Anderson, LL652 P/O Gibson, DS620 P/O Hammond, DS678 P/O McCann, LL695 P/O McKechnie, LL641 P/O Milgate, LL667 P/O Moon, LL694 P/O Vipond, DS682 W/O Hammond, DS781 W/O Treasure, LL624 F/S Cameron, LL666 F/S Campbell, LL646 F/S Chantler, DS664 F/S Newman, DS728 F/S Taylor and LL730 F/S Williams. The squadron was airborne between 18.30 and 19.00 hours, and set course for southern Denmark and the Baltic, before turning towards the target. An unexpected difficulty was the unprecedented strength of the winds at cruising altitude, which scattered the bomber stream, and drove the aircraft constantly south of the intended track. The method of updating crews during the outward flight could not cope with the pace at which this was happening, and it was only when landfall was made, that navigators discovered the extent to which they were off course. There were inevitable consequences at the target, both in the lack of concentrated markers, and the fact that many were carried beyond the city's south western extremities and into open country. Over 100 outlying communities were afflicted by bombs, while most of the damage within Berlin itself involved housing in the south-western corner. The bomber stream became even more scattered during the return flight, and many crews found themselves being blown over heavily defended areas of Germany, where the flak batteries took full advantage. Of the seventy-two missing aircraft, an estimated two-thirds fell to predicted flak, although all four 115 Squadron victims fell to nightfighters. The first to meet with trouble was LL730, which was set on fire by a nightfighter during the outward flight, and was steered by F/S Williams towards Sweden. Sadly, the Lancaster ran out of height, and only the bomb-aimer succeeded in abandoning it seconds before it crashed in northern Germany. DS678 was skirting Leipzig on the way home when the end came, and P/O McCann died with four others of his crew. LL694 had reached Holland before it was pounced upon by one of Germany's foremost aces, Hptm Drewes, and there were no survivors from the crew of P/O Vipond. Finally, DS664 was caught by a JU88 over Germany, and a fierce fire raged within the fuselage. F/S Newman gave the order to abandon ship at 18,000 feet, but the rear gunner, Sgt Alkemade, found his parachute destroyed, and the flames beginning to infiltrate his turret. Faced with the prospect of death by fire or descent from a great height, he opted for the latter, and departed the aircraft resigned to his fate. He lost consciousness on the way down, and awoke later in a snowdrift, suffering from burns and shrapnel wounds, but otherwise undamaged by the three mile fall to earth. His captors initially refused to believe his remarkable story, but ultimately found the necessary evidence to confirm his incredible escape, which was attributed to falling through fir trees and into deep soft snow while in a state of complete limpness. Shortly after he began his descent the Lancaster exploded, flinging the navigator and wireless operator into space, and they were the only other survivors from the crew.

A force of Halifaxes, Lancasters and Stirlings failed to find the mark at Aulnoye on the 25/26th, and the railway yards escaped serious damage. Although the Berlin campaign was now over, the winter offensive still had a week to run, and two more major operations for the crews to negotiate. The first of these was against Essen on the 26/27th, when over 1,700 houses were destroyed, and forty-eight industrial buildings were seriously damaged, thus continuing the remarkable run of successes at this once elusive target since the introduction of Oboe to main force operations a year earlier. A modest nine aircraft failed to return, and after its disastrous time at Berlin, 115 Squadron welcomed back all its participating crews. A hundred aircraft of 3, 4, 6 and 8 Groups were sent to bomb the railway yards at Courtrai on the same night, and although some damage was inflicted, traffic was running again within three days. Unfortunately, the town sustained heavy damage and civilian casualties, a situation which could not be avoided, and as already mentioned, a problem that would never be satisfactorily addressed.

The winter campaign was concluded on the night of the 30/31st with a standard maximum effort raid on Nuremberg. During a conference held early on the 30th, the Lancaster Group AOCs expressed a preference for a 5 Group inspired route, which would require the aircraft to fly a long, straight leg across Germany, to a point about fifty miles north of Nuremberg, from where the final run-in would commence. The Halifax AOCs were less convinced of the benefits, and AVM Bennett, the Pathfinder AOC, was positively overcome by the potential dangers. It was standard practice for 8 Group to prepare routes, feints and diversions, and Bennett, incandescent with rage at being overruled and apprehensive of the consequences, predicted a disaster. As the 795 aircraft, including fifty-six Lancasters of 3 Group, prepared for action, a Met Flight Mosquito crew transmitted information on the weather conditions, which differed markedly from those forecast at briefing. Operations staff expected the raid to be called off, but the warning went unheeded, and from around 21.45 for the next hour or so, the crews took off for the rendezvous area. Unknown to them they were heading into a conspiracy of circumstances, which would inflict upon Bomber Command its blackest night of the war. It was not long into the flight before the crews began to notice some unusual features in the conditions, which included uncommonly bright moonlight, and a crystal clarity of visibility, which allowed them to see the other aircraft in the stream. This was unsettling, as it was quite normal for crews to feel alone in the sky, and not see another aircraft until converging on the target. If they could see other bombers, so could the enemy. Once at cruising altitude the forecast cloud was conspicuous by its absence, and instead lay beneath them as a white tablecloth, against which they were silhouetted like flies. Condensation trails began to form in the cold, clear air to further advertise their presence to the enemy, and the jetstream winds, which had so adversely effected the Berlin raid a week earlier were also present, only this time from the south. As the final insult, the route into Germany passed close to two nightfighter beacons, which the enemy aircraft were orbiting awaiting their instructions.

The crews that either failed to detect the true strength of the wind, or simply refused to believe the evidence, were driven up to fifty miles north of their intended track, and consequently turned towards Nuremberg from a false position. This was not entirely their own fault but rather a weakness in the windfinder system. Selected 'windfinder' crews gauged the strength of the wind and transmitted their findings back to HQ, where they would be collated and retransmitted to the bomber stream as an average. The problem was that the existence of jetstreams was unknown at the time, and the windfinder crew members modified their readings lest they be considered incompetent. Even so, the modified figures were also not taken seriously by operations staff and were downgraded again before being sent back to the outward bound force. This led to more than 100 aircraft bombing at Schweinfurt in the belief that they were over Nuremberg some fifty miles further south. The carnage began over Charleroi in Belgium, and from there to the target the route was sign-posted by the burning wreckage on the ground of Bomber Command aircraft. At least eighty aircraft fell before the target was reached, and together with those attacking the wrong city this reduced considerably the numbers arriving at the briefed destination. Nuremberg escaped serious damage as many of the Pathfinder markers were carried beyond the built-up area and into open country. An unbelievable ninety-five aircraft failed to return, and many more either crashed at home or were written off with battle damage too severe to repair. 514 Squadron suffered the heaviest casualties in 3 Group, losing four Lancasters to the defences and two others to crashes on return. Unlike the bulk of the losses, both of 115 Squadron's occurred on the way home, which made them even more tragic. LL704 crashed south of Stuttgart through a combination of flak and a nightfighter, but F/S Fogaty and his crew escaped by parachute to be taken into captivity. They were halfway through their tour, but F/S Thomas and his crew all died on their first operation together, when LL622 became the last but one of the night's victims at the hands of a nightfighter over Belgium. Having carried 115 Squadron crews through the most intense twelve months of the war to date the end was now in sight for the MK II Lancaster. Merlin-powered examples of the type had been at Witchford since the 20th of March, and conversion was now complete.

That which now faced the crews of Bomber Command was in marked contrast to what had been endured over the winter months. In place of the long slog to Germany on dark, often dirty nights, shorter range hops to France and Belgium would become the order of the day in improving weather conditions, to prosecute the Transportation Plan. These operations would prove to be equally demanding in their way, however, and would require of the crews a greater commitment to accuracy to avoid civilian casualties. The main fly in the ointment was a dictate from on high, which decreed that most such operations were worthy of counting as just one third of a sortie towards the completion of a tour, and until this flawed policy was rescinded, an air of mutiny pervaded the bomber stations. Despite the prohibitive losses of the winter period, the Command was in remarkably fine fettle to face its new challenge, and Harris was in the enviable position of being able to achieve what his predecessor never could. This was to attack multiple targets simultaneously, with forces large enough to make an impact, and he could now assign targets to individual Groups, to Groups in tandem or to the Command as a whole, as dictated by operational requirements. While Harris was at the helm, of course, his preferred policy of city-busting would never be entirely shelved in favour of other considerations. 5 Group was about to go 'independent' with its low level visual marking method using Mosquitos, and a rejuvenated 3 Group would gain its own degree of autonomy later in the year with the G-H bombing device.

The new campaign got into full swing on the night of the 9/10th of April, when elements of 3, 4, 6 and 8 Groups attacked the Lille-Deliverance goods station, while all of the Groups contributed to a raid on railway yards at Villeneuve-St-George on the outskirts of Paris. The former, involving twenty-two Stirlings, was particularly effective, and destroyed over 2,000 items of rolling stock, and left buildings and track severely damaged. The success was marred by very heavy civilian casualties, and this was repeated to a lesser extent at the other target. The Command was active at five railway targets in France and Belgium on the 10/11th, and all but one of the attacks was concluded successfully. An area attack on Aachen on the 11/12th left devastation in its wake and 1,500 people dead, and this was followed by a period of minor operations for the next week. In the meantime, from the 14th, the Command became officially subject to the dictates of SHAEF, and would remain thus shackled until the Allied armies were sweeping towards the German frontier at the end of the summer. On the 15th W/C Watkins DSO, DFC, DFM was installed as the new commanding officer of XV Squadron, a tenure which would terminate in a PoW camp in November. He succeeded and swapped jobs with W/C Elliott, who took over as deputy station commander at Faldingworth, home to 1 Group's Polish 300 Masovian Squadron.

Attacks on railway targets resumed on the 18/19th, when elements of 1, 3 and 8 Groups were assigned to the marshalling yards at Rouen, which were left severely damaged, and the operation was concluded without loss until home airspace was regained. As 115 Squadron's LL667 was on final approach to Witchford shortly after 02.00, it was set upon by an enemy intruder and shot down, killing P/O Birnie and his crew. A little over an hour and a half later an identical fate befell the crew of F/L Eddy in LL867. Also on this night a large mining effort by 168 aircraft took place in northern waters. On a busy night on the 20/21st 1, 3, 6 and 8 Groups inflicted heavy punishment on Cologne, during which 115 Squadron's DS728 fell victim to flak in the target area. F/S Bertram and four of his crew escaped with their lives to become PoWs, but both gunners were killed. 5 Group, meanwhile, was carrying out its first fully-fledged independent operation with its own marker force at La Chapelle, and fourteen 218 Squadron Stirlings were conducting a G-H raid on the railway depot at Chambly. In the event only four aircraft bombed, and LJ448 crashed in France, killing F/L Doolan and one of his crew, while one man was taken prisoner and four others ultimately evaded capture.

Düsseldorf was pounded by well over 500 aircraft from all but 5 Group on the 22/23rd, and 2,000 houses were destroyed or seriously damaged, along with dozens of industrial premises. Among the twenty-nine missing aircraft were three Lancasters from 514 Squadron, two of which are believed to have collided in the target area after one was hit by flak. 115 Squadron's casualty was also the result of flak in the target area, and involved the crew of the now P/O Chantler. They, it will be remembered, had force-landed on return from Berlin on New Year's Night early on in their tour, but now all perished in the wreckage of ND753. This was the first 115 Squadron Merlin powered Lancaster to be lost. 5 Group, meanwhile, was trying out its low-level marking system for the first time at a heavily defended German target, Brunswick, although on this occasion with a disappointing outcome. Also on this night forty-eight Stirlings, including fourteen from 218 Squadron, joined other types from 4, 6 and 8 Groups for a two-wave attack on the railway yards at Laon, where severe damage was inflicted for the loss of nine aircraft.

Among these was the Lancaster carrying 635 Squadron's W/C Cousens, the Master Bomber, and former commanding officer of 115 Squadron. Also missing was 218 Squadron's EH942, which was despatched by a nightfighter, and crashed in France killing S/L Poulter and one of his gunners. This was the pilot's first operation for three years, but happily, the other five members of the crew escaped by parachute, and evaded the enemy's attempts to capture them.

EF137 became the final Stirling casualty for 75 (NZ) Squadron on the occasion of the unit's last operation with the type, another large mining effort in the Baltic on the 23/24th. It fell to a nightfighter in the target area, and P/O Lammas and his crew all perished. Thus ended an association which had begun in October 1942, but a new allegiance had begun, which would see the squadron through to the end of hostilities. It was probable that a misplaced feeling of confidence accompanied the arrival of the Lancaster, the losses of which, in a mixed force, were considerably lower than the poorer performing Halifaxes and Stirlings. When operating alone, however, Lancasters were equally at the mercy of the defences, as the succeeding months would graphically demonstrate. 5 Group had failed to deliver a telling blow at Brunswick, but Munich provided another opportunity on the 24/25th, and this time it was a resounding success that probably sealed the award of the Victoria Cross to W/C Cheshire of 617 Squadron at the conclusion of his tour in July. 3 Group Lancasters participated in a major assault on Karlsruhe on this night, when strong winds led to the main weight of the attack falling on the northern part of the city. Among the nineteen missing aircraft was DS734, the last Mk II Lancaster to be posted missing by 115 Squadron, which crashed in Belgium killing F/S Cagienard and his crew. HK542 was one of the squadron's new Mk I Lancasters, which also crashed in Belgium taking with it to their deaths F/S Bennett and his crew. Also on this night 218 Squadron sent four G-H Stirlings back to the railway yards at Chambly without loss. Essen was the target for an accurate attack by all but 5 Group on the 26/27th, while 5 Group went to the centre of Germany's ball-bearing production, Schweinfurt. This was the first time that 627 Squadron Mosquitos carried out the low-level marking in place of 617 Squadron, and it lacked the necessary accuracy. On the same night elements of 4, 6 and 8 Groups targeted railway yards at Villeneuve-St-Georges, while ten 218 Squadron G-H Stirlings returned to Chambly. Together with mining operations, this brought the squadron's monthly tally to 113 sorties for the loss of two aircraft. The highly industrialized town of Friedrichshafen was the target for over 300 Lancasters of 1, 3, 6 and 8 Groups on the 27/28th. Situated on the shores of the Bodensee close to the Swiss frontier, the town was associated particularly with the production of tank engines and gearboxes, and these factories were the principal objectives. Diversionary measures prevented the enemy nightfighters from making contact until the bombing was in progress, and the raid was highly successful, destroying over 60% of the town's built-up area. Eighteen Lancasters were shot down, however, and among them was

115 Squadron's ND803, which crashed into the Bodensee after being hit by flak, and there were no survivors from the crew of F/S Stewart.

The new month brought a change in command for 138 Squadron, as W/C Speare concluded his lengthy tour in the hot seat, and was replaced by the newly re-promoted W/C Russell, the A Flight commander. Sadly, the latter's period of tenure, in contrast to that of his predecessor, would be brief indeed. W/C Bill Russell was the same breed of warrior as S/L Robinson, who had been languishing in Hotel *Stalag Luft* since the previous May. Russell had been around for a long time, having joined up in the late twenties, and was, therefore, considerably older than most. Between October 1942 and August 1943 he had commanded 5 Group's 50 Squadron with distinction, and after six month's screening volunteered to return to operations with 138 Squadron in a reduced rank in March.

On the 1st of May 199 Squadron was posted to 100 Group to undertake bomber support duties, specifically radio countermeasures. Having closed 218 Squadron's April bombing account, it fell to Chambly to open that of May. Mounted on the night of the 1/2nd it was a 3 Group operation, predominantly with Lancasters, while 218 Squadron provided all sixteen Stirlings. The raid was outstandingly accurate, but cost the squadron three aircraft, one of which crashed in England. EF184 was caught by a nightfighter on the way home, and was crash-landed at the emergency strip at Woodbridge by P/O Scammell. The flight engineer was killed, but whether this was during the engagement or the landing is uncertain. The two missing Stirlings, EF259 and EF504 both crashed in France, three of the former's crew losing their lives, while F/O Eliot and three others evaded capture. Two also retained their freedom from the latter, but F/O Jones and the remaining four were killed. This proved to be the last bombing operation to be carried out by the squadron during the month, and the only other Stirling units now still operating in 3 Group, 90 and 149 Squadrons, would devote their energies during May entirely to mining and SOE operations. The gradual conversion to new equipment got underway for 90 Squadron with the arrival on station of the first Lancasters during the course of the month. Lancaster operations would begin in June, but in the meantime, the Stirling contingent continued its resistance support work.

The main force spent the month in the relentless campaign against the railway system, but also began to attack coastal batteries in the Pas-de-Calais, a long way from the planned invasion beaches in order to deceive the Germans. 218 Squadron was screened for a period, while some of its crews trained for a top secret operation to be undertaken on D-Day Eve. Deception was to play a major part in the actual landings, and 218 Squadron was one of a number of units, 617 Squadron was another, to be selected for an important and special role. For the remainder of the month the selected crews spent their time in preparing for the big day, the training flights being recorded in their log books as 'special local flying' or something similar.

Five small-scale bombing operations were in progress over France on the night of the 7/8th as 138 Squadron's W/C Russell headed for his target and encountered one of the nightfighters stirred up by the activity. LL280 was shot down some twenty-five miles from Le Mans, and all on board were killed. W/C Russell was the holder of a DFC and Bar, and only one member of his crew was not wearing the ribbon of a DFC, DFM or both. On the following day, or shortly thereafter, W/C Burnett DFC was installed as 138 Squadron's new commanding officer. Yet another Canadian, twenty-eight year old Burnett had gained his DFC while serving with 49 Squadron in 1940. Later, as an acting squadron leader with 408 (Goose) Squadron, he was seriously injured in a crash on return from Hamburg in a Hampden, and spent more than a year recovering before being declared fit for operations again. While 218 Squadron's select band trained for D-Day the rest of the squadron maintained its commitment to mining, an activity, which cost it another aircraft on the 9th, although fortunately, without crew casualties. Returning in the early hours from the Gironde coastal region of France, EF249 lost its port inner engine while approaching base, and the pilot, F/S Samuels, was unable to select full flap. On touch-down the Stirling swung off the runway losing its undercarriage, and was declared a write-off. Four railway targets, a military camp and a gun battery provided employment for around 700 aircraft on the 11/12th, as a result of which, 115 Squadron suffered its first loss of the month. A squadron element joined others from the Group for an attack on the railway yards at Louvain, during which, ND923 fell victim to a nightfighter in the target area, and there were no survivors from the eight-man crew of S/L Grant. The bombing caused damage mostly to workshops and other buildings, but a follow-up raid by 6 Group on the next night completed the job.

On the 12th 149 Squadron began to move out of Lakenheath, and by the 15th it had taken up residence at Methwold, which would be its home for the remainder of the war. W/C Sampson DFC concluded his tour as commanding officer of 514 Squadron, and was succeeded temporarily by S/L Reid until the appointment of W/C Wyatt DFC on the 24th. It will be recalled that W/C Wyatt had commanded 75 (NZ) Squadron between May and August 1943. It was possibly at this time that W/C Wigfall was posted from 149 Squadron to be replaced by W/C Pickford DFC*. Also in mid month S/L Leslie arrived at 75 (NZ) Squadron from Flying Training Command, and on promotion to Wing Commander he assumed command of the squadron at the departure of W/C Max to 3 Group HQ.

After the period of reduced activity in mid month five railway yards were bombed on the 19/20th, the Le Mans site assigned to 3 Group. As in the case of most operations other than some by 5 Group, marking was by the Pathfinders, sometimes relying solely on Oboe Mosquitos. On this night, 7 Squadron provided the Master Bomber and deputy. The previously mentioned New Zealander, Fraser Barron, now a Wing Commander and highly experienced Pathfinder, typified the 8 Group spirit. Sadly, both he and his deputy, S/L Dennis, were lost in the target area and killed, possibly as the result of a collision, and the only other failure to return from this successful operation was a 115 Squadron Lancaster. HK547 likewise went down over the target after being hit by flak, and P/O Atkin died with the other seven men on board. As far as industrial Germany was concerned, Duisburg received its first major raid for a year on the 21/22nd, when 1, 3 and 5 Groups provided a 500-strong main force. The Ruhr was still a dangerous region to visit, and the loss of twenty-nine Lancasters, including three from 514 Squadron, was an echo of the campaign of a year earlier. ND754 was the 115 Squadron representative among the missing, and this was sent crashing to earth in the target area by the local flak. It was another eight-man crew, captained by F/L Andersen, and only the wireless operator escaped with his life to become a PoW. Dortmund was also honoured with its first raid for a year on the following night, and although this operation, like the previous night's, was a success, eighteen aircraft failed to return, among them 115 Squadron's ND745, which crashed in Belgium, killing F/O Ward and three of his crew.

Two railway yards at Aachen were the aiming points for a raid by over 400 aircraft on the 24/25th, but it quickly developed into an area attack, which inflicted serious damage on the town and surrounding villages. It was considered necessary to target the Rothe Erde yards again, and this operation by 1 and 3 Groups took place on the 27/28th. 3 Group provided the main force for an attack on the railway yards at Angers on the following night, when a large proportion of the bombing strayed onto residential districts, destroying 800 buildings, and killing over 250 French civilians. A two wave assault on the railway yards at Trappes on the last night of the month was successfully concluded by elements from all but 5 Group, but LL936 failed to return to Witchford, having crashed in France, and there was total loss of life among the crew of F/S McLachlan. The last night of the month brought three missing crews from Tempsford, two in 138 Squadron Halifaxes and another in a 161 Squadron Hudson.

The weather at the start of June was not favouring the launch of the invasion, and the time was used up in further attacks on coastal batteries, radar and listening stations and railway yards. SOE operations to Belgium and France on the night of the 2/3rd cost 138 Squadron two Halifaxes and 90 Squadron a Stirling, the latter proving to be the final Stirling casualty for the squadron as conversion to Lancasters was now well underway. Training for 218 Squadron's part in Overlord continued with practice flights on the 2nd, 3rd and 4th, during which, twenty-eight sorties were flown by the eight selected crews. Their role was one of supreme importance, which would have a direct bearing on the enemy's response to the approaching invasion fleet. If Operations Glimmer and Taxable were successful, the latter a similar operation by 617 Squadron, it meant that the armada of Allied ships would probably reach its position off the Normandy beaches unopposed, and be able to disembark the invasion forces in relative peace. The plan was for six

218 Squadron aircraft in two lines of three abreast, to fly a meticulously accurate succession of overlapping elongated orbits for up to 2 hours, each one advancing gradually towards the coastal area between Boulogne and Le Havre, north of the genuine landing grounds. At precise intervals Window would be dispensed into the slipstream at a rate of a bundle every twelve minutes, and to the enemy radar, this would appear as a large convoy of ships heading across the Channel at a speed of 7 knots. These six aircraft plus two reserves would represent only a tiny fraction of the Command's contribution to the invasion, and in all, a record 1,211 sorties would be flown against coastal batteries, and in diversionary or other support operations during the night of the 5/6th, D-Day Eve and D-Day itself.

It was 23.39 hours when LJ522 took off from Woolfox Lodge in the hands of F/L Chaplin and F/L Webster to launch Operation Glimmer. Each aircraft carried a crew of thirteen men, comprised of two pilots, three navigators, one wireless operator, one flight engineer, two gunners, two windowers and two spare bods. Two minutes later S/L Brentnall and P/O Ecclestone departed in LJ472, to be followed at 23.44 by S/L Overton and F/L Funnell in EF133. The reserve aircraft were next away at 23.50, F/Ls Locke and Coram in LJ449, and F/L Knapman with the appropriately named F/L Stirling in LJ517, both of these pilot combinations RNZAF/RAAF. An hour after the departure of the first aircraft F/Ls McAllister and Young initiated the second wave in LK401, to be followed three minutes later by F/Ls Seller and Scammell in LJ632 and F/Ls King and Gillies in EF207 at 00.43. By the time the second wave reached its beat, the first wave had completed eight of its eventual twenty three orbits, and the final fifteen would be conducted in tandem. If a single crew faltered in its course or the timing of turns and windowing, the enemy would see the operation as a spoof, and be alerted to a landing elsewhere. In the event, the crews of both 218 and 617 Squadrons performed to the high standards expected and demanded of them, and the operations were a complete success.

Although no actual reference to the invasion was made at most briefings, crews were given strict flight levels, and were instructed not to jettison bombs over the sea. Among the special diversionary operations was the dropping of dummy parachutists in north-western France, well away from the invasion area, by Halifaxes and Stirlings of 90, 138, 149 and 161 Squadrons. W/C Pickford, in EF140, led a contingent of seven 149 Squadron aircraft with nine man crews, and two of them were shot down over France. Aircraft were taking off throughout the night, and some of those crews returning in dawn's early light were rewarded with a view of the armada ploughing its way sedately across the Channel below. Some 1,000 aircraft were involved in operations against communications targets near French towns on D-Day night. LM533 did not return home with the rest of the 115 Squadron contingent, and its fate, along with that of the crew of F/O Wesley, has never been determined. Similar activity involved smaller numbers of aircraft on the following two nights. On the 7/8th 115 Squadron put up eighteen Lancasters for a communications target at Chevreusse, and only twelve returned on a night when nightfighter activity was fierce. This turned out to be the squadron's blackest night of the war, and all six aircraft fell to nightfighters over France with only six men surviving to tell the tale. Five of these were in HK548, and although the bomb-aimer and one of the gunners perished in the crash, P/O Law and the remaining four escaped by parachute, and ultimately evaded capture. The only other survivor was the navigator in F/S Todd's crew, who were flying in HK552. ND760 was shot down over Paris during the outward flight with the crew of P/O Quinton on board, and the other crews were those of P/O Maude, F/L Norbury and P/O Francis in LL864, ND761 and ND790 respectively. During the course of the summer a number of squadrons would suffer similar or worse tragedies, but this would not be allowed to interfere with the business in hand. 138 Squadron also posted missing three Halifax crews from operations to France on this night, and a fourth Halifax was written off in a crash on take-off. Four airfields south of the beachhead were attacked by around 400 aircraft provided predominantly by 1, 4 and 6 Groups on the 9/10th, and then it was back to railways for most of the main force, including 115 Squadron on the 10/11th and 11/12th.

Two new campaigns began in quick succession at this time, the first, against Germany's oil industry, beginning on the night of the 12/13th at the hands of 1, 3 and 8 Groups. This outstandingly accurate attack halted all production at the Nordstern synthetic oil refinery at Gelsenkirchen for several weeks, costing the enemy war effort 1,000 tons per day of vital aviation fuel. Such installations were always hotly defended, and flak claimed 115 Squadron's HK545 in the target area. S/L Shadforth and his crew were all killed, and he became the squadron's second flight commander to be lost in the space of four weeks. This was the first operation for 115 Squadron under a new commanding officer, W/C Devas DFC, AFC having taken up his appointment earlier in the day. Also on this night mining sorties resulted in two 218 Squadron Stirlings being written off at home. EF181 crashed when a tyre burst during take-off for French coastal waters, but F/L young and his crew walked away, and EF299 came to grief when attempting to overshoot on return, and F/L Funnell and his crew also emerged unscathed. As events were to prove, these were the final Stirling casualties to be suffered by the squadron as its two and a half year association with the type neared its end.

The Command mounted the first daylight operations since the departure of 2 Group a year earlier on the evening of the 14th, when a two-phase attack was delivered on E-Boats and other light marine craft at Le Havre to prevent them harassing Allied shipping supplying the beachhead. A predominantly 1 Group force attacked first, to be followed by 3 Group at dusk, and the operation was entirely successful. Boulogne received similar treatment on the following evening with equally satisfying results. 3 Group was else-where on this night, however, attacking railway installations at Valenciennes. The bombing was accurate in good visibility, but five Lancasters were lost, among them 115 Squadron's HK550. The pilot, F/O Amaka, and his bomb-aimer were able to save themselves before the crash on French soil, and they ultimately evaded capture, but their crew colleagues all perished. Stirlings returned to bombing later that night, with an accurate raid on railway yards at Lens. Earlier on the 15th 1678 Conversion Flight had been disbanded, and any aircraft fit for operations were sent to 514 Squadron. The second new campaign was a renewal of the battle against flying bomb launching and storage sites in the Pas-de-Calais, only on a much larger scale than in December and January, and the first attacks were successfully carried out on the 16/17th. On the following night twelve Stirlings joined 300 other aircraft in raids on railway targets, although the 3 Group operation against a railway cutting near Montdidier was abandoned almost immediately because of cloud. Just one aircraft failed to return, and this was 115 Squadron's HK559, which crashed in France without survivors from the crew of P/O Traill. This proved to be the swan song for 90 Squadron's Stirlings, and now only 149 and 218 Squadrons were operating the type with 3 Group's main force. W/C Ogilvie DFC, AFC became 90 Squadron's latest commanding officer on posting from 3 Group HQ. He was another highly experienced officer, who had commanded XV Squadron during the second half of 1941. For the remainder of the month 3 Group participated in operations against flying bomb sites on the 23/24th, 24/25th and 27/28th, before concluding the month with a daylight operation in support of the ground forces on the 30th. A road junction at Villers-Bocage was attacked with great accuracy, and this prevented a planned German armoured advance towards British and American forces. The Stirlings, meanwhile, mostly mined the sea lanes and dropped supplies.

The first few days of the new month were dominated by daylight raids on flying bomb sites, 3 Group's involvement coming on the 2nd. On the 5th the King and Queen visited 115 Squadron, accompanied by the Princess Elizabeth, to present nineteen medals, and that night 3, 4, 6 and 8 Groups operated against two launching and two storage sites, 3 Group attacking one in the latter category at Wizernes. A major operation against fortified villages around Caen in support of the ground forces went ahead on the evening of the 7th without a 3 Group contribution, and then it was back to flying bomb launching sites during the early afternoon of the 9th. 3 Group was assigned to Lisieux, one of six targets, but cloud made concentrated bombing difficult. It was a similar story on the 10th, when 1, 3 and 8 Groups joined forces to try to eliminate a storage dump at Nucourt, but could produce only scattered bombing in the conditions. The same Groups provided aircraft for a switch to railway yards at Vaires on the outskirts of Paris on the 12th, but the Master Bomber abandoned the operation in the face of cloud after just twelve aircraft had bombed. With superiority over the battle area having been established, twenty-eight Stirlings had a rare opportunity to carry bombs when attacking flying bomb sites on the 17th. 3 Group was, in fact, the least employed during the second third of the month, but was out in force on the 18th, to help prepare the way for the British Second Army's armoured attack under Operation Goodwood. Over 900 aircraft got away at first light to target five fortified villages east of Caen, and the operation was a complete success. On return from Emieville, and a little under three hours after taking off, 115 Squadron's LM616 crashed at 07.15 in Hertfordshire, killing P/O Letts and his crew. American bombers had also been involved, but Bomber Command delivered the majority of the ordnance, amounting to more than 5,000 tons onto the enemy divisions below, and this enabled Goodwood to get off to an encouraging start.

That night, elements of the Group attacked a railway junction at Aulnoye, while 5 Group went to a similar target at Revigny, which had thwarted two earlier attempts by 1 Group. The 5 Group force was badly mauled by night-fighters, losing twenty-four aircraft, and this, together with extensive Bomber Command activity over the oil refineries at Wesseling and Scholven-Buer, may have contributed to the loss of just two 3 Group Lancasters. One of these, however, was 115 Squadron's LL943, which crashed on the Franco-Belgian border with no survivors from the crew of F/O Pellew. Over 140 Lancasters of 1, 3 and 8 Groups targeted the oil plant at Homberg to good effect on the 20/21st, but were badly mauled by nightfighters, which hacked down twenty of their number. It was a bad experience for 3 Group in particular, whose 75 (NZ) Squadron lost seven aircraft, 514 Squadron four, 90 Squadron three and 115 and 622 Squadrons two each. Fortunately, one of the 115 Squadron Lancasters made it back to the emergency landing strip at Woodbridge, where it was written off in a crash-landing. LM510 had been attacked by a nightfighter over the target, and during the engagement, most of the crew sustained wounds, which, as far as both gunners were concerned, proved to be fatal. The pilot, F/S Gaston, was awarded the DFM for his exploits, and was later commissioned. The other empty dispersal should have been occupied by C Flight's ND913, but this was now a shattered wreck in southern Holland, where it lay as an epitaph to the passing of F/O Clarey and his gallant crew.

The first raid on a German urban target for two months took place on the 23/24th, when a large force appeared suddenly and with complete surprise from behind a 100 Group RCM screen, and proceeded to inflict heavy damage on Kiel. This was followed by a three-raid series against Stuttgart over five nights, beginning on the 24/25th. By the end of the third attack on the 28/29th, the city's central districts lay in ruins. It was another costly night for 514 Squadron, however, with three more empty dispersals to contemplate at Waterbeach. On the evening of the 27th the two remaining Stirling squadrons had bombed flying bomb sites at Les Landes and Les Lanville-et-Neuss. Twenty Stirlings joined a predominantly Halifax force in a number of raids on flying bomb launching and storage sites in the Pas-de-Calais on the 28th, including one in the Foret de Nieppe, and this was attacked again on the following day with sixteen Stirlings in attendance. Almost 700 aircraft were involved in a push against six enemy positions in support of the advancing ground forces in the Villers-Bocage area on the 30th, but cloud created difficulties, leading to a curtailment, and only two of the sites were effectively bombed. Briefed to attack a position at Amaye, Sgt Thompson and his crew perished, when 115 Squadron's PB130 crashed in France.

Lancasters began to arrive at Woolfox Lodge during the second half of the month in preparation for 218 Squadron's conversion to the type. Despite this the squadron moved into Methwold early in August, so that all servicing of Stirlings could be centralized. As it was about to relinquish the type, one wonders why. Major daylight operations against flying bomb sites characterized the first week of August, 3 Group participating on the 1st and again on the 2nd, when both Stirling squadrons attacked the Mont Condon site. This proved to be the last operation by 218 Squadron with Stirlings, and within a matter of days they would be fully replaced by Lancasters. Operations against flying bomb sites on the 3rd involved over 1,100 sorties by the Command as a whole. While almost 300 aircraft of 6 and 8 Groups continued the campaign on the 4th, and the previously mentioned former 115 Squadron stalwart S/L Bazalgette lost his life, elements of 1, 3 and 8 Groups attacked oil storage depots at Bec-d'Ambes and Pauillac without loss. Pauillac and two similar sites were attacked by the same Groups on the following day, and, as twenty-four hours earlier, they operated under the umbrella of a 100 Group Mosquito escort. On the night of the 6/7th 149 Squadron sacrificed its last crew to a mining operation, when LK383 disappeared without trace with the crew of F/O Adams, and this was the last Stirling from a main force squadron to be lost in Bomber Command service. Over 1,000 aircraft were employed against five enemy positions in support of the Allied ground forces on the 7/8th, before elements of 1, 3 and 8 Groups returned to the oil offensive, with a successful raid on two storage dumps on the 8/9th. The single loss from the Forêt de Lucheux operation was 115 Squadron's LM166, which crashed in the Pas-de-Calais, killing W/O Leggett and two of his crew, while the four survivors landed in Allied held territory to return home. After its short period of screening 218 Squadron returned to the fray as a fully-fledged Lancaster unit on the night of the 9/10th, when S/L Brentnall led seven aircraft to attack a flying bomb storage site at Fort d'Englos. One Lancaster returned early, but the remainder carried out their assigned tasks before coming safely back home. During a heavy night of activity on the 12/13th, twelve 149 Squadron Stirlings joined an attack on a German troop concentration north of Falaise, an area upon which the 3rd Canadian Division was advancing.

The first operations of the month to industrial Germany took place on the 12/13th, when two forces were launched. A total of 379 aircraft were sent to Brunswick without a Pathfinder presence, in order to ascertain the ability of crews to establish themselves over a target on the strength of their own H2s equipment. This may have been an attempt to ease the enormous work load heaped upon 8 Group by the concurrent campaigns against railways, oil, flying bombs and city-busting, whilst also providing tactical support for the ground forces. In the event, the raid lacked concentration, and was inconclusive as an experiment, while costing twenty-seven aircraft. Two of these were from 115 Squadron, and both ND927 and PB127 crashed in Germany with one survivor each. In an unusual coincidence, it was the pilot in each case, F/O Hockey and F/L Belyea respectively, who escaped with their lives, which suggests the possibility that the Lancasters broke up in mid air before the other crew members had time to attach their parachutes. The night's second major operation to Germany was a standard Pathfinder-led raid on the Opel motor works at Rüsselsheim, but damage was not serious, and it would be necessary for the Command to return later in the month.

Further operations against enemy troop positions on the 14th led to the 'friendly fire' incident, in which thirteen Canadian soldiers were killed, and over fifty were wounded. In preparation for his new night offensive against Germany, Harris launched 1,000 aircraft by daylight on the 15th, to attack nine nightfighter airfields in Holland and Belgium. On the night of the 16/17th over 800 aircraft were involved in raids on Stettin and Kiel, the former in particular producing outstanding results. A total of 1,500 houses and twenty-nine industrial premises were destroyed, while five ships were sunk in the harbour, and a further eight sustained serious damage. The Kiel operation enjoyed moderate success, inflicting heavy damage on the town's dock area, but a proportion of the effort fell away from the target. A modest five aircraft were lost from each raid, and 3 Group came through unscathed. Bremen suffered catastrophic destruction on the 18/19th, which included over 8,500 houses and apartment blocks and an indeterminate number of industrial premises. Eighteen ships were also sunk in the harbour, and this was the city's worst night of the war. On the 25th six Lancasters arrived at Methwold to begin 149 Squadron's conversion, and within four days a full complement was on charge. The return to Rüsselsheim and the Opel Motor works was entrusted to elements of 1, 3, 6 and 8 Groups on the 25/26th, and although a greater degree of damage was inflicted than in the earlier raid, lorry production was not seriously compromised. As 115 Squadron's PD274 was leaving the target area, it collided with another Lancaster, losing both port engines. F/L Aldridge and his crew were forced to abandon their chariot to its fate, and all were taken prisoner on the ground. This final week of the month would prove to be expensive for 115 Squadron, which provided crews on the 26/27th for the second trip in eleven nights to Kiel. Another highly destructive assault ensued, but C Flight's HK556 and HK560 failed to return to Witchford, and were lost without trace with the crews of F/O Holder and F/S Braun respectively. On the 28th small scale operations were mounted against twelve flying bomb sites in the Pas-de-Calais, as Allied forces prepared to take the region, and this concluded the campaign which had begun in earnest in mid June. Stettin received its second visit of the month on the 29/30th, again suffering massive damage to housing, industry and shipping, but 115 Squadron once more had the sad task of posting missing two of its crews. ME718 crashed in Denmark, killing F/L Chatterton and his crew, while PB131 went down beyond the target in Poland. The consequences for the crew of F/O Berkeley were the same, however, and the wireless operator was only seventeen years old when he met his death.

September was a month devoted largely to the liberation of the three major French ports still in enemy hands, and six operations took place against enemy strong points around Le Havre between the 5th and the 11th. 149 Squadron sent five Stirlings against the port on the 5th, in company with 343 other aircraft, and all returned safely from an accurate attack. Two more completed their sorties against the same target on the 6th, and on the morning of the 8th four aircraft, LJ481, LJ632, LK396 and LK401 flew the final sorties by 149 Squadron Stirlings, F/O McKee having the honour of being the last to touch down back at Methwold at 09.25 hours in LK396. Thus was ended the career of this type with Bomber Command's main force. 115 Squadron's HK579 was one of two missing Lancasters from this operation, and fell to flak in the target area. F/S Kilsby and one of his gunners lost their lives, but the other five crew members landed safely in Allied-held territory. Within hours of the final attack on the 11th, the German garrison surrendered to British forces. A simultaneous operation against oil refineries at Castrop-Rauxel, Gelsenkirchen and Kamen was carried out under a huge fighter escort, and only one 3 Group aircraft was lost from the last mentioned target. Two city-busting operations were mounted on the night of the 12/13th against Frankfurt and Stuttgart, the former by 1, 3 and 8 Groups, the last major raid of the war on this city. Heavy damage was inflicted upon the western districts, where industrial and residential property suffered alike. The cost to Bomber Command was seventeen aircraft, three of them 218 Squadron Lancasters. It was a similar story of destruction at Stuttgart, where the northern and western districts were devastated, and a minor firestorm erupted. On the night of the 16/17th attacks were carried out in support of the ill-fated Operation Market Garden, which was to be launched later in the morning. While 1 and 8 Groups targeted airfields, a small force from 3 and 8 Groups attended to a flak position at Moerdijk, losing two Lancasters to a tragic collision in the process. One of them was LM693 of 115 Squadron bearing the crew of F/O Bickford, and the other was the 90 Squadron aircraft LM169, both of which plunged into the Dutch countryside without survivors.

It required just one day and 3,000 tons of bombs on the 17th to soften up the garrison at Boulogne sufficiently for the ground forces to go in, and the surrender of the port took place a little over a week later. This operation was the first by 149 Squadron in Lancasters, ten aircraft having been dispatched, and it signalled the completion of 3 Group's resurgence to the forefront of Bomber Command's offensive. Only Calais of the main French ports now remained in enemy hands, and the first of six operations to rectify this situation was mounted on the 20th. Over 600 aircraft took part, including ten Lancasters from 149 Squadron, and they all returned safely from a successful raid. On the 23/24th, over 500 aircraft from 1, 3, 4 and 8 Groups destroyed or seriously damage more than 600 buildings in Neuss. It was later on the 24th that the second operation took place on Calais and its environs, but cloud proved to be a major obstacle, and a third of the 188 strong force was unable to bomb. It was the same story on the 25th, when two thirds of the 872 participants were forced to return home with their bombs. The effort was divided on the 26th, when over 500 aircraft attacked four gun emplacements at Cap Gris Nez, while 191 others sought out enemy positions at Calais. Low cloud continued to be a problem for 1, 3, 4 and 8 Groups on the 27th, but the Master Bomber called the force in to bomb visually from below the cloud base, and an accurate attack ensued. Just one aircraft failed to return, 115 Squadron's LM738, which crashed in the target area, killing F/O Wibberley and all but his bomb-aimer, who landed safely, and was soon in Allied hands. 1, 3, 6 and 8 Groups concluded the campaign on the 28th, in another dual operation, which included six gun batteries at cap Gris Nez. Only a quarter of the Calais force bombed before the attack was called off, but the aim had been achieved, and within days Canadian forces took control of the port.

October would bring a full return to the bombing of industrial Germany, and from this point on an unprecedented tonnage was to be delivered onto its towns and cities. 3 Group added to its strength with two new squadrons during the first week. On the 1st 195 Squadron was formed, on paper at least, at Witchford under the command, on paper again, of W/C Dudley Burnside DFC*. The first crews to join the new squadron would come from 3 LFS on the 7th, but 115 Squadron would donate its C Flight as the nucleus in mid month. Burnside's previous command had been the RCAF's 427 (Lion) Squadron, now in 6 Group, which he had led from its formation in November 1942 until the following September. His DFC had been awarded for his service during operations in Waziristan in 1940. Since 427 Squadron he had been station commander at Woodbridge. On the 5th C Flight of 90 Squadron gave birth to 186 Squadron at Tuddenham, and W/C Giles DFC was appointed commanding officer, having held a similar post with the parent squadron between June and December 1943. Neither of these units had a tradition in bombing, in fact both had more of a fighter pedigree.

3 Group opened its October account on the 5/6th, when joining 1 Group to provide the main force for a raid on Saarbrücken. The aim was to cut the railway and block supply routes ahead of advancing American forces, and this was achieved, along with the destruction of almost 5,900 houses for the modest loss to 1 and 3 Groups of three aircraft. For the second time in three weeks a 115 Squadron Lancaster was involved in a mid-air collision, this time over Germany, and PD344 plummeted to earth before any of F/S Henderson's crew could save themselves. The other Lancaster, ND904 from 75 (NZ) Squadron, likewise crashed with total loss of life. A new Ruhr campaign began at Dortmund on the 6/7th, for which 3, 6 and 8 Groups put up over 500 aircraft. Only two 3 Group aircraft failed to return, and once again,

the unlucky squadrons were 115 and 75 (NZ). The former's LL880 contained a thirty-eight year old flight engineer, and he died along with the rest of W/O Erickson's crew. The frontier towns of Cleves and Emmerich were heavily bombed on the 7th, to prevent access by enemy forces to the exposed Allied right flank after the failure of Operation Market Garden. 3 Group was present at both targets, and extensive damage was inflicted.

The new Ruhr offensive led inexorably to Operation Hurricane, a demonstration to the enemy of the overwhelming superiority of the Allied air forces ranged against it. At first light on the 14th, over 1,000 aircraft took off for Duisburg, 957 of them arriving over the city shortly after breakfast time to deliver more than 4,000 tons of bombs. Fourteen aircraft failed to return, and 115 Squadron had the misfortune to be represented by two of them. Only the pilot, F/O Lister, survived the destruction by flak of HK599, and he was taken prisoner, while F/O Price and four of his crew perished in ND805, only the flight engineer and navigator coming through as PoWs. Late that night the Command returned in similar numbers to press home the point about superiority, and remarkably, this massive effort of launching 2,018 sorties in less than twenty-four hours was achieved without a contribution from 5 Group. Earlier in the day S/L Farquharson and his C Flight had been posted across the tarmac from 115 Squadron to 195 Squadron, again on paper, as the physical move would not take place until the 25th. However, five of the new unit's pilots flew to Duisburg that night as second dickies in 115 Squadron aircraft. On the following night 500 aircraft from all but the 'Independent Air Force' attacked Wilhelmshaven for the last time, and claimed severe damage. One of 115 Squadron's veteran Lancasters went missing without trace on this night, ME692 having clocked up sixty-nine operations, and it took with it the eight man crew of F/O Perry. The eighth crew member was S/L Franklin, who had joined 195 Squadron as a flight commander from 3 LFS on the 7th, and was flying as second pilot. The former 115 Squadron commander, W/C Rainsford, returned to Witchford temporarily from 33 Base on the 16th to sort out the new squadron's administration, and W/C Burnside arrived on the following day to take command physically. He was soon joined by S/L Brentnall from 218 Squadron as the replacement flight commander.

3 Group now prepared to embark upon its new career of independence with the G-H blind-bombing device. In this way it would be mimicking the independent role enjoyed by 5 Group since April, after it had developed the low-level visual marking system using Mosquitos. To establish its effectiveness it was important to select a virtually virgin target, and the city of Bonn presented itself as the ideal choice. The G-H blind bombing device had already been used in a limited way, but 3 Group was to pioneer mass attacks against targets obscured by cloud not exceeding 18,000 feet, and would develop an expertise in this role which would be put to good use particularly against the German oil industry. A third of the Group's Lancasters were now equipped with G-H, and their tail fins carried bold markings in the form of

two yellow horizontal bars to identify them to the rest of the force. Crews in non-equipped aircraft were to formate on G-H leaders, and release their bombs when the leaders' were seen to fall. Most such operations were intended to take place in daylight, but a number of night operations would also be undertaken. The operation against Bonn was mounted on the morning of the 18th by 128 aircraft, and was a complete success, which destroyed the city centre and many of the historic and cultural buildings. Just one aircraft was lost, 115 Squadron's HK544, which went missing without trace with the crew of F/O Smith.

Despite its new role the Group would still operate in tandem with others, and joined forces with 1, 6 and 8 Groups on the 19/20th for an effective two-phase attack on Stuttgart, while 5 Group attended to Nuremberg. This was the last operation by 218 Squadron to be presided over by W/C Fenwick-Wilson, who was posted to 31 Base on the 21st. W/C Smith arrived from 115 Squadron, where he had been a flight commander in the rank of Squadron Leader. It was the first operation to be presided over by 622 Squadron's new commanding officer, W/C Buckingham, who had arrived earlier in the day to replace the departing W/C Swales, who was posted to 3 Group HQ as Group Training Inspector. W/C Buckingham would see the squadron through to the end of hostilities. The Hurricane force moved on to Essen with 1,000 aircraft on the evening of the 23rd, and returned on the 25th in smaller numbers to carry out an even more destructive attack. A hundred 3 Group Lancasters carried out a G-H raid on Leverkusen on the 26th, with the aim of hitting the I G Farben chemicals factory, which was engaged in the production of synthetic oil. Returning crews believed the operation to be successful, but were prevented by cloud from making an assessment. Cologne's turn at the hands of the Hurricane force came initially on the 28th, when over 2,200 apartment blocks were destroyed, and further massive damage was inflicted on the city on the evenings of the 30th and 31st. 3 Group carried out G-H raids on oil refineries at Wesseling on the 30th and Bottrop on the 31st at a cost of just one 90 Squadron Lancaster from the latter.

As 3 Group was now operating a single type and all of its non-special duties squadrons were engaged in similar activities, we will dispense with the closer examination of 115 Squadron. November began for 3 Group in similar vein, with a daylight G-H attack on the oil refinery at Homberg on the 2nd. Large fires were reported by the returning crews, and five of the 184 participants failed to return. The Hurricane force visited Düsseldorf that night with over 900 aircraft, and destroyed more than 5,000 houses and some industrial buildings. A 3 Group raid on Solingen on the 4th was scattered and ineffective, and 195 Squadron lost three aircraft, two of them exploding over the target, probably as the result of direct hits by heavy flak. The operation was repeated on the following afternoon with great success, and 1,300 houses were destroyed, along with eighteen industrial premises. A night G-H attack on Coblenz followed on the 6/7th, when an estimated 58% of the town's built-up area was reduced to ruins. The busy start to the month continued with a return to the oil plant at Homberg on the 8th, but smoke from the early bombing quickly concealed the aiming point, and the remainder of the attack was scattered. On the 10th W/C Bannister was appointed as the new commanding officer of 90 Squadron. He was an armaments specialist, who had held his rank since March 1941, and had been on loan to the RCAF in Canada for eleven months up to February 1943. Thereafter, he commanded various training units until transferring to 3 Group for operational duties, and, therefore, had little if any operational experience. On the 11th, over 100 of the Group's Lancasters took off for another oil target at Castrop-Rauxel, and a similar plant at Dortmund occupied the Group on the 15th. Two days earlier 195 Squadron had moved from Witchford to Wratting Common. On the 16th, the three small towns of Düren, Jülich and Heinsberg were attacked to cut communications behind enemy lines ahead of advancing American ground forces. The last mentioned was assigned to 3 Group, and at the time of the attack, contained only a hundred or so civilians, half of whom were killed, and a handful of enemy soldiers. Only one Lancaster was lost, and this was XV Squadron's PB137, which contained the eight man crew of the commanding officer, W/C Watkins. He alone of his crew survived, and he spent the remainder of the war as a guest of the Reich. His replacement, and the last wartime commander of the squadron, was W/C MacFarlane, who took up his appointment on the 17th.

3 Group's assault on Homberg's oil production continued on the afternoon of the 20th, but bad weather hampered visibility and the G-H attack was scattered. It was another expensive operation for 75 (NZ) Squadron, which lost three Lancasters, at least one of them to heavy flak over the target. A follow-up attack by the Group twenty-four hours later began badly, but became concentrated, and the consensus was that the target had been dealt with once and for all. It did cost 514 Squadron two aircraft, however, and a third was written off in a crash-landing in Allied territory. On the 23rd the Nordstern oil refinery at Gelsenkirchen was the target for a G-H raid by over 150 aircraft, and it was believed to be a successful operation. The 26th brought an experimental raid to gauge the effective range of G-H. Seventy-five Lancasters raided railway yards at Fulda in central Germany south of Kassel, but the distance was too great, and the bombing was scattered. On the following day the Group carried out a G-H attack on the Kalk Nord railway yards at Cologne, which was well within range, and a successful outcome was claimed. Earlier on the 27th W/C Devas had been posted from 115 Squadron to 31 Base, from whence came his successor, W/C Shaw, who would see the squadron through to the end of the bombing war, and almost to the total cessation of hostilities. The Group ended the month with separate raids on a coking plant at Bottrop, and a benzol plant at Osterfeld on the 30th, each with sixty aircraft.

The main force began its December campaign on the 2/3rd, the night on which the previously mentioned former138/161 Squadron stalwart, W/C 'Sticky' Murphy, died in the wreckage of his 23 Squadron Mosquito. He was on bomber support duties, hunting the enemy nightfighters preying on almost 500 aircraft from 1, 4, 6 and 8 Groups as they pounded Hagen in the Ruhr. 3 Group opened its December account at Dortmund on the 3rd, where the Hansa benzol plant was the target. Cloud obscured Oberhausen on the 4th, so that no assessment of the results could be made, but it was later established that 472 houses were destroyed, and some industrial and public buildings sustained damage. Hamm, a major railway centre, was attacked by the Group on the 5th, and 39% of the town's built-up area was destroyed. This was on the day on which 218 Squadron changed address for the final time during the war, and took up residence at Chedburgh. 1 and 3 Groups provided the main force for a raid on the oil refinery at Leuna near Leipzig on the 6/7th, when over 400 aircraft completed the 1,000 mile round trip. The effort was worthwhile, and extensive damage was inflicted on the installation. W/C Newton DFC, MiD, a former flight commander with 75 (NZ) Squadron in 1942, returned in early December to assume command at the departure of W/C Leslie. Sadly, however, his tenure would be brief. 3 Group conducted operations against railway yards at Duisburg on the 8th, and Osterfeld on the 11th, before ineffectively targeting the Ruhrstahl steel works at Witten on the 12th. This last-mentioned operation cost 195 Squadron three Lancaster's and a fourth crash-landed in Allied territory.

A particularly sad event occurred on the 15th involving 3 Group in general and 149 Squadron in particular. A total of 138 of the Group's Lancasters set off for a daylight attack on Siegen, expecting to meet up with a fighter escort over the Channel. Bad weather over much of the UK prevented the fighters from taking off, however, and the 3 Group force was recalled at the French coast. At about the same time that the Lancasters were climbing and forming up for the sea crossing, a single engine Norseman took off into the fog from Twinwood Farm airfield in Bedfordshire. It and its two occupants, the pilot and Glenn Miller, the famous band leader, were never seen again. He was on his way to Paris ahead of his band to organise a concert to be broadcast over Christmas. As the Norseman approached the French coast in bright clear weather, the 3 Group Lancasters were high above, wheeling round to return home after being recalled, and at least some 149 Squadron crews jettisoned their bombs. One or more of these, it seems, struck the comparatively flimsy light aircraft and sent it crashing into the sea. It was only around fifty years after the tragedy, when a crewman told his story that the mystery of Glenn Miller's disappearance was finally solved.

During the remainder of the month the Group carried out G-H attacks on railway yards at Siegen on the 16th, Trier on the 19th, 21st and 23rd, Cologne/Gremberg on the 28th and Vohwinkel on the 31st. The Group also bombed Hangelar airfield near Bonn on the 24/25th, and participated in raids on troop positions at St Vith on Boxing Day, railway yards at Rheydt on the 27th, and a similar target at Coblenz on the 29th. In mid month 186 Squadron had moved from Tuddenham to Stradishall, and W/C Burnett concluded his tour as 138 Squadron's commanding officer on the 17th. He was succeeded by W/C Murray DSC, DFC, who would see the squadron through to the end of hostilities. A few days after Christmas Tempsford's station commander, Group Captain 'Mouse' Fielden, 161 Squadron's first commanding officer, was promoted to Air Commodore and posted as station commander to Woodhall Spa, a 5 Group airfield and home of 617 Squadron, better known as the Dambusters, and 627 Squadron, a Mosquito unit.

The year had begun with the Command at its lowest ebb during the winter offensive, but having risen phoenix-like from the ashes, it had become transformed into a juggernaut, smashing its way across the tortured Reich. Its peaking strength coincided with Germany's decline, and although the scent of victory was in the air, the heaviest bombardment of the war was still to come. The year had also seen the resurgence of 3 Group to the van, and from this point to the end of the war it would share fully in the continuing assault on the German homeland.

1945
Juggernaut; Thunderclap; victory

The New Year began with a bang, as the *Luftwaffe* launched its ill-conceived and ultimately ill-fated Operation Bodenplatte at first light on the 1st of January. The intention, to destroy elements of the Allied air forces on the ground at the recently liberated airfields of France, Holland and Belgium, was only modestly realized, and the cost in front-line fighters was around 250, and more critically, around 150 pilots were killed, wounded or taken prisoner. This was a setback from which the *Luftwaffe*'s day-fighter force would never fully recover, although enemy nightfighters would continue to take a toll of RAF bombers, even if not on the former scale. Inevitably, Operation Bodenplatte created itchy fingers among the American flak crews in the liberated territories, and any aircraft coming within range over the ensuing twenty-four hours were likely to receive a hot reception, irrespective of their nationality. Bomber Command operations went on throughout the day, and it was late afternoon when 152 Lancasters of 3 Group took off to return to the railway yards at Vohwinkel. The attack was successful, but on the way home over Namur in Belgium a number of aircraft were hit by American flak, and 115 Squadron's NG332 plunged to earth before S/L Miles and the other seven occupants could take to their parachutes. W/C Newton had been in the van of a twenty-one-strong contingent of 75 (NZ) Squadron Lancasters in ME321. It failed to return, having crashed in Holland, and he was killed along with the other seven men on board. He was replaced a few days later by the youthful W/C Baigent DFC*, who would see the squadron through to the end of hostilities. Born in 1923 he had earned his DFC with XV Squadron and the Bar with 115 Squadron. The Group contributed to a devastating raid on Nuremberg in company with 1, 6 and 8 Groups on the 2/3rd. Benzol plants at Dortmund and Castrop-Rauxel followed by daylight on the 3rd, and railway yards at Ludwigshafen on the 5th. An attack with 1 Group on the railway yards at Neuss on the 6/7th resulted in over 1,700 houses, nineteen industrial premises and twenty public buildings being destroyed or seriously damaged. The last major raid on Munich was mounted by 1, 3, 5, 6 and 8 Groups on the 7/8th, then 3 Group went alone to railway yards at Krefeld on the 11th, and left severe damage in that part of the town. Saarbrücken came next on the 13th, and this attack, too, appeared to be effective. Even so, 4, 6 and 8 Groups had another crack at it that night, and 3 Group returned on the 14th. Small-scale G-H raids on benzol plants at Bochum and Langendreer took place through complete cloud cover on the 15th, and similar conditions prevailed at Wanne-Eickel on the 16/17th, so that neither operation could be assessed. 1 and 3 Groups acted as the main force at Duisburg on the 22nd/23rd, for which 149 Squadron put up eleven Lancasters, and the Group ended the month with a G-H raid on the Gremberg railway yards at Cologne on the 28th, and the Uerdingen yards at Krefeld on the 29th. W/C Pickford was posted from 149 Squadron on this day, to be replaced with extreme brevity of tenure by W/C Kay DFC. W/C Wyatt departed 514 Squadron during the month and W/C Morgan MiD was installed as his successor to see the squadron through to the end of hostilities. W/C Boxer was posted from 161 Squadron to Bomber Command HQ during the second half of the month, and was succeeded by W/C Watson, who was promoted from his flight commander post with 138 Squadron. With the end of the war in sight 3 LFS was disbanded on the 31st.

3 Group was in action straight away in February, when 160 aircraft set off in the early afternoon of the 1st with Mönchengladbach as their destination. A main force drawn from 1, 3 and 6 Groups carried out the first major raid of the war on Wiesbaden through cloud on the 2/3rd, but most of the bombing found the mark, and 550 buildings were destroyed. The operation was costly for 3 Group, as two of its squadron commanders lost their lives. 90 Squadron's HK610 and PD336 collided near Bury St Edmunds shortly before 21.30 hours while outbound, and the former crashed, killing W/C Bannister and the seven others on board. Most records suggest that PD336 also went down, but in fact, it returned safely to base in the hands of F/O Harries with just one injured crew member. It proved to be only a temporary reprieve for this Lancaster, however, as it too would be lost in action seventeen days hence with the new commanding officer, W/C Dunham, on board. 149 Squadron's commanding officer, W/C Kay, was also killed on this, his first operation with the squadron just five days after being appointed to the post. The new commanding officer was W/C Chilton DFC, AFC, who would see the squadron through to the end of hostilities and beyond. He had formerly commanded 1678 Conversion Unit, and gained his DFC with 115 Squadron. To maintain the pressure on the oil industry, it was necessary to return to previous targets to undo any repairs, and the Hansa benzol plant at Dortmund provided the objective for a raid by the Group on

the 3/4th, on this occasion without success. The oil refinery at Wanne-Eickel likewise escaped damage on the 7th, when bad weather intervened and scattered the force. There was a similarly disappointing outcome at the Hohenbudberg railway yards at Krefeld on the 8/9th, after which, a lull in operations preceded one of the most controversial operations of the war.

The Churchill inspired series of attacks on Germany's eastern cities under Operation Thunderclap began at Dresden on the 13/14th, and was a two phase affair opened by 5 Group, employing its low level visual marking technique. A layer of cloud hampered the Mosquito marker force, but 244 Lancasters delivered over 800 tons of bombs, and started fires, which gained a hold and acted as a beacon to the 529 Lancasters of 1, 3, 6 and 8 Groups following three hours behind. By the time that the Pathfinders arrived over the city, the skies were clear, and a further 1,800 tons of bombs rained down onto this beautiful and historic centre of culture. It triggered the same chain of events, which had so devastated parts of Hamburg over eighteen months earlier, and a firestorm erupted of unimaginable fury. The city's population had been swelled by tens of thousands of refugees fleeing from the eastern front, and some of these were among the staggering number of people killed. A figure of 35,000 has been settled upon in recent years, although some believe the number to be substantially higher. On the following morning, the hapless inhabitants were subjected to a raid by American bombers, during which, escort fighters are alleged to have strafed the streets and open places where the survivors were sheltering, but this is unlikely. It was this operation more than any other, which unjustly earned Harris the hatred of German people. The operation was not his initiative, he had no interest in carrying it out, and he had to be pressed by Portal, the CAS, before he gave in. Over 700 aircraft were involved in a similar two phase operation aimed at Chemnitz twenty-four hours later, with 4 Group substituting for 5 Group, which was active elsewhere. Complete cloud cover and the use of skymarking led to a scattered raid, and much of the bombing fell into open country.

The town of Wesel lay close to the ground action, and was to suffer a merciless pounding over the ensuing five weeks, beginning on the 16th, with a raid by 100 Lancasters of 3 Group. It was attacked again on the 17th by 4 and 6 Groups, and on the 18th and 19th by 3 Group using G-H through cloud. This last operation was led by 90 Squadron's new commanding officer, W/C Dunham, flying in the previously mentioned PD336. On the final run-in to the target with bomb doors open the Lancaster received a direct hit by flak and disintegrated, killing all on board, and forcing the following gaggle to fly through the debris. This was the only aircraft to be lost from the operation. W/C Scott became the new commanding officer on the 26th, and he would see the squadron through to the end of hostilities. The southern half of Dortmund was subjected to a heavy raid by 1, 3, 6 and 8 Groups on the 20/21st, and Duisburg's turn came on the following night at the hands of 1, 6 and 8 Groups. Oil refineries at Gelsenkirchen and Osterfeld occupied the Group by daylight on the 22nd, and a return was made to the former on the 23rd, to attack the Alma Pluto benzol plant. The night of the 21/22nd was one of high activity emanating from Tempsford. A Hudson failed to return from a SIS operation, and on board was W/C Watson, the recently appointed commanding officer. He was one of two fatalities, and there is a suggestion that he died while in captivity. Watson had been awarded a DFM for service with 149 Squadron in 1942, and rose from Flight Sergeant to Wing Commander in just two years. He was succeeded at 161 Squadron by W/C Brogan, who was posted across from 138 Squadron, where he had been a flight commander. An attempt by 4, 6 and 8 Groups to destroy the oil refinery at Bergkamen on the 24th led to heavy damage in the nearby town of Kamen, and 3 Group was sent there on the following day to attack the site again by G-H. On the 25th it was the Hoesch benzol plant at Dortmund, on the 27th, the Alma Pluto plant at Gelsenkirchen again, and on the 28th, the Nordstern plant at the same location.

Mannheim received its final raid of the war on the 1st of March, while a 3 Group force returned to Kamen. Cologne was attacked for the last time on the morning of the 2nd, in what was planned as a two phase assault involving over 800 aircraft. The intention was for 155 Lancasters of 3 Group to follow a 700 strong opening assault, but the failure of a G-H station in England all but cancelled out the 3 Group effort. Despite this minor setback, the city was left in a state of paralysis, and was taken by American forces four days later. G-H attacks were carried out on oil targets at Wanne-Eickel and Gelsenkirchen on the 4th and 5th respectively. The night of the 4/5th brought the loss of another 161 Squadron commanding officer within weeks of his appointment. W/C Brogan's Stirling went down in the sea off Denmark without survivors, by which time he had completed at least fifty-eight sorties beginning back in the autumn of 1941 with 149 Squadron. W/C Len Ratcliff was Wing Commander Operations at Tempsford when the news of Brogan's loss was announced, and he was appointed to command 161 Squadron. Happily, he would remain in post until the end of hostilities. That night Operation Thunderclap returned to Chemnitz, where central and southern districts were left in flames. On the 6th a 3 Group force went to Salzbergen to attack the Wintershall oil refinery, and maintained the pressure on Wesel that night. 1, 3, 6 and 8 Groups delivered the only raid of the war on Dessau on the 7/8th, and on the 9th the Group went alone to Datteln to carry out a G-H attack on the Emscher Lippe benzol plant. This was the day 161 Squadron departed Bomber Command for a permanent posting to 38 Group.

The end had now arrived for 138 Squadron's illustrious career in clandestine operations, and a new role beckoned. As the Nazi sphere of influence shrank by the day, the requirement for SOE and SIS operations diminished accordingly, and could no longer support two squadrons. The 138 Squadron crews approaching the end of their tours were posted to 161 Squadron, while the remainder were packed off to 1662 HCU at Lindholme for conversion onto Lancasters. It had been decided that 138 Squadron would end the war as a standard 3 Group front-line bomber unit, and on the 10th it took up residence at Tuddenham, where it would share the facilities with 90 Squadron. Working up to operational status would now occupy almost the remainder of the month, and the squadron was sidelined, therefore, during some notable occasions.

An all-time record was set on the 11th, when 1,079 aircraft took off in the late morning to deliver the final raid of the war on Essen. The record stood for a little over twenty-four hours, and was surpassed, when 1,108 aircraft departed their stations in the early afternoon of the 12th, to attack Dortmund for the last time. Benzol plants at Datteln and Hattingen kept elements from the Group busy on the 14th, and similar targets and railway yards saw the squadron through to the end of the month. W/C Hancock assumed command of 186 Squadron on the 16th as successor to W/C Giles DFC, who was posted to RAF Staff College. 3 Group sent 160 Lancasters to attack railway yards at Münster on the 21st, along with a nearby railway viaduct, and all three of those missing belonged to 75 (NZ) Squadron. On the 28th briefing took place for three 138 Squadron crews to fly the squadron's first operational sorties from Tuddenham. According to the Operations Record Book they would fly with 90 Squadron as part of a 3 Group G-H raid on the Hermann Goering iron works at Hallendorf. In the event the operation was postponed and rescheduled for the 29th, when an operation did take place, but it is believed, that the target was more likely the Hermann Goering benzol plant at Salzgitter near Brunswick. The 138 Squadron crews, those of F/O Liddell in NF966, F/O Horsaman in HK606 and P/O Brand in NG409, all returned safely having bombed with the leader or on instruments. The A Flight commander, S/L Sephton, was posted out as tour expired on this day, and he was replaced by S/L Stanton from 149 Squadron.

April would bring an end to the bombing war for the heavy brigade, but the pressure on Germany's oil industry and communications was maintained for the first half of the month. 3 and 6 Groups provided the main force for a raid on the synthetic oil refinery at Leuna on the 4/5th, and 1 and 3 Groups performed a similar role at Kiel on the 9/10th. The Deutsche Werke U-Boat yards were severely damaged and other shipyards hit, while the pocket battleship *Admiral Scheer* capsized. The final area bombing raid of the war was delivered on Potsdam by 1, 3 and 8 Groups on the 14/15th, the first time since March 1944 that RAF heavy bombers had operated within the Berlin defence zone, and a proportion of the attack spilled over into the capital. Over 900 aircraft pulverized the island of Heligoland by daylight on the 18th, and left it looking like a moonscape. The honour of conducting the very last attack on an oil related target fell to 3 Group on the 20th, and this involved a long round trip to Regensburg by 100 Lancasters. The objective was a fuel storage depot, and it was effectively dealt with for the loss of just one aircraft. Two days ahead of an attack by the British XXX Corps, the south-eastern suburbs of Bremen were bombed by 1, 3, 6 and 8 Groups, and this was the last major activity of the war for 3 Group. 149 Squadron's commanding officer, W/C Chilton, was awarded the DSO for this operation.

W/C Burnside handed command of 195 Squadron to W/C Cairnes on the 25th, on the morning of which the other Groups concluded Bomber Command's heavy offensives by raiding the SS barracks at Hitler's Eaglesnest retreat at Berchtesgaden. Later in the day heavy gun emplacements were targeted on the island of Wangerooge to clear a path through to the north German ports. That night 5 Group attacked a refinery at Tonsberg in Norway, and then it was all over. Having spent just a month as a flight commander at 138 Squadron, Harley Stanton was promoted to Wing Commander and posted to command 115 Squadron on the 27th as successor to W/C Shaw. From the 29th 3 Group participated in the humanitarian Operation Manna, to drop food to the starving Dutch people still under German occupation, and in May began to ferry PoWs back to Britain as part of Operation Exodus.

A final word by Steve Smith
'Niet zonder arbyt' ('Nothing without labour')

As World War II and the bomber offensive came to an end, it would be entirely appropriate for the surviving members of 3 Group to look back at their achievements with a great deal of pride and satisfaction. None of the other bomber Groups had been through so many changes in roles and directions during the long and bitter conflict. Whatever role was handed down to it, the Group, or more accurately, the men and women who served it, rose to the challenge and on numerous occasions exceeded the expectations placed upon them by their masters.

At the forefront of operations from the very outset of hostilities, the squadrons of 3 Group participated in every campaign undertaken by RAF Bomber Command between 1939 and 1942, and incurred grievous losses for their pains in both men and aircraft. The Group's Wellingtons were active within hours of the declaration of war. During December 1939, the vulnerability of the poorly armed Vickers Wellington was tragically realised by both Group and Bomber Command HQ after savage encounters with German Bf109s and 110s over Northern Germany. It was the 'heavies' of 3 Group accompanied by the Whitley, which equipped 4 Group, that enabled Bomber Command to take the war to the heart of Nazi Germany throughout 1940–1941. They suffered considerable losses in experienced pre-war crews. In 1941 alone the Group lost 382 aircraft on operations, which was more than any other Group.

The year 1942 was the most important year in the Group's history. During this year, it provided over a quarter of the bombers sent on the first 1,000-bomber raid on Cologne on 30th of May 1942 for Operation Millennium. By August 1942 3 Group had expanded to fourteen front-line squadrons, a total it would never surpass, and its contribution in terms of operational sorties and tonnage dropped was unparalleled at that point during the war. The contribution is reflected in the fact that the Group lost more aircraft than any other Bomber Command Group during 1942, totalling over 500 aircraft and crews lost. The Group also carried out experiments in secret over the Isle of Man in 1942 with target flares, the results of which helped to define the role and tactics of the Pathfinder Force.

August and September would see the Group's strength almost halved when 7 Squadron, 156 Squadron, and 109 Squadron were posted out en-masse to help form the new Pathfinder Force. However, the year would bring a change in command, when after a brief spell as acting AOC-in-C Bomber Command, Air Vice Marshall Baldwin was replaced in September by Air Commodore Sir Ralph Cochrane. Cochrane's presence was immediately felt throughout the Group. Initially critical of the Group's performance with regard to service-ability, Cochrane and his staff set about getting the very best out of each of the Squadrons, and by February 1943 the evidence suggested that he had succeeded. Sir Ralph Cochrane's forthright approach and his tireless striving for operational perfection instilled a sense of pride in the weary aircrews and ground staff of the Group.

February 1943 witnessed the departure of Air Commodore Cochrane to command 5 Group, and his replacement was Air Vice Marshall Richard Harrison. The appointment of Harrison as AOC 3 Group was not a simple one. Prior to Baldwin's departure it was originally considered that the Group should be commanded by Harris's Deputy, Air Vice Marshal Saundby. Harris was opposed to the loss of his long-standing friend and right hand man, however he let Saundby decide, and his answer was 'no'. Saundby wanted to continue to serve with Harris. Harris and Air Chief Marshall Portal then considered Air Vice Marshal H P Lloyd, but by Lloyd's own admission he had gone 'maritime'.

The previous year, in a letter dated 5th of July 1942 to Portal, Harris wrote. 'Alternatively, Harrison my Deputy SASO, would entirely suite me as AOC 3 Group. He is a fine commander, though rather junior. He would be the first AOC in this war with personal operational experience of the war, and that in itself has many attractions ...'

The year 1943 would also see the decline of the Short Sterling's contri-bution toward the bomber offensive as its value as a front line bomber became questionable. Beset by numerous mechanical problems and burdened by design specifications set by the Air Ministry in 1936 which severely limited its operational ceiling, the Stirling was, by the start of 1943, struggling when compared to her more able sister 'heavies' the Halifax and Lancaster.

A letter from ACM Sir Arthur Harris, C in C Bomber Command, to the Secretary of State for Air, Sir Archibald Sinclair, sums up the despair felt at HQ Bomber Command and by Harris in particular:

> ... The Stirling and the Halifax are now our major worries. They presage disaster unless solutions are found. I understand that the Stirling is to go in favour of the Lancaster as fast as the changeover can be achieved. The

Stirling Group has now virtually collapsed. They make no worthwhile contribution to our war effort in return for their overheads. They are at half strength, and serviceability is such that in spite of the much-reduced operational rate and long periods of complete idleness due to weather I am lucky if I can raise 30 Stirling's from No. 3 Group for one night's work after doing a week of nothing, or 20 the night after. There should be a wholesale sacking of the incompetents who have turned out approximately 50% rogue aircraft from Short and Harland's, Belfast and Austin's, not forgetting the supervisors responsible at the parent firm. Much the same applies to the Halifax issue, nothing ponderable is being done to make this deplorable product worthy for war or fit to meet those jeopardises, which confront our gallant crews....

Undaunted, the Group continued the offensive. Throughout the successful Ruhr campaign in the spring of 1943, the Group flew 4,585 sorties and dropped 11,469 tons of bombs losing only 150 aircraft and crews. A series of devastating attacks on Hamburg during July and August 1943 were followed by the raid on the experimental rocket facility at Peenemünde while the contribution in numbers of aircraft dispatched was gradually dwindling.

Throughout the summer of 1943 it became increasingly apparent that the losses suffered by the Stirling-equipped squadrons were critical. A steady increase in operational losses and early returns during this period forced Bomber Command HQ and 3 Group to redeploy the squadrons to less distant targets. From November onwards the Stirling's fate had been decided – it had to be replaced. In the interim it was decided that the Stirlings should be used to attack targets in the occupied territories and step-up its mine-laying capability.

In early 1944, Group aircraft were occasionally used in the SOE supply-dropping role to supplement the Group's two established SOE squadron's, 138 and 161. Utilising the Stirling's superb low-level manoeuvrability, various front line squadrons were actively involved in the clandestine supply-dropping role.

Nos 138 and 161 Squadrons were the only units in the whole of Bomber Command to be tasked solely with this essential cloak and dagger work. Like the squadrons of 38 Group, they suffered grievous losses in both men and aircraft. Such was the strict secrecy that surrounded these operations and it was not until recently that the Group's contribution was in part realised.

During this relative period of inactivity, the Lancaster equipped units, XV, 115, 514 and 622 Squadrons continued to operate throughout the late summer and winter of 1943, and through the bloody and costly Berlin campaign. The period between November 1943 and June 1944 was perhaps the Group's lowest point throughout the war. Its contribution to the bomber offensive was, when compared to the other Groups, minimal. The Group's ability to adapt and continue to operate especially with the Stirling is a testament to the Group and all those who served within it. Not only did it continue to operate, but the Group was at the forefront of a new era in bombing techniques.

It was not until all the squadrons in the Group had finally converted to the Lancaster in mid-1944 that they once again took their rightful place in the Command's order of battle. A combination of factors decided the future role of the Group, a role that would see it attack, mark, and bomb targets independently of the other Groups. Firstly, the superlative Lancaster and the relatively new and accurate blind bombing aid G-H, provided the tools, and secondly, the attacks on the less than glamorous targets in France, Holland and Belgium equipped the crews with the 'know how'. Targets such as railway yards, communication centres and 'noball' sites (V1 Launch sites) were frequently attacked by the Group in early 1944, while the Lancaster and Halifax Groups continued to attack targets in Germany prior to the onset of the Transportation Plan in April 1944.

Between late 1943 and D-Day in 1944, the Group's Stirling squadrons were assigned targets mostly situated close to towns and cities in the occupied territories. Accuracy while attacking these targets was a necessity. The possibility of innocent civilians being killed due to inaccurate Allied bombing was an ever-present danger during these operations and the Group took every reasonable precaution to avoid civilian deaths. The lower than average losses suffered by the Group during this period meant that within its ranks there was a high number of officers and men with considerable operational experience – this experience would be used to the fullest from the late summer of 1944 onwards.

From October 1944 the Group independently attacked a variety of targets by day and night. The decision to equip the Group with G-H in late 1943 was a fortuitous one, and the first G-H operation was carried out on the night of the 3/4th of November 1943 against the Mannesmannrohrenwerkes, situated on the outskirts of Düsseldorf. The attack carried out by the Lancaster equipped 115 and 514 Squadrons was a complete success. This success was however short lived, as G-H was hastily withdrawn on the orders of Harris on the grounds that there were insufficient sets available and that until the appropriate time, no further operations would be undertaken with this equipment over occupied Europe. The other and perhaps more far reaching reason was the ever-present danger that such a valuable piece of equipment could fall into the hands of the Germans, allowing them to create a counter-measure and thus thwarting its true potential from the outset. It was reintroduced to the Group's aircraft from early 1944, but predominantly to assist minelaying operations. It would be much later in 1944 before the Group would re-equip on a large scale with G-H and use it against large German targets.

On 18th of October 1944, 128 Lancaster's drawn from nine squadrons carried out the Group's first independent 'G-H' bombing raid. The attack, carried out in daylight was directed against the German town of Bonn and was a complete success. The reason for the choice of Bonn was simple, it had until then received relatively little damage from bombing, and as a result of this raid the core of Bonn was burnt out and destroyed. Throughout the next seven months, raids were carried out almost daily against Germany's railway networks, marshalling yards, synthetic oil and benzyl installations, and communication networks. All of these targets received extensive damage due to the accuracy of 'G-H'.

Not only did the 'G-H' equipped Lancasters of the Group mark and attack their own targets independently of both 5 Group and 8 Group, but they would also often lead other bomber Groups. Unlike other Groups that were restricted by bad visibility, 10/10th cloud cover over the target area did not cause any unnecessary problems, as visual identification was not required with 'G-H'. Especially trained 'G-H' Leader crews would bomb on their equipment and the following gaggle would instantly release the G-H crew bombed, and the results were often accurate and impressive.

The Group's last bombing operation of the Second World War was carried out on the 24th of April 1945 when 107 Lancasters drawn from 31 Base and 33 Base attacked the railway yards located at Bad Oldesloe. No aircraft were lost. This was not quite the end however, as on the night of the 3–4th of May 1945, 15 Squadron, 622 Squadron, 90 Squadron, and 75 (NZ) Squadron dispatched a total of twelve aircraft to mine the waters off the Kattegat, but this operation was cancelled soon after take-off.

So ended 3 Group's war. This was a war where the tireless men and women who served in this Group were able to accept and overcome any task, and any aircraft. Their determination and spirit was unrivalled, thus honouring their Group motto 'Niet zonder arbyt' ('Nothing without labour').

CHAPTER TWO

Quick Reference Facts, Figures and General Information

AIR OFFICERS COMMANDING

Air Vice Marshal	J E A Baldwin	22.08.39 to 14.09.42
Air Vice Marshal	The Hon. R A Cochrane	14.09.42 to 27.02.43
Air Vice Marshal	R Harrison	27.02.43

OPERATIONAL STATIONS

Alconbury	Honington	Ridgewell
Bourn	Lakenheath	Stradishall
Chedburgh	Little Snoring	Tempsford
Downham Market	Marham	Tuddenham
East Wretham	Mepal	Waterbeach
Feltwell	Methwold	Witchford
Foulsham	Mildenhall	Woolfox Lodge
Gransden Lodge	Newmarket	Wratting Common (West Wickham)
Graveley	Oakington	Wyton

AIRCRAFT TYPES

Wellington	Stirling	Lancaster	Whitley (SD)
Halifax (SD)	Liberator (SD)	Hudson (SD)	Havoc (SD)
Ventura (SD)	Lysander (SD)	Mosquito (SD)	

GROUP STRENGTH

As of September 1939

Operational Squadrons
9, 37, 38, 99, 115, 149

Non-operational Squadrons
214, 215

GROUP STRENGTH

As of April 1945

Operational Squadrons
XV, 75 (NZ), 90, 115, 138, 149, 186, 195, 218, 514, 622

Quick Reference Station/Squadron

Alconbury	40, 156
Bourn	XV, 101
Chedburgh	214, 218, 620
Downham Market	214, 218, 623
East Wretham	115, 311
Feltwell	37, 57, 75 (NZ), 192
Foulsham	514
Gransden Lodge	192
Graveley	161
Honington	9, 214, 311
Lakenheath	149
Little Snoring	115
Marham	38, 109, 115, 218
Mepal	75 (NZ)
Methwold	149, 214, 218
Mildenhall	XV, 75 (NZ), 115, 149, 419, 622
Newmarket	75, 99, 138, 161
Oakington	7, 101
Ridgewell	90
Stradishall	101, 138, 186, 214
Tempsford	138, 161
Tuddenham	90, 138, 186
Waterbeach	99, 514
Witchford	115, 195, 196
Woolfox Lodge	218
Wratting Common (West Wickham)	90, 195
Wyton	XV, 40, 57, 109

Quick Reference Station/Squadron Dates

Alconbury	40	01.02.41 to 14.02.42
	156	14.02.42 to 15.08.42
Bourn	101	11.02.42 to 11.08.42
	XV	14.08.42 to 14.04.43
Chedburgh	214	01.10.42 to 17.06.43
	214, 620	17.06.43 to 23.11.43
	214	23.11.43 to 10.12.43
	218	05.12.44 to 10.08.45
Downham Market	218	07.07.42 to 10.08.43
	218, 623	10.08.43 to 06.12.43
	218, 214	10.12.43 to 16.01.44
	218	16.01.44 to 07.03.44
East Wretham	311	16.09.40 to 28.04.42
	115	08.11.42 to 06.08.43
Feltwell	37	26.04.37 to 04.09.39
	37, 75	04.09.39 to 04.04.40
	37, 75 (NZ)	04.04.40 to 15.08.40
	37	15.08.40 to 12.11.40
	57	20.11.40 to 01.01.41
	57, 75 (NZ)	01.01.41 to 05.01.42
	75 (NZ)	05.01.42 to 01.11.42
	192	05.04.43 to 25.11.43

Warriors of the Night
3 Group's stalwarts, the Vickers Wellington and Short Stirling, captured in the early evening sun, *circa* 1942.

Wing Commander Griffiths, DF
Wing Commander John Francis Griffiths DFC, commanding office of 99 Squadron, standing beside one of the squadron's Vickers Wellington Mk.IA. Canadian-bor Griffiths was awarded the DFC i recognition of his leadership qualities during the operation of December 1939. He was tragically killed in a road accident on the 9 of May 1945.

Wing Commander Kellett DFC, AFC
34-year-old Wing Commander Richard Kellett DFC AFC Commanding Officer of 149 Squadron. Kellett commanded the squadron from January 1939 until May 1940. He was shot down and taken Prisoner of War while flying as a second pilot on a raid on Tobruk, 13/14th September 1942. At the time he was a Group Captain serving as SASO 205 Group.

Air-Vice Marshall J.E. Baldwin, KBE,CB DSO DL
Seen here with Air Chief Marshal Sir Edgar Ludlow Hewitt, Air Officer Commanding-in-Chief, Bomber Command. AVM 'Jack' Baldwin commanded 3 Group from the 28th of August 1939 to the 14th of September 1942. Initially opposed to the formation of the Pathfinder Force, Baldwin reluctantly transferred two of his front line bomber squadrons, 7 and 156 and the Special Duties Squadron, 109. Baldwin took temporary command of RAF Bomber Command after the sacking of Air Marshall Sir Richard Peirse in 1942.

Wing Commander 'Moose' Fulton DSO DFC AFC

Born in Kamloops, British Columbia on the 4th of November 1912, Fulton began his military career as a trooper in the British Columbia Hussars. Appointed acting pilot officer on probation in 1935 Fulton spent his early wartime career with the Instrument Armament Defence Flight, Experimental Section. He flew operationally with 99 and 311 (Czechoslovak) Squadron, finally assuming command of 419 RCAF Squadron on the 21st of December 1941.

161 Squadron Pilots

A rather informal gathering of some of 161 Squadron's personalities, in the garden of the 'Cottage' Tangmere. From left to right: Flying Officer J.A. McCairns DFC, Squadron Leader H. Verity DFC, Group Captain Pickard DSO DFC commanding officer, Flight Commander P. Vaughan-Fowler DFC and Flying Officer F. 'Bunny' Rymills DFC DFM. Also in attendance Pickard's dog Ming, and Rymills' spaniel, Henry.

Air Vice Marshall R. Harrison CB CBE DFC AFC
Commanding Officer 3 Group from February 1943. Harrison was an experienced front line officer who had previously served as SASO HQ 1 Group and SASO HQ Bomber Command as Harris' deputy. Harris had this to say about his former deputy, 'the first AOC in this war with personal operational experience, and that in itself has many attractions'.

Wing Commander 'Jack' Little DFC
Wing Commander Little was a distinguished airman and athlete, playing cricket and rugby at county level. He was also a vibrant Christian. He 'failed to return' from the 31st of August raid on Berlin when accompanying a recently posted 623 Squadron crew.

Flying Officer John Basten RAFVR
Flying Officer Basten arrived on 218 (Gold Coast) Squadron on the 11th of June 1943, as bomber aimer to Sergeant Collingswood. The crew's first operation was a Gardening trip on the 23rd of June, tragically Collingswood FTR from a 2nd Dickie flight the next night. The pilotless crew were split up; Basten did not operate again until the 23rd of August 1943 when he volunteered to operate with Squadron Leader Hiles DSO DFC against Berlin; he failed to return.

218 (Gold Coast) Squadron Vickers Wellington.
Sir Alan Burns, Governor Designate of the Gold Coast with Squadron Leader Clyde-Smith, photographed during the former's visit to the squadron, soon after the formal adoption of the squadron by the peoples of the Gold Coast.

Cloak and Dagger Squadrons
Senior officers of RAF Tempsford. Wing Commander E. ('Mouse') Fielding DFC AFC, Officer Commanding 161 Squadron, and former captain of the King's Flight. Group Captain A.H. McDonald, Station Commander Tempsford, and Wing Commander R. Hockey, Commanding Officer 138 Squadron.

Wing Commander M.F.B. Read RAF

Wing Commander Read's role as Squadron Commander of 218 Squadron, lasted exactly one month before he met his death over the Danish Coast on the night of the 2nd of October 1942. 30-year-old Canadian Read, joined the RAF in 1933 and graduated from Royal Air Force College, Cranwell, in September 1933. He served with various squadrons pre-war, including 83 and 99 (Bomber) Squadrons, and was seconded to the American Legation based in Cairo, Egypt.

Wing Commander C.H. Baigent DFC & Bar

One of New Zealand's most decorated and outstanding bomber pilots was born in Ashburton New Zealand on the 16th of January 1923. Baigent volunteered for the RNZAF when he was 17. When still at the Victoria University College, too young to join up, he took flying lessons at the Wellington Aero Club. His operational career with Bomber Command would see him operate with 15 and 115 Squadrons before assuming command of 75 (NZ) Squadron in January 1945. At 21 he was Bomber Command's youngest squadron commander.

Flight Lieutenant A. Humphreys DFC

Flight Lieutenant Arthur Humphreys had, before his loss on the 18th of May 1942, flown 26 operations with 218 Squadron. The award of the DFC was in recognition of his flying ability in evading a persistent night fighter, while returning to Lubeck on the 28th of March 1942.

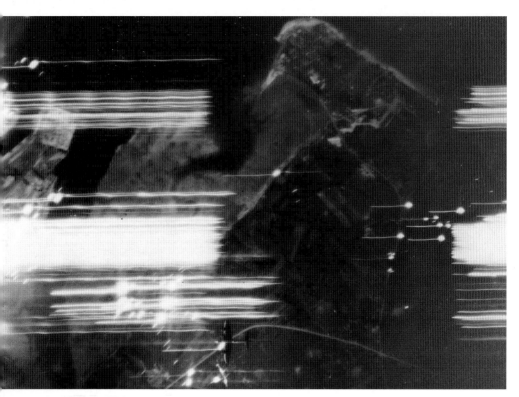

Stirling Over Lorient

This vertical photograph, graphically illustrates the dangers the low flying Short Stirling crews of the group encountered night after night from friendly bombs dropped from above. An unidentified Short Stirling passes over the German submarine base at Keroman (top) during RAF Bomber Command's heaviest raid on the U-Boat pens at Lorient, France 13/14 February 1943.

Unidentified Short Stirling of No. 1651 Conversion Unit being salvaged after crash landing at RAF Waterbeach circa 1942. *(Author's collection via Bob Collins)*

Flight Sergeant Aaron's Short Stirling at Bone Aerodrome
Flight Sergeant Aaron's Short Stirling after the tragic events unfolded on the Turin raid of 12 August. Ground personnel point to the bullet holes in the canopy. This is thought to be the only photograph of HA-O EF452.

Sting In The Tail
Manually operated rear turret of a 149 Squadron Wellington 1939.

The Queen of the Skies
With everything hanging, the mighty Short Stirling seen landing at an unidentified grass airfield, *circa* 1942.

Quiet Ulsterman
Squadron Leader R.A. Esler DSO DFC & Bar began his operational career with 149 Squadron on the 29th of October 1940. His first tour of 32 operations ended on the 30th of April 1941. He commenced his second tour with 109 Squadron Marham on the 3rd of February 1944. His pilot was F/Lt Robert Palmer with whom he flew unprecedented 74 consecutive operations. Esler completed a further 5 operations bringing his wartime total to an impressive 112 operations.

Squadron Leader Jeff Rothwell DFC & Bar
One of 3 Group's characters, Jeff had a long and distinguished association with the group which began in 1940 with 99 Squadron. He subsequently operated with 75 (NZ) and 218 (Gold Coast) Squadron where he completed his second tour. He was awarded a bar to his DFC in September 1943. He was shot down near Texel and made a PoW while operational with 138 (SD) Squadron on the 8/9th of September 1944.

Mining Operation Planning 1944.
Air Vice Marshall R. Harrison CB CBE DFC AFC and two of his squadron commanders, Wing Commander J.H. Giles DFC and Wing Commander W.J. Burnett DFC, preparing for a mining operation, *circa* 1944. Also in attendance is 3 Group's SASO Air Commodore H. Kirkpatrick DFC.

No. 1657 Heavy Conversion Unit Stirling
Flying Officer John Harris and crew pose beside a 1657 C.U. Short Stirling at RAF Stradishall in February 1943, just prior to their posting to 218 Squadron. Flying Officer Harris and crew failed to return from the 29th of March operation to Berlin.

Nuremburg Victim
The wreckage of Avro Lancaster Mk.II LL704 KO-H flown by Flight Sergeant Fogarty DFM. The victim of both flak and night-fighter, the abandoned aircraft crashed near Raidwangen, Germany. The crew were on their fourteenth operation. Fogarty was awarded an immediate DFM in recognition of his masterly handling of his Lancaster, on return from an attack on Brunswick when severely mauled by a JU88. It was Fogarty's first operation on the Avro Lancaster.

Early Daylight Operations
A XV Squadron Short Stirlings escorted by Hawker Hurricanes while attacking the Five-Lille Steel Works on Saturday, 5 July 1941. The operation was led by XV Squadron's Commanding Officer, Wing Commander Menaul. (*Via M. Ford Jones Collection*)

Tea & Wag
Short Stirling M-Mike of 90 Squadron RAF Tuddenham 1944.

I.C.U. Prang

Short Stirling BK601 of 1657 Conversion Unit at rest at USAAF Bury St Edmunds (Rougham) 29 January 1944. The previous evening, pupil pilot Sergeant Lemoine and crew were briefed for circuit and landings training, during the course of which the Stirling swung violently and left the runway. BK601 was struck off charge.

149 Squadron Loss 1940.

Vickers Wellington OJ-J P9218 of 149 Squadron crash landed at Limfjorden, Denmark, after being hit by Flak. Flying Officer F.T. Knight and crew, spent the rest of the war as PoWs.

3 Group G-H Aircraft
To identify a GH equipped aircraft two horizontal yellow bars were painted onto the Lancaster's rudders. Here are two examples of GH equipped aircraft.

623 Squadron Short Stirling
Short Stirling Mk.III IC-E LJ454 flown by Flying Officer Bennett RAAF the victim of barrage flak over Mannheim on the raid of the 18th of November 1943. The crew, on their fifth operation, all survived to become Prisoners of War.

Wing Commander Speare DSO DFC & Bar
Wing Commander 'Dickie' Speare assumed command of 138 (SD) Squadron on the 25th of May 1943. He undertook his first operation as Commanding Officer on 20/21st June 1943, delivering supplies to the code area PHYSICIAN 70 and 50. Tragically, Speare was killed in an accident while flying an Avro Anson on the 23rd of November 1945. He is buried in Bournemouth North Cemetery.

Group Captain H.J. Kirkpatrick CBE DFC MiD MA
Former member of the Oxford University Air Squadron, Kirkpatrick was granted a permanent commission in the RAF in February 1932. Pre-war, he occupied a number of staff jobs including the role of personnel assistant to the AOC RAF India. He assumed command of 218 Squadron on the 22nd of April 1941 were he was awarded the DFC. From March 1943 Kirkpatrick was S.A.S.O HQ, 3 Group.

Daylight over Le Havre
A 514 Squadron Lancaster, captured over the German fortified positions situated around the coastal town of Le Havre, 5th September 1944.

Bombing Up
A 500lb GP bomb hoisted upwards under the watchful gaze of a corporal armourer at RAF Marham, note the 115 Squadron Vickers Wellingtons dispersed.

Avro Lancaster Mk.B.I of 149 (East India) Squadron
A rare photo of TK coded machine of C Flight, 149 Squadron. This Vickers Armstrong built aircraft HK795 joined 149 Squadron on the 14th of February 1945; it was scraped on the 11th of November 1946. Note GH bars on rudder.

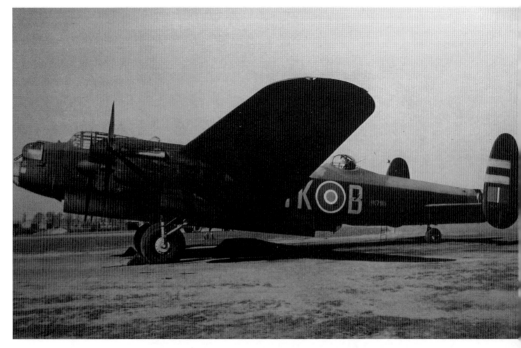

Foulsham	514	01.09.43 to 23.11.43
Gransden Lodge	192	14.01.43 to 05.04.43
Graveley	161	01.03.42 to 11.04.42
Honington	9	15.07.39 to 29.07.40
	9, 311	29.07.40 to 16.09.40
	9	16.09.40 to 05.01.42
	9, 214	05.01.42 to 12.01.42
	9	12.01.42 to 07.08.42
Lakenheath	149	12.04.37 to 06.04.42
	199	20.06.43 to 01.05.44
Little Snoring	115	06.08.43 to 26.11.43
Marham	38	05.05.37 to 15.06.37
	38, 115	15.06.37 to 22.11.40
	115	22.11.40 to 25.11.40
	115, 218	25.11.40 to 07.07.42
	115	07.07.42 to 24.09.42
Mepal	75 (NZ)	28.06.43 to 21.07.45
Methwold	214	03.09.39 to 12.02.40
	57	15.01.42 to 04.09.42
	14	15.05.44 to 04.08.44
	149, 218	04.08.44 to 05.12.44
	149	05.12.44 to 04.46
Mildenhall	99	15.11.34 to 12.04.37
	99, 149	12.04.37 to 09.09.39
	149	09.09.39 to 15.08.40
	149, 75 (NZ)	15.08.40 to 01.01.41
	149	01.01.41 to 15.12.41
	149, 419	15.12.41 to 06.04.42
	419	06.04.42 to 12.08.42
	115	24.09.42 to 08.11.42
	XV	14.04.43 to 10.08.43
	XV, 622	10.08.43 to 15.08.45
Newmarket	99	15.09.39 to 18.03.41
	1419Flt/138	22.05.41 to 12.41
	161	14.02.42 to 01.03.42
	75 (NZ)	01.11.42 to 01.03.42
Oakington	7	29.10.40 to 06.07.41
	7, 101	06.07.41 to 11.02.42
	7	11.02.42 to 24.07.45
Ridgewell	90	29.12.42 to 31.05.43
Stradishall	75	01.40 to 02.40
	214	12.02.40 to 19.10.40
	214, 419Flt/1419Flt/138	09.10.40 to 05.01.42
	138	05.01.42 to 12.01.42
	138, 214	12.01.42 to 14.03.42
	214	14.03.42 to 06.04.42
	214, 109	06.04.42 to 06.08.42
	214	06.08.42 to 11.08.42
	214, 101	11.08.42 to 22.09.42
	214	22.09.42 to 01.10.42
	186	17.12.44 to 17.07.45
Tempsford	109	19.01.42 to 14.03.42
	109, 138	14.03.42 to 06.04.42
	138	06.04.42 to 11.04.42
	138, 161	11.04.42 to 09.03.45
	161	09.03.45 to 02.06.45

Tuddenham	90	13.10.43 to 17.12.44
	90, 186	17.12.44 to 09.03.45
	90, 186, 138	09.03.45 to 17.07.45
Waterbeach	99	18.03.41 to 19.03.42
	514	23.11.43 to 22.08.45
Witchford	196	19.07.43 to 18.11.43
	115	26.11.43 to 01.10.44
	115, 195	01.10.44 to 13.11.44
	115	13.11.44 to 28.09.45
Woolfox Lodge	218	07.03.44 to 04.08.44
Wratting Common	90	31.05.43 to 13.10.43
(West Wickham)	195	13.11.44 to 14.08.45
Wyton	40	02.12.39 to 10.12.39
	40, XV	10.12.39 to 01.11.40
	40, XV, 57	01.11.40 to 20.11.40
	40, XV	20.11.40 to 01.02.41
	XV	01.02.41 to 06.08.42
	XV, 109	06.08.42 to 14.08.42

QUICK REFERENCE AIRCRAFT/SQUADRON
(New types)
7 Squadron

Stirling	First received		01.08.40
	First operation	Rotterdam	10.02.41

XV Squadron

Wellington	First received	N2871	07.11.40
	First operation	Antwerp	20.12.40
	Last operation	Hamburg	16.05.41
Stirling	First operation	Kiel	30.04.41
	Last operation	Cherbourg	22.12.43
Lancaster	First operation	Brunswick	14.01.44

75 (NZ) Squadron

Wellington	Last operation	Mining	25.10.42
Stirling	First operation	Turin	20.11.42
	Last operation	Mining	23.04.44
Lancaster	First received		13.03.44
	First operation	Villeneuve-St-Georges	09.04.44

90 Squadron

Stirling	First received		01.12.42
	First operation	Mining	08.01.43
	Last operation	Special duties	07.06.44
Lancaster	First operation	Dreux	10.06.44

115 Squadron

Wellington	Last operation	Essen	12.03.43
Lancaster	First operation	Mining	20.03.43

138 Squadron

Lancaster	First operation	Hallendorf	07.05.45

149 Squadron

Wellington	Last operation	Emden	26.11.41
Stirling	First operation	Ostend	26.11.41
Lancaster	First received		25.08.44
	First operation	Boulogne	17.09.44

186 Squadron

Lancaster	First received		16.10.44
	First operation	Bonn	18.10.44

195 Squadron

Lancaster	First received		01.10.44
	First operation	Leverkusen	26.10.44

196 Squadron

Stirling	First received		22.07.43
	First operation	Air Sea Rescue	24.08.43
	Last operation	Mining	26.10.43

199 Squadron

Stirling	First operation	Air Sea Rescue	27.07.43
	Last operation	Air Sea Rescue	25.04.44

214 Squadron

Wellington	Last operation	Kiel	29.04.42
Stirling	First operation	Mining	18.05.42
	Last operation	Mining	23.01.44

218 Squadron

Wellington	Last operation	Mining	12.02.42
Stirling	First operation	Mining	12.02.42
	Last operation	V-1 site Dieppe	02.08.44
Lancaster	First operation	Fort D'Englos	09.08.44

514 Squadron

Lancaster	First operation	Düsseldorf	03.11.43

620 Squadron

Stirling	First received		17.06.43
	First operation	Le Creusot	19.06.43
	Last operation	Leverkusen	19.11.43

622 Squadron

Stirling	First operation	Nuremberg	10.08.43
	Last operation	Mining	20.12.43
Lancaster	First operation	Brunswick	14.01.44

623 Squadron

Stirling	First operation	Nuremberg	10.08.43
	Last operation	Mining	04.12.43

3 Group Sorties and Losses

Aircraft	Sorties	Losses
Wellington	20,584	608 (3.0%)
Stirling	15,895	577 (3.6%)
Lancaster	26,462	380 (1.4%)
Other (SOE/SIS/RCM)	3,672 (approx.)	103 (2.8%)
Total	66,613	1,668 (2.5%)

VCs

F/S R H Middleton (A)	149 Squadron	Turin	November 1942
F/S A L Aaron	218 Squadron	Turin	August 1943

Quick Reference Records
Bomber Command

Most sorties	75 (NZ) Squadron (8,017)
Highest aircraft losses	115 Squadron (208)
Most mining operations	149 Squadron (160)

3 Group

Most overall operations	75 (NZ) Squadron (739)
Most bombing operations	XV Squadron (606)
Most sorties	75 (NZ) Squadron (8,017)
Highest aircraft operational losses	115 Squadron (208)
Highest % losses	196 Squadron (6.7)

CHAPTER THREE

The Squadrons

7 SQUADRON

Motto: Per diem, per noctem (By day and by night)   Code MG

No. 7 Squadron carries the lowest number of any unit to serve with Bomber Command during the Second World War. It was formed on the 1st of May 1914, and after the outbreak of the Great War it operated as an experimental unit until April 1915, at which point it moved to France. Reconnaissance and artillery spotting duties over the Western Front saw the squadron through to the end of hostilities, but it was September 1919 before it returned to the UK, where disbandment took place on the last day of the year. No. 7 Squadron was re-formed on the 1st of June 1923 as a bomber unit operating chronologically Vimys, Virginias, Heyfords, Wellesleys, Whitleys and finally Hampdens. On the 1st of June 1939 the squadron took on a training role, and this continued for the first six months of Second World War. On the 4th of April 1940 the squadron merged with 76 Squadron to form 16 OTU, but was re-formed with Hampdens a month later only to be disbanded again. On the 1st of August 1940 came off the shelf again at Leeming to begin the work of preparing the new Stirling bomber for operational service. Thus began an illustrious career with 3 Group, which came to an end in August 1942 as the squadron became a founder member of the Pathfinder Force. No. 7 Squadron continued in this role for the remainder of the war, converting to Lancasters in mid 1943.

STATIONS

Leeming	01.08.40 to 29.10.40
Oakington	29.10.40 to 24.07.45

COMMANDING OFFICERS

Wing Commander P I Harris DFC	01.08.40 to 13.04.41
Wing Commander H R Graham DSO DFC	13.04.41 to 09.04.42
Wing Commander B D Sellick DFC	10.04.42 to 01.10.42

AIRCRAFT

Stirling I	08.40 to 07.43
To Pathfinder Force	15.08.42

OPERATIONAL RECORD

Stirling

Operations	Sorties	Aircraft Losses	% Losses
267	1,744	78	4.5

Category of Operations

Bombing	Mining
249	18

TABLE OF STATISTICS

(Heavy squadrons)

17th highest number of overall operations in Bomber Command.
26th highest number of sorties in Bomber Command.
15th highest number of aircraft operational losses in Bomber Command.
10th highest number of bombing operations in Bomber Command.
28th highest number of mining operations in Bomber Command.

Out of 13 Stirling squadrons

4th highest number of Stirling overall operations in Bomber Command.
6th highest number of Stirling sorties in Bomber Command.
4th highest number of Stirling operational losses in Bomber Command..

Out of 28 bomber squadrons in 3 Group

12th highest number of overall operations in 3 Group.
16th highest number of sorties in 3 Group.
13th highest number of aircraft operational losses in 3 Group.

Out of 12 Stirling bomber squadrons in 3 Group

7th highest number of Stirling overall operations in 3 Group.
7th highest number of Stirling sorties in 3 Group.
7th highest number of Stirling operational losses in 3 Group.

AIRCRAFT HISTORIES

Stirling	From August 1940.
N3636 MG-A	Damaged at Oakington and became ground instruction machine.
N3637 MG-K/G	From Ringway. To AFEE.
N3638	From AMDP. To 15 Sqn.
N3640	Crashed on landing at Hodder Bridge Lancashire having been damaged by friendly AA fire while training 29.9.40.
N3641 MG-D	To 26CF.
N3642 MG-E	To 15 Sqn.
N3643 MG-G	From A&AEE. Crashed in Suffolk following fire sustained during operation to Calais 24.3.41.
N3644 MG-H	To 15 Sqn.
N3652 MG-M	To 1651CU.
N3653	FTR Brest 3/4.3.41. First Stirling lost on operations.
N3655	To 1651CU.
N3663	FTR Berlin 2/3.8.41.
N3664 MG-Z	FTR Hamburg 29/30.6.41.
N3666 MG-Z	Crashed on landing at Newmarket on return from Duisburg 29.8.41.
N3668 MG-B	To 15 Sqn.
N3669 MG-H/E/D	To 26CF.
N3670	From 15 Sqn. To 101CF.
N3672 MG-M/U	To 26CF and back. U/C collapsed during landing at Oakington while training 14.1.42.
N3677 MG-J	FTR Berlin 7/8.11.41.
N3679 MG-D	Crash-landed at Newmarket on return from Essen 13.4.42.
N3680 MG-Y	From 149 Sqn. FTR Brest 18.12.41.
N3700 MG-A	To 26CF and back. To 218 Sqn.

N3701	Crashed on landing at Oakington on return from air-sea rescue search 2.12.41.
N3705 MG-R/F	FTR from mining Borkum area 15/16.8.42. Crash-landed, recovered by Germans and test flown.
N3706 MG-S	From 218 Sqn. FTR Bremen 29/30.6.42.
N3708 MG-E	From 218 Sqn. To 1657CU 12.8.42.
N3709 MG-S/K	From 218 Sqn. FTR Essen 26/27.3.42.
N3710 MG-M	From 218 Sqn. FTR Stuttgart 5/6.5.42.
N3716 MG-A	FTR Mannheim 19/20.5.42.
N3720	To 218 Sqn.
N3727 MG-G	FTR from mining sortie to the Heligoland area 27/28.4.42.
N3750	FTR Essen 1/2.6.42.
N3754 MG-O	FTR Bremen 25/26.6.42.
N3757	To 15 Sqn.
N3760 MG-D	To 1657CU
N3764 MG-J	To 15 Sqn and back. FTR Hamburg 9/10.11.42.
N3765	To 1657CU.
N6001	From A&AEE. FTR Hamburg 29/30.6.41.
N6003MG-V	To 26CF.
N6004	To 15 Sqn.
N6005	To 26CF.
N6006 MG-G	To 101CF.
N6007	From 15 Sqn. FTR Bremen 28.6.41.
N6009	Crash-landed in Essex on return from Cologne 20/21.4.41.
N6010	FTR Berlin 10/11.5.41.
N6011	FTR Berlin 9/10.4.41.
N6012	Crashed in Cambridgeshire on return from Hamburg 3.5.41.
N6013	FTR Borkum 1.7.41.
N6014	Crash-landed in Suffolk on return from Berlin 1.5.41.
N6017	FTR Chocques Power Station 10.7.41.
N6019	Crashed on take-off from Oakington while training 9.5.41.
N6020 MG-B	FTR Karlsruhe 25/26.8.41.
N6022 MG-D	Abandoned over Norfolk on return from Hanover 15.7.41.
N6023	From DGRD. To 26CF.
N6032 MG-T	To 26CF.
N6033	Crashed in Northampton on return from Hanover 15.7.41.
N6034	FTR Mazingarbe 8.7.41.
N6035 MG-A	FTR Berlin 25/26.7.41.
N6036 MG-Q	To 214CF.
N6037	To 26CF.
N6039 MG-L	To 101CF.
N6041	Crashed at Oakington on return from Magdeburg 15.8.41.
N6042	Damaged in landing accident at Graveley on return from Magdeburg 15.8.41.
N6046	FTR Berlin 7/8.9.41.
N6048	To 7CF.
N6049	To 26CF.
N6073 MG-Y	FTR Mannheim 19/20.5.42.
N6074 MG-G	Ditched off North Wales on return from St Nazaire 26.3.42.
N6075	To 101CF.
N6085 MG-H	Shot down near Bourn on return from Brest 3.10.41
N6087 MG-M/A	Crash-landed in Cambridgeshire on return from Brest 18.11.41.
N6089 MG-L	To 26CF.

N6090	To A&AEE and back. To 15CF.
N6091 MG-K	FTR Berlin 7/8.11.41.
N6094	From 149 Sqn. To 15 Sqn via 26CF
N6095 MG-K	From 149 Sqn. Damaged beyond repair during an operation to Brest 18.12.41.
N6104	From 149 Sqn via 26CF. To 1651CU.
N6120	Crashed while attempting to land at Oakington following early return from Soesterburg 17.1.42.
N6121	To 101CF.
N6128	To 26CF.
N6129	To 218 Sqn.
R9143	To 149 Sqn.
R9147	To 1651CU.
R9149 MG-S	FTR Munich 9/10.3.43.
R9150 MG-A/O	FTR Turin 29/30.11.42.
R9154 MG-F	FTR Duisburg 6/7.8.42.
R9156 MG-H/S	To 1665CU.
R9158	Crashed on landing at Manston on return from Nuremberg 29.8.42.
R9169 MG-Y	FTR Hamburg 9/10.11.42.
R9192	To 15 Sqn.
R9193	To 15 Sqn.
R9199 MG-F/T	FTR Duisburg 8/9.4.43.
R9249	From TFU. To 1657CU.
R9251	To 1657CU.
R9252	From TFU. To NTU.
R9255 MG-Q	From TFU. Crashed on landing at Oakington on return from Berlin 28.3.43.
R9257 MG-C/E	From TFU. To 1657CU.
R9258 MG-K	To 214 Sqn.
R9259 MG-J	FTR Mannheim 6/7.12.42.
R9260 MG-O	From TFU. Damaged on landing at Oakington after aborting operation to Hamburg (Operation Gomorrah) 3.8.43.
R9261 MG-M	FTR Stettin 20/21.4.43.
R9262	FTR Munich 21/22.12.42.
R9263 MG-D	From TFU. FTR Bocholt 30.4/1.5.43.
R9264	FTR Cologne 2/3.2.43.
R9266 MG-J	From TFU. FTR Krefeld 21/22.6.43.
R9267 MG-S	Crash-landed in Cambridgeshire while training 14.6.43.
R9270 MG-S/Q	From TFU. FTR Nuremberg 8/9.3.43.
R9272 MG-W	From TFU. FTR Krefeld 21/22.6.43.
R9273	From TFU. To 1657CU.
R9275 MG-Y	From TFU. FTR Frankfurt 10/11.4.43.
R9277 MG-P/T	To NTU.
R9278 MG-E	From TFU. FTR Stuttgart 14/15.4.43.
R9280 MG-E	To BDU.
R9281 MG-V	FTR Wuppertal-Elberfeld 24/25.6.43.
R9283 MG-Q	To 214 Sqn.
R9284	To 214 Sqn.
R9286 MG-C	FTR Munster 11/12.6.43.
R9288	To 214 Sqn.
R9289	To 214 Sqn.
R9295	To 149 Sqn.

R9296	To 149 Sqn.
R9297 MG-P	From 218 Sqn. To 1657CU via 7CF.
R9298	From 218 Sqn. To 1651CU.
R9300 MG-L	To 1657CU via 7CF.
R9301 MG-Q	To 1657CU via 7CF.
R9305 MG-R	FTR Lübeck 28/29.3.42.
R9306	To 90 Sqn via 7CF.
R9324	FTR Essen 16/17.6.42.
R9328 MG-A	From 214 Sqn. FTR Hamburg 26/27.7.42.
R9331 MG-Y	Overshot while landing at Waterbeach during training 14.7.42.
W7430	FTR Berlin 2/3.6.41.
W7433 MG-U	FTR Stettin 29/30.9.41.
W7434 MG-E	Crashed on landing at Oakington on return from Hanover 15.8.41.
W7435	To 15 Sqn.
W7436 MG-D	FTR Brest 18.12.41.
W7438	FTR Duisburg 28/29.8.41.
W7440	To 101CF.
W7441 MG-J/Y	From 15 Sqn. FTR Stettin 29/30.9.41.
W7442 MG-M	To 1651CU.
W7443	To 15 Sqn.
W7444 MG-L/G	Crashed on landing at Oakington following early return from operation to Bremen 31.10.41.
W7445 MG-V	Crashed on take-off from Oakington bound for Kiel 15.11.41.
W7446 MG-S	Crashed on landing at Oakington while training 18.11.41.
W7447 MG-V	To 15 Sqn.
W7448 MG-Z	From 149 Sqn. To 26CF.
W7449 MG-J	From 149 Sqn. To 214 Sqn.
W7451 MG-D	From 149 Sqn. To 218CF via 7CF.
W7454 MG-S	To 26CF.
W7466 MG-B	From 218 Sqn. FTR Lübeck 28/29.3.42.
W7467	From 218 Sqn. Crashed in Cambridgeshire after colliding with a Hurricane during training 17.1.42.
W7468 MG-W	From 218 Sqn. To 1651CU.
W7470 MG-U	To 1657CU via 7CF.
W7471 MG-J	FTR Emden 6/7.6.42.
W7472 MG-C	FTR Emden 20/21.6.42.
W7500 MG-B	FTR Essen 1/2.6.42.
W7501 MG-Z	FTR Lübeck 28/29.3.42.
W7504	To 15 Sqn.
W7505	To 15 Sqn.
W7517 MG-Z	To 1657CU.
W7520 MG-S	FTR Mannheim 19/20.5.42.
W7522 MG-G/K	To 1651CU.
W7529 MG-R	To 1665CU.
W7533 MG-G	FTR Hamburg 28/29.7.42.
W7539	From 214 Sqn. FTR St.Nazaire 28/29.6.42.
W7563	Crashed on take-off from Oakington *en route* to Bremen 2.7.42.
W7564	Crash-landed in Essex on return from Düsseldorf 10/11.9.42.
W7565	FTR Hamburg 28/29.7.42.

W7569	FTR Essen 16/17.9.42.
W7574	From 149 Sqn. To 1657CU.
W7579 MG-Y	FTR from mining sortie 13/14.8.42.
W7581	To 1657CU.
W7616 MG-G	FTR Frankfurt 24/25.8.42.
W7617 MG-A/K	FTR Stuttgart 11/12.3.43.
W7620 MG-D/L	FTR from mining sortie 6/7.11.42.
W7629 MG-Z	FTR Duisburg 6/7.9.42.
W7630 MG-M	FTR Düsseldorf 10/11.9.42.
W7632 MG-N	FTR Munich 21/22.12.42.
BF316 MG-M	Crash-landed at Boscombe Down on return from Nuremberg 29.8.42.
BF317 MG-D/X	FTR Berlin 27/28.3.43.
BF321 MG-S	To 75 Sqn.
BF335 MG-E	Damaged beyond repair during an operation to Frankfurt 24/25.8.42.
BF336 MG-Z	FTR Frankfurt 24/25.8.42.
BF339 MG-C/F/L	To 1665CU.
BF340 MG-A	From 15 Sqn. To 1657CU.
BF342 MG-E	To 1657CU.
BF345 MG-H	To 1657CU.
BF354	To 1657CU.
BF358 MG-C	FTR Munich 21/22.12.42.
BF378 MG-W	To 15 Sqn.
BF379 MG-D	FTR Turin 11/12.12.42.
BF387 MG-U	FTR Hamburg 9/10.11.42.
BF390 MG-A	Shot down by friendly anti-aircraft fire at Gt Yarmouth on return from a mining sortie 21.10.42.
BF501 MG-N	To 218 Sqn.
BF526	To 90 Sqn.
BF532	To 90 Sqn.
BK592 MG-M/F	From 214 Sqn. FTR Essen 12/13.3.43.
BK602	To 75 Sqn.
BK610	Abandoned off Kent coast on return from Nuremberg 9.4.43.
BK621 MG-N	To 214 Sqn.
BK709 MG-F	FTR Stuttgart 14/15.4.43.
BK723 MG-E	To 90 Sqn.
BK724 MG-I	To 214 Sqn.
BK760 MG-X	FTR Frankfurt 10/11.4.43.
BK761	To 218 Sqn.
BK769 MG-G	FTR Stuttgart 14/15.4.43.
BK773 MG-T	FTR Dortmund 4/5.5.43.
BK779	To 90 Sqn.
EE945	To 620 Sqn.
EF361 MG-B	FTR Düsseldorf 25/26.5.43.
EF363 MG-G	To 214 Sqn.
EF364 MG-X	FTR Hamburg (Operation Gomorrah) 29/30.7.43.
EF366 MG-L	FTR Krefeld 21/22.6.43.
EF368 MG-A	To 214 Sqn.
EF369 MG-Z	Crashed at Oakington on return from Hamburg 28.7.43.
EF384	To 1665CU.
EF386	To 1657CU.
EF387 MG-D	FTR Krefeld 21/22.6.43.

EF388 MG-M	To 214 Sqn.
EF390 MG-T	To 214 Sqn.
EF392 MG-N	FTR Wuppertal-Elberfeld 24/25.6.43.
EF393 MG-W	To 214 Sqn.
EF401	To NTU.
EF402 MG-Y	To 214 Sqn.
EF406 MG-U	To 214 Sqn.

9 SQUADRON

Motto: Per noctem volamus (Through the night we fly)   Code WS

No. 9 Squadron has one of the longest histories in British military aviation, dating back to its original formation on the 8th of December 1914, when it became the first radio equipped unit, and was employed in the role of artillery spotting. A decision to equip all artillery spotting squadrons with a radio flight resulted in the dispersal of 9 Squadron, which eventually lost its identity and was disbanded in March 1915. Resurrected in April 1915 as a radio training unit the squadron also undertook coastal defence duties until moving to France in November. The squadron operated as a bomber and reconnaissance unit until the end of 1916, when it reverted to its former role of artillery spotting, but carried out some bombing operations from June 1918. On the last day of 1919 the squadron was again disbanded, only to reappear as a night bomber unit in April 1924. In February 1939, the squadron began converting to Wellingtons, the type with which it would enter the impending conflict, and in July took up residence at Honington as one of 3 Group's six Wellington equipped front line squadrons. No. 9 Squadron was involved in the very first raid undertaken by Wellingtons, which was to Brunsbüttel on the 4th of September, the second day of hostilities. As a result it sustained the first failures to return of the type after two were brought down. The squadron continued to serve 3 Group with distinction until posted to 5 Group in August 1942. After operating successfully with Lancasters as a standard squadron of the line, it was selected to operate with the Barnes Wallis designed Tallboy bomb, previously the preserve of 617 Squadron. Beginning in September 1944, 9 and 617 Squadrons undertook a series of joint operations, including the three against the German battleship *Tirpitz*. With an overall loss rate of 3% 9 Squadron suffered slightly higher than average casualties.

STATIONS

| Honington | 15.07.39 to 07.08.42 |
| Lossiemouth (Detachment) | 09.04.40 to 14.04.40 |

COMMANDING OFFICERS

Wing Commander H P Lloyd	02.01.39 to 27.09.39
Wing Commander R A A Cole	27.09.39 to 17.01.40
Wing Commander A Mckee	17.01.40 to 24.07.40
Wing Commander A E Healy	24.07.40 to 16.01.41
Wing Commander R G C Arnold	16.01.41 to 09.06.41
Wing Commander K M M Wasse	20.06.41 to 10.01.42
Wing Commander W I C Inness	10.01.42 to 27.05.42
Wing Commander L V James	27.05.42 to 21.06.42
Wing Commander J M Southwell	27.06.42 to 15.03.43

AIRCRAFT

Wellington I	02.39 to 09.39
Wellington Ia	09.39 to 03.40
Wellington Ic	03.40 to 09.41
Wellington II	03.41 to 08.42
Wellington III	09.41 to 08.42
To 5 Group	07.08.42

OPERATIONAL RECORD

Operations	Sorties	Aircraft Losses	% Losses
287	2,333	66	2.8

Category of Operations

Bombing	Mining	Other
272	7	8

TABLE OF STATISTICS

(Heavy squadrons)

14th highest number of overall operations in Bomber Command.
15th highest number of sorties in Bomber Command.
7th highest number of aircraft operational losses in Bomber Command.
7th highest number of bombing operations in Bomber Command.
27th highest number of mining operations in Bomber Command.

Out of 42 Wellington squadrons

4th highest number of overall Wellington operations in Bomber Command.
4th highest number of Wellington sorties in Bomber Command.
3rd highest number of Wellington operational losses in Bomber Command.

Out of 28 bomber squadrons in 3 Group

8th highest number of overall operations in 3 Group.
10th highest number of sorties in 3 Group.
8th equal (with 514 Sqn) highest number of aircraft operational losses in 3 Group.

Out of 18 Wellington squadrons in 3 Group

3rd highest number of Wellington overall operations in 3 Group.
3rd highest number of Wellington sorties in 3 Group.
3rd highest number of Wellington operational losses in 3 Group.

AIRCRAFT HISTORIES

Wellington	To August 1942.
L4260 KA-H	To 11 OTU.
L4261 KA-B	To 214 Sqn.
L4262 KA-P	To 11 OTU.
L4268	FTR Brunsbüttel 4.9.39.
L4269	To 214 Sqn.
L4273	To 11 OTU.
L4274 KA-K	To CGS.
L4275 KA-H	FTR Brunsbüttel 4.9.39.
L4276 KA-M	To 11 OTU.

L4277	To CGS.
L4278 KA-Z/A	To CGS.
L4279 KA-D	To 75 Sqn.
L4286	To 11 OTU.
L4287	Became ground instruction machine in April 1942.
L4288 KA-A	Crashed near Honington after collision with L4363 (9 Sqn) during training 30.10.39.
L4298	From 99 Sqn via SD Flt to 11 OTU.
L4320 KA-Z/B	Crashed in Suffolk while training 8.9.39.
L4358	From 214 Sqn. To 1GRU.
L4363	From 214 Sqn. Crashed near Honington after mid-air collision with L4288 (9 Sqn) 30.10.39.
L4364	From 214 Sqn. Returned to 214 Sqn.
L7777	Crashed on landing at Abingdon on return from Namur 23.5.40.
L7778 KA-U	To 311 Sqn.
L7785	To 311 Sqn.
L7786 WS-X	To 311 Sqn.
L7787 WS-J	FTR Pont-de-l'Arche 13/14.6.40.
L7788 WS-N	To 311 Sqn.
L7789 WS-Y	To 300 Sqn.
L7795 WS-G	FTR Wismar 19/20.7.40.
L7796 WS-C	Posted out 29.8.40. after 21 operations.
L7799 WS-D	From 148 Sqn. Crashed in Sussex during operation to Venice 21/22.12.40.
L7807 WS-J	Ditched in North Sea on return from Bremen 22.6.40.
L7814 WS-W	To 12 OTU.
L7817	From 149 Sqn. To 1505 BAT Flt.
L7852 WS-P	From 311 Sqn. FTR Berlin 14/15.11.40.
L7867 WS-U	To 18 OTU.
L7868	To 99 Sqn.
L7871 WS-B	Destroyed by fire at Honington while preparing for operations 16.6.41.
N2744 WS-U	FTR Bremen 12/13.3.41.
N2745 WS-O	FTR Cologne 17/18.4.41.
N2871 WS-B	From 214 Sqn. To 15 Sqn.
N2872	FTR from shipping search off Wilhelmshaven 18.12.39.
N2873 WS-C	To 20 OTU.
N2883 WS-O	To 20 OTU.
N2895 WS-R	To 75 Sqn.
N2896	To 20 OTU.
N2897 WS-P	FTR Leverkusen 18/19.6.40.
N2898 WS-O	To 3 BAT Flt.
N2939 WS-H	FTR from shipping search off Wilhelmshaven 18.12.39.
N2940	FTR from shipping search off Wilhelmshaven 18.12.39.
N2941	FTR from shipping search off Wilhelmshaven 18.12.39.
N2942 WS-R	Crashed on landing at Honington while training 10.10.40.
N2964 WS-D	To 15 OTU.
N2981 WS-F	To 15 OTU.
N2982	To 75 Sqn.
N2983	Ditched on return from Wilhelmshaven 18.12.39.
N2984	To 99 Sqn.
N2985	To 99 Sqn.
N2986	To 99 Sqn.

N3000 WS-L	From 99 Sqn. To 40 Sqn.
N3014	To 75 Sqn.
N3015	FTR Gelsenkirchen 16/17.5.40. Crew rescued.
N3016	WS-C To 15 OTU.
N3017	Crashed on take-off from Weybridge during ferry flight 8.3.40.
N3018	To 15 OTU.
P2520 WS-U	FTR from reconnaissance sortie to Norway 12.4.40.
P2521	No operations. Posted out 11.1.40.
P2523 WS-W	To 15 OTU.
P9205	Crashed near Honington during training 22.7.40.
P9228	To 300 Sqn via RAE.
P9231 WS-A	To 1 AAS.
P9232 WS-M	FTR Duisburg 5/6.6.40.
P9239 WS-H	To 214 Sqn.
P9278 WS-B	Crashed in Bedfordshire on return from Kiel 16/17.10.40.
P9283	To 115 Sqn.
R1023 WS-K	To 12 OTU.
R1040	From 57 Sqn. FTR Cologne 7/8.7.41.
R1096	Force-landed near Martlesham Heath on return from Hanover 11.2.41.
R1175 WS-A	To 15 OTU.
R1225 WS-P	From 311 Sqn. To 1505BAT Flt.
R1244	FTR Turin 11/12.1.41.
R1267 WS-Y	Crashed on landing at Honington on return from Boulogne 17.5.41.
R1279 WS-L	From 15 Sqn. FTR Genoa 28/29.9.41.
R1281	From 57 Sqn. FTR Emden 26/27.4.41.
R1284 WS-W	From 12 OTU. To 23 OTU.
R1286	To 15 OTU.
R1287	To 18 OTU.
R1288 WS-D	Crashed in the sea off Spurn Head on return from Cologne 2.3.41.
R1335 WS-K	From 12 OTU. FTR Cologne 27/28.3.41.
R1341 WS-Z	FTR Hanover 12/13.8.41.
R1455 WS-D	FTR Kiel 19/20.8.41.
R1499	Crash-landed at Honington on return from Berlin 8.9.41.
R1513	FTR Kiel 12/13.8.41.
R1591 WS-M	To 3Gp TF.
R1707	From 11 OTU. To 57 Sqn.
R1722	From 11 OTU. To 57 Sqn.
R1757 WS-Y	To 57 Sqn.
R1758	FTR from reconnaissance sortie to French and Belgian coastal area 9.6.41.
R1763 WS-N	To 57 Sqn,
R1764 WS-K	To 15 OTU.
R3161	To 149 Sqn.
R3173 WS-A	From 148 Sqn, To 18 OTU.
R3204 WS-J	Became ground instruction machine in July 1942.
R3216 WS-K	From 75 Sqn. To 18 OTU.
R3220 WS-L	FTR Düsseldorf Airfield 7/8.12.40.
R3230 WS-M	From 311 Sqn. To 22 OTU.
R3282 WS-G	Crashed off Suffolk coast on return from Berlin 2.10.40.
R3283	Became ground instruction machine in July 1942.

R3286 WS-V	To Czech TU.
R3296 WS-P	To 12 OTU.
T2458 WS-M	To 149 Sqn.
T2462 WS-A	Crashed on approach to Honington on return from Essen 7/8.11.40.
T2464 WS-K	From 75 Sqn. FTR Magdeburg 14/15.10.40.
T2468 WS-Y	From 75 Sqn. To 40 Sqn.
T2472 WS-G	Crashed on approach to Honington on return from Hanau 29.9.40.
T2473 WS-M	FTR Berlin 9/10.4.41.
T2477 WS-C	To 99 Sqn.
T2505 WS-W	FTR Cologne 28/29.9.40.
T2546	To 99 Sqn.
T2564 WS-X	From 311 Sqn to 11 OTU.
T2578 WS-Z	From 311 Sqn to 21 OTU.
T2579 WS-J	To 3 Gp TF.
T2619 WS-T	To 26 OTU.
T2620 WS-G	FTR from reconnaissance sortie to French and Belgian coastal area 9.6.41.
T2744	FTR Bremen 12/13.3.41.
T2900 WS-L	FTR Berlin 17/18.4.41.
T2964 WS-N	Damaged beyond repair during operation to Rotterdam 3/4.5.41. and SOC 14.5.41.
T2973 WS-G	FTR Münster 8/9.7.41.
W5445	From 218 Sqn to 57 Sqn.
W5703	FTR Cologne 26/27.8.41.
W5729 WS-J	FTR Cologne 10/11.7.41.
X3222	Crashed in Norfolk following recall from operation to Emden 26.9.41.
X3226 WS-B	To 101 Sqn and back. FTR Rostock 25/26.4.42.
X3275	To 22 OTU via Manufacturers.
X3276	FTR Boulogne 17/18.5.42.
X3277	To 419 Sqn.
X3280	FTR Hamburg 9/10.11.41.
X3281 WS-X	To 311 Sqn and back to 17 OTU.
X3283	To 150 Sqn.
X3285	To 101 Sqn.
X3287	Abandoned off Kent coast on return from Düsseldorf 27/28.11.41.
X3288 WS-N	To 150 Sqn.
X3289	Force-landed in Suffolk during training 6.12.41.
X3305 WS-G	To 57 Sqn.
X3332 WS-O	To 57 Sqn.
X3339	From 75 Sqn to 156 Sqn.
X3342	From 156 Sqn to 115 Sqn.
X3346	To 57 Sqn.
X3347	Crashed on approach to Honington on return from Hamburg 1.10.41.
X3348	From 115 Sqn. To 466 Sqn.
X3351	To 115 Sqn.
X3352 WS-M	Crashed on approach to East Wretham on return from Hamburg 9.11.41.
X3353 WS-K	To 57 Sqn.
X3354 WS-L	To 115 Sqn.

X3358	FTR Cologne 22/23.4.42.
X3367	From 75 Sqn. To 166 Sqn.
X3369	FTR Warnemünde 8/9.5.42.
X3370 WS-D	Crashed in Norfolk during training 19.1.42.
X3372 WS-R	To 1483Flt.
X3388	Crashed on approach to Honington on return from Brest 6.1.42.
X3389 WS-Y	From 57 Sqn. To 75 Sqn.
X3390	To 75 Sqn.
X3395	To 27 OTU.
X3397	To 75 Sqn.
X3398	Crashed in the sea off Essex coast while training 15.2.42.
X3407 WS-Y	To 101 Sqn.
X3411	FTR Essen 8/9.3.42.
X3415 WS-P	FTR Cologne 5/6.4.42.
X3416 WS-X	To 75 Sqn.
X3422 WS-G	To 156 Sqn.
X3423 WS-X	From 115 Sqn. Crashed in Berkshire on return from St Nazaire 24.6.42.
X3424 WS-O	From 114 Sqn. To 101 Sqn.
X3449	To MAEE.
X3451	To 75 Sqn.
X3452	To 75 Sqn.
X3456	FTR Hamburg 28/29.7.42.
X3457	To 101 Sqn.
X3463 WS-X	To 150 Sqn.
X3469	FTR Cologne 30/31.5.42.
X3470 WS-D	To 419 Sqn.
X3474 WS-B	From 57 Sqn. To 1 ECU.
X3475 WS-P	From 101 Sqn. FTR Hamburg 28/29.7.42.
X3594 WS-G	To 26 OTU.
X3603	Crashed on landing at Bodney on return from Kiel 12/13.3.42.
X3605	To 3FPP.
X3606 WS-M	FTR Hamburg 28/29.7.42.
X3638	FTR Cologne 22/23.4.42.
X3641	FTR Essen 8/9.3.42.
X3643	Crashed in Norfolk following early return from Essen 9.3.42.
X3649 WS-D	To 101 Sqn.
X3666 WS-N	To 115 Sqn.
X3695 WS-V	From 101 Sqn. FTR from mining sortie 11/12.6.42.
X3702	FTR Essen 10/11.4.42.
X3713 WS-J	FTR Emden 20/21.6.42.
X3716	FTR Kiel 28/29.4.42.
X3718 WS-B	To 115 Sqn.
X3722	FTR Essen 12/13.4.42.
X3759	Crashed in Norfolk during operation to Cologne 22/23.4.42.
X3794	To 75 Sqn.
X9660	To 214 Sqn.
X9750	From 214 Sqn. FTR Mannheim 5/6.8.41.
X9762	To 214 Sqn.
X9785 WS-K	To 214 Sqn.
X9786	To 57 Sqn.

X9923	To 57 Sqn.
X9924	To 57 Sqn.
Z1575 WS-V	Crashed soon after take-off from Honington bound for Emden 6/7.6.42.
Z1577 WS-T	FTR Duisburg 23/24.7.42.
Z1615 WS-H	FTR from mining sortie 15/16.5.42.
Z1658	To 101 Sqn.
Z1663	To 57 Sqn.
Z8373	From 214 Sqn. FTR Emden 26/27.11.41.
Z8845	From 311 Sqn. FTR Berlin 7/8.9.41.
Z8853	From 311 Sqn. To 115 Sqn.
Z8854	To 101 Sqn.
Z8856	To 12 OTU.
Z8858	To 75 Sqn.
Z8900 WS-C	To 214 Sqn and back. Crash-landed at Coltishall on return from Emden 15.11.41.
Z8943	From 214 Sqn. Returned to 214 Sqn.
Z8953	From 214 Sqn. FTR Emden 26/27.11.41.
BJ606 WS-R	To 101 Sqn.
BJ674	FTR Cologne 30/31.5.42.
BJ688	To 115 Sqn.
BJ725 WS-D	To 75 Sqn.
BJ876	FTR Düsseldorf 31.7/1.8.42.
BJ878	FTR Düsseldorf 31.7/1.8.42.

XV SQUADRON

Motto: Aim Sure
Codes LS, DJ

The history of XV Squadron, as it is traditionally depicted, stretches back to its original formation on the 1st of March 1915. As a reconnaissance unit it operated from French bases in an artillery spotting and photographic role, interspersed with ground attack operations during the German advance in March 1918. On the last day of 1919 the squadron was disbanded, only to be resurrected on the 24th of March 1924 to test armaments for the A&AEE. When this body undertook its own testing from the 1st of June 1934, XV Squadron was re-formed in the day-bomber role, exchanging its Hinds for Battles in June 1938, and it was with this type, that the squadron faced the impending conflict. The squadron moved to France on the eve of war, the 2nd of September 1939, as part of the Advanced Air Striking Force, but was withdrawn earlier than most to return home in December. A transfer to 2 Group brought daylight operations in Blenheims throughout most of 1940, before another move took place to 3 Group. Operating successively Wellingtons, Stirlings and Lancasters XV Squadron served 3 Group with distinction until war's end.

From 2 Group
01.11.40

STATIONS

Wyton	10.12.39 to 14.08.42
Alconbury (Satellite)	14.04.40 to 15.05.40
Alconbury/Warboys (Satellites)	08.41 to 01.42
Lossiemouth (Detachment)	28.01.42 to 07.02.42
Bourn	14.08.42 to 14.04.43
Mildenhall	14.04.43 to 08.46

COMMANDING OFFICERS

Wing Commander J Cox DFC	05.06.40 to 14.12.40
Wing Commander H R Dale	14.12.40 to 11.05.41
Wing Commander P B B Ogilvie DSO DFC	16.05.41 to 05.01.42
Wing Commander J C Macdonald DFC AFC	05.01.42 to 02.06.42
Wing Commander D J H Lay DSO DFC	02.06.42 to 07.12.42
Wing Commander S W B Menaul DFC	07.12.42 to 07.05.43
Wing Commander J D Stephens DFC	07.05.43 to 03.09.43
Wing Commander A J Elliott	03.09.43 to 15.04.44
Wing Commander N D G Watkins DSO DFC	15.04.44 to 16.11.44
Wing Commander N G Macfarlane DSO	17.11.44 to 12.03.46

AIRCRAFT

Wellington Ic	11.40 to 05.41
Stirling I	04.41 to 01.43
Stirling III	01.43 to 12.43
Lancaster I/III	12.43 to 03.47

OPERATIONAL RECORD

Operations	Sorties	Aircraft Losses	% Losses
617	5,244	139	2.7

Category of Operations

Bombing	Mining	Other
509	103	5

Wellingtons

Operations	Sorties	Aircraft Losses	% Losses
38	173	3	1.7

Stirling

Operations	Sorties	Aircraft Losses	% Losses
353	2,231	91	4.1

Category of Operations

Bombing	Mining	Other
263	85	5

Lancaster

Operations	Sorties	Aircraft Losses	% Losses
226	2,840	45	1.6

Category of Operations

Bombing	Mining
208	18

TABLE OF STATISTICS

(Heavy squadrons)

4th highest number of overall operations in Bomber Command.
16th highest number of sorties in Bomber Command.
14th highest number of aircraft operational losses in Bomber Command.
3rd highest number of bombing operations in Bomber Command.

Out of 42 Wellington squadrons

38th highest number of Wellington overall operations in Bomber Command.
2nd lowest number of Wellington sorties in Bomber Command.
Lowest equal (with 458 Sqn) number of Wellington operational losses in Bomber Command.

Out of 13 Stirling squadrons

2nd highest number of Stirling overall operations in Bomber Command.
3rd highest number of Stirling sorties in Bomber Command.
Highest equal (with 218 Sqn) highest number of Stirling operational losses in Bomber Command.

Out of 59 Lancaster squadrons

23rd highest number of Lancaster overall operations in Bomber Command.
26th highest number of Lancaster sorties in Bomber Command.
31st highest number of Lancaster operational losses in Bomber Command.

Out of 28 bomber squadrons in 3 Group

4th highest number of overall operations in 3 Group.
4th highest number of sorties in 3 Group.
3rd highest number of aircraft operational losses in 3 Group.

Out of 18 Wellington squadrons in 3 Group

Lowest number of Wellington overall operations in 3 Group.
Lowest number of Wellington sorties in 3 Group.
Lowest number of Wellington operational losses in 3 Group.

Out of 12 Stirling bomber squadrons in 3 Group

2nd highest number of Stirling overall operations in 3 Group.
3rd highest number of Stirling sorties in 3 Group.
Highest equal (with 218 Sqn) highest number of Stirling operational losses in 3 Group.

Out of 11 Lancaster squadrons in 3 Group

3rd highest number of Lancaster overall operations in 3 Group.
4th highest number of Lancaster sorties in 3 Group.
4th highest number of Lancaster operational losses in 3 Group.

AIRCRAFT HISTORIES

Wellington	From November 1940.
L4343	From 57 Sqn. To 311 Sqn.
L7797	From 75 Sqn. To 218 Sqn.
N2752	To 311 Sqn and back. To 4BAT Flt.
N2843	To 40 Sqn.
N2856	To 99 Sqn.
N2871	From 9 Sqn. To 311 Sqn.
N2954	From 38 Sqn. To 11 OTU.
R1066	From Wyton. To 40 Sqn.
R1169	To 20 OTU.
R1218 LS-H	Abandoned over Yorkshire on return from Kiel 24/25.4.41.

R1222	To 115 Sqn.
R1240	To 40 Sqn.
R1279	To 9 Sqn.
R1280	To 115 Sqn.
R1436	To 218 Sqn.
R1464	To 40 Sqn.
R1498	To 1504BAT Flt.
R1596	To 218 Sqn.
T2624	To Czech TU.
T2702 LS-H	FTR Hanover 10/11.2.41.
T2703 LS-A	FTR Bremen 31.3/1.4.41.
T2715	To 57 Sqn.
T2806 LS-N	To 218 Sqn.
T2847 LS-R	From 40 Sqn. FTR Sterkrade 15/16.2.41.
T2918	To 214 Sqn.
T2961	To 57 Sqn.
W5449	To 218 Sqn.

Stirling	From April 1941 to December 1943.
N3638	From 7 Sqn. To 149 Sqn 22.6.41.
N3642	From 7 Sqn. To 26CF 6.10.41.
N3644	From 7 Sqn. U/C collapsed at Wyton during training 21.5.41.
N3646	To 214 Sqn.
N3654 LS-B	From A&AEE. FTR Berlin 10/11.5.41.
N3656 LS-H	Crash-landed at Honington on return from Berlin 13.8.41.
N3658 LS-E	FTR Essen 7/8.8.41.
N3659 LS-N	FTR Berlin 12/13.8.41.
N3660 LS-M	Crashed while landing at Warboys during training 28.9.41.
N3661 LS-Q	Crashed at Wyton on return from Lille 11.7.41.
N3665 LS-B/S	FTR Brest 18.12.41.
N3667 LS-T	Crashed on landing at Wyton after early return from Nuremberg 12/13.10.41.
N3668	From 7 Sqn. Crashed on landing at Alconbury while training 8.1.42.
N3669 LS-H	From 7 Sqn via 26CF. To 1 AAS.
N3670	To 7 Sqn 24.2.42.
N3671	To 1651CU.
N3673 LS-D	FTR Essen 8/9.3.42.
N3674 LS-T	To 214CF 8.7.42.
N3675 LS-S	To 1427Flt via 15CF 22.1.42.
N3676 LS-U	To 1651CU 8.4.42.
N3683	To 7CF.
N3684 LS-O	From 149 Sqn. Conversion Flt only. FTR Bremen 13/14.9.42.
N3703 LS-G	Crashed near Wyton on return from Essen 11.4.42.
N3704 LS-A	To 75 Sqn and back. To 1651CU 16.10.42.
N3707 LS-M	To 1651CU.
N3728 LS-T	From R.A.E. FTR Essen 2/3.6.42.
N3756 LS-C	From 214 Sqn. Force-landed in Suffolk on return from Mainz 12.8.42.
N3757 LS-G	From 7 Sqn. FTR Bremen 29/30.6.42.
N3758 LS-V	To 1657CU.
N3759 LS-Q	FTR from mining sortie 18/19.9.42.

N3764	From 7 Sqn. To 214 Sqn.
N6004 LS-F	From 7 Sqn. To 1427Flt 11.6.41.
N6007	To 7 Sqn.27.4.41.
N6015 LS-A	FTR Hamburg 29/30.6.41.
N6016 LS-G	FTR Hamburg 29/30.6.41.
N6018 LS-C	FTR Lille 19.7.41.
N6021 LS-O	FTR Hamburg 15/16.9.41.
N6024 LS-K	To 1651CU 11.6.41.
N6029 LS-G/K	FTR Berlin 25/26.7.41.
N6030 LS-F/P	FTR from aborted operation to Wesel 18.7.41.
N6038 LS-R	Ditched in the Irish Sea returning from La Pallice 23.7.41.
N6040 LS-C	Crashed on landing at Wyton while training 25.10.41.
N6043 LS-G	Force-landed soon after take-off from Alconbury when bound for Hanover 14/15.8.41.
N6044 LS-O	To 1651CU via 15CF 27.3.42.
N6045 LS-U	FTR Berlin 7/8.9.41.
N6047 LS-P	FTR Nuremberg 12/13.10.41.
N6065 LS-D	To 149CF 8.7.42.
N6067 LS-E	Force-landed near Mildenhall on return from Kiel 26.2.42.
N6076 LS-D	From 218 Sqn. Crash-landed at Newmarket on return from Dortmund 15.4.42.
N6086 LS-F	To 101CF.
N6088 LS-G/Q/X	To 1651CU via 15CF 22.1.42.
N6090	From 7 Sqn. Conversion Flt only. Crashed on landing at Alconbury 18.4.42.
N6092	To 214 Sqn 5.4.42.
N6093 LS-C/P	From 7 Sqn. Crashed at Wyton on return from Münster 22.1.42.
N6094 LS-R	From 7 Sqn via 26CF. Crashed on landing at Wyton during transit 25.3.42.
N6096	To 26CF.
N6097 LS-C	Crashed on take-off from Warboys when bound for Kiel 15.11.41.
N6098 LS-G	Destroyed by fire at Lossiemouth 29.1.42.
R9144 LS-Q/R	To 1657CU 8.12.42.
R9151 LS-O	Crash-landed at Docking on return from Osnabrück 18.8.42.
R9153 LS-U	FTR Nuremberg 28/29.8.42.
R9168 LS-T	FTR Diepholz Aerodrome 16/17.12.42.
R9192 LS-E	From 7 Sqn. To 1657CU.
R9193 LS-S	From 7 Sqn. To 1651CU 5.10.43.
R9195 LS-P	To 1657CU.
R9201 LS-U	FTR from mining sortie 6/7.11.42.
R9268 LS-F/R	To 1665CU 5.6.43.
R9274 LS-B	FTR Hamburg 3/4.2.43.
R9279 LS-J	FTR Cologne 26/27.2.43.
R9302 LS-F	To 1651CU via 15CF.
R9303 LS-P	To 214 Sqn 5.4.42.
R9304 LS-U	To 1651CU 5.4.42.
R9308 LS-P	Crashed on landing at Waterbeach on return from Vegesack 20.7.42.
R9310	To 149 Sqn.
R9311	To 218 Sqn.
R9312 LS-C	FTR from mining sortie 16/17.10.42.

R9313	To 218 Sqn.
R9314	To 149 Sqn. 12.5.42.
R9315 LS-O	To 1657CU 17.11.42.
R9318 LS-B/J	FTR Essen 16/17.9.42.
R9319	To 214 Sqn.
R9351 LS-R	FTR from mining sortie 18/19.9.42.
R9352 LS-T	FTR Emden 19/20.6.42.
R9353 LS-B	To 1657CU.
W7426	From DGRD. To 26CF 26.9.41.
W7427	To 26CF 9.10.41.
W7428 LS-F/Z	FTR Brest 18.12.41.
W7429 LS-J/X	Crashed on landing at Warboys on return from Pilsen 28/29.10.41.
W7431 LS-A	Crashed near Methwold on return from Bremen 21.10.41.
W7432	To 1651CU.
W7435 LS-W	From 7 Sqn. Crashed on take-off from Alconbury *en route* to Magdeburg 14.8.41.
W7437 LS-L	FTR Magdeburg 14/15.8.41.
W7439 LS-N	To 26CF and back. To 106CF 15.12.41.
W7441	To 7 Sqn 8.9.41.
W7443 LS-W/J	From 7 Sqn. To 1651CU 21.1.42.
W7447	To TFU 8.12.41.
W7448 LS-M/E	From 26CF. To 15CF and back. FTR Essen 6/7.4.42.
W7450 LS-A	From 149 Sqn. Crashed on landing at Warboys on return from the Ruhr 25.11.41.
W7455	From 149CF. To 214 Sqn.
W7460	To 149 Sqn and back. Returned to 149 Sqn.
W7463 LS-B	From 149 Sqn. To 1651CU via 15CF 2.6.42.
W7464 LS-H	To 218 Sqn 4.4.42.
W7504 LS-A	From 7 Sqn. Crashed on landing at Wyton on return from Hamburg 27.7.42.
W7505 LS-V	From 7 Sqn. To 1651CU.
W7511 LS-T	Crashed on take-off from Wyton during air-test 8.4.42.
W7513 LS-R	To 149 Sqn 2.6.42.
W7514 LS-B	FTR Rostock 25/26.4.42.
W7515 LS-Q	FTR from mining sortie 29/30.5.42.
W7516 LS-S	To 1651CU.
W7518	FTR Berlin 1/2.3.43.
W7519 LS-O	FTR from mining sortie 13/14.4.42.
W7523 LS-C	Crashed soon after take-off from Wyton during air-test 19.5.42.
W7524 LS-D	FTR Lübeck 16.7.42.
W7525 LS-E	Crashed on approach to Bourn while training 22.8.42.
W7528 LS-G	FTR Warnemünde 8/9.5.42.
W7531 LS-F	FTR from mining sortie 17/18.5.42.
W7536 LS-G	Crashed on landing at Wyton while training 22.5.42.
W7561 LS-F	To 1651CU.
W7576 LS-G	FTR Duisburg 25/26.7.42.
W7578 LS-A	FTR Munich 19/20.9.42.
W7585 LS-T/U	Crashed in Cambridgeshire during air-test 29.12.42.
W7588 LS-J	Caught fire on landing at Coltishall on return from Hamburg 29.7.42.
W7611 LS-F	FTR Karlsruhe 2/3.9.42.
W7624 LS-E	FTR Kassel 27/28.8.42.

W7633 LS-P	To 1657CU.
W7634 LS-G	FTR Lübeck 1/2.10.42.
W7635 LS-V	FTR from mining sortie 8/9.12.42.
BF311	From 75 Sqn. To 1651CU.
BF327 LS-D	FTR Kassel 27/28.8.42.
BF329 LS-A	FTR Mainz 12/13.8.42.
BF340	To 7 Sqn.
BF347 LS-J	Crashed at West Malling on return from Düsseldorf 11.9.42.
BF350 LS-O	To 1657CU.
BF352 LS-U	Crashed on landing at Waterbeach when returning early from mining sortie 9.9.42.
BF353 LS-E	FTR Essen 16/17.9.42.
BF355 LS-F	To 1657CU 12.5.43.
BF356 LS-D	Crashed on landing at Bourn on return from mining sortie 17.12.42.
BF376 LS-N	To 90 Sqn 11.3.43.
BF378 LS-T	From 7 Sqn. FTR Wilhelmshaven 19/20.2.43.
BF380 LS-B	Crashed near Bourn on return from mining sortie 18.12.42.
BF384 LS-R	Crashed on take-off from Bourn bound for Turin 18.11.42.
BF386 LS-Q	Crashed near Downham Market during air-test 29.10.42.
BF389	To 149 Sqn.
BF392	To 149 Sqn.
BF411 LS-A	FTR Wilhelmshaven 19/20.2.43.
BF412	To 75 Sqn 13.3.43.
BF435	From 115 Sqn. To 90 Sqn.
BF436 LS-E	From 115 Sqn. To 1653CU 11.3.43.
BF439 LS-D	To 1653CU 28.12.43.
BF448 LS-T	FTR Cologne 14/15.2.43.
BF457 LS-B	FTR Wilhelmshaven 19/20.2.43.
BF460 LS-C	From 90 Sqn. FTR Nuremberg 10/11.8.43.
BF465	To 75 Sqn. 2.3.43.
BF469	To 214 Sqn. 5.3.43.
BF470 LS-G	FTR Kassel 3/4.10.43.
BF474 LS-H	FTR Mannheim 16/17.4.43.
BF475 LS-T	FTR Frankfurt 10/11.4.43.
BF476 LS-P	FTR Rostock 20/21.4.43.
BF482 LS-R	FTR Dortmund 23/24.5.43.
BF521 LS-P	From 90 Sqn. To 622 Sqn 10.8.43.
BF533 LS-K	To 1657CU 11.5.43.
BF534 LS-L	FTR Düsseldorf 25/26.5.43.
BF569 LS-O/V	FTR Montlucon 15/16.9.43.
BF571 LS-U	FTR Düsseldorf 11/12.6.43.
BF579 LS-B	FTR from mining sortie 3/4.7.43.
BK595 LS-A	FTR Turin 20/21.11.42.
BK597	To 149 Sqn.
BK611 LS-U	FTR Düsseldorf 25/26.6.43.
BK648 LS-J	FTR Cologne 3/4.7.43.
BK652 LS-V	To 622 Sqn 10.8.43.
BK654 LS-W	To 1661CU 4.12.43.
BK656 LS-A	FTR Mülheim 22/23.6.43.
BK657 LS-C	FTR Duisburg 26/27.4.43.
BK658 LS-K	FTR Dortmund 4/5.5.43.
BK667 LS-H	Crashed in Wiltshire following early return from St.Nazaire 22.3.43.

BK691 LS-F	FTR Mannheim 16/17.4.43.
BK694 LS-C	FTR Cologne 28/29.6.43.
BK695 LS-X	To 75 Sqn.
BK697 LS-P	FTR Nuremberg 8/9.3.43.
BK698	To 149 Sqn.
BK699 LS-M/E	FTR Gelsenkirchen 25/26.6.43.
BK703	To 149 Sqn.
BK704 LS-Z	FTR Bochum 13/14.5.43.
BK707 LS-G	From 214 Sqn. FTR Mannheim 18/19.11.43.
BK719 LS-B	To 1661CU 13.12.43.
BK764 LS-R	FTR Mönchengladbach 30/31.8.43.
BK766 LS-T	To 622 Sqn 10.8.43.
BK774 LS-T/K	FTR from mining sortie 3/4.9.43.
BK782 LS-X	FTR Dortmund 4/5.5.43.
BK805 LS-U	FTR Essen 25/26.7.43.
BK815 LS-V	FTR Krefeld 21/22.6.43.
BK816	To 622 Sqn.
BK818 LS-R	To 1661CU 4.12.43.
EE877	To 149 Sqn.
EE907 LS-C	To 1661CU 8.12.43.
EE908 LS-V	FTR Peenemünde 17/18.8.43.
EE910	To 199 Sqn. 19.7.43.
EE912 LS-U	FTR Berlin 31.8/1.9.43.
EE913	To 199 Sqn 19.7.43.
EE940 LS-Y	From 199 Sqn. FTR Hanover 27/28.9.43.
EE954 LS-J	From 199 Sqn. FTR Frankfurt 4/5.10.43.
EE974 LS-O	To 90 Sqn 23.12.43.
EF131	Crashed on landing at Mildenhall during air-test 19.9.43.
EF133 LS-U	To 218 Sqn 23.12.43.
EF161 LS-Y	From 622 Sqn. To 199 Sqn 23.12.43.
EF177 LS-S	From 622 Sqn. To 1661CU 8.12.43.
EF183 LS-D	To 90 Sqn 9.1.44.
EF186 LS-W	From 622 Sqn. To 1661CU 8.12.43.
EF195	Crashed on take-off from Mildenhall during air-test 15.10.43.
EF333 LS-X	FTR Hamburg 3/4.3.43.
EF339 LS-Y	Crash-landed at Coltishall on return from Hamburg 30.7.43.
EF345 LS-M	FTR Dortmund 4/5.5.43.
EF347 LS-T	FTR Berlin 1/2.3.43.
EF348 LS-N	FTR Mülheim 22/23.6.43.
EF351 LS-L	To 622 Sqn 10.8.43.
EF354 LS-Q/C	To 1665CU 6.6.43.
EF355 LS-A	To 1665CU 21.6.43.
EF359 LS-B	FTR Duisburg 8/9.4.43.
EF391 LS-M/N	To 622 Sqn 10.8.43.
EF399 LS-Y	To 75 Sqn 6.6.43.
EF411	To 149 Sqn 14.6.43.
EF412	To 149 Sqn 14.6.43.
EF427 LS-A	FTR Remscheid 30/31.7.43.
EF428 LS-N	FTR Remscheid 30/31.7.43.
EF437	Crashed near Mildenhall on return from Hamburg 28.7.43.
EF453	To 199 Sqn 24.7.43.
EF459 LS-S	To 90 Sqn 4.10.43.

EF460 LS-B	From 199 Sqn. To 622 Sqn.
EF461	To 622 Sqn 14.8.43.
EF490 LS-B	To 622 Sqn 10.8.43.
EF518 LS-P	To 1661CU 8.12.43.
EH875 LS-S	FTR Berlin 23/24.8.43.
EH879	To 149 Sqn 22.5.43.
EH888 LS-Z	FTR Cologne 28/29.6.43.
EH890 LS-U	Ditched off East Anglia on return from Wuppertal 24/25.6.43.
EH893 LS-J	FTR Hamburg 27/28.7.43.
EH897	To 622 Sqn.
EH929 LS-F	From 75 Sqn. To 1661CU 8.12.43.
EH930 LS-A	From 75 Sqn. To 199 Sqn 8.12.43.
EH940 LS-H/U	To 218 Sqn 23.12.43.
EH941 LS-D	FTR Mannheim 23/24.9.43.
EH980	To 1654CU 2.12.43.
EH985 LS-O	FTR Nuremberg 27/28.8.43.
EH990 LS-K	FTR from mining sortie 7/8.10.43.
LJ451 LS-K	To 622 Sqn 13.12.43.
LJ453	To 75 Sqn 27.1.44.
LJ462	To 75 Sqn 9.11.43.
LJ464	To 1654CU 2.12.43.
LK386	To 149 Sqn.
LK393	To 1661CU.
MZ264 DJ-A	To 622 Sqn 18.8.43.

Lancaster	From December 1943.
L7527 LS-A	From 1654CU. FTR Essen 26/27.3.44.
R5490 LS-U	From 622 Sqn.
R5508 LS-C	From 1660CU. SOC.
R5692 LS-S	From 1667CU. To 75 Sqn.
R5739 LS-K	From 1654CU. To 622 Sqn and back. FTR Leipzig 19/20.2.44.
R5846	From 1654CU. To 622 Sqn.
R5896 LS-N	From 1660CU. SOC 7.4.44.
R5904 LS-G/L	From 9 Sqn via 1661CU. FTR Homberg 20/21.7.44.
R5906 LS-D	From 106CF. To 622 Sqn.
W4174LS-P	From 207 Sqn via 1660CU. To 622 Sqn and back. To 75 Sqn.
W4181LS-Q	From 49 Sqn via 1660CU. To 3LFS.
W4272LS-P	From 61 Sqn via 1654CU. To 622 Sqn.
W4355LS-A	From 97 Sqn. FTR Stuttgart 15/16.3.44.
W4852LS-B	From 103 Sqn via 1654CU. FTR Magdeburg 21/22.1.44.
W4885	From 622 Sqn. To 90 Sqn via 5LFS.
W4980LS-R/W	From 622 Sqn. To 90 Sqn via 3LFS.
ED310 LS-M/N	From 97 Sqn via 1654CU. To 75 Sqn.
ED323 LS-D	From 97 Sqn via 1661CU. FTR Berlin 27/28.1.44.
ED376 LS-F	From 100 Sqn via 1662CU. To 3LFS.
ED383 LS-C	From 622 Sqn. Crashed at Lakenheath on return from Augsburg 26.2.44.
ED473 LS-H/D	From 50 Sqn via 1667CU. FTR Nantes 7/8.5.44.
ED610 LS-C	From 622 Sqn. FTR Berlin 18/19.1.44.
ED628 LS-O	From 1662CU. FTR Berlin 15/16.2.44.
ED727	From 1662CU. To 622 Sqn.

ED808	From 1660CU. To 622 Sqn.
ED826	From 61 Sqn via 1654CU. Crashed in the Wash on return from a mining sortie 12/13.1.44.
HK612 LS-L	FTR Homberg 2.11.44. Collided with PB115 (15 Sqn).
HK614	To 622 Sqn.
HK615	To 622 Sqn.
HK616	To 622 Sqn.
HK617	To 622 Sqn.
HK618 LS-G	FTR Cologne 28.1.45.
HK619 LS-O/V/Y	
HK620 LS-W/V	FTR Hohenbudburg railway yards Krefeld 8/9.2.45.
HK622	To 90 Sqn.
HK625	To 90 Sqn.
HK626 LS-M/W	From 622 Sqn. FTR Oberhausen 4.12.44.
HK627 LS-Q/F	FTR Witten 12.12.44.
HK647 LS-E/K/L	
HK648 LS-F/H	
HK693 LS-B	
HK695 LS-V	To GH Flt January 1945.
HK765 DJ-Z	
HK772 LS-A/B/G	
HK773 LS-W	Crashed in Norfolk when bound for Bocholt 22.3.45.
HK789 LS-R	
HK799 LS-D	
JB475	From 514 Sqn. To 195 Sqn.
LL752 LS-A	FTR Louvain 11/12.5.44.
LL754 LS-P	FTR Cologne 20/21.4.44.
LL781 LS-B/L	Crash-landed at Friston on return from Maisey Palaiseau 8.6.44.
LL801 LS-J	FTR Friedrichshaven 27/28.4.44.
LL805 LS-M	FTR Friedrichshaven 27/28.4.44.
LL806 LS-J	Completed 134 operations with XV Sqn.
LL827 LS-O/P/Q	FTR Chalons-sur-Marne 15/16.7.44.
LL854 LS-Q/S	To 186 Sqn.
LL858 LS-N	Crashed on take-off from Mildenhall while training 30.4.44.
LL889 LS-L/B	FTR Le Havre 14/15.6.44.
LL890 LS-T	FTR Wizernes 5/6.7.44.
LL923 LS-O	From 115 Sqn. FTR Ludwigshafen 5.1.45.
LL945 LS-M	From 75 Sqn. FTR Maisy Palaiseau 7/8.6.44.
LM109 LS-E	FTR Calais 24.9.44.
LM110 LS-G	From 90 Sqn. FTR Frankfurt 12/13.9.44.
LM113 LS-K	From 626 Sqn.
LM121 LS-C	FTR Trappes 31.5/1.6.44.
LM142 LS-A	FTR Stuttgart 24/25.7.44.
LM156 LS-R	FTR Gelsenkirchen 12/13.6.44.
LM160 LS-D	From 626 Sqn.
LM167 LS-R	To 622 Sqn.
LM238 LS-T	
LM240 LS-R	To 149 Sqn.
LM441 LS-T	FTR Berlin 24/25.3.44.
LM456 LS-C	FTR Stuttgart 20/21.2.44.
LM465 LS-U	FTR Gelsenkirchen 12/13.6.44.
LM468 LS-F	FTR Dreux 10/11.6.44.
LM473 LS-P	To 5LFS.

LM490 LS-L	FTR Berlin 24/25.3.44.
LM533 LS-Y	FTR Lisieux 6/7.6.44.
LM534 LS-A	From 115 Sqn. FTR Maisy Palaiseau 7/8.6.44.
LM575 LS-H	From 90 Sqn. FTR Maisy Palaiseau 7/8.6.44.
LM576 LS-D	Crashed soon after take-off from Mildenhall while training 21.6.44.
ME434 LS-D	FTR Wanne-Eickel 7.2.45.
ME455 LS-O	
ME695 LS-R	To 1653CU.
ME844 LS-C/W	To 44 Sqn.
ME847	From 300 Sqn.
ME848 LS-N	To 103 Sqn.
ME849 LS-C/F/L	
ME850 LS-O/D	Damaged by American flak during operation to Vohwinkel 1.1.45.
ND763 LS-W	Crash-landed at Woodbridge on return from Düsseldorf 23.4.44.
ND955 LS-W	FTR Aachen 24/25.5.44.
ND958 LS-H	To 3LFS.
NF916 LS-Z	From 218 Sqn. FTR Solingen 5.11.44.
NF952 LS-Q	FTR Kiel 27/28.8.44.
NF953 LS-A	To 149 Sqn.
NF957 LS-X	To 1659CU.
NF958 LS-M	FTR Frankfurt 12/13.9.44.
NG338 LS-M/DJ-U	
NG357 LS-G/K	
NG358 LS-H/DJ-U	
NG364 LS-P	
NG365 LS-N	
NG444 LS-B/Y/Z	
NN700 LS-Q	FTR Rocquecourt 7/8.8.44.
NN704	
NX561 LS-L	
PA170 LS-N	FTR Oberhausen 4.12.44.
PA235 LS-E	
PB112 LS-K	To 195 Sqn
PB115 LS-W	FTR Homberg 2.11.44. Collided with HK612 (XV Sqn).
PB137 LS-U	FTR Heinsburg 16.11.44.
PB139 LS-B	To 195 Sqn.
PB259 LS-Q	From 218 Sqn.
PB674	To 218 Sqn.
PB802 LS-F	From 622 Sqn. Crashed in Norfolk during a night training exercise 17.1.45.
PD122	
PD125	
PD234 LS-E	From 218 Sqn.
PD285	To 622 Sqn and back.
PD404 LS-H	From 626 Sqn.
PD419 LS-P/V	FTR Dortmund 3/4.2.45.
PP664 LS-A/U	
PP672 LS-N	Crashed on take-off from Juvincourt for ferry flight 13.5.45.
RA543 LS-A	From 626 Sqn.
RF184	To 90 Sqn.
RF185	To 90 Sqn.

37 SQUADRON

Motto: Wise Without Eyes   Code LF

First formed on the 15th of April 1916 in an experimental role, 37 Squadron soon became absorbed into another unit, and had to be re-formed as a home defence squadron in mid September. A variety of aircraft types were operated, firstly against Zeppelins and then later the Gotha bombers based in Belgium. After the war the squadron lost its identity by being renumbered 39 Squadron in July 1919. On the 26th of April 1937 214 Squadron donated its B Flight to form a new 37 Squadron, a bomber unit initially operating Harrows until the arrival of Wellingtons in May 1939. As one of 3 Group's front line squadrons, 37 operated on the very first day of the war. The squadron's future lay overseas, however, and it flew out to the Middle East in November 1940. The squadron operated against enemy ports and bases in Libya, and a detachment was sent to Greece. Later targets were added in Sicily and southern Italy, and in February 1943 the squadron moved to Libya to increase its radius of operations. Further moves took place to Tunisia and Italy, where Wellingtons were finally phased out at the end of 1944 in favour of Liberators.

STATIONS

Feltwell   26.04.37 to 12.11.40

COMMANDING OFFICERS

Wing Commander F J Fogarty DFC AFC   08.09.38 to 03.06.40
Wing Commander W H Merton   03.06.40 to 18.01.41

AIRCRAFT

Wellington I	05.39 to 10.40
Wellington Ia	09.39 to 10.40
Wellington Ic	10.40 to 03.43
To Middle East	12.11.40

OPERATIONAL RECORD

Operations	Sorties	Aircraft Losses	% Losses
88	688	15	2.2

Category of Operations

Bombing	Leaflets
80	8

TABLE OF STATISTICS

Out of 42 Wellington Squadrons

22nd equal (with 419 Sqn) highest number of Wellington overall operations in Bomber Command.
21st highest number of Wellington sorties in Bomber Command.
32nd highest number of Wellington operational losses in Bomber Command.

Out of 28 bomber squadrons in 3 Group

21st highest number of overall operations in 3 Group.
19th highest number of sorties in 3 Group.
20th highest number of aircraft operational losses in 3 Group.

Out of 18 Wellington squadrons in 3 Group

14th equal (with 419 Sqn) highest number of Wellington overall operations in 3 Group.
13th highest number of Wellington sorties in 3 Group.
14th highest number of Wellington operational losses in 3 Group.

AIRCRAFT HISTORIES

Wellington	To November 1940.
L4326	To 214 Sqn.
L4327	To 214 Sqn.
L4328	To 11 OTU.
L4329	To 11 OTU.
L4331	To 215 Sqn.
L4332	To 214 Sqn.
L4336	To 215 Sqn.
L4337	To 214 Sqn.
L4338	To 214 Sqn.
L4339	To 38 Sqn via 215 Sqn and 11 OTU.
L4347	To 148 Sqn.
L4348	To 148 Sqn.
L4349	To 15 OTU.
L4351	To 215 Sqn.
L4352	To 3GRU.
L4353	To 215 Sqn.
L7779	To 15 OTU.
L7780	To 11 OTU.
L7781	Destroyed by fire at Feltwell 3.8.40.
L7782	To 15 OTU.
L7783	To 214 Sqn.
L7784	To 75 Sqn.
L7790	Destroyed in air raid on Feltwell 24.9.40.
L7791	FTR Nieuwpoort 31.5/1.6.40.
L7792	FTR Hamburg 14/15.7.40.
L7793	FTR from attack on enemy communications in Belgium 25/26.5.40.
L7794	To 108 Sqn.
L7806	To 75 Sqn.
L7850	To 15 OTU.
L7865	To Middle East.
L7866	To Middle East.
N2757	To Middle East.
N2777	From 75 Sqn.
N2882	To Hendon.
N2888	FTR from armed reconnaissance to Wilhelmshaven 18.12.39.
N2889	TR from armed reconnaissance to Wilhelmshaven 18.12.39.
N2890	To CGS.
N2903	To 214 Sqn.
N2904	FTR from armed reconnaissance to Wilhelmshaven 18.12.39.
N2905	To 11 OTU.
N2935	FTR from armed reconnaissance to Wilhelmshaven 18.12.39.

N2936	FTR from armed reconnaissance to Wilhelmshaven 18.12.39.
N2937	To 75 Sqn.
N2938	To 57 Sqn.
N2951	To 38 Sqn.
N2952	To 38 Sqn.
N2953	To 38 Sqn.
N2954	To 38 Sqn.
N2980	From 149 Sqn. To 20 OTU.
N2992	FTR Hanover 1/2.9.40.
N2993	To 214 Sqn.
N2994	To 214 Sqn.
N3019	To CGS.
P2515	FTR from leafleting sortie 23/24.3.40.
P2516	To 15 OTU.
P2517	To 149 Sqn via Hendon/Yeadon.
P2525	To 214 Sqn.
P9213	From 214 Sqn. FTR Stavanger 30.4/1.5.40.
P9215	From 214 Sqn. FTR Stavanger 30.4/1.5.40.
P9216	From 214 Sqn. To 305 Sqn via 11 OTU.
P9217	From 214 Sqn. To 11 OTU.
P9288	FTR Niewpoort 31.5/1.6.40.
R1020	To 75 Sqn.
R1033	From 38 Sqn. Returned to 38 Sqn.
R1067	From 15 OTU. To Middle East.
R1095	From 75 Sqn. To Middle East.
R1290	From RAE. To Middle East.
R1387	To Middle East.
R3150	From 115 Sqn. To 149 Sqn and back. FTR Bitterfeld 29/30.9.40.
R3179	To Middle East.
R3195	From 115 Sqn. To 75 Sqn.
R3200	To 99 Sqn.
R3210	FTR Gelsenkirchen 20/21.7.40.
R3211	To 75 Sqn.
R3224	To 75 Sqn.
R3231	To 75 Sqn.
R3236	FTR Bremen 6/7.7.40.
R3239	To 75 Sqn and back. To Middle East.
R3275	To 75 Sqn.
R3281	To ATA.
R3284	To 75 Sqn.
T2503	To 75 Sqn.
T2504	To 75 Sqn.
T2508	To 75 Sqn and back. To Malta.
T2512	To Middle East.
T2547	To 75 Sqn.
T2575	To Malta
T2580	To 38 Sqn.
T2607	To Middle East.
T2609	To 3METS.
T2614	From 108 Sqn. To Middle East.
T2616	To Middle East.
T2711	To Middle East.

T2728	To Middle East.
T2730	From 70 Sqn. To ASR Flt.
T2801	From 15 OTU. To Middle East.
T2812	To Middle East.
T2818	From 148 Sqn. To Middle East.
T2821	From 75 Sqn. To Middle East.
T2822	From 75 Sqn. To Middle East.
T2837	From 75 Sqn. To Middle East.

38 SQUADRON

Motto: Ante Lucem (Before the dawn)   Code HD

No. 38 Squadron was formed on the 1st of April 1916, but was redesignated during the following month. The process began again in July, when the squadron was re-formed as a home defence unit to protect the Midlands from Zeppelin incursions. Later in the year the squadron added night flying training to its role, and this was how it spent its time until moving to France as a night-bomber unit in May 1918. The squadron returned to the UK in February 1919, and was disbanded in July. Re-formation took place in September 1935 when 99 Squadron donated its B Flight as the nucleus at Mildenhall. The squadron was equipped with Heyfords until becoming the only unit to operate Hendons. The latter were replaced by Wellingtons at the end of 1938. The squadron had a low-key introduction to the war, and bombing operations did not begin in earnest until the German march into the Low Countries. In November 1940 the squadron moved to Egypt for operations over Libya, Italy and the Balkans. The year 1942 found the squadron carrying out night torpedo and mining operations, and although torpedo attacks ceased in January 1943, mining, reconnaissance/bombing and anti-submarine operations continued. Towards the end of 1944 the squadron moved to Greece and finally Italy, from where operations were flown against coastal shipping for what remained of the war.

STATIONS

Marham   05.05.37 to 22.11.40

COMMANDING OFFICER

Wing Commander C D Adams   08.02.39 to 29.11.40

AIRCRAFT

Wellington I	11.38 to 12.39
Wellington Ia/Ic	09.39 to 01.42
To Middle East	12.11.40

OPERATIONAL RECORD

Operations	Sorties	Aircraft Losses	% Losses
91	659	7	1.1

Category of Operations

Bombing	Leaflets
88	3

TABLE OF STATISTICS

Out of 42 Wellington squadrons

19th highest number of Wellington overall operations in Bomber Command.
22nd highest number of Wellington sorties in Bomber Command.
39th highest number of Wellington operational losses in Bomber Command.

Out of 28 bomber squadrons in 3 Group

18th highest number of overall operations in 3 Group.
20th highest number of sorties in 3 Group.
26th highest number of aircraft operational losses in 3 Group.

Out of 18 Wellington squadrons in 3 Group

12th highest number of Wellington overall operations in 3 Group.
14th highest number of Wellington sorties in 3 Group.
16th highest number of Wellington operational losses in 3 Group.

AIRCRAFT HISTORIES

Wellington	To November 1940.
L4218	From 99 Sqn. To 15 OTU.
L4219	From RAE. To 15 OTU.
L4230	To 75 Sqn.
L4231	To 75 Sqn.
L4234	To 218 Sqn via 20 OTU.
L4235	To RAE.
L4236	To 148 Sqn.
L4237	To 148 Sqn.
L4238	Became ground instruction machine.
L4239	Crashed in Norfolk during ferry flight 5.11.39.
L4241	To 20 OTU.
L4242	To 148 Sqn.
L4245	To 15 OTU.
L4248	To 15 OTU.
L4295	To 115 Sqn.
L4296	To 20 OTU.
L4307	From 115 Sqn. Became ground instruction machine.
L4335	From A&AEE. To 215 Sqn.
L4339	From 37 Sqn via 215 Sqn and 11 OTU. FTR from reconnaissance Sortie 13/14.4.40.
L4391	To RAE.
L7808	To Middle East.
L7809	FTR Hamburg 24/25.10.40.
L7810	To 115 Sqn.
L7854	To 115 Sqn.
N2740	To Middle East.
N2756	From 115 Sqn. To Middle East.
N2759	From 115 Sqn. To Middle East.
N2760	From 115 Sqn. Returned to 115 Sqn.
N2855	From 115 Sqn. FTR Ostend 11/12.9.40.
N2878	From 115 Sqn. To 12 OTU.
N2879	To FTU.

N2880	To 311 Sqn.
N2881	To CGS.
N2884	From 115 Sqn. To 20 OTU.
N2900	From 115 Sqn. To 20 OTU.
N2906	To 214 Sqn.
N2907	To 20 OTU.
N2908	To 20 OTU.
N2909	To 221 Sqn.
N2910	To 221 Sqn.
N2951	From 37 Sqn. FTR from armed reconnaissance of enemy shipping 20/21.2.40.
N2952	From 37 Sqn. To 150 Sqn.
N2953	From 37 Sqn. FTR Black Forest 14/15.6.40.
N2954	From 37 Sqn. To 15 Sqn.
N2956	To 99 Sqn.
N2957	To 99 Sqn.
N2958	To 99 Sqn.
N2963	To 1 AAS.
N2995	To 11 OTU.
N2996	To 103 Sqn.
N2997	To 103 Sqn.
N2998	To 150 Sqn.
P2526	Abandoned over Norfolk on return from armed reconnaissance of Enemy shipping 21.2.40.
P9207	From NZ Flt. To 115 Sqn.
P9220	To 1 AAS.
P9226	To 115 Sqn.
P9227	To 115 Sqn.
P9235	To 115 Sqn.
P9249	Crashed in Norfolk during ferry flight 16.6.40.
P9250	To Middle East.
P9265	To Malta.
P9269	FTR from reconnaissance sortie to Norwegian coast 12.4.40.
P9284	From 115 Sqn. Returned to 115 Sqn.
P9285	From 115 Sqn. Returned to 115 Sqn.
P9286	To 115 Sqn.
P9287	FTR Berlin 7/8.10.40.
P9290	To 115 Sqn.
P9291	To 115 Sqn.
P9292	To 115 Sqn.
P9293	To Middle East.
P9294	To 108 Sqn.
P9295	To 1AAS.
P9296	To 115 Sqn.
P9297	To 115 Sqn.
P9299	From 115 Sqn. Returned to 115 Sqn.
R1018	To 148 Sqn.
R1033	From 115 Sqn. To 37 Sqn and back. To Middle East.
R1034	From 115 Sqn. Returned to 115 Sqn.
R1139	From 15 OTU. To Middle East.
R1180	To Middle East.
R1182	To 40 Sqn.
R3162	FTR Dijksmuide 30/31.5.40.

R3198	To 115 Sqn.
R3213	To 115 Sqn.
R3219	FTR Leipzig 30.9/1.10.40.
R3291	From 115 Sqn. To Middle East.
R3293	To OADF.
T2465	To 115 Sqn.
T2507	From 115 Sqn.
T2551	From 115 Sqn. To Middle East.
T2570	To Middle East.

40 SQUADRON

Motto: Hostem Coelo Expellere (To drive the enemy from the sky)   Code BL

Formed on the 26th of February 1916, 40 Squadron moved to France as a fighter unit in August of that year and conducted patrols over the Western Front. A change of role to low-level ground attack followed the German offensive in March 1918, and in February 1919, the squadron returned to the UK for eventual disbandment at the end of June. Re-formation took place on the 1st of April 1931, and after operating a number of types, Fairey Battles were taken on charge in July 1938. The squadron moved to France on the 2nd of September 1939, the final day of peace, as part of the Advanced Air Striking Force. Its time away from the UK was relatively brief and its few operational sorties were uneventful. No. 40 Squadron was brought home in December 1939 along with XV Squadron, and joined 2 Group to fly operations with Blenheims. The squadron suffered heavy losses in the cauldron of the Battle of France, and after the country's fall 40 Squadron took part in raids on invasion barges in the occupied ports. A move to 3 Group in November 1940 saw the squadron convert to Wellingtons, with which type it operated at night against German industrial targets. A temporary posting to the Middle-Eastern theatre in October 1941 became permanent, and a home echelon began to rebuild. After some political posturing it was decided to renumber the home echelon, and allow the overseas element to retain the coveted 40 Squadron badge. The home echelon was built up to full squadron status, and in February 1942 became 156 Squadron. Six months later 156 Squadron was posted to the newly formed Pathfinder Force as a founder member, and served in that role until war's end.

From 2 Group   11.40

STATIONS

Wyton	02.12.39 to 01.02.41
Alconbury	01.02.41 to 14.02.42

COMMANDING OFFICERS

Wing Commander D H F Barnett	04.06.40 to 23.12.40
Wing Commander E J B Davy	23.12.40 to 23.08.41
Wing Commander L J Stickley	23.08.41 to 23.10.41
Squadron Leader G J Spence	06.11.41 to 26.11.41
Wing Commander P G R Heath	26.11.41 to 14.02.42

AIRCRAFT

Wellington   11.40 to 02.42
Remnant renumbered as 156 Squadron   12.02.42

OPERATIONAL RECORD

Operations	Sorties	Aircraft Losses	% Losses
90	730	31	4.2

Category of Operations
Bombing
90

TABLE OF STATISTICS

Out of 42 Wellington squadrons

20th highest number of Wellington overall operations in Bomber Command.
20th highest number of Wellington sorties in Bomber Command.
15th highest number of Wellington operational losses in Bomber Command.

Out of 28 bomber squadrons in 3 Group

20th highest number of overall operations in 3 Group.
18th highest number of sorties in 3 Group.
15th highest number of aircraft operational losses in 3 Group.

Out of 18 Wellington squadrons in 3 Group

13th highest number of Wellington overall operations in 3 Group.
12th highest number of Wellington sorties in 3 Group.
9th highest number of Wellington operational losses in 3 Group.

AIRCRAFT HISTORIES

Wellington	From November 1940.
L4343	From 214 Sqn via 418 Sqn and 15 OTU. To 57 Sqn.
L7772	From 75 Sqn via 15 OTU. To 161 Sqn.
L7854	From 115 Sqn. To 20 OTU.
N2843 BL-L	From 15 Sqn. FTR Münster 6/7.7.41.
N3000	From 9 Sqn. To 311 Sqn.
P9280	From 75 Sqn. To 4BAT Flt and back. To 1429Flt.
R1007 BL-L	FTR Kiel 7/8.4.41.
R1013 BL-B	FTR Berlin 12/13.3.41.
R1030 BL-R	Ditched in North Sea on return from Ostende 2/3.9.41.
R1066 BL-K	From 15 Sqn. To Middle East.
R1166 BL-M	Crashed on landing at Alconbury on return from Berlin 24.3.41.
R1167 BL-N	FTR Hanover 15/16.5.41.
R1168 BL-B	To 156 Sqn.
R1182 BL-D	From 38 Sqn. To Middle East.
R1239	From 214 Sqn. To 20 OTU.
R1240	From 15 Sqn. To 57 Sqn and back. To 1429Flt.
R1312 BL-J	
R1323 BL-J	FTR Düsseldorf 11/12.6.41.
R1328 BL-T	From 214 Sqn. FTR Frankfurt 12/13.9.41.

R1330 BL-H	FTR Hamburg 11/12.5.41.
R1331 BL-R	Crashed in Devon on return from Berlin 18.4.41.
R1338	To 101 Sqn.
R1406 BL-C	FTR Cologne 26/27.6.41.
R1436 BL-U	
R1438	Crashed in Alconbury circuit on return from Düsseldorf 3.6.41.
R1456	To 1503BAT Flt.
R1461 BL-Z	FTR Hamburg 11/12.5.41.
R1464 BL-L	From 15 Sqn. FTR Düsseldorf 11/12.6.41.
R1493 BL-P	FTR Merignac 10/11.4.41.
R1643	To 99 Sqn.
R1647 BL-M	To 27 OTU.
R1770 BL-C	FTR Osnabrück 9/10.7.41.
R1793	From 15 OTU. To 1503BAT Flt.
T2468	From 9 Sqn. To 311 Sqn.
T2514 BL-D	FTR Karlsruhe 25/26.8.41.
T2515 BL-U	FTR Boulogne 12/13.3.41.
T2701 BL-S	To 16 OTU.
T2718	Crashed on take-off from Wyton while training 12.12.40.
T2847	To 15 Sqn.
T2911 BL-A	To 21 OTU.
T2912 BL-S	FTR Wilhelmshaven 16/17.1.41.
T2986 BL-A	FTR Brest 24.7.41.
W5454	To 99 Sqn.
W5456BL-P	FTR Hamburg 29/30.6.41.
W5704	To 57 Sqn.
W5718	From 99 Sqn. To 304 Sqn.
W5727	To 218 Sqn.
X3174	To 149 Sqn.
X3220 BL-H	Crashed in Norfolk when bound for Hamburg 16.7.41.
X9619 BL-M	FTR Nuremberg 12/13.10.41.
X9630 BL-J	FTR Hamburg 16/17.7.41.
X9662 BL-U	To Malta.
X9669 BL-F	Crashed on landing at Alconbury following early return from Frankfurt 2.9.41.
X9742	From 215 Sqn. FTR Hamburg 14/15.1.42.
X9749 BL-J	FTR Karlsruhe 25/26.8.41.
X9763 BL-U	To Malta.
X9765 BL-A	To Malta.
X9785	From 214 Sqn. To 218 Sqn.
X9822 BL-T/J	FTR Bremen 12/13.10.41.
X9824	From 149 Sqn. Returned to 149 Sqn and back. FTR Wilhelmshaven 10/11.1.42.
X9871	From 215 Sqn. To 150 Sqn.
X9882 BL-W	FTR Nuremberg 14/15.10.41.
X9889	To Malta.
X9907	To Malta.
X9909	From 115 Sqn. SOC 15.1.42.
X9911	To 27 OTU.
X9912	From 99 Sqn. To Malta.
X9919	To Malta.
X9921	SOC 15.1.42.
X9926	BL-T FTR Nuremberg 14/15.10.41.

X9974		From 214 Sqn. Crashed soon after take-off from Hampstead Norris for ferry flight to Gibraltar 26.10.41.
Z1046		To Middle East.
Z1073		To 26 OTU.
Z1079		To Malta.
Z1081		To 101 Sqn.
Z1083		To 75 Sqn.
Z1084		To 115 Sqn.
Z8782	BL-E/H	FTR Nuremberg 14/15.10.41.
Z8837		From 149 Sqn. To 11 OTU.
Z8838		From 149 Sqn. Returned to 149 Sqn.
Z8839	BL-L	FTR Duisburg 28/29.8.41.
Z8853		From 115 Sqn. Returned to 115 Sqn.
Z8855		From 99 Sqn. SOC 24.1.42.
Z8859		From 75 Sqn. To 156 Sqn.
Z8862	BL-B	FTR Duisburg 16/17.10.41.
Z8894		To 218 Sqn.
Z8904		Abandoned over Essex following early return from Mannheim 11.2.42.
Z8959		To Malta.
Z8968		From 75 Sqn. To 12 OTU.
Z8977		From 75 Sqn. To 18 OTU.
Z8981		To 57 Sqn.

57 SQUADRON

Motto: Corpus Non Animum Muto (I change my body not my spirit)   Code DX

The history of 57 Squadron can be traced back to its original formation as a flying training unit on the 8th of June 1916. In December of that year it moved to France and became a fighter squadron, before changing roles yet again in the summer of 1917, and spending the remainder of the war as a bomber and reconnaissance unit, eventually undergoing disbandment on the last day of 1919. The squadron remained on the shelf until its re-formation as a light bomber unit in October 1931, and continued in this role, eventually taking delivery of Blenheims at the end of March 1938. It was with this type that the squadron faced the impending conflict in September 1939. No. 57 Squadron was in action from the start of hostilities flying Blenheims with the Advanced Air Striking Force in France. On return to the UK the squadron joined 2 Group, before spending a short time with Coastal Command and ultimately converting to the Wellington for a move to 3 Group. In the autumn of 1942 the squadron underwent another metamorphosis, joining 5 Group as a Lancaster unit. Its C Flight became the nucleus of 617 Squadron in March 1943, and of 630 Squadron in November. In whichever aircraft and Group 57 Squadron operated it sustained higher than average percentage casualties. That not withstanding it remained at the forefront of operations, serving with distinction until war's end.

From 2 Group   12.11.40

STATIONS

Wyton	01.11.40 to 20.11.40
Feltwell	20.11.40 to 05.01.42
Methwold	05.01.42 to 04.09.42

COMMANDING OFFICERS

Wing Commander A H Garland   07.02.40 to 24.02.41
Wing Commander S S Bertram DFC   24.02.41 to 08.05.41
Wing Commander J M Southwell   08.05.41 to 19.03.42
Wing Commander M V Peters-Smith DFC   19.03.42 to 27.07.42
Wing Commander E J Laine DFC   30.07.42 to 23.09.42

AIRCRAFT

Wellington Ic   11.40 to 02.42
Wellington II   07.41 to 02.42
Wellington III   02.42 to 09.42

To 5 Group   04.09.42

OPERATIONAL RECORD

Operations	Sorties	Aircraft Losses	% Losses
173	1,056	54	5.1

Category of Operations

Bombing	Mining
166	7

TABLE OF STATISTICS

(Heavy squadrons)

15th highest number of overall operations in Bomber Command.
23rd highest number of sorties in Bomber Command.
9th highest number of aircraft operational losses in Bomber Command.
17th highest number of bombing operations in Bomber Command.
21st highest number of mining operations in Bomber Command.
Highest percentage loss rate in Bomber Command.

Out of 42 Wellington squadrons

11th highest number of Wellington overall operations in Bomber Command.
15th highest number of Wellington sorties in Bomber Command.
5th highest number of Wellington operational losses in Bomber Command.

Out of 28 bomber squadrons in 3 Group

13th highest number of overall operations in 3 Group.
15th highest number of sorties in 3 Group.
10th highest number of aircraft operational losses in 3 Group.

Out of 18 Wellington squadrons in 3 Group

7th highest number of Wellington overall operations in 3 Group.
9th highest number of Wellington sorties in 3 Group.
4th highest number of Wellington operational losses in 3 Group.

AIRCRAFT HISTORIES

Wellington	From November 1940.
L4343	From 40 Sqn. To 15 Sqn.
N2783	To 149 Sqn.

N2784 DX-N	Crashed on approach to Feltwell on return from Duisburg 16.7.41.
N2810	To 9FPP.
N2841 DX-C	To 27 OTU.
N2853	To 149 Sqn.
N2938	From 37 Sqn. To 311 Sqn.
P9209	From 311 Sqn. To CGS.
R1040	To 9 Sqn.
R1240	From 40 Sqn. Returned to 40 Sqn.
R1271 DX-P	Ditched during operation to Berlin 20/21.9.41.
R1281	To 9 Sqn.
R1369	FTR Kiel 24/25.7.41.
R1437 DX-X	FTR Vegesack 9/10.4.41.
R1441	From 311 Sqn. Crashed on approach to East Wretham on return from Cologne 28.3.41.
R1462	To 214 Sqn.
R1508	To 20 OTU.
R1589 DX-M	From 75 Sqn. Crashed near Feltwell when bound for Essen 4.7.41.
R1592	From 150 Sqn. To 22 OTU.
R1605 DX-A	To 1503BAT Flt.
R1608	FTR Kiel 24/25.6.41.
R1624 DX-U	FTR Duisburg 15/16.7.41.
R1706 DX-W	Damaged beyond repair following operation to Frankfurt 20/21.9.41.
R1707	From 9 Sqn. To 156 Sqn.
R1722	From 9 Sqn. Crash-landed in Suffolk on return from Hamburg 27.10.41.
R1757	From 9 Sqn. FTR Nuremberg 12/13.10.41.
R1763	From 9 Sqn. To 18 OTU.
R1792	From 75 Sqn. Crashed on take-off from Feltwell when bound for Brest 13.9.41.
R1794 DX-R	FTR Bremen 27/28.6.41.
R1799 DX-F	To 1503BAT Flt.
R3169	From 75 Sqn. Returned to 75 Sqn.
R3195 DX-O	From 75 Sqn. To 20 OTU.
R3231	From 75 Sqn. To 11 OTU.
R3275	From 75 Sqn. To 12 OTU.
R3297	From 75 Sqn. To 25 OTU.
T2504	From 75 Sqn. Destroyed by enemy action at Feltwell 7.5.41.
T2713 DX-Q	To 149 Sqn.
T2715 DX-S	From 15 Sqn. To 16 OTU.
T2721 DX-S	To 99 Sqn.
T2804	FTR Berlin 9/10.4.41.
T2957 To 99 Sqn.	
T2959 DX-D	Crashed near East Wretham on return from Le Havre 11.12.41.
T2961 DX-Q	From 15 Sqn. To 18 OTU.
T2962 DX-L	To 311 Sqn.
T2970	FTR Hamburg 13/14.3.41.
W5434	From 218 Sqn. Crashed in Cambridgeshire on return from Frankfurt 3.9.41.
W5445	From 9 Sqn. FTR Hamburg 30.9/1.10.41.

W5616 DX-K	Crashed on approach to Methwold during air-test 7.7.41.
W5704 DX-G	From 40 Sqn. To AFDU.
X3162	FTR Ostend 21/22.3.41.
X3221	From 311 Sqn. To 103 Sqn.
X3278	To 3 OTU.
X3284	To 424 Sqn.
X3285	From 101 Sqn. To 75 Sqn and back. To 23 OTU.
X3305	From 9 Sqn. To 150 Sqn.
X3331 DX-F	FTR Kassel 27/28.8.42.
X3332	From 9 Sqn. To 25 OTU.
X3333	To 156 Sqn.
X3346	From 9 Sqn. To 23 OTU.
X3353	From 9 Sqn. To 25 OTU.
X3371	FTR Flensburg 18/19.8.42.
X3387	Force-landed near Lakenheath when bound for Cologne 31.5.42.
X3389	To 9 Sqn.
X3390	From 419 Sqn. Returned to 419 Sqn.
X3402	From 115 Sqn. To 75 Sqn and back. To 1483Flt.
X3410	FTR Hanau 1/2.4.42.
X3425	FTR Hanau 1/2.4.42.
X3448	To 115 Sqn.
X3450	To 115 Sqn.
X3460	To 424 Sqn.
X3474	To 9 Sqn.
X3478	FTR Hamburg 17/18.4.42.
X3542	FTR Hamburg 17/18.4.42.
X3558	To 75 Sqn.
X3584 DX-B	From 115 Sqn. To 75 Sqn and back. FTR Duisburg 21/22.7.42.
X3599	Crashed in Ireland during training 16.3.42.
X3600	To 426 Sqn.
X3607	FTR Hanau 1/2.4.42.
X3608	To 23 OTU.
X3640	FTR Gennevilliers 29/30.4.42.
X3653	FTR Bremen 27.7.42.
X3658 DX-P	To 12 OTU.
X3665	FTR Essen 26/27.3.42.
X3696	To 426 Sqn.
X3698 DX-M	
X3726	From 419 Sqn. To 115 Sqn.
X3745	From 150 Sqn. Returned to 150 Sqn.
X3746	Force-landed at Feltwell during training 17.6.42.
X3747	To 75 Sqn.
X3748	FTR Hanau 1/2.4.42.
X3755	From 150 Sqn. To 75 Sqn.
X3756	Abandoned near Weston-Super-Mare during training 3.5.42.
X3757	FTR Hamburg 8/9.4.42.
X3758	FTR Emden 22/23.6.42.
X3946	To 75 Sqn.
X9642 DX-A	To 18 OTU.
X9744	From 214 Sqn. To 99 Sqn.
X9745	To 218 Sqn.

X9748		To 419 Sqn.
X9756		FTR Cologne 10/11.10.41.
X9760		From 75 Sqn. To 311 Sqn.
X9786		From 9 Sqn. To 26 OTU.
X9787		From 311 Sqn. FTR Essen 2/3.6.42.
X9874		To 419 Sqn.
X9923		From 9 Sqn. Crashed on landing at Marham on return from Hamburg 16.9.41
X9924		From 9 Sqn. To 99 Sqn.
X9978		FTR Cologne 15/16.10.41.
X9982		To 16 OTU.
Z1053		From 75 Sqn. To 419 Sqn.
Z1067		To 419 Sqn.
Z1085		To 1503BAT Flt.
Z1087	DX-Q	From 75 Sqn. To 20 OTU.
Z1091		From 75 Sqn. To 419 Sqn.
Z1093		From 75 Sqn. To 1506BAT Flt.
Z1096		From 75 Sqn. Crashed soon after take-off from Feltwell when bound for Brest 6.1.42.
Z1097		FTR Düsseldorf 27/28.12.41.
Z1145		From 75 Sqn. To 419 Sqn.
Z1147		To 311 Sqn.
Z1564		FTR from mining sortie 7/8.5.42.
Z1565		FTR Hanau 1/2.4.42.
BJ619		FTR Nuremberg Z1567 To 25 OTU.
Z1568		To TFU.
Z1569		To 101 Sqn.
Z1578		FTR Bremen 29/30.6.42.
Z1611		FTR Emden 19/20.6.42.
Z1618		FTR Bremen 29/30.6.42.
Z1650		FTR Hamburg 28/29.7.42.
Z1652		To 75 Sqn.
Z1653		To 115 Sqn.
Z1654		FTR Hamburg 26/27.7.42.
Z1656		FTR Mainz 11/12.8.42.
Z1657	DX-A	To 115 Sqn.
Z1663		From 9 Sqn. To 115 Sqn.
Z1747		To 75 Sqn.
Z8403		To 12 Sqn.
Z8429		To 75 Sqn.
Z8704	DX-V	FTR Mannheim 6/7.8.41.
Z8789		Crashed on landing at Feltwell on return from Genoa 29.9.41.
Z8792		Force-landed in Suffolk on return from Mannheim 23.10.41.
Z8794	DX-H	FTR Hüls 6/7.9.41.
Z8800		To 419 Sqn.
Z8868		From 75 Sqn. FTR Genoa 28/29.9.41.
Z8893		To 23 OTU.
Z8897		FTR Cologne 10/11.10.41.
Z8903		FTR from Rover patrol to Münster 7/8.11.41.
Z8904		To 75 Sqn.
Z8946		FTR Hamburg 26/27.10.41.
Z8951		To 214 Sqn.

Z8961	To 75 Sqn.
Z8965	To 218 Sqn.
Z8968	To 75 Sqn.
Z8972	To 15 OTU.
Z8977	To 75 Sqn.
Z8978	To 75 Sqn.
Z8980	To 99 Sqn.
Z8981	From 40 Sqn. To 419 Sqn.
Z8985	FTR from Rover patrol to Münster 7/8.11.41.
BJ581	To 101 Sqn.
BJ582	To 199 Sqn via 11 OTU.
BJ593	Crashed on approach to Methwold while training 11.8.42.
BJ596	To 75 Sqn.
BJ607	FTR Düsseldorf 31.7/1.8.42.
BJ612	To 16 OTU. 28/29.8.42.
BJ667	To 23 OTU.
BJ673	FTR Duisburg 23/24.7.42.
BJ701	FTR Nuremberg 28/29.8.42.
BJ705	To 101 Sqn.
BJ707	To 75 Sqn.
BJ711	To 101 Sqn.
BJ770	To 115 Sqn.
BJ771	To 115 Sqn.
BJ830	FTR Mainz 11/12.8.42.
BJ833	To 115 Sqn.
DV759	To 304 Sqn via 18 OTU.
DV806	Ditched off Kent coast during operation to Boulogne 17/18.5.42.
DV809	To 1483Flt.
DV816	FTR Essen 1/2.6.42.
DV819	To 109 Sqn.
DV845	To 109 Sqn.
DV865	To 1429Flt.
DV870	To 109 Sqn.
DV883	To 1429Flt.
DV884	To 1429Flt.
HF915	FTR Essen 5/6.6.42.
HF921	To 311 Sqn.

75 (NZ) SQUADRON

Motto: Ake ake kia kaha (For ever and ever be strong)   Codes AA, JN

The original 75 Squadron was formed as a home defence anti-Zeppelin unit on the 1st of October 1916. Moves to East Anglia and later the London area saw the squadron through to the end of the Great War. Disbandment came in June 1919, and the squadron remained on the shelf until March 1937, when it was reborn from B Flight of 215 Squadron. After initially training on Virginias and Ansons the squadron took on Harrows, but added Ansons again to its strength when becoming a group pool training squadron in March 1939. On the 4th of April 1940 the squadron lost its identity by being absorbed into 15 OTU. On the same day the New Zealand Flight acquired the number 75, and the words New Zealand were added. As 75

(New Zealand) Squadron, and populated as far as possible by New Zealanders, the unit served with distinction with 3 Group for the remainder of the war, and flew over 8,000 sorties, the highest in the Command. It also sustained heavy casualties, losing the second highest number of aircraft in the Command.

STATIONS

As New Zealand Flight

Harwell	09.39 to 01.40
Stradishall	01.40 to 02.40
Feltwell	02.40 to 04.40

As 75 (New Zealand) Squadron

Feltwell	04.04.40 to 15.08.40
Mildenhall	15.08.40 to 01.01.41
Feltwell	01.01.41 to 01.11.42
Oakington (Detachment)	15.10.42 to 12.42
Newmarket	01.11.42 to 28.06.43
Mepal	28.06.43 to 21.07.45

COMMANDING OFFICERS

Wing Commander M W Buckley	04.04.40 to 11.40
Wing Commander C E Kay	11.40 to 09.41
Wing Commander R Sawrey-Cookson	09.41 to 06.04.42
Wing Commander E G Olson	06.04.42 to 07.42
Wing Commander V Mitchell	07.42 to 18.12.42
Squadron Leader G T Fowler (Temp)	18.12.42 to 01.43
Wing Commander G A Lane	01.43 to 03.05.43
Wing Commander M Wyatt	03.05.43 to 08.43
Wing Commander R D Max	08.43 to 05.44
Wing Commander R J A Leslie	05.44 to 12.44
Wing Commander R J Newton	12.44 to 02.01.45
Wing Commander C H Baigent	02.01.45 to 10.45

AIRCRAFT

Wellington I	07.39 to 04.40
Wellington Ia	04.40 to 09.40
Wellington Ic	04.40 to 01.42
Wellington III	01.42 to 10.42
Stirling I	10.42 to 08.43
Stirling III	02.43 to 04.44
Lancaster I/III	03.44 to 10.45

OPERATIONAL RECORD

Operations	Sorties	Aircraft Losses	% Losses
739	8,017	193	2.4

Category of Operations

Bombing	Mining	Other
584	149	6

Wellingtons

Operations	Sorties	Aircraft Losses	% Losses
320	2,540	74	2.9

Category of Operations

Bombing	Mining	Other
291	24	5

Stirlings

Operations	Sorties	Aircraft Losses	% Losses
210	1,736	72	4.1

Category of Operations

Bombing	Mining	Other
103	107	0

Lancaster

Operations	Sorties	Aircraft Losses	% Losses
209	3,741	47	1.3

Category of Operations

Bombing	Mining	Other
190	18	1

TABLE OF STATISTICS

(Heavy squadrons)
2nd highest number of overall operations in Bomber Command.
Highest number of sorties in Bomber Command.
5th highest number of bombing operations in Bomber Command.
3rd highest number of mining sorties in Bomber Command
2nd highest number of aircraft operational losses in Bomber Command.

Out of 42 Wellington squadrons

3rd highest number of Wellington overall operations in Bomber Command.
2nd highest number of Wellington sorties in Bomber Command.
2nd highest number of Wellington operational losses in Bomber Command.

Out of 59 Lancaster squadrons

26th highest number of Lancaster overall operations in Bomber Command.
18th highest number of Lancaster sorties in Bomber Command.
30th highest number of Lancaster operational losses in Bomber Command.

Out of 28 bomber squadrons in 3 Group

Highest number of overall operations in 3 Group.
Highest number of sorties in 3 Group.
2nd highest number of aircraft operational losses in 3 Group.

Out of 18 Wellington squadrons in 3 Group

2nd highest number of Wellington overall operations in 3 Group.
2nd highest number of Wellington sorties in 3 Group.
2nd highest number of Wellington operational losses in 3 Group.

Out of 12 Stirling bomber squadrons in 3 Group

6th highest number of Stirling overall operations in 3 Group.
5th highest number of Stirling sorties in 3 Group.
4th highest number of Stirling operational losses in 3 Group.

Out of 11 Lancaster squadrons in 3 Group

5th highest number of Lancaster overall operations in 3 Group.
2nd highest number of Lancaster sorties in 3 Group.
3rd highest number of Lancaster operational losses in 3 Group.

AIRCRAFT HISTORIES

Wellington	To October 1942.
L4330	To 3BAT Flt via 75 Sqn.
L7784	From 37 Sqn. To CGS.
L7797	To XV Sqn.
L7806	From 37 Sqn. To 149 Sqn.
L7818 AA-R	To 15 OTU.
L7847	From 214 Sqn. To 99 Sqn.
L7848	To 21 OTU.
L7857	Abandoned over Cumberland on return from Kiel 17.10.40.
N2747	To 214 Sqn.
N2777	To 37 Sqn.
N2854	FTR Brest 24.7.41.
N2877	From 115 Sqn. To 15 OTU.
N2894	On loan from CGS. FTR Cologne 30/31.5.42.
N2895	From 9 Sqn. To 15 OTU.
N2901	From 115 Sqn. To 15 OTU.
N2913	From 99 Sqn. To 15 OTU.
N2937	From 37 Sqn. To 218 Sqn.
N2982	From 9 Sqn. To 15 OTU.
N2985	From 99 Sqn. To 15 OTU.
N3014	From 9 Sqn. To 215 Sqn.
P9206	From NZ Flt. To 20 OTU.
P9207	From NZ Flt. To 38 Sqn.
P9209	From NZ Flt. To 311 Sqn.
P9210	From NZ Flt. To RAE.
P9212	From NZ Flt. To 311 Sqn.
P9209	From NZ Flt. To 311 Sqn.
P9280	From 99 Sqn. To 40 Sqn.
P9292	From 115 Sqn. FTR Berlin 23/24.10.40.
R1020	From 37 Sqn. Crashed on landing at Feltwell during training 18.11.40.
R1038	FTR Kiel 11/12.9.41.
R1095	To 37 Sqn.
R1161	To 311 Sqn.
R1162	To 27 OTU.
R1163	From 15 Sqn. To 103 Sqn.
R1177 AA-F	Abandoned over Essex on return from Frankfurt 29.9.41.
R1237	To 21 OTU.
R1409	From 15 OTU. To 1505BAT Flt.
R1457	To 156 Sqn.
R1466	From 311 Sqn. To 15 OTU.

R1518	Abandoned over Norfolk on return from Berlin 21.9.41.
R1589	To 57 Sqn.
R1648	FTR Mannheim 6/7.8.41.
R1771	To 311 Sqn.
R1792	To 57 Sqn.
R3156	From 115 Sqn. Became ground instruction machine.
R3157 AA-H	From 115 Sqn. FTR Dinant 21/22.5.40.
R3158	From 115 Sqn. Crashed on landing at Manston on return from Eindhoven 22.10.40.
R3159	From 115 Sqn. Crashed on approach to East Wretham on return from Hanover 2.9.40.
R3165	From 149 Sqn. FTR Horst 20/21.7.40.
R3166	To 311 Sqn.
R3167	To 99 Sqn.
R3168	Force-landed in Devon on return from Leipzig 30.9.40.
R3169	To 57 Sqn and back. Crashed in the Humber River on return from Hamburg 6/7.5.41.
R3171	From 214 Sqn. FTR Duisburg 15/16.7.41.
R3172	From 148 Sqn. To 11 OTU.
R3176	Force-landed in Suffolk on return from Horst 4.8.40.
R3195	From 37 Sqn. To 57 Sqn.
R3211	From 37 Sqn. FTR Hamm 29/30.12.40.
R3216	To 9 Sqn.
R3218	To 311 Sqn.
R3224	From 37 Sqn. To 22 OTU.
R3231	From 37 Sqn. To 57 Sqn.
R3235	FTR Kassel 25/26.7.40.
R3239	From 37 Sqn. Returned to 37 Sqn.
R3275	From 37 Sqn. To 57 Sqn.
R3277	From 311 Sqn. To 12 OTU.
R3284	From 37 Sqn. To 11 OTU.
R3297	To 57 Sqn.
T2463	FTR from attack on invasion ports 20/21.9.40.
T2464	To 9 Sqn.
T2468	To 9 Sqn.
T2474	FTR Mannheim 22/23.12.40.
T2503	From 37 Sqn. FTR Wilhelmshaven 21/22.2.41.
T2504	From 37 Sqn. To 57 Sqn.
T2508	From 37 Sqn. Returned to 37 Sqn.
T2547	From 37 Sqn. Crashed on landing at Feltwell on return from Wilhelmshaven 22.2.41.
T2550 AA-L	Crashed in Cambridgeshire during air-test 10.1.41.
T2575	To 37 Sqn.
T2736	Abandoned over Yorkshire on return from Kiel 19.3.41.
T2741	To 15 OTU.
T2805	From 115 Sqn. Force-landed in Norfolk on return from Berlin 21.9.41.
T2820	Force-landed near Methwold on return from Hamburg 21.10.40.
T2821	To 37 Sqn.
T2822	To 37 Sqn.
T2835	To 1503BAT Flt.
T2837	To 37 Sqn.
W5618	From OADF. To 21 OTU.

W5621		FTR Essen 3/4.7.41.
W5663		FTR Cologne 15/16.10.41.
W5718		From 149 Sqn. To 99 Sqn.
X3176		From 149 Sqn. To 1504Flt.
X3194		SOC 26.3.42.
X3205		FTR Hamburg 15/16.9.41.
X3282		From A&AEE. FTR Kiel 12/13.3.42.
X3285		From 57 Sqn. Returned to 57 Sqn.
X3339		To 9 Sqn.
X3355	AA-Y	Crashed in Norfolk during air-test 28.2.42.
X3359		To 419 Sqn.
X3367		To 9 Sqn.
X3389		From 9 Sqn. FTR Nuremberg 28/29.8.42.
X3390		From 9 Sqn. To 419 Sqn.
X3396		FTR Emden 3/4.9.42.
X3397		From 9 Sqn. To 115 Sqn.
X4302		From 57 Sqn. Returned to 57 Sqn.
X3403		To 1418Flt.
X3408		From 115 Sqn. To 1418Flt and back. FTR Essen 2/3.6.42.
X3416		From 9 Sqn. To 115 Sqn.
X3420		To 419 Sqn.
X3451		From 9 Sqn. To 150 Sqn and back via 419 Sqn. To 150 Sqn.
X3452		From 9 Sqn. FTR Hamburg 28/29.7.42.
X3459		To 150 Sqn.
X3461		To 466 Sqn.
X3462	AA-N	FTR Lübeck 28/29.3.42.
X3464		To 101 Sqn.
X3468		From 115 Sqn. To 23 OTU.
X3475		To 156 Sqn.
X3476		To A&AEE.
X3477		To 419 Sqn.
X3479		To 156 Sqn.
X3480		To 429 Sqn.
X3482	AA-J	FTR from mining sortie 15/16.5.42.
X3487		Crash-landed at Feltwell on return from Cologne 22/23.4.42.
X3488		From 115 Sqn. To 419 Sqn.
X3489		FTR Cologne 5/6.4.42.
X3538		Crashed on approach to Mildenhall during training 27.8.42.
X3539		To 115 Sqn and back. FTR Bremen 29/30.6.42.
X3540		To 115 Sqn and back. To 115 Sqn.
X3557		FTR Wilhelmshaven 8/9.7.42.
X3558		From 57 Sqn. FTR Hamburg 28/29.7.42.
X3584		To 115 Sqn and back via 57 Sqn. To 57 Sqn.
X3585		FTR Kiel 12/13.3.42.
X3586		To 23 OTU.
X3587		FTR Essen 8/9.6.42.
X3588		FTR Kiel 12/13.3.42.
X3595		To Manufacturers for conversion.
X3597		To 115 Sqn.
X3636		To 1483Flt.
X3637		To 9 Sqn.
X3646		FTR Mainz 11/12.8.42.
X3652	AA-O	FTR Essen 25/26.3.42.

X3661	FTR Cologne 5/6.4.42.
X3664	FTR Hamburg 28/29.7.42.
X3667 AA-D	FTR Le Havre 22/23.4.42.
X3705	To 29 OTU.
X3714	FTR Hamburg 26/27.7.42.
X3720	FTR Düsseldorf 10.7.42.
X3747	From 57 Sqn. To 12 OTU.
X3751	To 23 OTU.
X3755	From 57 Sqn. To 150 Sqn.
X3760	FTR Emden 20/21.6.42.
X3794	From 9 Sqn. FTR Emden 3/4.9.42.
X3867	FTR Duisburg 6/7.9.42.
X3931	To 1483Flt.
X3936	To 156 Sqn.
X3946	From 57 Sqn. To 115 Sqn.
X3954	FTR Kiel 13/14.10.42.
X3959	To 156 Sqn.
X9628	FTR Essen 8/9.11.41.
X9634	Ditched off Suffolk coast bound for Bremen 13/14.7.41.
X9742	From 311 Sqn. To 115 Sqn.
X9757	To 419 Sqn.
X9759	FTR Hamburg 15/16.9.41.
X9760	To 57 Sqn.
X9764 AA-V	To 304 Sqn.
X9767 AA-A	FTR Hüls 6/7.9.41.
X9806	From 101 Sqn. To 311 Sqn.
X9825	To 1505BAT Flt.
X9834	FTR Karlsruhe 17/18.9.41.
X9914	FTR Mannheim 22/23.10.41.
X9916	FTR Cologne 15/16.10.41.
X9918	To 21 OTU.
X9951	FTR Berlin 7/8.11.41.
X9975	To 156 Sqn.
X9976	FTR Berlin 7/8.11.41.
X9977	FTR Essen 8/9.11.41.
X9981	FTR Nuremberg 12/13.10.41.
Z1053	To 57 Sqn.
Z1068	To 156 Sqn.
Z1077	To 419 Sqn.
Z1083	From 40 Sqn. To 419 Sqn.
Z1087	To 57 Sqn.
Z1091	To 57 Sqn.
Z1093	To 57 Sqn.
Z1096	To 57 Sqn.
Z1099	FTR Emden 30.11/1.12.41.
Z1108	To 156 Sqn.
Z1114	To 156 Sqn.
Z1144	Abandoned over Lincolnshire on return from Emden 26.11.41.
Z1145	To 57 Sqn.
Z1149	To 18 OTU.
Z1153	Crashed 29.11.41. Details uncertain.
Z1168	FTR Hamburg 26/27.10.41.
Z1566	Crashed in Staffordshire while training 22.5.42.

Z1570 AA-B	FTR Hamburg 28/29.7.42.
Z1572	From 115 Sqn. To 419 Sqn.
Z1573	FTR Essen 8/9.6.42.
Z1592	To 18 OTU.
Z1596	FTR Hamburg 26/27.7.42.
Z1616 AA-D	Crashed soon after take-off from Feltwell bound for Bremen 29.6.42.
Z1652	From 57 Sqn. FTR Milan 24/25.10.42.
Z1738	To 115 Sqn.
Z1747	From 57 Sqn. To 1483Flt.
Z8429	From 57 Sqn. To 158 Sqn.
Z8441	To 158 Sqn.
Z8495	To 305 Sqn.
Z8834	Crashed in Suffolk on return from Brest 23.12.41.
Z8854	From 101 Sqn. To 1429Flt.
Z8858	From 9 Sqn. To 214 Sqn.
Z8859	To 40 Sqn.
Z8868	To 57 Sqn.
Z8904	From 57 Sqn. To 40 Sqn.
Z8909	FTR Cologne 10/11.10.41.
Z8942	FTR Essen 8/9.11.41.
Z8945	FTR Cologne 10/11.10.41.
Z8961	From 57 Sqn. To 25 OTU.
Z8968	From 57 Sqn. To 40 Sqn.
Z8971	Crashed in Devon on return from Brest 27/28.12.41.
Z8977	From 57 Sqn. To 40 Sqn.
Z8978	From 57 Sqn. To 156 Sqn.
BJ584	To 115 Sqn.
BJ596	From 57 Sqn. FTR Frankfurt 8/9.9.42.
BJ599	From 1483Flt. FTR Hamburg 28/29.7.42.
BJ625	FTR Mainz 11/12.8.42.
BJ661	FTR Hamburg 28/29.7.42.
BJ707	From 57 Sqn. To 156 Sqn.
BJ708	FTR Kassel 27/28.8.42.
BJ721	To 29 OTU.
BJ725	From 9 Sqn. FTR Milan 24/25.10.42.
BJ756	To 115 Sqn.
BJ758	To 1483Flt.
BJ765	FTR Duisburg 6/7.9.42.
BJ766	To 150 Sqn.
BJ767	FTR Mainz 11/12.8.42.
BJ772	Destroyed on the ground at Mildenhall by exploding 88 Sqn Boston Z2285 28.9.42.
BJ773	Force-landed in Cambridgeshire while training 11.8.42.
BJ774	FTR from mining sortie 20/21.8.42.
BJ790	To 82 OTU.
BJ828	FTR Düsseldorf 10/11.9.42.
BJ832 AA-Z	From 115 Sqn. Returned to 115 Sqn.
BJ837	Crash-landed at Lakenheath on return from Kiel 13/14.10.42.
BJ898	To 115 Sqn.
BJ968 AA-W	FTR Düsseldorf 10/11.9.42.
BJ974	FTR Düsseldorf 10/11.9.42.
BK206	To 115 Sqn.

BK207	To 18 OTU.
BK274	To 115 Sqn.
BK275	To 115 Sqn.
BK341	FTR from mining sortie 11/12.10.42.
BK362	To 115 Sqn.
BK386	To 156 Sqn.
DF639	FTR Osnabrück 6/7.10.42.
DF673	FTR Nuremberg 28/29.8.42.

Stirling — From October 1942.

N6123 AA-Q	From 1657CU. FTR from mining sortie 3/4.3.43.
N3683	From 1657CU. Returned to 1657CU.
N3704	From 15 Sqn. Returned to 15 Sqn.
R9200 AA-S	From 149 Sqn. SOC 19.7.45.
R9243 AA-C	To 1651CU.
R9245 AA-N	Crashed soon after take-off from Newmarket when bound for a mining sortie 16.12.42.
R9246 AA-S	Crash-landed in Huntingdonshire while training 24.11.42.
R9247 AA-W	FTR Fallersleben 17/18.12.42.
R9248 AA-H	FTR Lorient 23/24.1.43.
R9250 AA-C/W	FTR Hamburg 3/4.2.43.
R9290 AA-Y/X	FTR from mining sortie 28/29.4.43.
R9316 AA-K	From 214 Sqn. FTR Lorient 13/14.2.43.
W7469AA-O	From 149 Sqn. FTR Mannheim 16/17.4.43.
W7513AA-G	From 149 Sqn. FTR from mining sortie 28/29.4.43.
BF311	From 149 Sqn. To 15 Sqn.
BF321	To 1657CU.
BF377 AA-J	From CRD. To 1651CU.
BF396 AA-X	From 1657CU. FTR Fallersleben 17/18.12.42.
BF397	From 1657CU. To 1657CU.
BF398 AA-F/P	Partially abandoned over Staffordshire and crashed while training 17.5.43.
BF399 AA-O	Crashed near Oakington while training 28.11.42.
BF400 AA-G	FTR Fallersleben 17/18.12.42.
BF412 AA-F/Y	From 15 Sqn. To 1665CU.
BF434 AA-X	To 1665CU.
BF437 AA-L	FTR Nuremberg 8/9.3.43.
BF443 AA-V	To 1651CU.
BF451 AA-Z	FTR Mannheim 16/17.4.43.
BF455 AA-Y	Ditched off Sussex coast on return from Frankfurt 11.4.43.
BF456 AA-J	FTR Frankfurt 10/11.4.43.
BF458 JN-P	FTR Remscheid 30/31.7.43.
BF459 JN-G	FTR Mannheim 23/24.9.43.
BF461 AA-B	FTR from mining sortie 4/5.11.43.
BF465 JN-K	From 15 Sqn. FTR Berlin 23/24.8.43.
BF467 AA-W	To 214 Sqn and back. FTR from mining sortie 28/29.4.43.
BF473	From 90 Sqn. To 199 Sqn.
BF506 AA-P	FTR Rostock 20/21.4.43.
BF513 AA-E	FTR Stuttgart 14/15.4.43.
BF516	To 214 Sqn.
BF517	To 1657CU.
BF518 AA-E	Crashed on landing at West Malling during transit flight 1.9.43.
BF561 AA-O	FTR Wuppertal 29/30.5.43.

BF564 JN-W	FTR Berlin 23/24.8.43.
BF573	To 149 Sqn.
BF575 AA-H	To 295 Sqn.
BF577 JN-M	FTR Hamburg 2/3.8.43.
BK602 AA-R	From 7 Sqn. FTR Düsseldorf 25/26.5.43.
BK604 AA-S	From 1657CU. FTR Hamburg 3/4.2.43.
BK608 AA-T	Crashed on landing at Stradishall on return from Turin 29.11.42.
BK609 AA-R/T	Crashed on landing at Bradwell Bay on return from Turin 30.11.42.
BK614 JN-H	FTR from mining sortie 6/7.8.43.
BK615	To RAE.
BK617 AA-D	Crashed in the sea off Cromer when bound for mining sortie 5.2.43.
BK618 AA-Q	FTR Frankfurt 2/3.12.42.
BK619 AA-O/X	To 1651CU.
BK620 AA-A	FTR Fallersleben 17/18.12.42.
BK624 AA-A	From 1651CU. Returned to 1651CU.
BK646 AA-N	FTR from mining sortie 14/15.6.43.
BK647 AA-M	Crash-landed soon after take-off from Newmarket when bound for Essen 5/6.3.43.
BK664 AA-M	Crashed on landing at Newmarket on return from Mannheim 16/17.4.43.
BK695 AA-X	From 15 Sqn. To 199 Sqn.
BK721 AA-Z	Crashed soon after take-off from Newmarket when bound for Duisburg 13.5.43.
BK768 AA-L	FTR Gelsenkirchen 25/26.6.43.
BK770 AA-L	Crashed in Norfolk on return from Duisburg 8/9.4.43.
BK776 JN-B	FTR Wuppertal 29/30.5.43.
BK777 AA-U	To 1653CU.
BK778 JN-U	FTR from mining sortie 4/5.11.43.
BK783 AA-Q	FTR Dortmund 23/24.5.43.
BK807 AA-M	FTR from mining sortie 28/29.4.43.
BK809 AA-T	Crashed at Mepal on take-off for Boulogne 8.9.43.
BK810 AA-G	FTR Mülheim 22/23.6.43.
BK817 AA-B	FTR Düsseldorf 11/12.6.43.
EE878 AA-P/F	FTR Berlin 31.8/1.9.43.
EE881	To 1657CU.
EE886 AA-L	Crashed on landing at Oakington on return from Aachen 14.7.43.
EE890 AA-L	FTR Hamburg 24/25.7.43.
EE891 AA-Q	FTR from mining sortie 15/16.8.43.
EE892 AA-F	Crashed off Suffolk coast on return from Essen 25/26.7.43.
EE893 JN-N	FTR Mannheim 5/6.9.43.
EE897 AA-G	FTR from mining sortie 4/5.11.43.
EE898 AA-D	To 1651CU.
EE915 AA-X	FTR Remscheid 30/31.7.43.
EE918 AA-D	FTR Berlin 31.8/1.9.43.
EE938 AA-X/F	FTR Berlin 23/24.8.43.
EE955 AA-D	FTR Nuremberg 27/28.8.43.
EE958	To 513 Sqn and back. To 1653CU.
EF130 JN-M	FTR Frankfurt 4/5.10.43.
EF135 JN-W	Crashed on landing at Mepal on return from Hanover 28.9.43.

EF137 AA-E	FTR from mining sortie 23/24.4.44.
EF142 AA-C	Crashed near Mepal on return from mining sortie 24/25.10.43.
EF148 AA-R	FTR Berlin 22/23.11.43.
EF152	To 1653CU.
EF163 JN-L	Crashed in Cambridgeshire on return from mining sortie 16/17.12.43.
EF181	To 218 Sqn.
EF200	To 513 Sqn.
EF201	To 513 Sqn.
EF205	To 513 Sqn.
EF206	To 513 Sqn.
EF207	To 218 Sqn.
EF211	To 513 Sqn.
EF215 AA-M	From 214 Sqn. FTR Special Operations 5/6.3.44.
EF217	From 622 Sqn. To 1653CU.
EF233	From 214 Sqn. To 218 Sqn.
EF236 AA-J	Crashed on landing on return from mining sortie 13/14.4.44
EF251	To 90 Sqn.
EF254	To 90 Sqn.
EF327	To 149 Sqn.
EF337	To 149 Sqn.
EF340 AA-Q	From 149 Sqn. FTR from mining sortie 5/6.5.43.
EF398 AA-A	FTR Wuppertal 29/30.5.43.
EF399 AA-O	From 15 Sqn. FTR Mülheim 22/23.6.43.
EF400	To 149 Sqn.
EF408 AA-P	FTR Mülheim 22/23.6.43.
EF435 AA-J	SOC 5.6.47.
EF436 AA-A	FTR from mining sortie 5/6.7.43.
EF440	To 620 Sqn.
EF451	To 620 Sqn.
EF454 AA-A	To 1657CU.
EF456	To 620 Sqn.
EF458	To 90 Sqn.
EF462	To 218 Sqn.
EF465 AA-H	To 513 Sqn.
EF466	From A&AEE. To 1653CU.
EF491 AA-O	Crash-landed at Coltishall on return from Berlin 31.8/1.9.43.
EF501 AA-K	FTR Berlin 31.8/1.9.43.
EF507 AA-P	To 1332CU.
EF512 AA-A	To 1661CU.
EF513 AA-E	To 1657CU.
EF514 AA-D	To 199 Sqn.
EF515 AA-F	FTR Hanover 27/28.9.43.
EH877 JN-C	FTR Hanover 27/28.9.43.
EH880 AA-J	Crashed in Northumberland during approach to land on return from mining sortie 1/2.12.43.
EH881 AA-Z	FTR Wuppertal 29/30.5.43.
EH889 AA-Z	FTR Mülheim 22/23.6.43.
EH901 AA-O	To 1657CU.
EH902 AA-K	FTR Wuppertal 24/25.6.43.
EH905 AA-R	FTR Berlin 31.8/1.9.43.
EH928 AA-A	FTR Hamburg 2/3.8.43.

EH929	To 15 Sqn.
EH930	To 15 Sqn.
EH935 JN-K	FTR Mannheim 23/24.9.43.
EH936 JN-W	FTR Mannheim 23/24.9.43.
EH938 AA-F	FTR Mönchengladbach 30/31.8.43.
EH939 AA-J	To 90 Sqn.
EH946	To 620 Sqn.
EH947	To 90 Sqn.
EH948 AA-Q	FTR from mining sortie 24/25.2.44.
EH949 AA-P	To 1651CU.
EH955 AA-K	FTR from mining sortie 18/19.4.44.
EJ108 AA-C	To 1657CU.
LJ441	To 1653CU.
LJ442 JN-F	FTR Leverkusen 19/20.11.43.
LJ453 AA-K	From 15 Sqn. FTR Berlin 22/23.11.43.
LJ457	To 1657CU.
LJ462 AA-O	From 15 Sqn. FTR from mining sortie 13/14.3.44.
LJ473 AA-R	Crash-landed at Mepal on return from mining sortie 4/5.1.44.
LK378	To 1657CU.
LK384 AA-X	To 1653CU.
LK389	To 1661CU.
LK396	From 622 Sqn. To 218 Sqn.
LK540	To 1651CU.
Lancaster	From March 1944.
R5692	From 15 Sqn. To 90 Sqn.
R5846	From 622 Sqn. To 5LFS.
W4174	From 15 Sqn. To 1654CU.
ED310	From 15 Sqn. To 1LFS.
ED425	From 622 Sqn. To 5LFS.
HK541	From 300 Sqn. To 115 Sqn.
HK542	From 156 Sqn. To 115 Sqn.
HK544	From 626 Sqn. To 115 Sqn.
HK551 JN-E	To 115 Sqn.
HK553 AA-S	FTR Dreux 10/11.6.44.
HK554 JN-Z/F	
HK557	To 5MU.
HK558 AA-D	FTR Amaye-sur-Seulles 30.7.44.
HK561 JN-Y	
HK562 JN-Y/L	
HK563 JN-W	
HK564 AA-P	From 115 Sqn. FTR Rüsselsheim 12/13.8.44.
HK565 JN-C	To 115 Sqn.
HK567 AA-C	FTR from tactical operation to Mare du Magne 7/8.8.44.
HK568 AA-K	FTR Stuttgart 24/25.7.44.
HK569 AA-Q	FTR Homburg 20/21.7.44.
HK573 JN-H	
HK574 JN-R	Ditched in the River Orwell on return from Leuna (Merseburg) 6/7.12.44.
HK575 AA-O	FTR Stuttgart 24/25.7.44.
HK576 JN-G	
HK593 JN-X	
HK594 AA-G	FTR Stettin 29/30.8.44.

HK596 AA-O	FTR Walcheren (Flushing) 21.10.44.
HK597 JN-P/N	To 46MU
HK600 JN-D/K	
HK601 JN-J/D	To 10MU.
HK697	To 195 Sqn.
HK751	To 1667CU.
HK792	From 138 Sqn.
HK806 JN-B	
JA903	From 44 Sqn.
LL864	To 115 Sqn.
LL865	
LL866 AA-S	FTR Rüsselsheim 25/26.8.44.
LL867	To 115 Sqn.
LL880	To 115 Sqn.
LL888 AA-X	FTR Valenciennes 15/16.6.44.
LL921 AA-E	From 115 Sqn. FTR Aulnoye 19/20.7.44.
LL942	Blew up at Mepal 30.6.44.
LL945	To 15 Sqn.
LM104 AA-Z	FTR Dortmund 6/7.10.44.
LM265	To 514 Sqn.
LM266 AA-F	
LM268 AA-D	FTR from mining sortie 11/12.9.44.
LM276 AA-S	
LM510	To 115 Sqn.
LM544 JN-D	From 115 Sqn. To 138 Sqn. Returned to 75 Sqn.
LM593 AA-N	To 622 Sqn and back. FTR Rüsselsheim 25/26.8.44.
LM728 AA-R	From 514 Sqn. Crashed on landing at Mepal 14.4.45.
LM733 AA-R	From 514 Sqn. FTR Münster 21.3.45.
LM740 AA-D/B	FTR Kamen 25.2.45.
ME321 AA-N	FTR Vohwinkel 1/2.1.45.
ME450 AA-W	Crashed in Cambridgeshire on return from Dortmund 26.2.45.
ME531 AA-K	
ME682 AA-E	From 625 Sqn. To 1662CU.
ME689 AA-Y	FTR Chambly 1/2.5.44.
ME690 AA-Z	FTR Dortmund 22/23.5.44.
ME691 AA-R	FTR Homburg 20/21.7.44.
ME692	To 115 Sqn.
ME702 AA-Q	FTR Dreux 10/11.6.44.
ME751 AA-M/P	From 115 Sqn. To 138 Sqn.
ME752 AA-E/M/Z	From 115 Sqn. FTR Homburg 20/21.7.44.
ME753	From 115 Sqn. To 1651CU.
ME754 AA-A	From 115 Sqn. To 166 Sqn.
ME834	To 115 Sqn.
ND745	To 115 Sqn.
ND747 AA-O	To 5LFS.
ND752 AA-O	FTR Homburg 20/21.7.44.
ND753	To 115 Sqn.
ND754	To 115 Sqn.
ND756 AA-M	FTR Stuttgart 28/29.7.44.
ND758	To 115 Sqn.
ND760	To 115 Sqn.
ND761	To 115 Sqn.
ND768 AA-F	FTR Dortmund 22/23.5.44.

ND782	To 3LFS.
ND796 AA-J	FTR Friedrichshaven 27/28.4.44.
ND800 AA-J	From 115 Sqn. FTR Homburg 20/21.7.44.
ND801 JN-X	Crashed while landing at Mepal 3.2.45.
ND802 AA-D	FTR Aachen 27/28.5.44.
ND804 AA-K	FTR Duisburg 21/22.5.44.
ND904 AA-B	From 115 Sqn. FTR Saarbrücken 5/6.10.44.
ND908 AA-M	FTR Aachen 27/28.5.44.
ND911 AA-D	FTR Homburg 20.11.44.
ND914	Crashed during landing at Mepal 28.5.44.
ND915 AA-A	FTR Homberg 20/21.7.44.
ND917 AA-O	From 115 Sqn. FTR Solingen 4.11.44.
ND918 AA-Y	To 1654CU.
ND919 AA-D	FTR Louvain 11/12.5.44.
ND920 AA-P	From 115 Sqn. FTR Rimeux 24/25.6.44.
NE148 AA-H	From 115 Sqn. FTR Stuttgart 28/29.7.44.
NE181 AA-M	To 514 Sqn.
NF935 AA-P	
NF980 AA-F	FTR Osterfeld 30.11.44.
NF981 AA-Y/D	
NG113 AA-D	FTR Chemnitz 14/15.2.45.
NG322 JN-F	
NG448 JN-P	
NG449 JN-T	FTR Münster 21.3.45.
NN710 AA-Q	FTR Rheydt 27.12.44.
NN745 AA-A	FTR from mining sortie 21/22.11.44.
NN747 JN-D/O	
NN773 AA-G	From 514 Sqn.
PA967 AA-D	From 115 Sqn. FTR Homburg 20/21.7.44.
PB132 AA-T/JN-X	
PB380 JN-V	From 44 Sqn.
PB418 AA-C	
PB421 AA-U/K/P	
PB424 AA-O	From 44 Sqn.
PB427 AA-U	
PB430 AA-P	Crashed while landing at Hawkinge on return from Boulogne 17.9.44.
PB520 AA-G	FTR Homburg 20.11.44.
PB689 AA-X	FTR Homburg 20.11.44.
PB741 AA-E	FTR Hattingen 14.3.45.
PB761 AA-Y	Crashed in Suffolk on return from Wanne-Eickel 16/17.1.45.
PB763 AA-A	
PB767	To 514 Sqn.
PB820 AA-V	
PD327	From 630 Sqn.
PD422	From 44 Sqn.
PP663	
RA510 AA-E	
RA541 AA-J	To 514 Sqn.
RA564 JN-P	FTR Münster 21.3.45.
RF127 AA-W	
RF129 AA-M	
RF157 AA-X	
RF190 AA-F	From 115 Sqn.

90 SQUADRON

Motto: Celer (Swift)   Codes WP, XY

First formed on the 8th of October 1917, 90 Squadron was originally a fighter unit, which never achieved operational status before being disbanded on the 3rd of August 1918. Eleven days later it re-formed in the home defence role, but was never brought into action, and was again disbanded on the 13th of June 1919. Resurrected in March 1937, the squadron received Blenheims in May, and fulfilled a training role, which eventually saw it lose its identity by being absorbed into 17 OTU on the 4th of April 1940. On the 7th of May 1941 the squadron was again re-formed, this time at Watton, and became part of 2 Group. It was tasked with the introduction of the B17C to RAF service under the designation Fortress I. Ultimately, the type failed to match expectation in the high-level bombing role, and this, together with a poor rate of serviceability, saw it withdrawn from the UK theatre in the autumn of 1941. The squadron took on Blenheims thereafter, but did not become operational before yet another disbandment in February 1942. Reborn for the fifth time in November 1942, 90 Squadron joined 3 Group with which it would remain until the end of hostilities. Initially operating Stirlings the squadron converted to Lancasters in mid 1944.

Re-formed   07.11.42

STATIONS

Bottesford	07.11.42 to 29.12.42
Ridgewell	29.12.42 to 31.05.43
West Wickham (Wratting Common)	31.05.43 to 13.10.43
Tuddenham	13.10.43 to 31.05.46

COMMANDING OFFICERS

Wing Commander J C Claydon	07.11.42 to 13.06.43
Wing Commander J H Giles	13.06.43 to 06,12.43
Wing Commander G T Wynne-Powell	06.12.43 to 06.01.44
Wing Commander F M Milligan	09.01.44 to 15.06.44
Wing Commander A J Ogilvie	15.06.44 to 10.11.44
Wing Commander W G Bannister	10.11.44 to 02.02.45
Wing Commander P F Dunham	03.02.45 to 19.02.45
Wing Commander E G Scott	26.02.45

AIRCRAFT

Stirling I	11.41 to 05.43
Stirling III	02.43 to 06.44
Lancaster I/III	05.44 to 12.47

OPERATIONAL RECORD

Operations	Sorties	Aircraft Losses	% Losses
392	4,561	83	1.8

Category of Operations

Bombing/SOE	Mining
273	119

Stirlings

Operations	Sorties	Aircraft Losses	% Losses
211	1,937	58	3.0

Category of Operations

Bombing/SOE	Mining
111	100

Lancasters

Operations	Sorties	Aircraft Losses	% Losses
181	2,624	25	1.0

Category of Operations

Bombing	Mining
162	19

TABLE OF STATISTICS

The fifth highest number of mining operations in Bomber Command.

Out of 59 Lancaster squadrons

34th highest number of Lancaster overall operations in Bomber Command.
30th highest number of Lancaster sorties in Bomber Command.
41st highest number of Lancaster operational losses in Bomber Command.

Out of 28 bomber squadrons in 3 Group

7th highest number of overall operations in 3 Group.
6th highest number of sorties in 3 Group.
7th highest number of aircraft operational losses in 3 Group.

Out of 12 Stirling bomber squadrons in 3 Group

7th highest number of Stirling overall operations in 3 Group.
5th highest number of Stirling sorties in 3 Group.
6th highest number of Stirling operational losses in 3 Group.

Out of 11 Lancaster squadrons in 3 Group

6th highest number of Lancaster overall operations in 3 Group.
6th highest number of Lancaster sorties in 3 Group.
6th highest number of Lancaster operational losses in 3 Group.

AIRCRAFT HISTORIES

Stirling	From December 1942.
R9198	From 214 Sqn. To 1665CU.
R9256 WP-G	To 1651CU.
R9271 WP-Q	From 149 Sqn. FTR Essen 5/6.3.43.
R9276 WP-G	From 149 Sqn. FTR Wilhelmshaven 19/20.2.43.
R9306 WP-J	From 7 Sqn via 7CF. Crashed in Dorset on return from Lorient 16.2.43.
R9349 WP-U	From 218 Sqn. FTR St Nazaire 28.2/1.3.43.
W7510	From 149 Sqn. To 1657CU.
W7575	From 214 Sqn. To 1657CU.
W7623	From CRD. To 1665CU.
W7627 WP-A/E	From 214 Sqn. Crashed on take-off from Ridgewell while training 18.3.43.

BF324 WP-H	From 214 Sqn. To 1657CU
BF346 WP-G	From 218 Sqn. FTR from mining sortie 28/29.4.43.
BF376	From 15 Sqn. To 1657CU.
BF383 WP-T	FTR Duisburg 26/27.4.43.
BF404 WP-A	From 218 Sqn. To 214 Sqn.
BF407 WP-S	To 1657CU.
BF409 WP-R	Crashed on landing at Ridgewell while training 5.4.43.
BF410 WP-E	FTR Nuremberg 25/26.2.43.
BF414 WP-F/R	Crashed on landing at Ridgewell while training 19.5.43.
BF415 WP-S	FTR Hamburg 3/4.2.43.
BF435 WP-X	From 15 Sqn. To 1657CU.
BF438 WP-D	FTR Cologne 14/15.2.43.
BF442 WP-K	FTR Rostock 20/21.4.43.
BF449 WP-J	Crashed on landing at Ridgewell following early return from mining sortie 9.3.43.
BF454 WP-W	Crashed on take-off from Ridgewell while training 13.4.43.
BF460	To 15 Sqn.
BF462 WP-P	FTR Stuttgart 14/15.4.43.
BF463 WP-Q	FTR Rostock 20/21.4.43.
BF464 WP-E	To 570 Sqn.
BF466	To 214 Sqn.
BF471 WP-L	Crash-landed near Manston on return from Frankfurt 11.4.43.
BF473 WP-D	From 218 Sqn. To 75 Sqn.
BF503	From 149 Sqn. To 620 Sqn.
BF504 WP-F	Crashed on landing at West Wickham on return from Cologne 4.7.43.
BF508 WP-S	FTR Rostock 20/21.4.43.
BF521	To 15 Sqn.
BF523 WP-G	FTR Duisburg 12/13.5.43.
BF524 WP-N/U	FTR from SOE sortie to France 8/9.5.44.
BF526 WP-R/G	From 7 Sqn. To 1651CU.
BF527 WP-K	To 1657CU.
BF529	To 196 Sqn.
BF532 WP-W	From 7 Sqn. To 1657CU.
BF566 WP-T/G	FTR Hanover 22/23.9.43.
BF574 WP-F	From 214 Sqn. To 1660CU.
BK598 WP-N	From 149 Sqn. To 1657 Sqn.
BK625 WP-D	Crash-landed at Ridgewell while training 29.12.42.
BK626 WP-C/W	Crash-landed at Shipdham on return from air-sea rescue sortie 25.5.43.
BK627 WP-F/P	FTR Wilhelmshaven 19/20.2.43.
BK628 WP-G	FTR Wuppertal 24/25.6.43.
BK644 WP-T	FTR from mining sortie 5/6.2.43.
BK655 XY-X	FTR Bremen 8/9.10.43.
BK661 WP-O	FTR Duisburg 12/13.5.43.
BK665 WP-V/D	From 149 Sqn. FTR Mülheim 22/23.6.43.
BK693 WP-A	To 214 Sqn and back. Crashed on landing at Stradishall on return from Hamburg 28.7.43.
BK718 WP-M	FTR Cologne 3/4.7.43.
BK723 WP-D	From 7 Sqn. FTR Kassel 3/4.10.43.
BK725 WP-M	FTR Mannheim 16/17.4.43.
BK775 WP-H	FTR Remscheid 30/31.7.43.

BK779 WP-L	From 7 Sqn. FTR Berlin 23/24.8.43.
BK780 WP-L	Crashed on landing at Ridgewell while training 25.4.43.
BK781 WP-E	To 149 Sqn.
BK784 WP-P/O/M	Crashed in Cambridgeshire soon after take-off for a mining sortie 23.5.44.
BK804 WP-J	FTR Mülheim 22/23.6.43.
BK811 WP-V	To 1653CU.
BK813 WP-O	FTR Wuppertal 24/25.6.43.
BK814 WP-T	FTR Dortmund 4/5.5.43.
BK816 WP-B	From 199 Sqn. To 149 Sqn.
EE871 WP-Q	From 214 Sqn. FTR Berlin 31.8/1.9.43.
EE873 WP-D	FTR Aachen 13/14.7.43.
EE887 WP-T	FTR Krefeld 21/22.6.43.
EE889	To 190 Sqn.
EE896 WP-J/O	To 1653CU.
EE900 WP-Y	To 190 Sqn.
EE901 XY-U	From 214 Sqn. FTR Kassel 3/4.10.43.
EE904 WP-S	FTR Essen 25/26.7.43.
EE916 WP-F	Crashed on take-off from West Wickham when bound for Hamburg 29.7.43.
EE939	To 1651CU.
EE951 WP-B	Crashed on take-off from Wratting Common (formerly West Wickham) for air-test 3.9.43.
EE952 WP-F	Crashed near Cambridge on return from Hanover 28.9.43.
EE974 WP-M	From 15 Sqn. Abandoned over Suffolk on return from SOE sortie to France 28/29.4.44.
EF129 WP-Q	FTR Mannheim 5/6.9.43.
EF147 WP-J	FTR from SOE sortie to France 5/6.3.44.
EF159 WP-B	From 620 Sqn. FTR Laon 22/23.4.44.
EF162 WP-K	FTR from SOE sortie to France 12/13.4.44.
EF179 WP-V	Ditched off Cromer on return from mining sortie 8.10.43.
EF182 WP-V/M	To 1651CU.
EF183 WP-Z	From 15 Sqn. To 1657CU.
EF188 WP-Z	To 149 Sqn.
EF191 WP-H	FTR from mining sortie 1/2.12.43.
EF193 WP-Q	To 149 Sqn.
EF196 WP-L	To 1651CU.
EF198 WP-F/H	Crashed in Suffolk on return from mining sortie 25/26.2.44.
EF251 WP-P	From 75 Sqn. To 1653CU.
EF254 XY-Q	From 75 Sqn. FTR from SOE sortie to France 9/10.5.44.
EF294 WP-B	FTR from SOE sortie to France 2/3.6.44.
EF302	To 1651CU.
EF328	Crash-landed at Ridgewell after early return from mining sortie 8/9.3.43.
EF334 WP-U	To 1657CU.
EF336	To 149 Sqn.
EF346 WP-G	From 218 Sqn. To 1665CU.
EF349 WP-Y	From 218 Sqn. FTR Wuppertal 29/30.5.43.
EF397 WP-K	Crashed near Stradishall on return from Wuppertal 30.5.43.
EF426 WP-S/W	Crashed while landing at Wratting Common during air-test 12.10.43.
EF431 WP-X	To 149 Sqn.
EF439 WP-C/H	FTR Nuremberg 27/28.8.43.
EF441 WP-G	To 1653CU.

EF443 XY-M	FTR from mining sortie 28/29.1.44.
EF446 WP-O	To 570 Sqn.
EF458 XY-Y	From 75 Sqn. FTR Mannheim 23/24.9.43.
EF459	From 15 Sqn. To 199 Sqn.
EF497 WP-L	Crashed in Oxfordshire during air-test 20.10.43.
EF509 XY-X	FTR from SOE sortie to France 9/10.5.44.
EF510	To 1654CU.
EF511 WP-C	Crashed near Bury-St-Edmunds on return from mining sortie 26.11.43.
EH876 WP-J	FTR Düsseldorf 25/26.5.43.
EH900 WP-Y	FTR Gelsenkirchen 25/26.6.43.
EH906 XY-T	FTR from SOE sortie to France 4/5.3.44.
EH907 WP-O	FTR Cologne 3/4.7.43.
EH908 WP-R/U	Crashed in Suffolk while training 12.11.43.
EH937 WP-S	FTR Berlin 23/24.8.43.
EH939 WP-P	From 75 Sqn. To 1653CU.
EH944 WP-A	Crash-landed at Lakenheath on return from Hanover 23.9.43.
EH947 XY-S	From 75 Sqn. Crashed in Suffolk on return from SOE sortie 10/11.4.44.
EH958 WP-O	To 1660CU.
EH982 WP-Y	To 218 Sqn.
EH989 WP-N/P	Crashed in Northamptonshire after collision with an OTU Wellington on return from Amiens 15/16.3.44.
EH996 WP-H	FTR Mannheim 18/19.11.43.
EJ115 WP-K	From 199 Sqn. To 149 Sqn.
EJ122 WP-E	To 149 Sqn.
LJ460 WP-E/XY-U	FTR from SOE sortie to France 10/11.4.44.
LJ470 WP-C	To 1332CU.
LJ474	From 214 Sqn. To 149 Sqn.
LJ483 XY-V	From 1657CU. FTR from SOE sortie to France 12/13.4.44.
LJ506 WP-F	To 218 Sqn.
LJ509 WP-F	From 214 Sqn. FTR from SOE sortie to France 10/11.3.44.
LJ579 WP-O	To ECFS.
LJ581	To 1654CU.
LJ625	To 218 Sqn.
LK379 WP-F	FTR Mannheim 18/19.11.43.
LK380 WP-Y XY-Y	Crashed near Mildenhall after collision with a Hurricane while training 9.11.43.
LK383 WP-W	To 149 Sqn.
LK392 WP-A	To 149 Sqn.
LK516 WP-J	From 149 Sqn. To 1651CU.
LK568	From 149 Sqn. To 218 Sqn.
LK569	To 1651CU.
LK570	To 1651CU.
LK571	To 1653CU.
MZ262 WP-K	Crashed in Suffolk when bound for Hanover 22.9.43.
Lancaster	From May 1944.
L7532	From 3LFS. No operations. To 1656CU.
R5514	From 3LFS.
R5631	From 3LFS. Became ground instruction machine.
R5692	From 75 Sqn. To 3LFS.
R5845	From 3LFS. To 1656CU.

W4885	From 15 Sqn via 5LFS.
W4980 WP-R	From 15 Sqn via 3LFS. To 1661CU.
HK602 WP-E/X	FTR Walcheren 29.10.44.
HK603 WP-E/D	FTR Ludwigshafen 5.1.45.
HK604 WP-G	FTR Kiel 26/27.8.44.
HK605 WP-A	FTR Frankfurt 12/13.9.44.
HK606 WP-Y XY-V	To 186 Sqn.
HK607 WP-Y	To 1654CU.
HK608 WP-G/P	Force-landed in Allied territory on return from Gelsenkirchen 19.3.45.
HK609 WP-F	To 10MU.
HK610 WP-Z	Collided with PD336 (90 Sqn) and crashed near Bury-St-Edmunds when bound for Wiesbaden 2.2.45.
HK611	To 10MU.
HK613 WP-Y XY-Y	To 186 Sqn.
HK622	From 15 Sqn. To 186 Sqn.
HK625	From 15 Sqn. To 10MU.
HK664 WP-V	FTR Trier 23.12.44.
HK685	
HK692	To 186 Sqn.
HK694	To 186 Sqn.
HK696	To 115 Sqn.
LM110	To 15 Sqn.
LM111 WP-C/G	FTR Mare de Magne 7/8.8.44.
LM128 WP-Y	Crashed in Suffolk on return from Stettin 29/30.8.44.
LM157 WP-C	Crash-landed near Newmarket during an air-test 6.2.45.
LM158 WP-P	FTR Gelsenkirchen 12/13.6.44.
LM159 WP-H	
LM160 XY-W	To 186 Sqn.
LM164 WP-V XY-V	FTR Mare de Magne 7/8.8.44.
LM165 WP-T	FTR Duisburg 14/15.10.44.
LM169 WP-R	FTR Moerdyk 16/17.9.44.
LM179 WP-M	FTR Rimeux 24/25.6.44.
LM183 WP-L	FTR Homburg 20/21.7.44.
LM184 WP-K	FTR Stettin 29/30.8.44.
LM185 WP-D	FTR Homburg 20/21.7.44.
LM187	To 218 Sqn.
LM188 WP-S XY-S	To 186 Sqn.
LM189 WP-U	FTR Homburg 20/21.7.44.
LM280 WP-F	
LM575	To 15 Sqn.
LM576	To 15 Sqn.
LM588 WP-W/F	FTR Rüsselsheim 25/26.8.44.
LM615 WP-B	To 1653CU.
LM617 WP-X XY-X	Completed 58 operations.
LM618 WP-U XY-U	To 186 Sqn.
LM692 XY-R	From 90 Sqn.
ME802 WP-S	FTR Rüsselsheim 25/26.8.44.

ME838 WP-D	FTR from mining sortie 11/12.9.44.
ME852 WP-Q	FTR Brunswick 12/13.8.44.
ME860	To 218 Sqn.
ME862	To 625 Sqn.
ND387	From 7 Sqn. Shot down by intruder near Woolfox Lodge on return from mining sortie 4.3.45.
NE145 WP-K/D	Shot down by an intruder over Suffolk on return from Biennais 27/28.6.44.
NE149 WP-A	FTR Dreux 10/11.6.44.
NE177 WP-H	FTR Dreux 10/11.6.44.
NE178	To 1651CU.
NF987 XY-R	
NG137 XY-D	
NG138 WP-C/U	
NG140	
NG146	
NG148 XY-B	
NG149 XY-D	
NG175	To 186 Sqn.
NG176 XY-H	To 186 Sqn.
NG306 WP-B	
NG323 WP-G	Crashed on landing at Tuddenham while in transit from Lossiemouth 21.12.44.
NG408	From TFU.
NG465	From SIU.
NG467	From SIU.
NN698 WP-U	FTR Cologne (crash-landed in France) 27.11.44.
XY-A	
NN720 XY-K	
NN753	
NN761 WP-V	From 115 Sqn.
NN762 WP-V/Y	From 115 Sqn.
NN783 WP-E	
PA158 WP-S	FTR Dortmund 3/4.2.45.
PA159 WP-V	To 1651CU.
PA167 WP-K	
PA193	
PA239 WP-S	
PA252	
PA253 WP-B/Z	
PA254 WP-C/A	FTR Datteln 9.3.45.
PB193 WP-N	FTR Frankfurt 12/13.9.44.
PB196 WP-A	To 195 Sqn.
PB198 WP-M	FTR Stuttgart 28/29.7.44.
PB204 WP-R	To 1653CU.
PB488	From 149 Sqn. To 186 Sqn.
PD269 WP-Q	FTR Bottrop 31.10.44.
PD336 WP-P	Collided with HK610 (90 Sqn) over Suffolk when bound for Wiesbaden 2.2.45. and landed safely. FTR Wesel 19.2.45.
PD341 WP-P	FTR Wilhelmshaven 15/16.10.44.
PD400	From 115 Sqn.
PD402 WP-G	From 115 Sqn.
PD430 WP-A	
PD433 WP-P/R	

PP679	To 138 Sqn.
PP680 WP-D	
PP682 WP-J	
RF184 WP-C	From 15 Sqn.
RF185 WP-T	From 15 Sqn.
SW267/SW272	To 186 Sqn.

99 (Madras Presidency) SQUADRON

Motto: Quisque Tenax (Each tenacious)   Code LN

First formed in August 1917, 99 Squadron moved to France at the end of April 1918 as a day bomber unit. It spent the remainder of the Great War operating against German industrial targets. The squadron moved to India in May 1919, and subsequently lost its identity by being renumbered in April 1920. Re-formation took place on the 1st of April 1924. Throughout the inter-war years the squadron operated various types of bombers until October 1938, when it became the first recipient of the Wellington. The squadron remained at the forefront of 3 Group operations until January 1942, and shortly afterwards departed the UK for India. Night operations against Japanese bases in Burma began in November, and in September 1944 Liberators replaced Wellingtons for long-range operations.

STATIONS

Mildenhall	15.11.34 to 09.09.39
Elmdon	09.09.39 to 15.09.39
Newmarket	15.09.39 to 18.03.41
Waterbeach	18.03.41 to 19.03.42

COMMANDING OFFICERS

Wing Commander H E Walker MC DFC	21.06.37 to 26.09.39
Wing Commander J F Griffiths DFC	26.09.39 to 29.06.40
Wing Commander R J A Ford	29.06.40 to 16.01.41
Wing Commander F W Dixon-Wright DFC	16.01.41 to 12.12.41
Wing Commander P Heath	12.12.41 to 14.06.42

AIRCRAFT

Wellington I/Ia/Ic	10.38 to 10.42
Operations ceased	14.01.42
To India	19.03.42

OPERATIONAL RECORD

Operations	Sorties	Aircraft Losses	% Losses
233	1,786	43	2.4

Category of Operations

Bombing	Leaflet
228	5

TABLE OF STATISTICS

Out of 42 Wellington squadrons

6th highest number of overall Wellington operations in Bomber Command.
5th highest number of Wellington sorties in Bomber Command.
10th highest number of Wellington operational losses in Bomber Command.

Out of 28 bomber squadrons in 3 Group

10th highest number of overall operations in 3 Group.
11th highest number of sorties in 3 Group.
12th highest number of operational losses in 3 Group.

Out of 18 Wellington squadrons in 3 Group

4th highest number of overall Wellington operations in 3 Group.
4th highest number of Wellington sorties in 3 Group.
6th highest number of Wellington operational losses in 3 Group.

AIRCRAFT HISTORIES

Wellington	To January 1942.
L4215	To 148 Sqn.
L4216	To 11 OTU.
L4218	To 38 Sqn.
L4219	To RAE.
L4220	To 15 OTU.
L4222	To 214 Sqn.
L4224	To 214 Sqn.
L4225	To 20 OTU.
L4227	To RAE.
L4228	To 215 Sqn.
L4229	To 149 Sqn.
L4232	Crashed on take-off at Carew Cheriton while Training 19.9.39.
L4233	To 11 OTU.
L4244	To RAE.
L4246	To 15 OTU.
L4247	To 11 OTU.
L4297	To 11 OTU.
L4298	From A&AEE. To 9 Sqn via SD Flt.
L4309	To 51MU.
L7770	To 15 OTU.
L7783 LN-D	From 214 Sqn. Crashed while trying to land at Newmarket during training 4.1.41.
L7802	To 25 OTU.
L7803	FTR Dinant 21/22.5.40.
L7804	To 15 OTU.
L7847	From 75 Sqn. To 311 Sqn.
L7851	From 214 Sqn via 5BAT Flt. To 1505BAT Flt.
L7868	From 9 Sqn. Crashed soon after take-off from Newmarket when bound for Calais 26.9.40.
L7873 LN-J	FTR Emden 15/16.11.41.
L7896 LN-G	Destroyed by fire at Honington on return from Berlin (149 Sqn crew) 7/8.10.40.

N2767	Ditched off Sussex coast on return from Düsseldorf 9.11.40.
N2768	To 101 Sqn.
N2774	To 149 Sqn.
N2856	From 15 Sqn. To 12 OTU.
N2870	FTR from a reconnaissance sortie off Wangerooge after colliding with N2911 during fighter attack 14.12.39.
N2885	To 115 Sqn.
N2886	FTR from a reconnaissance sortie off Wangerooge 14.12.39.
N2887	To 11 OTU.
N2891	From 149 Sqn. To CGS.
N2911	FTR from a reconnaissance sortie off Wangerooge after a collision with N2870 during a fighter attack 14.12.39.
N2912	To 215 Sqn.
N2913	To 75 Sqn.
N2914	To 1AAS.
N2956	From 38 Sqn. FTR from a reconnaissance sortie off Wangerooge 14.12.39.
N2957	From 38 Sqn. Crashed while trying to land at Newmarket on return from a reconnaissance sortie off Wangerooge 14.12.39.
N2958	From 38 Sqn. To 1AAS.
N2959	To CGS.
N2960	To 149 Sqn.
N2961	To 149 Sqn.
N2962	To 149 Sqn.
N2984	From 9 Sqn. To 149 Sqn.
N2985	From 9 Sqn. To 75 Sqn.
N2986	From 9 Sqn. FTR from a reconnaissance sortie off Wangerooge 14.12.39.
N2999	To 1 AAS.
N3000	To 9 Sqn.
N3001	To 11 OTU.
N3002	To 11 OTU.
N3003	To 11 OTU.
N3004	Force-landed in Belgium during a leafleting sortie to Hamburg 23/24.2.40 and interned.
N3005	To 214 Sqn.
N3006	Crashed in Suffolk following recall from a leafleting sortie 3.3.40.
N3008	To 1AAS.
N3009	To 20 OTU.
N3013	From 149 Sqn. To 301 Sqn.
P9219	Force-landed in Cambridgeshire on return from a reconnaissance sortie 20/21.2.40.
P9221	To 18 OTU.
P9222	To 214 Sqn via 20 OTU.
P9233	To 214 Sqn.
P9234	From 149 Sqn. FTR Stavanger 17/18.4.40.
P9240	From 149 Sqn. To 21 OTU.
P9241	From 149 Sqn. Partially abandoned then force-landed in Norfolk on return from St Omer 30.5.40.
P9242 LN-B	FTR from operation to NW Germany 18/19.9.40.
P9243	FTR Wilhelmshaven 13/14.10.40.
P9272	To 149 Sqn.

P9273	To 149 Sqn.
P9274	Crashed while landing at Newmarket following early return from operation to NW Germany 26.7.40.
P9275	FTR from operation to NW Germany 25/26.7.40.
P9276	Crashed in The Wash during an operation to Stavanger 30.4/1.5.40
P9277	To OADF.
P9279	To 22 OTU.
P9280	To 75 Sqn.
P9281	FTR Düsseldorf 11/12.6.41.
P9282 LN-P	Abandoned over Essex on return from St Omer 30.5.40.
R1176 LN-B	FTR Kiel 25/26.11.40.
R1181	To 149 Sqn.
R1293	To 22 OTU.
R1332	From 12 OTU. To 115 Sqn.
R1333	Crashed soon after take-off from Newmarket bound for Ludwigshaven 18.12.40.
R1372	FTR Bremen 25/26.6.41.
R1407	To 11 OTU.
R1411 LN-N	Shot down by intruder on approach to Mildenhall on return from Cologne 1.9.41.
R1440	FTR Vegesack 9/10.4.41.
R1472	To 22 OTU.
R1503	Crashed soon after take-off from Waterbeach when bound for Boulogne 12/13.8.41.
R1519 LN-Q	Crashed off Dorset coast during operation to Brest 3/4.1.42.
R1537	FTR Cologne 19/20.6.41.
R1643	From 40 Sqn. To 11 OTU.
R2701	To RAE.
R2702	To 15 OTU.
R3167	From 75 Sqn. Abandoned over Middlesex on return from operation to NW Germany 14.11.40.
R3170	FTR Kiel 5/6.7.40.
R3196	Abandoned over Norfolk on return from St Omer 30.5.40.
R3197	To 12 OTU.
R3199	FTR Berlin 9/10.4.41.
R3200 LN-O	From 37 Sqn. Ditched off Yarmouth on return from operation to the Ruhr area 20.6.40.
R3201	To 21 OTU.
R3203	To OADF.
R3214	To 18 OTU.
R3217	From 214 Sqn. To FPP.
R3222	FTR Bremen 20/21.10.41.
R3228	Became ground instruction machine 7.42.
R3287	Became ground instruction machine 7.42.
R3289	Shot down off Suffolk coast on return from an operation to the Ruhr 6/7.11.40.
R3295	To 101 Sqn.
T2460	To 149 Sqn.
T2461	Crashed in Sussex on return from Mannheim 17.12.40. Became ground instruction machine.
T2477	From 9 Sqn. Crashed just after take-off from Waterbeach when bound for Mannheim 5/6.5.41.
T2501 LN-F	FTR Düsseldorf 4/5.12.40.

T2516	FTR Berlin 7/8.11.41.
T2541 LN-O	Force-landed in Suffolk and burnt out during training 31.1.41.
T2546	From 9 Sqn. Crashed in Northumberland during operation to Berlin 29/30.10.40.
T2549	To 115 Sqn.
T2554 LN-F	FTR Berlin 7/8.11.41.
T2611	To 15 OTU.
T2708	From 214 Sqn. Returned to 214 Sqn.
T2721	From 57 Sqn. FTR Mannheim 29/30.4.41.
T2739	From 149 Sqn. To 218 Sqn.
T2803	From 115 Sqn. Ditched off Thorney Island on return from Mannheim 18/19.12.40.
T2850	From 301 Sqn. To 214 Sqn.
T2879	FTR Frankfurt 28/29.9.41.
T2880	FTR Cologne 7/8.7.41.
T2888 LN-R	Abandoned over Cambridgeshire during operation to Bremen 11/12.2.41.
T2957	From 57 Sqn. FTR Cologne 30/31.7.41.
T2984	FTR Essen 3/4.7.41.
T2997	Crashed off Suffolk coast on return from Cologne 21.4.41.
W5400	From 218 Sqn. FTR Berlin 8/9.5.41.
W5436	Crashed in Suffolk on return from Frankfurt 29.9.41.
W5454	From 40 Sqn. FTR Mannheim 22/23.10.41.
W5458	To 12 Sqn.
W5460	To 12 Sqn.
W5494	To 142 Sqn.
W5529	From 40 Sqn. To 305 Sqn.
W5680	FTR Düsseldorf 11/12.6.41.
W5716	From 101 Sqn. To 1504BAT Flt.
W5718	From 75 Sqn. To 40 Sqn.
X9635	To 27 OTU.
X9643	Crashed near Waterbeach while training 21.6.41.
X9667	To 22 OTU.
X9674	From 218 Sqn. To 1483Flt.
X9679	From 218 Sqn. To 22 OTU.
X9700 LN-B	FTR Duisburg 16/17.8.41.
X9703 LN-G	Crashed just after taking-off from Waterbeach when bound for Brest 13.9.41.
X9739	FTR Berlin 7/8.11.41.
X9740 LN-O	Crash-landed in Cambridgeshire after aborting an operation to Kiel 15/16.11.41.
X9744	From 57 Sqn. To 11 OTU.
X9754	To 1438Flt.
X9761	FTR Frankfurt 28/29.9.41.
X9787	From 218 Sqn. To 156 Sqn.
X9912	To 40 Sqn.
X9924	From 57 Sqn. To 22 OTU.
Z1084	From 115 Sqn. To 12 OTU.
Z1090	From 101 Sqn. To 156 Sqn.
Z1107	To 16 OTU.
Z1143	To 214 Sqn.
Z1156	To 214 Sqn.
Z1161	To 458 Sqn.

Z8855	To 40 Sqn.
Z8869	Crashed in Suffolk on return from Frankfurt 29.9.41.
Z8891	From 214 Sqn. Ditched off Suffolk coast on return from Bremen 20/21.10.41.
Z8894	From 218 Sqn. To 214 Sqn.
Z8899	From 20 OTU. To 419 Sqn.
Z8947 LN-J	Crash-landed in Suffolk on return from Emden 14.1.42.
Z8958	Crashed during emergency landing at Waterbeach shortly after taking-off for Aachen 8.12.41.
Z8963	To 20 OTU.
Z8964	To 419 Sqn.
Z8967	To 419 Sqn.
Z8969	To 156 Sqn.
Z8973	To 156 Sqn.
Z8975 LN-X	FTR Emden 15/16.11.41.
Z8980	From 57 Sqn. To 419 Sqn.
AD633	From 15 OTU. Returned to 15 OTU.
AD653	To Middle East.
DV484	Posted overseas.
DV498	Posted overseas.
DV504	Posted overseas.
DV510	To OADU.
DV513	Posted overseas.
DV547	Posted overseas.
DV549	Posted overseas.
DV553	To 15 OTU.
DV554	To OADU.

101 SQUADRON

Motto: Mens Agitat Molem (Mind over matter)   Code SR

No. 101 Squadron was formed in July 1917 as a night bomber unit, and spent the remainder of the Great War operating against enemy communications, bases and stores. After returning to the UK the squadron was disbanded on the last day of 1919. It was resurrected in March 1928. Eventually equipping with Sidestrands and later Overstrands, 101 Squadron was the only unit for an eight-year spell to operate twin engine bombers. In June 1938 conversion began to Blenheims, and the squadron began the Second World War as a training unit. Operations under the banner of 2 Group began in early July 1940, with Channel ports as the main objective. The squadron received Wellingtons in April 1941, while still with 2 Group, and was, therefore, the only unit to operate the type with that Group. A posting to 3 Group followed in July 1941, and the squadron carried out night bombing from then on, and was earmarked for conversion to the Stirling. In the event a further posting took the squadron to 1 Group in September 1942 and ultimately on to Lancasters. A year later the squadron added the role of radio countermeasures (RCM) to its bombing duties, using 'Mandrel' or Airborne Cigar (ABC). This required an extra crew member to listen in to enemy night fighter broadcasts and jam the frequencies with noise. From October 1943 onwards a sprinkling of 101 Squadron Lancasters accompanied most major operations, whether or not 1 Group was on the order of battle, and as a result, 101 Squadron sustained the highest casualties of any heavy squadron.

From 2 Group   06.07.41

STATIONS

Oakington	06.07.41 to 11.02.42
Bourn	11.02.42 to 11.08.42
Stradishall	11.08.42 to 29.09.42

COMMANDING OFFICERS

Wing Commander D R Biggs	16.05.41 to 14.01.42
Wing Commander T H L Nicholls	14.01.42 to 01.06.42
Wing Commander E C Eaton DFC	01.06.42 to 26.01.43

AIRCRAFT

Wellington 1C	04.41 to 10.42
Wellington III	02.42 to 10.42
To 1 Group	29.09.42

OPERATIONAL RECORD

Operations	Sorties	Aircraft Losses	% Losses
135	1,161	42	3.6

Category of Operations

Bombing	Mining
122	13

TABLE OF STATISTICS

(Heavy squadrons)

15th highest number of overall operations in Bomber Command.
4th highest number of sorties in Bomber Command.
10th equal highest number (with 12 Sqn) of aircraft operational losses in Bomber Command.
13th highest number of bombing operations in Bomber Command.
26th highest number of mining operations in Bomber Command.

Out of 42 Wellington squadrons

15th highest number of Wellington overall operations in Bomber Command.
9th highest number of Wellington sorties in Bomber Command.
10th equal highest number (with 99 Sqn) of Wellington operational losses in Bomber Command.

Out of 28 squadrons in 3 Group

15th highest number of overall operations in 3 Group.
14th highest number of sorties in 3 Group.
13th highest number of operational losses in 3 Group.

Out of 18 Wellington squadrons in 3 Group

9th highest number of Wellington overall operations in 3 Group.
8th highest number of Wellington sorties in 3 Group.
7th highest number of Wellington operational losses in 3 Group.

AIRCRAFT HISTORIES

Wellington	From April 1941.
L7869 SR-P	From 214 Sqn. To 29 OTU.
N2768	From 99 Sqn. To 23 OTU.
R1088 SR-O	Crashed in Kent on return from Hamburg 3.8.41.
R1219 SR-R	From 115 Sqn. FTR Cologne 10/11.10.41.
R1338	From 40 Sqn. To 25 OTU.
R1505	From 115 Sqn. To 214 Sqn.
R1699 SR-D	From 105 Sqn. FTR Turin 10/11.9.41.
R1700 SR-X	To 18 OTU.
R1701 SR-K	FTR Berlin 7/8.11.41.
R1702 SR-F	FTR Brest 24.7.41.
R1703 SR-J	FTR Cologne 31.8/1.9.41.
R1778 SR-G	FTR Hamburg 30.11/1.12.41.
R1780 SR-B/U	To 11 OTU.
R1781 SR-C	To 12 OTU.
R1800 SR-T	FTR Hamburg 2/3.8.41.
R1801 SR-U	To 419 Sqn.
R3295 SR-P	From 99 Sqn. FTR Hamburg 30.11/1.12.41.
T2846 SR-S	From 149 Sqn. FTR Düsseldorf 13/14.10.41.
T2963 SR-R	
W5715SR-N	To 301 Sqn and back. FTR Kiel 19/20.8.41.
W5716	To 99 Sqn.
X3206 SR-H	To 214 Sqn.
X3226	From 9 Sqn. Returned to 9 Sqn.
X3277	From 419 Sqn. To ECU.
X3285 SR-R	From 9 Sqn. To 57 Sqn.
X3312 SR-U	FTR Duisburg 21/22.7.42.
X3356 SR-P	FTR Hamburg 17/18.4.42.
X3366 SR-H	To 23 OTU.
X3368	To 29 OTU.
X3391 SR-A	From 115 Sqn. FTR Nuremberg 28/29.8.42.
X3407	From 9 Sqn. To 150 Sqn.
X3424	From 9 Sqn. To 23 OTU.
X3447	From 115 Sqn. Returned to 115 Sqn.
X3455 SR-V	From 156 Sqn. To 142 Sqn.
X3457 SR-R	From 9 Sqn. FTR from mining sortie 21/22.9.42.
X3464	From 75 Sqn. To 115 Sqn.
X3472 SR-D	From 115 Sqn. FTR Mannheim 19/20.5.42.
X3473 SR-S	FTR Bremen 3/4.6.42.
X3475	From 156 Sqn. To 9 Sqn.
X3541 SR-E	From 419 Sqn. To 18 OTU.
X3547 SR-P	
X3559 FTR	Nuremberg 28/29.8.42.
X3634 FTR	Wilhelmshaven 8/9.7.42.
X3642 SR-G	From 115 Sqn. Crashed on landing at Oakington on return from Essen 10.3.42.
X3647	To 115 Sqn.
X3648	To 425 Sqn.
X3649	From 9 Sqn. Ditched off Hull following early return from Kassel 27.8.42.
X3650 SR-B	To 27 OTU.
X3651 SR-Z	Crashed on landing at Bourn while training 15.3.42.

X3654 SR-K	FTR Osnabrück 17/18.8.42.
X3655 SR-V	FTR Hamburg 17/18.4.42.
X3656 SR-L	FTR Essen 8/9.3.42.
X3657 SR-Q	Crash-landed at Martlesham Heath on return from Kassel 28.8.42.
X3663	Crashed in Berkshire while training 26.2.42.
X3668 SR-G	Crashed in Cambridgeshire after a collision with 101 Sqn CF Stirling N6121 when bound for Hamburg 28.7.42.
X3669 SR-H	FTR Emden 19/20.6.42.
X3670 SR-F	FTR Cologne 30/31.5.42.
X3694 SR-U	FTR Dortmund 15/16.4.42.
X3695	From 156 Sqn. To 9 Sqn.
X3701 SR-X	FTR Rostock 23/24.4.42.
X3709 SR-J	FTR from mining sortie 2.4.42.
X3753	To 29 OTU.
X3754 SR-R	FTR Nuremberg 28/29.8.42.
X3812	To 142 Sqn and back via 12 Sqn. To 199 Sqn.
X3815	FTR from mining sortie 21/22.9.42.
X3960	To 142 Sqn.
X3965	To 150 Sqn.
X9601 SR-V	Crashed soon after take-off from Bourn while training 18.11.41.
X9806 SR-A	To 75 Sqn.
X9818	To 16 OTU.
X9819 SR-V	To 419 Sqn.
X9828 SR-K	FTR Frankfurt 24/25.10.41.
X9920 SR-F	To 419 Sqn.
X9922	Crashed in Northamptonshire on return from Ostend 20.9.41.
Z1080	To 156 Sqn.
Z1081	From 40 Sqn. To 214 Sqn.
Z1090	To 99 Sqn.
Z1095	To 419 Sqn.
Z1110	From 311 Sqn. FTR Emden 20/21.1.42.
Z1115	FTR Düsseldorf 27/28.12.41.
Z1146	To 419 Sqn.
Z1148	To 214 Sqn.
Z1569	From 57 Sqn. Destroyed by fire after landing at Waterbeach following operations 13.4.42.
Z1594	FTR Frankfurt 24/25.8.42.
Z1612 SR-Z	From 156 Sqn. FTR Cologne 30/31.5.42.
Z1625 SR-H	To 150 Sqn.
Z1658	From 9 Sqn. Damaged beyond repair in accident at Bourn 6.8.42.
Z1661 SR-F	To 150 Sqn.
Z1662 SR-D	To 16 OTU.
Z1726	To 142 Sqn.
Z1748	To 12 Sqn.
Z1751	FTR from mining sortie 11/12.7.42.
Z8373	To 214 Sqn.
Z8716 SR-D	
Z8840	To 150 Sqn.
Z8842 SR-T	To 214 Sqn.
Z8854	From 9 Sqn. To 75 Sqn.

Z8860	Crashed in Cambridgeshire during an operation to Hamburg 30/31.8.41.
Z8891	To 214 Sqn.
BJ581	From 57 Sqn. To 142 Sqn.
BJ583	FTR from mining sortie 11/12.7.42.
BJ590 SR-H	FTR Hamburg 26/27.7.42.
BJ606	From 9 Sqn. To 12 Sqn.
BJ659 SR-T	To 23 OTU.
BJ689 SR-O	FTR Saarbrücken 19/20.9.42.
BJ698 SR-U	FTR Kassel 27/28.8.42.
BJ705	From 57 Sqn. To 142 Sqn.
BJ711	From 57 Sqn. To 142 Sqn.
BJ715	To 196 Sqn.
BJ768 SR-U	To 142 Sqn.
BJ769	FTR Duisburg 6/7.9.42.
BJ796	To 115 Sqn.
BJ797	To 115 Sqn.
BJ841	FTR Düsseldorf 31.7/1.8.42.
BJ844 SR-C	Ditched in the North Sea on return from Osnabrück 17/18.8.42.
BJ847	To 16 OTU.
BJ891	FTR Bremen 4/5.9.42.
BJ897	FTR Essen 16/17.9.42.
BJ961	To 150 Sqn.
BJ972	To 150 Sqn.
BJ991	To 199 Sqn.
BK298	To 142 Sqn.
BK299	To 142 Sqn.
BK309	To 150 Sqn.
BK310	To 150 Sqn.
BK311	To 150 Sqn.
DV507	To 156 Sqn.
DV509	To 419 Sqn.

115 SQUADRON

Motto: Despite the Elements　　　　　　　　　　　　　　Code KO, IL, A4

Formed on the 1st of December 1917, 115 Squadron did not see action until it arrived in France in September 1918, from where it conducted bombing operations against German industrial targets for what remained of the Great War. Following its return to England, it was disbanded in October 1919, and spent most of the inter-war years on the shelf. Re-formation took place on the 15th of June 1937 at Marham, and on the 3rd of April 1939, it became the fifth unit in the Command to re-equip with Wellingtons. With this type on charge, and as one of 3 Group's front line squadrons, 115 Squadron spent the last few months of peace preparing for the inevitable impending conflict. After a low-key beginning the squadron was at the forefront of 3 Group operations for the remainder of the war, becoming the first unit in the Command to operate the Hercules-powered Lancaster II. By war's end 115 Squadron had lost 208 aircraft on operations, the highest overall losses by any squadron, and this figure included the highest Wellington losses.

STATIONS

Marham	15.06.37 to 24.09.42
Mildenhall	24.09.42 to 08.11.42
East Wretham	08.11.42 to 06.08.43
Little Snoring	06.08.43 to 26.11.43
Witchford	26.11.43 to 28.09.45

COMMANDING OFFICERS

Wing Commander H G Rowe DFC	15.03.39 to 27.12.39
Wing Commander G H Mills DFC	27.12.39 to 25.06.40
Wing Commander H I Dabinett	25.06.40 to 20.01.41
Wing Commander A C Evans-Evans	20.01.41 to 14.08.41
Wing Commander T O Freeman Dso DFC	14.08.41 to 20.06.42
Wing Commander F W Dixon-Wright DFC	20.06.42 to 27.07.42
Wing Commander A G S Cousens DFC	30.07.42 to 16.12.42
Wing Commander A F M Sisley	16.12.42 to 30.03.43
Wing Commander J B Sims	30.03.43 to 01.06.43
Wing Commander F F Rainsford DFC	01.06.43 to 21.12.43
Wing Commander R H Annan DSO	21.12.43 to 12.06.44
Wing Commander W G Devas DFC AFC	12.06.44 to 27.11.44
Wing Commander R H Shaw	27.11.44 to 27.04.45
Wing Commander H Stanton	27.04.45 to 21.07.45

AIRCRAFT

Wellington I	04.39 to 11.39
Wellington Ia	09.39 to 08.40
Wellington Ic	04.40 to 03.42
Wellington III	11.41 to 03.43
Lancaster II	03.43 to 05.44
Lancaster I/III	03.44 to 09.49

OPERATIONAL RECORD

Operations	Sorties	Aircraft Losses	% Losses
678	7,753	208	2.7

Category of Operations

Bombing	Mining	Leaflet
593	81	4

Wellingtons

Operations	Sorties	Aircraft Losses	% Losses
390	3,075	98	3.2

Category of Operations

Bombing	Mining	Leaflet
332	54	4

Lancasters

Operations	Sorties	Aircraft Losses	% Losses
288	4,678	110	2.4

Category of Operations

Bombing	Mining
261	27

TABLE OF STATISTICS

(Heavy squadrons)

6th highest number of overall operations in Bomber Command.
2nd highest number of sorties in Bomber Command.
Highest aircraft operational losses in Bomber Command.
4th highest number of bombing raids in Bomber Command.

Out of 59 Lancaster squadrons

16th equal (with 405 Sqn) highest number of Lancaster overall operations in Bomber Command.
4th highest number of Lancaster sorties in Bomber Command.
11th highest number of Lancaster operational losses in Bomber Command.

Out of 42 Wellington squadrons

Highest number of Wellington operations in Bomber Command.
Highest number of Wellington sorties in Bomber Command.
Highest number of Wellington operational losses in Bomber Command.

Out of 28 squadrons in 3 Group

3rd highest number of overall operations in 3 Group.
2nd highest number of sorties in 3 Group.
Highest number of aircraft operational losses in 3 Group.

Out of 18 Wellington squadrons in 3 Group

Highest number of Wellington overall operations in 3 Group.
Highest number of Wellington sorties in 3 Group.
Highest number of Wellington operational losses in 3 Group.

Out of 11 Lancaster squadrons in 3 Group

Highest number of Lancaster overall operations in 3 Group.
Highest number of Lancaster sorties in 3 Group.
Highest number of Lancaster operational losses in 3 Group.

AIRCRAFT HISTORIES

Wellington	To March 1943.
L4221	From A&AEE. To 3GRU.
L4295	From 38 Sqn. Became ground instruction machine.
L4299	To 20 OTU.
L4300	To 20 OTU.
L4301	To 18 OTU.
L4305	To 20 OTU.
L4306	To 214 Sqn.
L4307	To 38 Sqn.
L4317	To 15 OTU.
L4318	To 15 OTU.
L4319	To 148 Sqn.
L4321	To 20 OTU.
L4323	To 15 OTU.
L4324	To 11 OTU.
L4325	To CGS.
L4333	To 215 Sqn.
L4334	To 15 OTU.

L7774	From 214 Sqn. Returned to 214 Sqn.
L7796	To 9 Sqn.
L7798	From 148 Sqn. To 218 Sqn.
L7801	From 148 Sqn. To 15 OTU.
L7810 KO-R	From 38 Sqn. FTR Boulogne 23/24.2.41.
L7812	To 149 Sqn.
L7845	From 149 Sqn. To 40 Sqn.
L7854	From 38 Sqn. To 29 OTU.
L7895	From 311 Sqn. To 29 OTU.
N2755	To 12 OTU.
N2756	To 38 Sqn.
N2759	To 38 Sqn.
N2760	To 38 Sqn and back. To 27 OTU.
N2855	To 38 Sqn.
N2875	To 305 Sqn.
N2876	To 11 OTU.
N2877	To 75 Sqn.
N2878	From 214 Sqn. To 38 Sqn.
N2884	To 38 Sqn.
N2885	From 99 Sqn. To 311 Sqn.
N2899	To 304 Sqn.
N2900	To 38 Sqn.
N2901	To 75 Sqn.
N2902	To 3FPP.
N2947	To 1 AAS.
N2948 KO-A	Crashed on take-off from Marham while training 24.2.40.
N2949 KO-H	FTR from reconnaissance sortie off Denmark 7.4.40.
N2950 KO-J	Crashed during emergency landing at Marham while training 23.3.40.
N2987 KO-O	Crashed in Huntingdonshire while in transit 19.3.40.
N2988	To CGS.
N2989 KO-V	To 304 Sqn.
N2990	To 11 OTU.
P2524 KO-F	FTR from reconnaissance sortie off Denmark 7.4.40.
P9207	From 38 Sqn. To 218 Sqn.
P9224	From 149 Sqn. To 311 Sqn.
P9226	From 38 Sqn. To 311 Sqn.
P9227	From 38 Sqn. FTR Bremen 18/19.7.40.
P9229 KO-S	To 12 OTU.
P9230	To 311 Sqn.
P9235	From 38 Sqn. To 311 Sqn.
P9236	Lost 20.7.40. Details uncertain.
P9271	To 12STT.
P9283	From 9 Sqn. Force-landed at Oulton 27.10.40.
P9284 KO-J	To 38 Sqn and back. FTR Stavanger 11.4.40.
P9285	To 38 Sqn and back. To 27 OTU.
P9286 KO-K	From 38 Sqn. FTR Hamburg 16/17.11.40.
P9290	From 38 Sqn. To 12 OTU.
P9291	From 38 Sqn. To 218 Sqn.
P9292	From 38 Sqn. To 75 Sqn.
P9296	From 38 Sqn. To 218 Sqn.
P9297 KO-F	From 38 Sqn. FTR Dinant 21/22.5.40.
P9298 KO-H	FTR Cambrai 20/21.5.40.
P9299	To 38 Sqn and back. To 218 Sqn.

P9300	To 12 OTU.
R1004 KO-U	Abandoned near Cambridge on return from Bremen 11/12.2.41.
R1033	To 38 Sqn.
R1034	From 311 Sqn. To 38 Sqn and back. To 22 OTU.
R1063 KO-D	FTR Münster 6/7.7.41.
R1084 KO-Q	Crash-landed in Norfolk on return from Hanover 11.2.41.
R1094	To Malta.
R1179	To 15 OTU.
R1219	To 101 Sqn.
R1221 KO-F	Crashed on approach to Marham on return from Brest 23.2.41.
R1222 KO-H	From 15 Sqn. FTR Duisburg 15/16.7.41.
R1238 KO-A	Crashed on approach to Finningley on return from Bremen 12.2.41.
R1269	To 1429Flt.
R1280 KO-H	From 15 Sqn. Crash-landed near Oakington on return from Brest 4.5.41.
R1332 KO-X	From 99 Sqn. FTR Emden 26/27.9.41.
R1379 KO-B	FTR Hamburg 10/11.5.41.
R1468 KO-Q	Crashed while trying to land at West Raynham on return from Mannheim 28.8.41.
R1470 KO-H	Shot down by intruder over Norfolk on return from Brest 4.4.41.
R1471 KO-T	FTR Mannheim 5/6.8.41.
R1474	To 149 Sqn.
R1500 KO-K	FTR Hanover 14/15.8.41.
R1501 KO-X	Crashed on take-off from Marham when bound for Cologne 26/27.6.41.
R1502 KO-W	FTR Bremen 13/14.7.41.
R1505	To 101 Sqn.
R1508 KO-T	Crash-landed at Manby on return from Hamburg 30.6.41.
R1509 KO-P	FTR Hamburg 29/30.6.41.
R1517 KO-Z	Crashed soon after take-off from Marham for air-test 17.6.41
R1713	To 218 Sqn.
R1721 KO-R	From 22 OTU. Crashed on approach to Marham on return from Hamm 13.6.41.
R1772 KO-M	FTR Kiel 7/8.9.41.
R1798 KO-B	FTR Berlin 7/8.9.41.
R1805	Damaged beyond repair on operations 27.6.41.
R3150	To 37 Sqn.
R3151	To 20 OTU.
R3152 KO-J	FTR Dinant 21/22.5.40.
R3153	To 218 Sqn.
R3154 KO-Q	Crashed in Yorkshire on return from Stavanger 1.5.40.
R3155	To A&AEE.
R3156	To 75 Sqn.
R3157	To 75 Sqn.
R3158	To 75 Sqn.
R3159	To 75 Sqn.
R3160	To 149 Sqn.
R3198	From 38 Sqn. To 22 OTU.
R3202 KO-J	FTR Hamburg 2/3.8.40.

R3213 KO-S	From 38 Sqn. FTR Hamburg 16/17.11.40.
R3232	To 214 Sqn.
R3238 KO-H	Abandoned over Essex on return from Bremen 11/12.2.41.
R3276 KO-B	Force-landed in Norfolk on return from Mannheim 23.8.40.
R3278	To 148 Sqn.
R3279 KO-D	FTR Brest 2/3.3.41.
R3291	To 38 Sqn.
R3292 KO-F	FTR Osnabrück 30.9/1.10.40.
T2465 KO-O	From 38 Sqn. FTR Hamm 29/30.12.40.
T2466 KO-C	FTR Mannheim 11/12.12.40.
T2509 KO-W	Ditched on return from Berlin 15.11.40.
T2520 KO-A	Crashed in Wales on return from Bordeaux 9.12.40.
T2549 KO-K	From 99 Sqn. FTR Osnabrück 30.9/1.10.40.
T2551	To 38 Sqn.
T2560 KO-E	Crashed in Wiltshire during operation to Brest 22/23.4.41.
T2563 KO-D	Shot down by intruder near Norwich on return from Essen 13.8.41.
T2606	o 17 OTU.
T2613 KO-R	From 311 Sqn. Crashed in Buckinghamshire during ferry flight 30.10.40.
T2713	From 149 Sqn. To 20 OTU.
T2742	To 38 Sqn.
T2803	To 99 Sqn.
T2805	To 75 Sqn.
T2887	To 218 Sqn.
T2963 KO-A	From 15 OTU. Crashed on approach to Woodbridge on return from Cologne 24.6.41.
W5459KO-L	FTR Bremen 29/30.6.41.
W5526	To 218 Sqn.
W5566	To 305 Sqn.
W5684KO-G	Abandoned over Devon on return from Brest 3/4.9.41.
W5710KO-J	Abandoned over Norfolk on return from Mannheim 28.8.41.
X3341 KO-W	FTR Lübeck 28/29.3.42.
X3342	From 9 Sqn. To 23 OTU.
X3343	To 23 OTU.
X3344	To 419 Sqn.
X3345	To 156 Sqn.
X3348	To 9 Sqn.
X3351 KO-T	From 9 Sqn. FTR from mining sortie 31.12.42/1.1.43.
X3354	From 9 Sqn. To 27 OTU.
X3364	To 425 Sqn.
X3365	To 20 OTU.
X3391	To 101 Sqn.
X3392	To 420 Sqn.
X3393 KO-H	To 425 Sqn and back. To BDU via 1483Flt and back. FTR Turin 9/10.12.42.
X3394	Crashed in Norfolk while training 11.11.41.
X3397	From 75 Sqn. To 16 OTU via manufacturers.
X3402	To 57 Sqn.
X3408	To 75 Sqn.
X3412 KO-L	FTR Hamburg 26/27.7.42.
X3413	To 150 Sqn.
X3414	To 103 Sqn.

X3416	From 75 Sqn. To 419 Sqn.
X3417	To 156 Sqn.
X3419 KO-T	FTR Essen 8/9.3.42.
X3423	To 9 Sqn.
X3424	To 9 Sqn.
X3445	To 17 OTU.
X3447	To 101 Sqn and back. To 16 OTU.
X3448	From 57 Sqn. To 103 Sqn.
X3450	From 57 Sqn. To 150 Sqn.
X3464 KO-B	From 101 Sqn. FTR Nuremberg 28/29.8.42.
X3466 KO-N	FTR Stuttgart 6/7.5.42.
X3468	To 75 Sqn.
X3471	To 16 OTU.
X3472	To 101 Sqn.
X3488	To 75 Sqn.
X3539	From 75 Sqn. Returned to 75 Sqn.
X3540 KO-X	From 75 Sqn. To 75 Sqn and back. FTR Essen 29.10.42.
X3554 KO-Q	FTR Bremen 25/26.6.42.
X3555 KO-W	FTR Emden 22/23.6.42.
X3560 KO-K	From 9 Sqn. FTR Duisburg 13/14.7.42.
X3561 KO-X	FTR Duisburg 21/22.7.42.
X3565	To 30 OTU.
X3584	From 75 Sqn. To 57 Sqn.
X3589 KO-F	FTR Essen 26/27.3.42.
X3591 KO-K	FTR Stuttgart 6/7.5.42.
X3592	To 419 Sqn.
X3593 KO-C	FTR Gennevilliers 29/30.4.42.
X3596 KO-B	FTR Essen 12/13.4.42.
X3597 KO-Q	From 75 Sqn. FTR from mining sortie 16/17.11.42.
X3601	Lost 31.8.42. Details unknown.
X3602	Crashed in Norfolk while training 11.5.42.
X3604 KO-Y	FTR Essen 26/27.3.42.
X3633 KO-Y	FTR Rostock 25/26.4.42.
X3635 KO-J	FTR Bremen 3/4.6.42.
X3639 KO-K	FTR Cologne 27/28.4.42.
X3642	To 101 Sqn.
X3644 KO-A	FTR from mining sortie 17/18.5.42.
X3647 KO-A	From 101 Sqn. FTR Nuremberg 28/29.8.42.
X3662	To 20 OTU.
X3666	From 9 Sqn. To 23 OTU.
X3675 KO-D	FTR Nuremberg 28/29.8.42.
X3718 KO-Q	From 9 Sqn. FTR from mining sortie 18/19.9.42.
X3721 KO-F	FTR Essen 1/2.6.42.
X3724 KO-T	FTR Bremen 3/4.6.42.
X3726 KO-A	From 57 Sqn. FTR Duisburg 21/22.7.42.
X3749 KO-D	Crash-landed at Marham on return from Bremen 4.6.42.
X3750 KO-B	FTR Duisburg 21/22.7.42.
X3878	From 156 Sqn. To 15 OTU.
X3924	To 26 OTU.
X3936 KO-X	From 156 Sqn. Abandoned over Gloucestershire on return from a mining sortie 28.1.43.
X3946 KO-Q	From 75 Sqn. FTR from mining sortie 16/17.10.42.
X3989 KO-V	FTR from mining sortie 20/21.8.42.
X9616	From 301 Sqn. To 26 OTU.

X9632	To 20 OTU.
X9663	From 218 Sqn. To 149 Sqn.
X9671	To 21 OTU.
X9672 KO-F	From 218 Sqn. Abandoned over Norfolk on return from Mannheim 28.8.41.
X9673 KO-B	FTR Hamburg 29/30.9.41.
X9677	To 218 Sqn.
X9733 KO-L	To 149 Sqn.
X9742	From 75 Sqn. To 215 Sqn.
X9751	To 218 Sqn.
X9755	To 218 Sqn.
X9826 KO-D	Shot down by intruder over Suffolk on return from Mannheim 30.8.41.
X9831	To 1505BAT Flt.
X9871	From 218 Sqn. To 215 Sqn.
X9873 KO-P	FTR Bremen 31.10/1.11.41.
X9875 KO-J	To 218 Sqn and back. To 23 OTU.
X9877	To 149 Sqn.
X9888 KO-F	From 311 Sqn. FTR Emden 15/16.11.41.
X9909	To 40 Sqn.
X9910 KO-Y	FTR Hamburg 29/30.9.41.
Z1069	To 218 Sqn.
Z1070 KO-B	To 218 Sqn.
Z1084 KO-A	From 40 Sqn. To 99 Sqn.
Z1563 KO-G	Crashed in Marham circuit while training 15.1.42.
Z1572	To 75 Sqn.
Z1574 KO-S	Damaged beyond repair during operation to Genoa 23/24.10.42.
Z1605 KO-R	FTR Hamburg 28/29.7.42.
Z1606 KO-J	FTR Duisburg 25/26.7.42.
Z1607 KO-T	Crash-landed in Norfolk on return from Nuremberg 29.8.42.
Z1609	From 156 Sqn. To 1483Flt.
Z1614 KO-R	FTR Cologne 30/31.5.42.
Z1620 KO-T	From 156 Sqn. FTR Hamburg 3/4.3.43.
Z1624 KO-D	FTR Hamburg 28/29.7.42.
Z1648 KO-A	To 23 OTU.
Z1649	To 83 OTU.
Z1653	From 57 Sqn. To 18 OTU.
Z1657 KO-R	From 57 Sqn. To CGS.
Z1663 KO-J	From 57 Sqn. FTR Lingen (Dortmund-Ems Canal) 28.9.42.
Z1694 KO-G	To 23 OTU.
Z1738 KO-M	From 75 Sqn. FTR Essen 29.10.42.
Z8375	To 218 Sqn.
Z8788 KO-H	FTR Mannheim 21/22.7.41.
Z8796	To 20 OTU.
Z8799 KO-Z	To 20 OTU.
Z8802	To 20 OTU.
Z8804	To 20 OTU.
Z8809	To 20 OTU.
Z8830	To TFU.
Z8835 KO-U	FTR Essen 12/13.8.41.
Z8841	To 20 OTU.
Z8844 KO-S	FTR Munich 13/14.10.41.

Z8846	To 20 OTU.
Z8848 KO-H	Ditched off Yorkshire coast on return from Kiel 16.11.41.
Z8852	To 20 OTU.
Z8853	From 9 Sqn. To 40 Sqn and back. To 218 Sqn.
Z8857	To 20 OTU.
Z8863 KO-G	Crashed in Cambridgeshire while training 24.11.41.
BJ584	From 75 Sqn. To 36 OTU.
BJ589	To 156 Sqn.
BJ595 KO-S	Ditched off Lincolnshire coast during operation to Duisburg 23/24.7.42.
BJ615 KO-G	FTR Hamburg 26/27.7.42.
BJ660 KO-H	FTR Essen 29.10.42.
BJ663 KO-N	FTR Bremen 4/5.9.42.
BJ670 KO-K	FTR Hamburg 26/27.7.42.
BJ688 KO-R	From 9 Sqn. FTR Nuremberg 28/29.8.42.
BJ693 KO-J	FTR Wilhelmshaven 14/15.9.42.
BJ706	To 22 OTU.
BJ710 KO-L	FTR Kassel 27/28.8.42.
BJ722	To TFU.
BJ723 KO-B	FTR Hamburg 26/27.7.42.
BJ724 KO-P	Blew up in the air over Norfolk when bound for Duisburg 6.9.42.
BJ756 KO-Q	From 75 Sqn. FTR Essen 12/13.3.43.
BJ770	From 57 Sqn. To 18 OTU.
BJ771 KO-L	From 57 Sqn. FTR Bremen 4/5.9.42.
BJ796 KO-H	From 101 Sqn. Ditched in North Sea off the Suffolk coast during operation to Bremen 29/30.6.42.
BJ797	From 101 Sqn. To 17 OTU.
BJ832 KO-F	To 75 Sqn and back. To 29 OTU.
BJ833	From 57 Sqn. To 26 OTU.
BJ842 KO-W	FTR Stuttgart 22/23.11.42.
BJ879	To 26 OTU.
BJ880	To 82 OTU.
BJ893 KO-C	FTR Saarbrücken 1/2.9.42.
BJ898 KO-C	From 75 Sqn. FTR Mannheim 6/7.12.42.
BJ962 KO-D	FTR from mining sortie 21/22.9.42.
BJ965	To 12 OTU.
BJ990	To 17 OTU.
BK127 KO-D	FTR Hamburg 3/4.2.43.
BK128	To 30 OTU.
BK166 KO-C	FTR Lorient 13/14.2.43.
BK206 KO-R	From 75 Sqn. FTR Stuttgart 22/23.11.42.
BK271 KO-A	FTR Krefeld 2/3.10.42.
BK272	To 17 OTU.
BK274 KO-T	From 75 Sqn. FTR Fallersleben 17/18.12.42.
BK275	From 75 Sqn. To 26 OTU.
BK306 KO-K	FTR Milan 24/25.10.42.
BK307	To 29 OTU.
BK312	FTR from mining sortie 16/17.10.42.
BK313 KO-B	FTR Osnabrück 6/7.10.42.
BK314	To 17 OTU.
BK336 KO-D	FTR Fallersleben 17/18.12.42.
BK338 KO-A	FTR Frankfurt 2/3.12.42.
BK362	From 75 Sqn. To CGS.

BK495 KO-N	FTR from mining sortie 2/3.3.43.
BK513 KO-V	FTR Mannheim 6/7.12.42.

Lancaster — From March 1943. (Mk II*)

DS603*	From 61 Sqn. No operations. To 1657CU.
DS604*KO-B	From 61 Sqn. FTR Frankfurt 10/11.4.43.
DS607*	From 61 Sqn. To 1657CU.
DS608*KO-C	From 61 Sqn. To 1657CU.
DS609*KO-M	FTR Duisburg 26/27.4.43.
DS610*	From 61 Sqn. To 1657CU.
DS612*KO-F/H	From 61 Sqn. To 426 Sqn.
DS613*KO-Y	From 61 Sqn. To 1668CU.
DS614*KO-A	To 1666CU.
DS615*KO-N	To 1659CU.
DS616*KO-G	Crashed on landing at East Wretham on return from Wuppertal and collided with DS618 (115 Sqn) 30.5.43.
DS617*KO-N	To 1657CU.
DS618*KO-P	From 1657CU. Destroyed on ground in accident at East Wretham 30.5.43. (See DS616).
DS619*	To 1657CU.
DS620*KO-V/W	To 1668CU.
DS621*KO-U	From 61 Sqn. To 426 Sqn.
DS622*KO-F/Q/T	To 1668CU.
DS623*KO-R	To 1678CU.
DS624*KO-L	To 426 Sqn.
DS625*KO-W	FTR Berlin 29/30.3.43.
DS626*KO-J	To 426 Sqn.
DS627*A4-D/KO-R	From 1657CU. FTR Wuppertal 29/30.5.43.
DS629*KO-D/M	Crash-landed at Coltishall on return from Frankfurt 19.3.44.
DS630*KO-H	FTR Peenemünde 17/18.8.43.
DS631*KO-Z	To 1679CU.
DS633*	From 432 Sqn via 1678CU. To 514 Sqn.
DS634*KO-K	To 426 Sqn.
DS635*KO-G	To 1679CU.
DS647*KO-N	FTR Düsseldorf 11/12.6.43.
DS652*KO-B	FTR Bochum 12/13.6.43.
DS653*KO-S	To 1679CU.
DS654*	To 1657CU.
DS655*KO-M	FTR Essen 27/28.5.43.
DS656*KO-X	To 426 Sqn.
DS657*	To 426 Sqn.
DS658*KO-K	Wrecked on landing at Little Snoring on return from Berlin 4.9.43.
DS659*KO-T	FTR Nuremberg 27/28.8.43.
DS660*KO-P	FTR Aachen 13/14.7.43.
DS661*KO-F/Z	Crashed on take-off from Witchford while training 20.3.44.
DS662*KO-L	FTR Cologne 3/4.7.43.
DS663*KO-C	FTR from mining sortie 25/26.6.43.
DS664*KO-X/D	FTR Berlin 24/25.3.44. A4-K
DS665*KO-N	Crashed near Cambridge on return from Nuremberg 11.8.43.
DS666*KO-J	FTR Gelsenkirchen 25/26.6.43.
DS667*A4-G	FTR Berlin 2/3.1.44.

DS668*KO-R	FTR from mining sortie 19/20.6.43.
DS669*KO-L	To 514 Sqn.
DS670*KO-U	To 1678 Sqn.
DS671*	To BDU 6.43.
DS672*	To BDU 6.43.
DS673*KO-V	FTR Hamburg 2/3.8.43.
DS675*KO-E	FTR Hanover 22/23.9.43.
DS678*KO-J	FTR Berlin 24/25.3.44.
DS680*KO-L	FTR Berlin 18/19.11.43.
DS682*KO-Y/A	To 514 Sqn.
DS683*KO-R	Crash-landed at Little Snoring on return from Hanover 18.10.43.
DS684*KO-M	FTR Turin 16/17.8.43.
DS685*KO-A	FTR Hamburg 2/3.8.43.
DS690*KO-P/C	FTR Aachen 13/14.7.43.
DS691*KO-F/B	FTR Hanover 8/9.10.43.
DS715*KO-Q	FTR Hamburg 2/3.8.43.
DS720*KO-D	FTR Brunswick 14/15.1.44.
DS721*KO-U	FTR from air-sea search sortie 4.10.43.
DS722*KO-N	From 426 Sqn. FTR Berlin 23/24.8.43.
DS725*KO-F	FTR Leipzig 20/21.10.43.
DS728*KO-P/C/T	FTR Cologne 20/21.4.44.
DS734*KO-Y	FTR Karlsruhe 24/25.4.44.
DS761*KO-W	To 408 Sqn.
DS764*KO-S	FTR Berlin 22/23.11.43.
DS765*KO-A	FTR Leipzig 3/4.12.43.
DS766*KO-Q/R	Crashed on approach to Woodbridge on return from Frankfurt 23.3.44.
DS769*KO-H	FTR Hanover 18/19.10.43.
DS773*KO-T	FTR Berlin 23/24.12.44.
DS777*A4-C	FTR Magdeburg 21/22.1.44.
DS780*	Crashed in Norfolk during air-test and training 14.9.43.
DS781*KO-W	To 514 Sqn.
DS782*KO-K	FTR Berlin 22/23.11.43.
DS784*	To 514 Sqn.
DS793*KO-L	FTR Berlin 26/27.11.43.
DS795*A4-E	To 514 Sqn and back. To 38MU.
DS796*KO-E	From 514 Sqn. Force-landed in Cambridgeshire on return from Berlin 2.1.44.
DS825*	From 514 Sqn. Crashed on take-off from Little Snoring when bound for mining sortie 8.11.43.
DS827*KO-B	Crashed in Essex during bombing practice 5.2.44.
DS833*KO-S	FTR Berlin 28/29.1.44.
DS834*KO-F	From 514 Sqn. FTR Berlin 29/30.12.43.
DS835*KO-K	FTR Berlin 16/17.12.43.
DS836*KO-R	To 514 Sqn.
ED491	From 50 Sqn. To A&AEE Boscombe Down.
ED631 KO-B	From 617 Sqn. To 1651CU.
HK541 KO-P	From 75 Sqn. To 3LFS.
HK542 KO-J	From 75 Sqn. FTR Karlsruhe 24/25.4.44.
HK544 KO-U	From 75 Sqn. FTR Bonn 18.10.44.
HK545 KO-E	From 622 Sqn. FTR Gelsenkirchen 12/13.6.44.
HK546 A4-H	To 149 Sqn.
HK547 A4-F	FTR Le Mans 19/20.5.44.

HK548 KO-W	FTR Chevreusse 7/8.6.44.
HK549 KO-Q	To 149 Sqn.
HK550 KO-Y	FTR Valenciennes 15/16.6.44.
HK551 A4-E	From 75 Sqn. To 149 Sqn.
HK552 KO-J	FTR Chevreusse 7/8.6.44.
HK555 KO-E	To 149 Sqn and back. Collided over Germany with RA533 (186 Sqn) while returning from Leuna 4/5.4.45
HK556 A4-F	FTR Kiel 26/27.8.44.
HK559 A4-H	FTR Montdidier 17/18.6.44.
HK560 A4-K	FTR Kiel 27.8.44.
HK564	To 75 Sqn.
HK565 KO-L	From 75 Sqn. To 1659CU.
HK566	To 1654CU.
HK572 KO-Y	To 149 Sqn and back. To 1661CU.
HK578 IL-C	To 149 Sqn.
HK579 A4-B	FTR Le Havre 8.9.44.
HK595 KO-A	FTR Dortmund 15.11.44.
HK598	To 149 Sqn.
HK599 KO-K	FTR Duisburg 14.10.44.
HK624 IL-J	From 149 Sqn. FTR Cologne 27.11.44.
HK653	From 149 Sqn. Returned to 149 Sqn.
HK656 KO-Q	From 149 Sqn.
HK691 KO-R	
HK696	From 90 Sqn.
HK698 IL-A/K	
HK766 KO-F	
HK768	
HK790 KO-Y	
HK798 KO-H/L	
IL-L	
LL621*	To 426 Sqn.
LL622*A4-F/KO-J	FTR Nuremberg 30/31.3.44.
LL624*KO-D	To 514 Sqn.
LL626*A4-N	
LL639*	To 514 Sqn.
LL640*A4-C	FTR Frankfurt 18/19.3.44.
LL644*KO-N	From 514 Sqn. FTR Schweinfurt 24/25.2.44.
LL646*KO-G	To 46MU following forced-landing.
LL648*A4-B	FTR Berlin 30/31.1.44.
LL649*A4-G	FTR Berlin 28/29.1.44.
LL650*A4-J	From 514 Sqn. FTR Berlin 20/21.1.44.
LL651*A4-A	FTR Berlin 15/16.2.44.
LL652*A4-Q	To 514 Sqn.
LL666*KO-U	To 514 Sqn.
LL667*KO-R	Shot down by intruder over Witchford on return from Rouen 19.4.44.
LL668*A4-H	FTR Berlin 27/28.1.44.
LL669*	To 514 Sqn.
LL670*	To 514 Sqn.
LL673*KO-G	FTR Brunswick 14/15.1.44.
LL678*	To 514 Sqn.
LL680*	To 514 Sqn.
LL681*A4-A	To 514 Sqn.
LL682*KO-P	FTR Berlin 27/28.1.44.

LL685*	To 514 Sqn.
LL687*	From 426 Sqn. To 408 Sqn.
LL689*KO-P	FTR Berlin 15/16.2.44.
LL691*	To 514 Sqn.
LL692*KO-F	To 514 Sqn.
LL693*KO-I/A4-K	FTR Stuttgart 15/16.3.44.
LL694*KO-N	FTR Berlin 24/25.3.44.
LL695*	To 514 Sqn.
LL701*KO-F	FTR Schweinfurt 24/25.2.44.
LL702*	Damaged in accident and SOC 15.1.44.
LL704*KO-H	FTR Nuremberg 30/31.3.44.
LL716*	To 514 Sqn.
LL726*KO-G A4-A	To 514 Sqn.
LL729*A4-B	Crashed in Bedfordshire on return from Stuttgart 21.2.44.
LL730*KO-G	From 514 Sqn. FTR Berlin 24/25.3.44.
LL734*	To 514 Sqn.
LL804	To 300 Sqn.
LL864 A4-H	From 75 Sqn. FTR Chevreusse 7/8.6.44.
LL867 KO-U/A4-J	From 75 Sqn. Shot down by intruder over Witchford on return from Rouen 19.4.44.
LL880 KO-D	From 75 Sqn. FTR Dortmund 6/7.10.44.
LL921	To 75 Sqn.
LL923	To XV Sqn.
LL935 KO-N IL-N	From 57 Sqn. To 3LFS.
LL936 KO-V	FTR Trappes 31.5/1.6.44.
LL943 KO-C	FTR Aulnoye 18/19.7.44.
LL944 KO-Z	FTR Siegen 16.12.44.
LM127 KO-H	FTR Kiel 26/27.8.44.
LM166 KO-Y	FTR Foret de Lucheux 8/9.8.44.
LM510 KO-A/K	From 75 Sqn. Crash-landed at Woodbridge on return from Homberg 21.7.44.
LM533 KO-T	From XV Sqn. FTR Lisieux 6/7.6.44.
LM534	To XV Sqn.
LM544	To 75 Sqn.
LM616 KO-J	Crashed in Hertfordshire on return from Emieville 18.7.44.
LM693 KO-T	FTR Moerdijk 16/17.9.44.
LM696 KO-F/U A4-F	
LM725 KO-X	FTR Chemnitz 14/15.2.45.
LM734 IL-J	From 514 Sqn.
LM738 A4-B	FTR Calais 27.9.44.
LM743	To 195 Sqn.
LM744	To 195 Sqn.
LM753	To 195 Sqn.
ME692 KO-G A4-G	From 75 Sqn. FTR Wilhelmshaven 15/16.10.44.
ME718 KO-G	FTR Stettin 29/30.8.44.
ME751	To 75 Sqn.
ME752	To 75 Sqn.
ME753	To 75 Sqn.
ME754	To 75 Sqn.

ME756 A4-U/V	To 1651CU. 11.44.
ME803 KO-D/L A4-D/IL-B	
ME834	From 75 Sqn.
ME836 KO-S A4-C	Completed 99 operations.
ND677 KO-X	From 49 Sqn.
ND745 A4-D	From 75 Sqn. FTR Dortmund 22/23.5.44.
ND753 KO-K	From 75 Sqn. FTR Düsseldorf 22/23.4.44.
ND754 KO-F	From 75 Sqn. FTR Duisburg 21/22.5.44.
ND758 KO-Y A4-A	From 75 Sqn. To 3LFS 11.44.
ND760 A4-K	From 75 Sqn. FTR Chevreusse 7/8.6.44.
ND761 A4-C	From 75 Sqn. FTR Chevreusse 7/8.6.44.
ND790 KO-H	FTR Chevreusse 7/8.6.44.
ND800 A4-C	To 75 Sqn.
ND803 A4-D/B	FTR Friedrichshafen 27/28.4.44.
ND805 A4-J	FTR Duisburg 14.10.44.
ND900 KO-S	To 1651CU.
ND904 KO-M	To 75 Sqn.
ND913 KO-N A4-M	FTR Homberg 20/21.7.44.
ND917	To 75 Sqn.
ND920	To 75 Sqn.
ND923 KO-C	FTR Louvain 11/12.5.44.
ND927 KO-B	FTR Brunswick 12/13.8.44.
NE148	To 75 Sqn.
NF960 KO-R	FTR Cologne 28.10.44.
NG122	
NG124 KO-U A4-L	
NG130 IL-V	
NG162	To 195 Sqn.
NG168	
NG205 KO-K IL-D	
NG332 IL-D	FTR Vohwinkel 1/2.1.45.
NN706 KO-B	FTR Dortmund 15.11.44.
NN754 IL-F/J	
NN755	To 195 Sqn.
NN761	
NN762	
NN806	From 576 Sqn. Crashed on take-off from Fiskerton 8.5.45.
NX559 KO-D	
PA181 KO-A	
PA224 KO-L	
PA967	To 75 Sqn.
PB127 KO-T	FTR Brunswick 12/13.8.44.
PB130 KO-A	FTR Amaye-sur-Seulles 30.7.44.
PB131 KO-W	FTR Stettin 29/30.8.44.
PB373	From 49 Sqn.
PB433 KO-E	From 49 Sqn.
PB455	From 49 Sqn.
PB524 KO-C	To 1659CU.

PB571	From 49 Sqn.
PB577	To GH Flt at Feltwell.
PB647	From 227 Sqn.
PB686 KO-D	FTR Dresden 14.2.45.
PB721 KO-U	From 218 Sqn.
PB756 IL-A/H	
PB757 IL-E	
PB767 KO-T	From 514 Sqn.
PB789 KO-C	From 514 Sqn.
PB798 IL-G	From 514 Sqn.
PB818 KO-X	To 195 Sqn.
PB907 KO-O	From 49 Sqn.
PD274 KO-Y	FTR Rüsselsheim 26/27.8.44.
PD276 KO-X	FTR Essen 25.10.44.
PD277 KO-C	From 218 Sqn.
PD293 KO-O	FTR from training sortie 26.11.44.
PD344 KO-M	FTR Saarbrücken 5/6.10.44.
PD345	From 227 Sqn.
PD367 KO-H	FTR Osterfeld 30.11.44.
PD370	To 138 Sqn.
PD400	To 90 Sqn.
PD401	
PD402	To 90 Sqn.
PD444	From 1662CU.
PP666 KO-W	
IL-K	
PP670	
RF190	To 75 Sqn.

138 SQUADRON

Motto: For Freedom   Codes NF, AC

Formation of 138 Squadron began on the 1st of May 1918, but it was still only a nucleus when the process was suspended on the 4th of July to provide crews for front line units. Re-formation took place at Chingford on the 30th of September, but the squadron failed to achieve operational status as a fighter/reconnaissance unit before hostilities ended, and it was eventually disbanded on the 1st of February 1919. It was August 1941 before the squadron number was resurrected, but in the meantime, what might properly be viewed as its conception took place in the dark days of 1940, as Britain stood alone against the might of all-conquering Germany. A protracted war required long-term measures, including encouraging and arming resistance organisations in occupied Europe, and the Special Operations Executive (SOE) was formed to oversee all aspects. No. 419 Flight was set up to drop agents and arms, and pick up returning agents. It joined 3 Group and became 1419 Flight, before gaining full squadron status as 138 Squadron in August 1941. Operating a variety of types from Lysanders to Halifaxes, Stirlings, and for a period, Liberators, the squadron's crews displayed amazing airmanship in the most difficult of conditions. Polish airmen played a significant role, carrying out many hazardous operations to their homeland and elsewhere. Once the liberation of the occupied countries reduced the need for secret operations 138 Squadron converted to Lancasters in March 1945 and became a standard 3 Group front-line unit.

STATIONS

419 Flight

North Weald	21.08.40 to 03.09.40
Stapleford Tawney	03.09.40 to 09.10.40
Stradishall	09.10.40 to 03.41

1419 Flight

Stradishall	03.41 to 22.05.41
Newmarket	22.05.41 to 25.08.41

138 Squadron

Newmarket	25.08.41 to 12.41
Stradishall	12.41 to 14.03.42
Tempsford	14.03.42 to 09.03.45
Tangmere (Lysander Flight)	25.08.41 to 02.42
Tuddenham	09.03.45 to 11.46

COMMANDING OFFICERS

419 Flight

Flight Lieutenant W R Farley	21.08.40 to 12.40
Flight Lieutenant F J B Keast	12.40 to 17.02.41
Squadron Leader E V Knowles DFC	02.41 to 03.41

1419 Flight

Squadron Leader E V Knowles DFC	03.41 to 25.08.41

138 Squadron

Wing Commander E V Knowles DFC	25.08.41 to 17.11.41
Wing Commander W R Farley DFC	18.11.41 to 21.04.42
Wing Commander R C Hockey DSO DFC	21.04.42 to 21.02.43
Wing Commander K S Batchelor DFC	28.02.43 to 24.05.43
Wing Commander R D Speare DFC	25.05.43 to 30.04.44
Wing Commander W Mcf Russell DFC*	01.05.44 to 07.05.44
Wing Commander W J Burnett DFC	09.05.44 to 17.12.44
Wing Commander T B C Murray DSO DFC*	17.12.44 to 04.46
Squadron Leader H W Wilkie (Temp)	26.04.45 to 06.05.45

AIRCRAFT

Whitley V	08.40 to 10.42
Lysander IIIa	08.40 to 02.42
Halifax I	10.41 to 12.42
Halifax II	10.42 to 08.44
Liberator	08.43 to 10.43
Stirling	06.44 to 03.45
Lancaster	03.45 to 09.47

OPERATIONAL RECORD

419 and 1419 Flights

Sorties	Aircraft Losses
111	1

138 Squadron
Special Duties

Operations	Sorties	Aircraft Losses	% Losses
438	2,572	91	3.5

Sorties by Aircraft Type

Halifax	Stirling	Whitley	Lysander	Liberator	Wellington
1,788	503	219	64	3	1

It is not possible to be absolutely accurate with the above figures

Operational Losses by Aircraft Type

Halifax	Stirling	Whitley	Lysander	Liberator	Wellington
62	13	12	3	1	0

Lancaster

Operations	Sorties	Aircraft Losses	% Losses
9	105	1	1.0

TABLE OF STATISTICS

(non-special duties)

Out of 59 Lancaster squadrons

Lowest number of overall Lancaster operations, sorties and losses in Bomber Command.

Out of 28 squadrons in 3 Group

Lowest number of overall operations, sorties and losses in 3 Group.

Out of 11 Lancaster squadrons in 3 Group

Lowest number of overall Lancaster operations, sorties and losses in 3 Group.

AIRCRAFT HISTORIES

419 Flight

Whitley	From August 1940 to March 1941.
P5025	Crashed on landing at Stradishall after local flight 11.10.40.
P5029	To 1419Flt.
T4166	From 78 Sqn. To 1419Flt.
T4264	FTR from SOE operation to Belgium 17/18.2.41.
Z6473	From A&AEE. To 1419Flt.
Lysander	From August 1940 to March 1941.
R2625	From 13 Sqn. To 1419Flt.
R2626	From 13 Sqn. To 1419Flt.
R9027	Force-landed in Scotland on return from pick-up operation to France 21.10.40.

1419 Flight

Whitley	From March 1941 to August 1941.
P5029	From 419Flt. To 138 Sqn.
T4165	From 78 Sqn. To 138 Sqn.
T4166	From 419Flt. To 138 Sqn.
Z6473	From 419Flt. To 42 OTU.

Z6727	Crashed in Cambridgeshire during secret equipment test 25.7.41.
Z6728	To 138 Sqn.
Z9125	To 138 Sqn.

Lysander — From March 1941 to August 1941.

R2625	From 419Flt. To 138 Sqn.
R2626	From 419Flt. To 138 Sqn.
T1508	To 138 Sqn via TFU.
T1770	To 138 Sqn via SDF and TFU Newmarket.

Whitley — From August 1941 to October 1942.

P5029 NF-E	From 1419Flt. Ditched off Sussex coast on return from SOE sortie to France 22/23.10.42.
T4165	From 1419Flt. Crashed while landing at Tangmere on return from SOE operation to France 10/11.4.41.
T4166 NF-B	From 1419Flt. FTR from SOE operation to Holland 27/28.3.42.
Z6728	From 1419Flt. FTR from SOE operation to Belgium 28/29.1.42.
Z6959	From 102 Sqn. To 161 Sqn.
Z9125	From 1419Flt. Crashed on take-off from Stradishall when bound for SOE operation to France 10.3.42.
Z9140	From 51 Sqn. Destroyed by enemy action at Luqa airfield Malta 3.1.42.
Z9146 NF-P	From 51 Sqn. SOC 25.2.44.
Z9148	From 77 Sqn. Returned to 77 Sqn.
Z9158 NF-V	Crashed in Wiltshire on return from leaflet sortie to France 21.4.42.
Z9159 NF-D	FTR from SOE operation to France 31.10/1.11.42.
Z9223	Crashed while trying to land at Stradishall on return from a training flight 29/30.10.41.
Z9230 NF-N	From 51 Sqn. FTR from SOE operation to Holland 29/30.7.42.
Z9232 NF-L	From 78 Sqn. FTR from SOE operation to France 24/25.8.42.
Z9275 NF-G	From 78 Sqn. To OADU and back. FTR from SOE operation to Belgium 26/27.9.42.
Z9282 NF-M	From 102 Sqn. FTR from bombing operation to France 25/26.7.42.
Z9286 NF-H	
Z9287 NF-K	To PTS.
Z9288 NF-J	To 13MU.
Z9295	From 58 Sqn. Destroyed by enemy action at Luqa airfield Malta 3.1.42.
Z9298	From 51 Sqn. Returned to 51 Sqn.
Z9385	Crashed on landing at Stradishall on return from Special Duties operation to France 28.12.41.
Z9428 NF-F/W	From 161 Sqn. To 24 OTU.
BD260 NF-S	From 51 Sqn. To 10 OTU.
BD504 NF-F	To Royal Aircraft Establishment.
LA763 NF-L	To 10 OTU.
LA764 NF-M	To 10 OTU.

Wellington

P2521   From 1 GRU. To 161 Sqn.

Lysander   From August 1941 to February 1942.

R2625   From 1419Flt.

R2626   From 1419Flt. To 161 Sqn.

T1508   From 1419Flt via TFU. FTR from SOE operation to France 28/29.1.42.

T1770   From 1419Flt via SDF and TFU Newmarket. To 161 Sqn.

T1771   Crashed in Surrey during training 28.11.41.

Halifax   From October 1941 to August 1944.

L9611   From 76 Sqn. Returned to 76 Sqn.

L9612   From AFEE. Force-landed in Sweden on return from Special Duties operation to Poland 2.11.41.

L9613 NF-V   To 1661CU.

L9618 NF-W   From AFEE. Lost over Mediterranean while in transit to Malta 15.12.42.

R9376   From 10 Sqn. Returned to 10 Sqn.

V9976   From AFEE. FTR from SOE operation to Austria 20/21.4.42.

W1002 NF-Y   From AFEE. Crashed in Western Desert during transit from Malta to Gibraltar 17.12.42.

W1007   From 78 Sqn. To 1666CU.

W1012 NF-Z   From 161 Sqn. FTR from SIS/SOE operation to France 19/20.2.43.

W1046   From 161 Sqn. To 1666CU.

W1229 NF-A   Crashed on landing at Tempsford during training 19.6.43.

W7773 NF-S   FTR from SOE operation to Poland 29/30.10.42.

W7774 NF-T   Ditched off Norfolk coast on return from SOE operation to Poland 30.10.42.

W7775 NF-R   FTR from SOE operation to Holland 22/23.12.42.

W7776 NF-B   Force-landed in Yorkshire on return from SOE operation to Poland 1/2.10.42.

BB281 NF-O   FTR from SOE operation to Czechoslovakia 14/15.3.43.

BB309 NF-T   FTR from SOE operation to Poland 16/17.9.43.

BB313 NF-M   FTR from SOE operation to France 12/13.5.43.

BB316   To 1662CU.

BB317 NF-N   FTR from SOE operation to Holland 19/20.9.43.

BB328 NF-U   FTR from SOE operation to France 13/14.5.43.

BB329 NF-Z   From 161 Sqn. FTR from SOE operation to Holland 21/22.5.43.

BB330   Damaged beyond repair in accident 25.2.44.

BB334 NF-X   To 405 Sqn and back. FTR from SOE operation to France 12/13.8.43.

BB335   From 301FTU. To 148 Sqn.

BB340 NF-D   FTR from SOE operation to France 12/13.4.43.

BB363 NF-T   FTR from SOE operation to Belgium 13/14.4.43.

BB364 NF-R   Crashed in Bedfordshire while training 19.12.43.

BB378 NF-D   FTR from SOE operation to Denmark 10/11.12.43.

BB379 NF-J   FTR from SOE operation to Holland 23/24.6.43.

DG252 NF-B   FTR from SOE operation to Holland 19/20.9.43.

DG253 NF-F   From 408 Sqn. Crashed on landing at Tempsford following early return from SOE operation 18/19.8.43.

DG271 NF-C	Crashed on take-off from Tangmere for transit flight to Tempsford 4.2.43.
DG272	To 161 Sqn.
DG285	To 161 Sqn.
DG286	To 161 Sqn and back. Crashed on take-off from Tempsford during training 23.5.44.
DG287	To 1660CU.
DG316	To 518 Sqn.
DG996	To 161 Sqn.
DK119	To 161 Sqn.
DT542 NF-Q	Crashed on take-off from Luqa for transit flight to Gibraltar 17.12.42.
DT543	Believed crashed 17.7.44. Details unknown.
DT620 NF-T	FTR from SOE operation to Poland 14/15.3.43.
DT627 NF-P	FTR from SOE operation to Holland 11/12.5.43.
DT725 NF-J	FTR from SOE operation to France 17/18.4.43.
DT726 NF-H	FTR from SOE operation to France 3/4.11.43.
DT727 NF-K	Crashed on landing at Tempsford during training 22.6.43.
HR665 NF-L	FTR from SOE operation to Holland 24/25.3.43.
HR666 NF-E	FTR from SOE operation to Poland 14/15.9.43.
HX161	To 1586Flt.
JB802 NF-S	Crashed on landing at Maison Blanche Algeria during transit 18.5.43.
JB855	To 78 Sqn.
JD154 NF-V	FTR from SOE operation to Poland 14/15.9.43.
JD155 NF-M	FTR from SOE operation to France 12/13.7.43.
JD156 NF-W	FTR from SOE operation to Poland 16/17.9.43.
JD171	Details unknown.
JD172	To MAC.
JD179 NF-F	FTR from SOE operation to France 17/18.8.43.
JD180 NF-O	FTR from SOE operation to France 14/15.8.43.
JD269 NF-Q	FTR from SOE operation to Poland 14/15.9.43.
JD312 NF-J	FTR from SOE operation to France 16/17.8.43.
JD319	To 1586Flt.
JD362	To 1586Flt.
JN910 NF-K	FTR from SOE operation to Poland 14/15.9.43.
JN911	To 1586Flt.
JN921 NF-B	FTR from SOE operation to France 6/7.11.43.
LK736	Crash-landed in Bedfordshire during training 17.5.44.
LK742	To 1667CU.
LK743 NF-J	Crashed in Bedfordshire on return from SOE operation to Belgium 7/8.1.44.
LL114 NF-P	FTR from SOE operation to France 7/8.2.44.
LL115 NF-A	Crashed while trying to land at Woodbridge on return from SOE operation to France 16/17.12.43.
LL118	From 161 Sqn. To 1663CU.
LL119 NF-L	Abandoned over Sussex on return from SOE operation to France 16/17.12.43.
LL183 MA-W	On loan from 161 Sqn. FTR from SOE operation to France 9/10.5.44.
LL187	To 1663CU.
LL192 NF-A	FTR from SOE operation to Denmark 7/8.5.44.
LL236	
LL249	From 161 Sqn. To 1659CU.

LL250	From 161 Sqn. To 1FU.
LL251 NF-N	From 161 Sqn. Ditched in the Mediterranean during SOE operation from Blida, Algeria to France 11/12.7.44.
LL252 NF-K	From 161 Sqn. FTR from SIS/SOE operation to France 31.3/1.4.44.
LL254	From 161 Sqn. To 2 OADU.
LL276 NF-F	FTR from SOE operation to Belgium 31.5/1.6.44.
LL279 NF-R	FTR from SOE operation to France 3/4.3.44.
LL280 NF-O	FTR from SOE operation to France 7/8.5.44.
LL282	To 1FU.
LL284 NF-E	Crash-landed in Bedfordshire when bound for SOE operation to Belgium 2/3.6.44.
LL287 NF-S	FTR from SOE operation to Belgium 30/31.3.44.
LL289 NF-P	From 1658CU. FTR from SOE operation to France 1/2.6.44.
LL290	To 1667CU.
LL306 NF-R	FTR from SIS operation to France 7/8.6.44.
LL307 NF-J	FTR from SOE operation to Belgium 2/3.6.44.
LL308 NF-Q	FTR from SOE operation to Belgium 8/9.8.44.
LL354	To 2 OADU.
LL356 NF-U	FTR from SOE operation to Belgium 27/28.4.44.
LL359	To 301FTU.
LL364 NF-B	From 161 Sqn. FTR from SOE operation to France 18/19.7.44.
LL380	To 1FU.
LL381	From 161 Sqn. To 2 OADU.
LL385	To 161 Sqn.
LL387 NF-P	From 161 Sqn. FTR from SOE operation to France 18/19.7.44.
LL388	From 161 Sqn. Returned to 161 Sqn.
LL390 NF-S	Crashed on take-off from Tempsford when bound for SOE operation to France 7.6.44.
LL392	From 161 Sqn. To 1FU.
LL409	To 298 Sqn.
LL416 NF-O	FTR from SOE operation to France 7/8.6.44.
LL419 NF-V	FTR from SOE operation to Belgium 31.5/1.6.44.
LL465	To 161 Sqn.
LL466 NF-T	FTR from SOE operation to France 7/8.6.44.
LL467	To 161 Sqn.
LL468	To 1FU.
LL483	To 161 Sqn.
LL484	To 2 OADU.
LW272	To 1586Flt.
LW275 NF-O	FTR from SOE operation to France 7/8.2.44.
LW276	To MAC.
LW280 NF-K	Abandoned and crashed off Essex coast on return from SOE operation to France 16/17.12.43.
LW281 NF-W	FTR from SOE operation to Holland/Belgium 18/19.10.43.
LW284	To 1586Flt.
Liberator	From August 1943 to October 1943.
BZ858 NF-F	FTR from SOE operation to Poland 9/10.10.43.
BZ859	To 1586Flt.
BZ860	To 1586Flt.
BZ949	To 1586Flt.

Stirling	From June 1944 to March 1945.
LJ503 NF-P	From CRD. FTR from SOE operation to France 31.8/1.9.44.
LJ932 NF-N	Crash-landed on approach to Ludford Magna on return from SOE operation to Denmark 29.9.44.
LJ990 NF-O	
LJ993 NF-M	FTR from SOE operation to Norway 8/9.11.44.
LJ999 NF-Q	FTR from SOE operation Denmark 4/5.3.45.
LK119 NF-R	To 161 Sqn.
LK125 NF-S	
LK131 NF-T	FTR from SOE operation to Holland 31.8/1.9.44.
LK139 NF-A	
LK143 NF-B	FTR from SOE operation to Denmark 2/3.12.44.
LK145	
LK149 NF-D	FTR from SOE operation to Denmark 23/24. 2.45.
LK151 NF-E	FTR from SOE operation to Denmark 26/27.11.44.
LK192	
LK194	
LK198 NF-H	FTR from SOE operation to Norway 8/9.11.44.
LK200 NF-J	FTR from SOE operation to Holland 8/9.9.44.
LK204 NF-U	
LK206	To 161 Sqn 5.9.44.
LK207	To 161 Sqn 5.9.44.
LK208	To 161 Sqn 5.9.44.
LK209	To 161 Sqn 5.9.44.
LK210	To 161 Sqn 5.9.44.
LK232	To 299 Sqn.
LK235	To 4 OAPU.
LK272 NF-P	FTR from SOE operation to Norway 26/27.2.45.
LK274 NF-N	To 161 Sqn 10.3.45.
LK278	From 161 Sqn.
LK279 NF-L	FTR from SOE operation to Denmark 9/10.2.45.
LK283 NF-S	FTR from SOE operation to Norway 30/31.12.44.
LK285 NF-T	To 161 Sqn 25.3.45.
LK309	
LK329	To 161 Sqn 8.3.45.
PW395	To 161 Sqn 6.3.45.
Lancaster	From March 1945.
HK606 AC-D	From 186 Sqn. To 46MU.
HK615 AC-J	From 622 Sqn. To 15MU.
HK661	From 186 Sqn. To 10MU.
HK682	From 186 Sqn.
HK692 AC-Q	From 186 Sqn.
HK694 AC-S	From 186 Sqn.
HK792 AC-C	From 149 Sqn. To 75 Sqn.
LM275 AC-V	From 514 Sqn.
LM282	From 218 Sqn.
LM544	From 75 Sqn. Returned to 75 Sqn.
ME350	From 218 Sqn.
ME751 AC-R	From 75sqn.
NF966 AC-T	From 514 Sqn.
NG224	From 149 Sqn. Returned to 149 Sqn.
NG248	From 626 Sqn.

NG365 AC-K	From XV Sqn.
NG407 AC-B	From 149 Sqn.
NG409 AC-P	From 149 Sqn.
NX571 AC-J/X	
PA193 AC-H	From 149 Sqn.
PD370	From 115 Sqn.
PP675 AC-F	
PP678	
PP679 AC-L	From 90 Sqn.
RF142 AC-A	From 149 Sqn.
RF143 AC-O	From 149 Sqn. FTR Potsdam 14/15.4.45.

149 (EAST INDIA) SQUADRON

Motto: Fortis Nocte (Strong by night)   Codes OJ, TK

First formed as a night bomber unit on the 3rd of March 1918, 149 Squadron moved to France in June, and conducted operations against German units in Belgium and France. It was disbanded in Ireland on the 1st of August 1919, and remained on the shelf until its re-formation from B Flight of 99 Squadron at Mildenhall on the 12th of April 1937. Conversion from Heyfords to Wellingtons began on the 20th of January 1939, The squadron was thus the third in Bomber Command to receive the type after 99 and 38 Squadrons. One of 3 Group's six frontline squadrons at the outbreak of war, 149 Squadron was in action on the very first day. It remained with 3 Group throughout the war, and was one of only two squadrons to give unbroken service to Bomber Command from the first day of hostilities to the last. Having converted to Stirlings in 1941 the squadron was the last in the Group to relinquish the type, in the late summer of 1944, having employed it extensively on bombing, mining and special operations on behalf of SOE. Lancasters enabled the squadron to remain at the vanguard of Bomber Command's offensives right through to the end.

STATIONS

Mildenhall	12.04.37 to 06.04.42
Lakenheath	06.04.42 to 15.05.44
Methwold	15.05.44 to 04.46

COMMANDING OFFICERS

Wing Commander G H Russell DFC	05.01.39 to 06.11.39
Squadron Leader R Kellett AFC	06.11.39 to 10.05.40
Wing Commander J R Whitley AFC	10.05.40 to 24.11.40
Squadron Leader G W Heather	24.11.40 to 28.11.40
Wing Commander J A Powell	28.11.40 to 09.05.41
Wing Commander W R Beaman	09.05.41 to 26.11.41
Wing Commander G J Spence	26.11.41 to 05.42
Wing Commander C Charlton-Jones	05.42 to 28.08.42
Wing Commander K M Wasse DFC	29.08.42 to 04.43
Wing Commander G E Harrison DFC	04.43 to 25.10.43
Wing Commander C R B Wigfall	25.10.43 to 05.44
Wing Commander M E Pickford	05.44 to 29.01.45
Wing Commander L H Kay DFC	29.01.45 to 02.02.45
Wing Commander Chilton	03.02.45

AIRCRAFT

Wellington I/Ia/Ic	20.01.39 to 12.41
Stirling I	12.10.41 to 06.43
Stirling III	02.43 to 09.44
Lancaster I/III	08.44 to 11.49

OPERATIONAL RECORD

Operations	Sorties	Aircraft Losses	% Losses
738	5,905	131	2.2

Category of Operations

Bombing	Mining	Other
567	160	11

Wellingtons

Operations	Sorties	Aircraft Losses	% Losses
218	1,647	40	2.4

Category of Operations

Bombing	Mining	Other
213	0	5

Stirlings

Operations	Sorties	Aircraft Losses	% Losses
410	2,628	87	3.3

Category of Operations

Bombing	Mining	Leaflet
244	160	6

Lancaster

Operations	Sorties	Aircraft Losses	% Losses
110	1,630	4	0.2

All Bombing

TABLE OF STATISTICS

3rd highest number of overall operations in Bomber Command.
6th highest number of bombing operations in Bomber Command.
Highest number of mining operations in Bomber Command.
13th highest number of sorties in Bomber Command.
26th equal (with 77 Sqn) highest number of aircraft operational losses in Bomber Command.

Out of 42 Wellington squadrons

7th highest number of overall Wellington operations in Bomber Command.
7th highest number of Wellington sorties in Bomber Command.
12th highest number of Wellington operational losses in Bomber Command.

Out of 28 squadrons in 3 Group

2nd highest number of overall operations in 3 Group.
3rd highest number of sorties in 3 Group.
4th highest number of aircraft operational losses in 3 Group.

Out of 18 Wellington squadrons in 3 Group

5th highest number of Wellington overall operations in 3 Group.
5th highest number of Wellington sorties in 3 Group.
8th highest number of Wellington operational losses in 3 Group.

Out of 12 Stirling bomber squadrons in 3 Group

Highest number of overall Stirling operations in 3 Group.
Highest number of Stirling sorties in 3 Group.
3rd highest number of Stirling operational losses in 3 Group.

Out of 11 Lancaster squadrons in 3 Group

8th highest number of overall Lancaster operations in 3 Group.
8th highest number of Lancaster sorties in 3 Group.
10th highest number of Lancaster operational losses in 3 Group.

AIRCRAFT HISTORIES

Wellington	To December 1941.
L4214	From RAE via manufacturers. To 11 OTU.
L4229	From 99 Sqn. To 214 Sqn.
L4249	To 75 Sqn.
L4252	To GRU. Took part in squadron's first operation 3.9.39.
L4253	To 215 Sqn.
L4254	To 75 Sqn. Took part in squadron's first operation 3.9.39.
L4255	To 15 OTU.
L4256	To 75 Sqn.
L4259	To 15 OTU.
L4263	To 11 OTU.
L4264	To 15 OTU. Took part in squadron's first operation 3.9.39.
L4265	To 15 OTU.
L4266	To 11 OTU.
L4270	To 11 OTU.
L4271	Became ground instruction machine 4.42.
L4272 OJ-A/C	To 9BAT Flt.
L4374	To RAE.
L7800	From 148 Sqn. FTR Soissons 10/11.6.40.
L7805	FTR Bremen 11/12.7.40.
L7806	From 75 Sqn. To 311 Sqn.
L7811 OJ-C	Abandoned over England on return from Bremen 12.2.41.
L7812	From 115 Sqn. To RAE.
L7817	From 300 Sqn. To 9 Sqn.
L7845	To 115 Sqn.
L7846	To OADF.
L7855 OJ-W	To 25 OTU.
L7858 OJ-H/A	FTR Gelsenkirchen 14/15.3.41.
L7896 LN-G	On loan from 99 Sqn. Crash-landed at Honington and burned out on return from Berlin 8.10.40.
N2769 OJ-N	To 9BAT Flt.
N2774 OJ-A	From 99 Sqn. FTR Berlin 19/20.11.40.
N2775 OJ-B	To 311 Sqn.
N2783	From 57 Sqn. To 25 OTU.
N2853 OJ-R	From 57 Sqn. Crashed in Suffolk on return from Cologne 18.7.41.

N2866	To 215 Sqn.
N2867	To 214 Sqn and back. To CGS.
N2868	To 75 Sqn.
N2869	To 75 Sqn.
N2891	To 99 Sqn.
N2892	To 7 Sqn.
N2893	To CGS.
N2894	To 215 Sqn.
N2943	FTR from reconnaissance sortie 2.1.40.
N2944	To CGS.
N2945	To 215 Sqn.
N2946	FTR from reconnaissance sortie 2.1.40.
N2960	From 99 Sqn. To 215 Sqn.
N2961	From 99 Sqn. FTR from armed reconnaissance operation 18.12.39.
N2962	From 99 Sqn. FTR from armed reconnaissance operation 18.12.39.
N2980	To 37 Sqn.
N2984 OJ-H	From 99 Sqn. Crashed in Suffolk when bound for leaflet sortie to Bremen 2.3.40.
N3012	To 215 Sqn.
N3013	To 99 Sqn.
P2517	From 37 Sqn via Hendon and Yeadon. To 3Gp TF.
P2527	To 215 Sqn.
P2528	To 215 Sqn.
P9218 OJ-O	From 214 Sqn. FTR Aalborg 21/22.4.40.
P9224	To 115 Sqn.
P9225	FTR from reconnaissance sortie to Mittelland Canal 23/24.3.40.
P9234	To 99 Sqn.
P9240	To 99 Sqn.
P9241	To 99 Sqn.
P9244 OJ-E	Crashed on final approach to Mildenhall on return from Gelsenkirchen 12.8.40.
P9245 OJ-W	Crashed off Essex coast on return from Boulogne 9.9.40.
P9246	FTR from reconnaissance sortie to Norway 12.4.40.
P9247 OJ-M	Crashed in Lincolnshire on return from Hanover 12.2.41.
P9248 OJ-D/G	FTR Cologne 17/18.4.41.
P9266	FTR from reconnaissance sortie to Norway 12.4.40.
P9267	Crashed on approach to Mildenhall during training 4.4.40.
P9268 OJ-A	Crashed while landing at Mildenhall on return from Mannheim 17.12.40.
P9270 OJ-G	Crashed in Suffolk on return from France 24.5.40.
P9272 OJ-A	From 99 Sqn. FTR Kiel 27/28.8.40.
P9273 OJ-V	From 99 Sqn. FTR Herringen 9/10.10.40.
P9289	To 18 OTU.
R1024 OJ-V	FTR Hanover 12/13.8.41.
R1045 OJ-E/M	FTR Wilhelmshaven 21/22.2.41.
R1159 OJ-N	Crash-landed in Suffolk on return from Cologne 19.3.41.
R1181 OJ-W	From 99 Sqn. Crashed soon after take-off from Mildenhall for training flight 10.4.41.
R1229 OJ-H	Crashed while landing at Mildenhall on return from Emden 1.4.41.

R1294	Crashed near Mildenhall during air-test 16.12.40.
R1339	To 218 Sqn.
R1343 OJ-B	FTR Brest 1/2.7.41.
R1391	To 15 OTU.
R1408 OJ-J	FTR Brest 1/2.7.41.
R1439 OJ-U	FTR Kiel 15/16.4.41.
R1449	To 20 OTU.
R1469	To 150 Sqn.
R1474 OJ-M	From 115 Sqn. Shot down by intruder on final approach to Mildenhall on return from Bremen 18.3.41.
R1506 OJ-D	FTR Hamburg 8/9.5.41.
R1512 OJ-H	FTR Hamburg 10/11.5.41.
R1514 OJ-H	To 16 OTU.
R1524 OJ-P	FTR Mannheim 5/6.8.41.
R1587 OJ-P	Collided with a Hurricane during training and crashed in Cambridgeshire 17.5.41.
R1593 OJ-N	To 1483Flt.
R1627 FTR	Emden 15/16.11.41.
R1629	To RAE.
R1802 OJ-F	To 311 Sqn.
R3150	From 37 Sqn. Returned to 37 Sqn.
R3160 OJ-E	From 115 Sqn. FTR Le Havre 18/19.9.40.
R3161 OJ-O	From 9 Sqn. To 23 OTU.
R3163 OJ-G	FTR Black Forest 5/6.9.40.
R3164 OJ-B	FTR Hanau 28/29.9.40.
R3165	To 75 Sqn.
R3174 OJ-A/V	From 148 Sqn. FTR Koleda 16/17.8.40.
R3175 OJ-V	From 148 Sqn. FTR Boulogne 8/9.9.40.
R3206 OJ-M	To 311 Sqn.
R3212 OJ-T	To 300 Sqn.
R3280	From Mildenhall. To 18 OTU.
R3285	To 17 OTU.
T2458 OJ-D	From 9 Sqn. To 21 OTU.
T2460 OJ-T	From 99 Sqn. To 18 OTU.
T2713 OJ-G	From 57 Sqn. To 115 Sqn.
T2716 OJ-W	From 40 Sqn. Crash-landed in Suffolk on return from Hanover 13.8.41.
T2737 OJ-J/A	FTR Bremen 14/15.7.41.
T2739	To 99 Sqn.
T2740 OJ-E	Crashed in Essex while trying to make an emergency landing on return from Emden 24.10.40.
T2747	To 16 OTU.
T2807 OJ-R	FTR from Italian target 12/13.1.41.
T2846	To 101 Sqn.
T2881	To 23 OTU.
T2897 OJ-O	FTR Merignac Airfield 12/13.4.41.
T2898 OJ-F	To 18 OTU.
T2899 OJ-G	To 27 OTU.
T2994 OJ-A	To 23 OTU.
W5399OJ-Q	To 12 Sqn.
W5439OJ-X	FTR Düsseldorf 11/12.6.41.
W5567	To 305 Sqn.
W5573	To 305 Sqn.
W5718	To 75 (NZ) Sqn.

W5724	To 27 OTU.
X3165 OJ-C	To 14 OTU.
X3167 OJ-H	FTR Kiel 8/9.4.41.
X3174	From 40 Sqn. To 27 OTU.
X3176 OJ-O	To 75 (NZ) Sqn.
X3201	From 18 OTU. To 419 Sqn.
X9633 OJ-R	FTR Mannheim 6/7.8.41.
X9663	From 115 Sqn. To 218 Sqn.
X9679	From 301 Sqn. To 218 Sqn.
X9704 OJ-B	FTR Duisburg 18/19.8.41.
X9705 OJ-J	FTR Berlin 7/8.9.41.
X9733	From 115 Sqn. To 311 Sqn.
X9746 OJ-A	Damaged beyond repair during operation to Duisburg 18/19.8.41.
X9758	To 214 Sqn.
X9817 OJ-B/N	To 214 Sqn.
X9823	To 26 OTU.
X9824	To 40 Sqn and back. To 40 Sqn.
X9832	To 150 Sqn.
X9877	From 115 Sqn. To 311 Sqn.
X9878 OJ-A	FTR Berlin 7/8.11.41.
X9879 OJ-V	FTR Kiel 11/12.9.41.
X9880	To 156 Sqn.
X9890 OJ-G	To 214 Sqn.
Z1052	To 156 Sqn.
Z8795 OJ-C	FTR Bremen 20/21.10.41.
Z8837	To 40 Sqn.
Z8838	To 40 Sqn and back. To 311 Sqn.
Stirling	From November 1941 to September 1944.
N3638	From XV Sqn. To 106CF 3.1.42.
N3680	To 7 Sqn 7.11.41.
N3682 OJ-F/U	To 1657CU via 149CF 23.4.42.
N3684	To XV Sqn CF.
N3719 OJ-S	Crashed on landing at Lakenheath on return from Cologne 23.4.42.
N3723 OJ-E	Abandoned after crossing the south coast, and crashed in Berkshire on return from Mannheim 7.12.42.
N3726 OJ-G	Crashed on landing at Lakenheath after early return from Essen 7.4.42.
N3752 OJ-O	FTR from mining sortie 17/18.5.42.
N3755 OJ-S	To Conversion Flight and back. Crashed in Kent on return from Aachen 5/6.10.42.
N3766	To 214 Sqn.
N6065 OJ-Z	From XV Sqn. Conversion Flight only.
N6066	To 26CF.
N6068 OJ-T	FTR Dortmund 15/16.4.42.
N6079 OJ-F	To 1657CU via 149CF 16.8.42.
N6080 OJ-G	To 1657CU.
N6081 OJ-G/H	FTR Nuremberg 28/29.8.42.
N6082 OJ-Q	FTR Bremen 29/30.6.42.
N6083 OJ-N	Crashed soon after take-off from Lakenheath when bound for Frankfurt 24.8.42.
N6084 OJ-C	FTR Essen 8/9.6.42.

N6093	To 7 Sqn.
N6094	To 7 Sqn.
N6095	To 7 Sqn. 8.11.41.
N6099 OJ-C	To 1651CU 28.3.42.
N6100	To 26CF.
N6101	To 26CF and back. To 1651CU.
N6102 OJ-G	To 1651CU.
N6103 OJ-E	To 1651CU 10.5.42.
N6104	To 26CF 11.12.41.
N6122 OJ-Q	To 149CF. Crashed on landing at Mildenhall 21.6.42.
N6123 OJ-F	To 1657CU via 149CF 3.9.42.
N6124 OJ-R	FTR Stuttgart 4/5.5.42.
N6125	To 214 Sqn via 149CF 8.1.42.
N6126 OJ-U	From 218 Sqn. FTR Essen 10/11.3.42.
N6127 OJ-N	From 218 Sqn. To 1651CU.
R9142 OJ-B/R	To 1657CU.
R9143 OJ-O	From 7 Sqn. To 1665CU 6.7.43.
R9161 OJ-T	FTR Saarbrücken 29/30.7.42.
R9162 OJ-Q	FTR from mining sortie 10/11.8.42.
R9163 OJ-A	To 214 Sqn.
R9164 OJ-Q	FTR Essen 16/17.9.42.
R9167 OJ-N	FTR Krefeld 2/3.10.42.
R9170 OJ-H	FTR Düsseldorf 10/11.9.42.
R9200 OJ-P	From 214 Sqn. To 75 (NZ) Sqn.
R9202 OJ-K	FTR Turin 29/30.11.42.
R9203 OJ-D	To 218 Sqn.
R9242 OJ-B	To 214 Sqn.
R9253 OJ-C	FTR from mining sortie 8/9.12.42.
R9265 OJ-N	Crashed in Bedfordshire during air-test 19.12.42.
R9271 OJ-K	To 90 Sqn.
R9276 OJ-F	To 90 Sqn.
R9287	To 218 Sqn.
R9295 OJ-G	From 7 Sqn. Crashed near Mildenhall on return from Essen 11.3.42.
R9296 OJ-D	From 7 Sqn. To 1657CU via 149CF.
R9299	To 149CF. Crashed in Cambridgeshire 16.7.42.
R9307	Crashed on take-off from Lakenheath when bound for Le Havre 22.4.42.
R9310 OJ-P	From XV Sqn. FTR from mining sortie 17/18.5.42.
R9314 OJ-R/T	From XV Sqn. FTR Essen 5/6.6.42.
R9320 OJ-S	FTR from mining sortie 17/18.5.42.
R9321 OJ-R	FTR Essen 5/6.6.42.
R9327 OJ-M	From RAE. FTR Kiel 4/5.4.43.
R9329 OJ-V	Crashed in Devon on return from mining sortie 20/21.8.42.
R9330 OJ-O	Crashed on take-off from Lakenheath when bound for Bremen 29.8.42.
R9334 OJ-G	Crashed near Lakenheath while training 3.1.43.
R9358	To 214 Sqn.
W7448	To 7 Sqn.
W7449	To 7 Sqn.
W7450	To XV Sqn.
W7451	To 7 Sqn.
W7452 OJ-A	Crashed on landing at Ayr while training 9.3.42.

W7453	To 26CF.
W7455 OJ-B	To XV Sqn via 149CF.
W7456	Crash-landed in Cambridgeshire during training 22.11.41.
W7457	To 149CF. Crashed on landing at Lakenheath 11.2.42.
W7458	Crashed on landing at Mildenhall while training 28.1.42.
W7459	To 26CF.
W7460	From XV Sqn. To XV Sqn and back. To 1657CU via 149CF.
W7461 OJ-N	Force-landed in Yorkshire on return from Hamburg 16.1.42.
W7462 OJ-T	Crashed on landing at Lossiemouth on return from attacking Tirpitz 29/30.1.42.
W7463	To XV Sqn.
W7465 OJ-V	From 1651CU. To 214 Sqn.
W7469	From 218 Sqn. To 75 (NZ) Sqn.
W7508 OJ-D	FTR Essen 5/6.6.42.
W7509 OJ-U	To 1651CU.
W7510 OJ-B	To 90 Sqn.
W7512 OJ-A	FTR Rostock 26/27.4.42.
W7513	From XV Sqn. To 75 (NZ) Sqn.
W7526 OJ-V	To 214 Sqn and back. To 149CF and back. FTR Cologne 15/16.10.42.
W7530	To 218 Sqn.
W7566 OJ-C	FTR from mining sortie 16/17.11.42.
W7567	To 214 Sqn.
W7572 OJ-R	FTR Frankfurt 24/25.8.42.
W7574	To 7 Sqn.
W7580 OJ-D	FTR Duisburg 23/24.7.42.
W7582 OJ-F/S	Crashed in Suffolk during training 10.11.42.
W7589 OJ-P	Crashed in Norfolk on return from Osnabrück 18.8.42.
W7619 OJ-A	To 1651CU.
W7628 OJ-B	Crashed in Kent on return from Genoa 24.10.42.
W7638 OJ-R	FTR Cologne 14/15.2.43.
W7639 OJ-Q	Crashed in Suffolk following early return from a mining sortie 8.12.42.
BF310 OJ-H	FTR Bremen 29/30.6.42.
BF311 OJ-G	To 75 (NZ) Sqn.
BF312 OJ-A	FTR Lübeck 16.7.42.
BF320 OJ-H	FTR Saarbrücken 29/30.7.42.
BF323	To 1651CU.
BF325 OJ-A	To 1651CU.
BF328 OJ-D	FTR from mining sortie 30.9/1.10.42.
BF334 OJ-R	To 149CF. Ditched off Ramsgate on return from Munich 20.9.42.
BF348 OJ-P	Crashed while trying to land at Watton following early return from a mining sortie 10.10.42.
BF349 OJ-R	To 218 Sqn.
BF357 OJ-T	To 214 Sqn.
BF372 OJ-H	Crashed in sea off Kent on return from Turin 29.11.42. F/S Middleton awarded posthumous VC.
BF389 OJ-S	From XV Sqn. Crashed on take-off from Lakenheath during training 27.10.42.
BF391 OJ-T	FTR from mining sortie 8/9.12.42.
BF392 OJ-D	From XV Sqn. FTR from mining sortie 16/17.10.42.

BF416	From 115 Sqn. To 218 Sqn.
BF444 OJ-G	To 214 Sqn.
BF477 OJ-B	FTR Mannheim 5/6.9.43.
BF479 OJ-E	FTR Bochum 13/14.5.43.
BF483 OJ-C	FTR Cologne 28/29.6.43.
BF500 OJ-M	FTR Stuttgart 14/15.4.43.
BF503 OJ-U	To 90 Sqn.
BF507 OJ-S	FTR Wuppertal 29/30.5.43.
BF509 OJ-N/B/R	To 1653CU.
BF510 OJ-P	FTR from mining sortie 21/22.5.43.
BF512 OJ-E	Crashed while landing at Lakenheath after air-test 9.8.43.
BF520 OJ-B	To 196 Sqn.
BF530 OJ-B	FTR Cologne 3/4.7.43.
BF531 OJ-M	Crashed on landing at Lakenheath while training 14.6.43.
BF570 OJ-T/H	To 1651CU.
BF573 OJ-W	From 75 (NZ) Sqn. To 620 Sqn.
BF576 OJ-Y	To 620 Sqn.
BF580	To 620 Sqn.
BK597 OJ-F	From XV Sqn. To 218 Sqn.
BK598	To 90 Sqn.
BK601 OJ-N	From 214 Sqn. To 1657CU.
BK612 OJ-E	To 214 Sqn.
BK665	To 90 Sqn.
BK692 OJ-W	FTR Berlin 1/2.3.43.
BK696 OJ-K/L	Abandoned over Hampshire on return from mining sortie 2.5.43.
BK698 OJ-O	From XV Sqn. FTR Rostock 20/21.4.43.
BK701 OJ-G	FTR from mining sortie 17/18.5.43.
BK703 OJ-K	From XV Sqn. FTR Cologne 28/29.6.43.
BK708 OJ-P	FTR Berlin 29/30.3.43.
BK710 OJ-A	FTR Düsseldorf 25/26.5.43.
BK711 OJ-O	FTR Mannheim 5/6.9.43.
BK713 OJ-N	To 620 Sqn.
BK714 OJ-L	FTR Rostock 20/21.4.43.
BK715 OJ-D	Destroyed by fire at Lakenheath after air-test 31.3.43.
BK726 OJ-Z	FTR Bochum 13/14.5.43.
BK759 OJ-X	FTR Stuttgart 14/15.4.43.
BK765 OJ-P	FTR Berlin 23/24.8.43.
BK772 OJ-T	To 199 Sqn.
BK781 OJ-L	From 90 Sqn. To 1651CU.
BK798 OJ-Q	FTR from mining sortie 20/21.12.43.
BK799 OJ-O	FTR Krefeld 21/22.6.43.
BK806 OJ-V	To 199 Sqn.
BK812	Crashed on take-off from Lakenheath for ferry flight to XV Sqn at Mildenhall 11.5.43.
BK816	From 90 Sqn. To 1651CU.
DJ972 OJ-T	Crashed on landing at Lakenheath on return from Stuttgart 7.5.42.
EE872 OJ-N	FTR Mannheim 5/6.9.43.
EE875	To 620 Sqn.
EE877 OJ-E	From XV Sqn. FTR Nuremberg 27/28.8.43.
EE879 OJ-G	FTR Berlin 31.8/1.9.43.
EE880 OJ-O	FTR Cologne 28/29.6.43.
EE894 OJ-R	FTR Berlin 23/24.8.43.

EE953	From 199 Sqn.
EE963 OJ-N	To 1653CU.
EE969 OJ-E	FTR from mining sortie 27/28.1.44.
EF124	From 218 Sqn. To 1653CU.
EF133	From 218 Sqn. To 1651CU.
EF140 OJ-B	FTR Ruisseauville 24/25.6.44.
EF161	From 199 Sqn. To 1657CU.
EF185 OJ-D	From 218 Sqn. To 1653CU.
EF187 OJ-C	FTR from SOE operation to France 5/6.2.44.
EF188 OJ-M	From 90 Sqn. FTR from mining sortie 23/24.6.44.
EF192 OJ-F	From 199 Sqn. To 1653CU.
EF193 OJ-D	From 90 Sqn. To 1653CU.
EF202 OJ-L	FTR from mining sortie 25/26.11.43.
EF207 OJ-F	From 218 Sqn. To 1653CU.
EF233 OJ-D	From 218 Sqn. To 1657CU.
EF238 OJ-H	Crash-landed at Methwold on return from SOE operation to France 29.4.44.
EF262	From 214 Sqn. To 199 Sqn and back. To 1653CU.
EF307 OJ-E	FTR from mining sortie 24/25.2.44.
EF308 OJ-R	FTR from mining sortie 25/26.2.44.
EF327 OJ-M	From 75 (NZ) Sqn. Crashed on landing at Lakenheath on return from Stuttgart 12.3.43.
EF328 OJ-R	From 90 Sqn. Crash-landed in Suffolk on return from Nuremberg 9.3.43.
EF330 OJ-P	FTR Essen 12/13.3.43.
EF332	From 214 Sqn. To 75 (NZ) Sqn.
EF335 OJ-E/H	From 214 Sqn. To 1665CU.
EF336 OJ-F	From 90 Sqn. To 620 Sqn.
EF337	From 75 (NZ) Sqn. To 1657CU.
EF338 OJ-Q	To 620 Sqn.
EF340 OJ-D	From 218 Sqn. To 75 (NZ) Sqn.
EF341	To 1665CU.
EF342 OJ-A	To 1665CU.
EF343 OJ-B	FTR Dortmund 4/5.5.43.
EF344 OJ-R	To 1657CU.
EF357 OJ-V	FTR Duisburg 12/13.5.43.
EF360 OJ-H	To 1651CU.
EF389 OJ-Q	To 1651CU.
EF395 OJ-L	To 1651CU.
EF396 OJ-E	To 1651CU.
EF400 OJ-C	From 75 (NZ) Sqn. Crashed on landing at Lakenheath after early return from Cologne 4.7.43.
EF411 OJ-K	From XV Sqn. To 1653CU.
EF412 OJ-F	From XV Sqn. Crashed on take-off from Lakenheath while training 13.11.43.
EF431	From 90 Sqn. To 1651CU.
EF438 OJ-D	FTR Mönchengladbach 30/31.8.43.
EF450	To 199 Sqn.
EF495 OJ-R	FTR Hanover 27/28.9.43.
EF502 OJ-G	FTR from SOE operation to France 10/11.4.44.
EH879	From XV Sqn. To 1651CU.
EH883 OJ-A	FTR Mannheim 23/24.9.43.
EH885 OJ-V	Crashed on take-off from Lakenheath for air-test 9.6.43.
EH903 OJ-L	FTR Mannheim 18/19.11.43.

EH904 OJ-P	Undercarriage collapsed while taxying at Pembrey during training 16.12.43.
EH909	To 199 Sqn.
EH922 OJ-O/V	To 1653CU.
EH927	To 199 Sqn.
EH934	To 199 Sqn.
EH943OJ-B	FTR Laon 22/23.4.44.
EH982OJ-S	From 218 Sqn. To 1653CU.
EH987OJ-P	Crash-landed at Lakenheath while training 4.10.43.
EH993OJ-D	Belly landed 4.6.44.
EJ106 OJ-O	FTR from mining sortie 7/8.10.43.
EJ107 OJ-K	To 1657CU.
EJ109 OJ-H/M	To 1657CU.
EJ115	From 90 Sqn. To 1653CU.
EJ122 OJ-Q	From 90 Sqn. To 1657CU.
EJ124 OJ-C	From 214 Sqn. FTR Amiens 15/16.3.44.
LJ447	From 218 Sqn. To 1657CU.
LJ449	From 218 Sqn. To 1651CU.
LJ472 OJ-Q	From 218 Sqn. To 1651CU.
LJ477 OJ-M	Crashed while trying to land at Thorney Island on return from special SOE operation 6.7.44.
LJ481 OJ-U	From 218 Sqn. To 1653CU.
LJ501 OJ-H	From 199 Sqn. FTR from mining sortie 31.5/1.6.44.
LJ504 OJ-K	FTR from mining sortie 18/19.4.44.
LJ511 OJ-Q	To 1332CU.
LJ522 OJ-N	From 218 Sqn. To 1657CU.
LJ526 OJ-P	FTR from mining sortie 23/24.4.44.
LJ568 OJ-A	From 218 Sqn. To 199 Sqn.
LJ577	To 1651CU.
LJ580	To 199 Sqn.
LJ582	To 199 Sqn.
LJ621 OJ-M	FTR from special D-Day support operation 5/6.6.44.
LJ623 OJ-P	To 1661CU.
LJ625	From 218 Sqn. To 1657CU.
LJ632 OJ-P	From 218 Sqn. To 1653CU.
LK382 OJ-Q	FTR from SOE operation to France 9/10.4.44.
LK383 OJ-A	From 90 Sqn. FTR from mining sortie 6/7.8.44.
LK385 OJ-C	From 199 Sqn. FTR special D-Day support operation 5/6.6.44.
LK386 OJ-T/P/J/O	From XV Sqn. Crashed on landing at Hartford Bridge on return from a mining sortie 24.6.44.
LK388 OJ-L	Crash-landed at Methwold while training 17.7.44.
LK392 OJ-O	From 90 Sqn.
LK394 OJ-D	FTR Ruisseauville 24/25.6.44.
LK396 OJ-M	From 218 Sqn. To 1657CU.
LK397 OJ-K	From 199 Sqn.
LK401 OJ-G	From 218 Sqn. To 1653CU.
LK445 OJ-C	From 214 Sqn. To 1657CU.
LK499 OJ-R	To 1653CU.
LK500 OJ-S	Crashed on take-off from Lakenheath 11.5.44.
LK516	To 90 Sqn.
LK568	To 218 Sqn via 90 Sqn and back. To 1653CU.
MZ260OJ-C	Crashed while landing at Lakenheath during training 17.11.43.

Lancaster	From August 1944.
HK546 TK-K	From 115 Sqn.
HK549 OJ-L	From 115 Sqn. To 1651CU.
HK551 OJ-M/TK-J	From 115 Sqn.
HK555	From 115 Sqn. Returned to 115 Sqn.
HK572	From 115 Sqn. Returned to 115 Sqn.
HK577 TK-H/W	To 10MU.
HK578	From 115 Sqn. To 46MU.
HK598	From 115 Sqn. To G-H Flt.
HK624	To 115 Sqn.
HK645 TK-D/OJ-R	FTR Witten 12.12.44.
HK649 OJ-J/S/F/X TK-F	
HK652 OJ-E/W	
HK653 OJ-Y	To 115 Sqn and back. FTR Witten 12.12.44.
HK654 TK-G	
HK655	To 1651CU.
HK656	To 115 Sqn.
HK657 OJ-S	To 46MU.
HK699 OJ-H/C/C2 TK-C/H	To 54MU and back.
HK792	To 138 Sqn.
HK793 OJ-B/A TK-A	
HK795 OJ-O/TK-B	
LM240 OJ-O	From XV Sqn.
LM692 OJ-P/S	To 90 Sqn.
LM697 OJ-E	
LM721 OJ-O	To 150 Sqn.
ME352 OJ-E/K/S/T	From 218 Sqn.
NF927 OJ-D	
NF953	From XV Sqn.
NF969 OJ-F	
NF970 OJ-O/R	
NF971 OJ-P/S	
NF972 OJ-H	FTR Gelsenkirchen 5.3.45.
NF973 OJ-K/B	
NG224OJ-J/V/K	To 138 Sqn and back.
NG299OJ-A/T	From 622 Sqn.
NG355OJ-F/G/Q/U/L	From 218 Sqn.
NG356OJ-C/O/V	
NG361 OJ-E	
NG362 OJ-S	From 218 Sqn. Crashed on landing at Methwold on return from Nuremberg and burned out 2/3.1.45.
NG387 OJ-L	
NG388	To 195 Sqn.
NG407 OJ-X	
NG409 OJ-Q	
NN708 OJ-Q	FTR Wiesbaden 2/3.2.45.
NN756 OJ-R	
NN760 OJ-G/W	
PA166 OJ-B/G/U	
PA186 OJ-X	From 514 Sqn.
PB483 OJ-B/G/J	To 186 Sqn.

PB487 OJ-A/V	To 1656CU.
PB488 OJ-A	To 90 Sqn.
PB506 OJ-B	To G-H Flt at Feltwell.
PB508 OJ-U	To G-H Flt at Feltwell.
PB509 OJ-C	To 186 Sqn.
PB697	From 83 Sqn.
PB838 OJ-M	
PB902 OJ-H	From 514 Sqn.
PD284 OJ-N	
PD364	From 218 Sqn.
PP673 OJ-B	
PP677	
PP681 OJ-C	
PP684 OJ-A	
PP685 OJ-G	
PP686 TK-J	
PP687 OJ-F	
RF142	To 138 Sqn.
RF143 OJ-A	To 138 Sqn.

156 SQUADRON

Motto: We Light The Way   Code GT

First formed on the 12th of October 1918, 156 Squadron had received no aircraft by the end of the Great War and was disbanded immediately thereafter. On the 14th of February 1942 the home echelon of 40 Squadron was renumbered and 156 Squadron was reborn. After serving 3 Group as a Wellington unit the squadron became a founder member of the Pathfinder Force in mid August 1942. It represented 1 Group, despite never having served in it, and 1 Group would keep it supplied with fresh crews. From that point on 156 Squadron was at the forefront of operations, converting to Lancasters in January 1943. The squadron sustained heavy casualties during the winter campaign of 1943/44, ending the war with the second highest aircraft losses in 8 Group.

STATIONS

Alconbury   14.02.42 to 15.08.42

COMMANDING OFFICERS

Wing Commander P G R Heath	14.02.42 to 30.05.42
Wing Commander H L Price DFC	30.05.42 to 29.07.42
Wing Commander R N Cook	30.07.42 to 28.10.42

AIRCRAFT

Wellington Ic	14.02.42 to 01.43
Wellington III	03.42 to 01.43
To Pathfinder Force	15.08.42

OPERATIONAL RECORD

Operations	Sorties	Aircraft Losses	% Losses
43	346	22	6.4

Category of Operations

Bombing	Mining	Other
38	4	1

TABLE OF STATISTICS

Out of 28 bomber squadrons in 3 Group

25th highest number of overall operations in 3 Group.
24th highest number of sorties in 3 Group.
16th highest number of aircraft operational losses in 3 Group.

Out of 18 Wellington squadrons in 3 Group

16th highest number of overall Wellington operations in 3 Group.
16th highest number of Wellington sorties in 3 Group.
10th highest number of Wellington operational losses in 3 Group.

AIRCRAFT HISTORIES

Wellington	From February 1942 to January 1943.
R1168	From 40 Sqn. To 20 OTU.
R1457	From 75 Sqn. To 22 OTU.
R1588	From 103 Sqn. To 22 OTU.
R1707	From 57 Sqn. To 20 OTU.
X3333	From 57 Sqn. Crashed on landing at Alconbury during ferry flight 8.3.42.
X3339	From 9 Sqn. FTR Essen 5/6.6.42.
X3342	To 9 Sqn.
X3345	From 115 Sqn. FTR from mining sortie 6/7.7.42.
X3367	From 166 Sqn. FTR Kassel 27/28.8.42.
X3417	From 115 Sqn. FTR from mining sortie 16/17.4.42.
X3422	From 9 Sqn. FTR Genoa 7/8.11.42.
X3455	From 1418Flt. To 101 Sqn.
X3475	From 75 Sqn. To 101 Sqn.
X3479	From 75 Sqn. To AFEE.
X3485	FTR from mining sortie 19/20.4.42.
X3598	FTR Cologne 30/31.5.42.
X3671	FTR Mannheim 19/20.5.42.
X3672	FTR Stuttgart 22/23.11.42.
X3677	To 27 OTU.
X3695	To 101 Sqn.
X3697	FTR Dortmund (Squadron's first loss) 15/16.4.42.
X3704	To 196 Sqn.
X3706 GT-C	FTR Gennevilliers 29/30.5.42.
X3708	Crashed on landing at Warboys on return from mining sortie 19/20.4.42.
X3710 GT-W	FTR Hamburg 28/29.7.42.
X3728	FTR Nuremburg 28/29.8.42.
X3741	To 30 OTU.
X3742	To 15 OTU.

X3798	FTR Mainz 11/12.8.42.
X3811	Abandoned over Huntingdonshire during operation to Aachen 5.10.42.
X3822	Crash-landed at Warboys on return from Essen 16/17.9.42.
X3878	To 115 Sqn.
X3936	From 75 Sqn. To 115 Sqn.
X3959	From 75 Sqn. To 12 OTU.
X9787	From 99 Sqn. To 311 Sqn.
X9880	From 149 Sqn. To 311 Sqn.
X9975	From 75 Sqn. To 20 OTU.
Z1052	From 149 Sqn. To 214 Sqn.
Z1068	From 75 Sqn. To 214 Sqn.
Z1080	From 101 Sqn. To 1483Flt.
Z1090	From 99 Sqn. To 311 Sqn.
Z1108	From 75 Sqn. To 103 Sqn.
Z1114	From 75 Sqn. To 214 Sqn.
Z1571	FTR Gennevilliers 29/30.4.42.
Z1576	FTR from mining sortie 6/7.7.42.
Z1595	FTR Mainz 11/12.8.42.
Z1609	To 115 Sqn.
Z1612	To 101 Sqn.
Z1613	FTR Kassel 27/28.8.42.
Z1619	FTR Bremen 27/28.6.42.
Z1620	To 115 Sqn.
Z1622	FTR Düsseldorf 31.7/1.8.42.
Z1659	FTR Bremen 27.7.42.
Z1660	FTR Duisburg 20/21.12.42.
Z1673	To 16 OTU.
Z1690	To 23 OTU.
Z1723	To 23 OTU.
Z1727	From 419 Sqn. To 428 Sqn.
Z8837	From 40 Sqn via 11 OTU. To 311 Sqn.
Z8859	From 40 Sqn. To Malta.
Z8969	From 99 Sqn. To 11 OTU.
Z8973	From 99 Sqn. To 12 OTU.
Z8978	From 75 Sqn. To 20 OTU.
BJ589	From 115 Sqn. FTR Duisburg 20/21.12.42.
BJ592	FTR Hamburg 28/29.7.42.
BJ594	Crashed on landing at Alconbury following abortive sortie to Bremen 25/26.6.42.
BJ600	FTR Bremen 13/14.9.42.
BJ603	FTR Mainz 11/12.8.42.
BJ613	To 12 OTU.
BJ617	To 12 OTU.
BJ643	From 419 Sqn. To Defford.
BJ646	To 17 OTU.
BJ655	From 425 Sqn via 1483Flt. To 1483Flt.
BJ669	To 425 Sqn.
BJ707	From 75 Sqn. To 12 OTU.
BJ709	To 12 OTU.
BJ716	Crashed soon after take-off from Alconbury *en route* to Saarbrücken 1/2.9.42.
BJ766	From 150 Sqn. To 26 OTU.

BJ775	FTR Kiel 13/14.10.42.
BJ789	FTR Bremen 13/14.9.42.
BJ840	FTR Hamburg 28/29.7.42.
BJ883	FTR Saarbrücken 19/20.9.42.
BK203	Abandoned over Suffolk during operation to Aachen 5/6.10.42.
BK302	To 27 OTU.
BK315	To 26 OTU.
BK339	FTR Cologne 15/16.10.42.
BK386	From 75 Sqn. FTR Munich 21/22.12.42.
BK397	To 26 OTU.
BK508	To 27 OTU.
BK534	To 23 OTU.
DF624	To 429 Sqn.
DF626	From 420 Sqn. Returned to 420 Sqn.
DF635	To 428 Sqn.
DF666	FTR Dusseldorf 15/16.8.42.
DF667	FTR Kassel 27/28.8.42.
DV507	From 101 Sqn. To 311 Sqn via 15 OTU.
DV518	From 214 Sqn. Returned to 214 Sqn.
DV715	FTR Cologne 30/31.5.42.
DV739	To 15 OTU.
DV776	From 214 Sqn. To 15 OTU.
DV785	To 22 OTU.
DV786	FTR Essen 2/3.6.42.
DV799	To 311 Sqn.
DV812	FTR Essen 5/6.6.42.
DV813	To 11 OTU.
DV814	To 11 OTU.
HF918	FTR Emden 6/7.6.42.

161 SQUADRON

Motto: Liberate   Code MA

The first formation of 161 Squadron as a day bomber unit began on the 1st of June 1918, and lasted a little over a month. It remained on the shelf from July 1918 until the 15th of February 1942, when it was reborn from a nucleus provided by 138 Squadron to fly secret operations on behalf of Special Operations Executive (SOE) and Special Intelligence Service (SIS). The squadron took over the Lysander Flight from 138 Squadron, while also flying a variety of twin and four engined aircraft for delivery and collection of agents and dropping of arms to resistance groups. The squadron continued in this work until war's end, although as part of 38 Group from the 9th of March 1945.

STATIONS

Newmarket	14.02.42 to 01.03.42
Graveley	01.03.42 to 11.04.42
Tempsford	11.04.42 to 02.06.45
Tangmere (Lysander Flight)	26.02.42 to 08.44
Exeter (Lysander Flight)	08.44

COMMANDING OFFICERS

Wing Commander E H Fielden MVO AFC	14.02.42 to 01.10.42
Wing Commander P C Pickard DSO	01.10.42 to 05.43
Wing Commander L Mcd Hodges DSO DFC	05.43 to 13.03.44
Wing Commander A H C Boxer	13.03.44 to 01.45
Wing Commander G Watson DFM	01.45 to 21.02.45
Wing Commander M A Brogan DFC	22.02.45 to 04.03.45
Wing Commander L F Ratcliff DSO DFC AFC	05.03.45 to 02.06.45

AIRCRAFT

Lysander III	14.02.42 to 02.06.45
Whitley V	14.02.42 to 12.42
Havoc	02.42 to 12.43
Halifax V	11.42 to 10.44
Hudson III/V	10.43 to 02.06.45
Stirling III/IV	09.44 to 02.06.45

KNOWN OPERATIONAL RECORD

Sorties

Halifax	Stirling	Havoc	Lysander	Hudson	Whitley
786	379	125	266	179	139

Aircraft Losses

Halifax	Stirling	Havoc	Lysander	Hudson	Whitley
17	6	0	10	10	6

% Losses

Halifax	Stirling	Havoc	Lysander	Hudson	Whitley
2.2	1.6	0.0	3.8	5.6	4.3

The actual number of sorties is higher than those shown

AIRCRAFT HISTORIES

Lysander	From February 1942.
R2626	From 138 Sqn. To 4AGS.
R9106	Crashed and burned out while trying to land at Tempsford during training 16.5.43.
R9117	From 6 OTU after role conversion.
R9125	From Central Navigation School.
T1446	From 1 APC.
T1503	From Fleet Air Arm.
T1618	From CGS after role conversion.
T1651	From 90 AFU.
T1688	From 16 APC. To 357 Sqn.
T1707	From CGS. Force-landed in Sussex 18.10.44.
T1770	From 138 Sqn. SOC 6.8.44.
V9283	From 13 Sqn.
V9297	From 278 Sqn.
V9326	From Eastchurch.
V9353	
V9367 MA-B	Crashed on approach to Tangmere on return from SIS sortie to France 17.12.43.

V9375	From 309 Sqn. SOC 3.2.45.
V9405	From 275 Sqn. FTR from SOE sortie Caen 4.3.44.
V9428	From 613 Sqn. SOC 8.7.44.
V9490 MA-H	From 286 Sqn. FTR from SIS sortie to France 7/8.7.44.
V9548 MA-D	From 241 Sqn. FTR from SIS sortie to France 16/17.11.43.
V9595	From 225 Sqn. FTR from SOE sortie to France 29.5.42.
V9597	From 24 Sqn. Lost during course of SOE operation 1.9.42.
V9605 MA-B	FTR from SIS sortie to France 3/4.3.44.
V9614	From 1 AAS.
V9664	From 8 AACU. FTR from SOE sortie to France 3/4.5.44.
V9673 MA-J	From 286 Sqn. FTR from SOE sortie to France 10/11.12.43.
V9674 MA-K	From 286 Sqn. Crashed on approach to Ford on return from SIS sortie to France 17.12.43.
V9718	From 26 OTU. To India.
V9723 MA-H	From 41 OTU. Crashed on landing at Tangmere on return from SIS sortie to France 9.11.43.
V9737	From 275 Sqn. SOC 28.7.44.
V9738	From 516 Sqn. To India.
V9748 MA-D	From 275 Sqn. FTR from SOE sortie to France 4/5.8.44.
V9749 MA-M	From 275 Sqn. Disappeared while in transit from France 29.9.44.
V9822 MA-E	From 1489Flt. FTR from SIS sortie to France 10/11.2.44.
V9858	From 4 OTU.
Whitley	From February 1942 to December 1942.
Z6629 MA-N	From 77 Sqn. FTR from SOE sortie 22/23.11.42.
Z6653 MA-O	From 102 Sqn. FTR from SOE sortie 2/3.10.42.
Z6747	From 102 Sqn. To 42 OTU.
Z6814	From 77 Sqn. To 81 OTU.
Z6828	From 102 Sqn. To Gibraltar.
Z6940	From 102 Sqn. To TFU and back. FTR from SOE operation to France 19/20.9.42.
Z6952	From 77 Sqn. To 10 OTU.
Z6959	From 138 Sqn. To 10 OTU.
Z9131 MA-Q	From 51 Sqn. FTR from SOE sortie to France 24/25.9.42.
Z9160	From 10 Sqn. Force-landed in Portugal during ferry flight from Gibraltar 19.11.42.
Z9218	From 296 Sqn. To 42 OTU.
Z9224	From 78 Sqn. To TFU and back. Crashed soon take-off from Tempsford when bound for an SOE sortie 22.6.42.
Z9428	From TFU. To 138 Sqn.
Z9438	From 77 Sqn. To 10 OTU.
BD202	From 77 Sqn. To 10 OTU.
BD228 MA-S	From 77 Sqn. Crashed on approach to Tempsford on return from SOE sortie 22.10.42.
BD276	To 10 OTU.
BD363	From 296 Sqn. To 10 OTU.
Wellington	
P2521	From 138 Sqn. To 303FTU.
L7772	From 40 Sqn. Became ground instruction machine 12.43.

Hudson	From October 1943.
N7221	From 220 Sqn. Crashed 28.3.44.
N7263	From King's Flight. Crashed on landing at Tempsford while Training 1.8.44.
T9405	From 269 Sqn. FTR from SOE sortie 22.2.45.
T9436	From ATA.
T9439 MA-R	From 1444Flt. Force-landed in Sweden while training 19.4.44.
T9445	From 233 Sqn. FTR from SOE sortie 21.3.45.
T9453	From 233 Sqn.
T9463 MA-L	From 1404Flt. FTR from SOE sortie to Germany 26/27.11.44.
T9465 MA-T	From 269 Sqn. Damaged beyond repair in ground accident at Blida following SOE sortie to France 16/17.7.43. SOC 21.7.43.
V9155 MA-Q	From 1404Flt. FTR from SOE sortie to Holland 30.5/1.6.44.
V9169	From 233 Sqn.
AE505	From 233 Sqn. FTR from SOE sortie 21.3.45.
AE537	From ATA.
AE559	From 279 Sqn.
AM931	From 233 Sqn. Damaged beyond repair 19.1.45.
FH357	From 520 Sqn.
FH406	From 24 Sqn. Returned to 24 Sqn.
FK763	Abandoned over Surrey 12.4.45.
FK767	Crashed in Bedfordshire while training 28.3.44.
FK790 MA-R	FTR from SIS sortie to Holland 5/6.7.44.
FK797	SOC 18.4.45.
FK803	FTR presumably from SOE sortie 21.3.45.
Boston	From February 1942 to December 1943.
AW399	From 88 Sqn.
Havoc	From February 1942 to December 1943.
BJ477	From 23 Sqn. Became ground instruction machine 12.43.
Ventura	From February 1942 to May 1943.
AE881	From 487 Sqn. To 1575Flt.
AE948	From RAE. To 1575Flt.
Halifax	From November 1942 to October 1944.
W1012	From TFU. To 138 Sqn.
W1046	From 35 Sqn. To 138 Sqn.
BB329	To 138 Sqn.
BB429	To 301FTU.
BB431	To 148 Sqn.
BB432	To 148 Sqn.
BB433	To 301FTU.
BB435	To MAC.
BB436	To OAPU.
BB437	To 148 Sqn.
BB438	To 624 Sqn.
BB440	To 301FTU.
BB441	To OAPU.

DG244 MA-Y	FTR from SIS operation to Norway 19/20.3.43.
DG245 MA-W	FTR from SIS operation to Czechoslovakia 14/15.3.43.
DG272 MA-U	From 138 Sqn. FTR from air-sea rescue sortie off east coast 23.1.44.
DG283 MA-Y	Crashed in Buckinghamshire when bound for SOE sortie to France 14.3.43.
DG284	To 1660CU.
DG285 MA-X	From 138 Sqn. FTR from SOE operation to France 15/16.1.43.
DG286 MA-Z	From 138 Sqn. Returned to 138 Sqn.
DG405 MA-Y	FTR from SIS/SOE operation to Holland 22/23.6.43.
DG406 MA-V	FTR from SOE operation 11/12.6.43.
DG409 MA-W	Crashed almost immediately after take-off from Tempsford when bound for an air-test 13.4.43.
DG996	From 138 Sqn. To 1663CU.
DK119 MA-U	From 138 Sqn. FTR from SOE operation to France 22/23.7.43.
DK206 MA-V	Crashed while trying to land at Ford on return from SOE sortie to France 17.12.43.
DK232 MA-T	Crashed on take-off from Tempsford when bound for SOE sortie 5.11.43.
EB127	To 1663CU.
EB129 MA-W	FTR from SOE operation to France 10/11.11.43.
EB147	From 1575Flt. To 624 Sqn.
EB239 MA-Y	FTR from SOE operation to France 20/21.10.43.
LK695	
LK738 MA-T	FTR from SOE operation to France 10/11.4.44.
LK899 MA-T	Crashed on mudflats near Felixstowe on return from SOE sortie to France 17.12.43.
LL118	To 138 Sqn.
LL120 MA-W	Abandoned over Lincolnshire following early return from SOE operation 17.12.43.
LL182 MA-V	FTR from air-sea rescue search off east coast 23.1.44.
LL183 MA-W	FTR from SOE sortie to France while on loan to 138 Sqn 9/10.5.44.
LL248 MA-U	FTR from SOE operation to France 4/5.8.44.
LL249	To 138 Sqn.
LL250	To 138 Sqn.
LL251	To 138 Sqn.
LL252	To 138 Sqn.
LL254	To 138 Sqn.
LL300 MA-Z	Destroyed by fire at Tempsford 30.5.44.
LL358 MA-Y	FTR from SOE operation to France 8/9.8.44.
LL364	To 138 Sqn.
LL367	To 1FU.
LL381	To 138 Sqn.
LL385	From 138 Sqn. To 1FU.
LL387	To 138 Sqn.
LL388 MA-W	To 138 Sqn and back. FTR from SOE operation to Holland 28/29.8.44.
LL392	To 138 Sqn.
LL453	To 1FU.
LL465	From 138 Sqn. To 1FU.
LL467	From 138 Sqn. To 1FU.

LL483	From 138 Sqn. To 1FU.
LL534	To 1FU.

Mosquito

DD796	To 140 Sqn.

Stirling — From September 1944.

EF245	To 214 Sqn.
LK119 MA-Y	From 138 Sqn. FTR from SOE sortie to Norway 31.3.45.
LK206	From 138 Sqn.
LK207 MA-W	From 138 Sqn. Crashed in Bedfordshire during training 19.10.44.
LK208 MA-X	From 138 Sqn. Crashed on take-off from Tempsford when bound for SOE sortie to Belgium 21.9.44.
LK209 MA-T	From 138 Sqn. FTR from SOE sortie to Holland 23.3.45.
LK210	From 138 Sqn.
LK236 MA-Y	Crashed in Bedfordshire after collision with USAAF Mustang 14.2.45.
LK237	
LK238 MA-X	FTR from SOE sortie to Denmark 6/7.10.44.
LK274	From 138 Sqn.
LK278	To 138 Sqn.
LK285	From 138 Sqn.
LK308	To 299 Sqn.
LK312 MA-W	FTR from SOE sortie to Denmark 5.3.45.
LK329	From 138 Sqn.
PW395	From 138 Sqn. To 23MU.

186 SQUADRON

No motto   Codes XY, AP

No. 186 Squadron first saw the light of day on the same day as the Royal Air Force, the 1st of April 1918. Its original brief was to train personnel for home defence night fighting squadrons. In July 1919 the squadron was engaged in development work for naval co-operation, and lost its identity through renumbering. The squadron was re-formed at the end of April 1943 as a Hurricane fighter-bomber unit, receiving its first aircraft in August, before converting to Typhoons in November and Spitfires in the following February. Its first operation came on the 15th of March, but three weeks later the squadron was again renumbered. No. 186 Squadron was re-formed again on the 5th of October 1944 from C Flight of 90 Squadron, and began Lancaster operations two weeks later. It remained at the forefront of 3 Group operations until the war's end.

STATIONS

Tuddenham	05.10.44 to 17.12.44
Stradishall	17.12.44 to 17.07.45

COMMANDING OFFICERS

Wing Commander J H Giles DFC	07.10.44 to 16.03.45
Wing Commander E L Hancock	16.03.45 to 08.05.45

AIRCRAFT

Lancaster I/III   07.10.44 to 17.07.45

OPERATIONAL RECORD

Operations	Sorties	Aircraft FTR	% Losses
98	1,254	8	0.6

4 further aircraft destroyed in crashes

Category of Operations

Bombing	Mining
96	2

TABLE OF STATISTICS

Out of 59 Lancaster squadrons

44th highest number of overall Lancaster operations in Bomber Command.
43rd highest number of Lancaster sorties in Bomber Command.
50th equal highest number (with 432 Sqn) of Lancaster operational losses in Bomber Command.

Out of 28 squadrons in 3 Group

18th highest number of overall operations in 3 Group.
13th highest number of sorties in 3 Group.
25th highest number of aircraft operational losses in 3 Group.

Out of 11 Lancaster squadrons in 3 Group

9th highest number of Lancaster overall operations in 3 Group.
10th highest number of Lancaster sorties in 3 Group.
9th highest number of Lancaster operational losses in 3 Group.

AIRCRAFT HISTORIES

Lancaster	From October 1944.
HK606 XY-V	From 90 Sqn. To 138 Sqn.
HK613 XY-Y	From 90 Sqn. To 195 Sqn.
HK622 XY-P	FTR Homburg 20.11.44.
AP-Z	
HK650 AP-T	FTR Hohenbudburg railway yards Krefeld 8/9.2.45.
HK659 XY-Q	
HK661	To 138 Sqn.
HK662 AP-P	
HK680 AP-H	FTR Leuna (Merseburg) 6/7.12.44.
HK682	To 138 Sqn.
HK684 XY-O	To 195 Sqn.
HK688 AP-W	FTR Dortmund 3/4.2.45.
HK692	From 90 Sqn. To 138 Sqn.
HK694	From 90 Sqn. To 138 Sqn.

HK759	To 195 Sqn.
HK767 AP-A	Crashed while landing at Stradishall on return from Leuna 4/5.4.45.
HK794	To 195 Sqn.
HK796	To 195 Sqn.
HK801	From 195 Sqn. No operations. To 550 Sqn.
HK802	To 195 Sqn.
JB475 XY-X	From 195 Sqn.
LL854	From 15 Sqn.
LM160 XY-W	From 90 Sqn. To 300 Sqn.
LM188 XY-S	From 90 Sqn. To 1656CU.
LM216	From 630 Sqn. To 189 Sqn.
LM543	From 195 Sqn.
LM617 XY-X	From 90 Sqn after 58 operations.
LM618 AP-U	From 90 Sqn. Crash-landed in Holland on return from Homburg 2.11.44.
LM692 XY-R	From 90 Sqn.
LM697 XY-A	From 149 Sqn.
NG137 XY-D	From 90 Sqn.
NG147 AP-C	Crashed soon after take-off from Stradishall when bound for Wanne-Eickel 16.1.45.
NG148 XY-B	From 90 Sqn. To 149 Sqn.
NG149 XY-D	From 90 Sqn.
NG174	
NG175 AP-J	From 90 Sqn. FTR Gelsenkirchen 27.2.45.
NG176 AP-H	From 90 Sqn. FTR Stuttgart 19/20.10.44.
NG284	
NG293 XY-U	
NG353 AP-X	FTR Dresden 13/14.2.45.
NG354	
NN720 XY-K	From 90 Sqn.
PB483 AP-X	From 149 Sqn. Collided with PB488 of 186 Sqn near Stradishall on return from Kiel 13/14.4.45.
PB488 AP-J	From 90 Sqn. Collided with PB483 of 186 Sqn near Stradishall on return from Kiel 13/14.4.45.
PB509 XY-Y	From 149 Sqn.
PB790 XY-B/S	From 195 Sqn.
PB858 XY-O	From 195 Sqn.
PB896	From 195 Sqn.
PD429 XY-Z	From 106 Sqn.
PP668	
PP669	
RA522	To 218 Sqn.
RA533 AP-P	Crashed in Germany following a collision with HK555 of 115 Sqn on return from Leuna 4/5.4.45.
RA569	From SIU.
RA570 AP-K	From SIU.
RA577	From SIU.
RA580	From SIU.
RF126 XY-V	
RF198 XY-N	
SW267	From 90 Sqn.
SW272	From 90 Sqn.
SW275	From 90 Sqn.

192 SQUADRON

Motto: Dare to discover   Code DT

No. 192 Squadron was originally formed as an advanced night-flying training unit in September 1917 to supply pilots for night bombing and home defence duties. The squadron fulfilled this role until the end of the Great War and was disbanded in the following month. The squadron was reborn from 1474 Flight on the 4th of January 1943 for radar countermeasures (RCM) duties. This required operations over Germany and the occupied countries to identify the wavelengths in use by the enemy. When 100 Group was formed on the 23rd of November 1943, 192 Squadron was posted to it from 3 Group.

STATIONS

Gransden Lodge	04.01.43 to 05.04.43
Feltwell	05.04.43 to 25.11.43

COMMANDING OFFICERS

Wing Commander C D V Willis DFC   04.01.43 to 12.03.44

AIRCRAFT

Wellington Ic	04.01.43 to 02.43
Wellington III	04.01.43 to 02.43
Wellington X	04.01.43 to 03.45
Mosquito IV	04.01.43 to 03.45
Halifax II	01.43 to 03.45
Halifax V	08.43 to 11.43
To 100 Group	25.11.43

OPERATIONAL RECORD

Operations	Sorties	Aircraft Losses	% Losses
141	346	5	1.4

Wellington

Sorties	Aircraft Losses	% Losses
291	4	1.4

Halifax

Sorties	Aircraft Losses	% Losses
55	0	0.0

Mosquito

Sorties	Aircraft Losses	% Losses
48	1	2.1

TABLE OF STATISTICS

Because of the unique nature of the squadron in conducting bomber support operations, sometimes with a bomb load and sometimes without, it is not possible to produce an accurate table of statistics.

AIRCRAFT HISTORIES

Wellington	From January 1943 to March 1945.
N2772	From 1474Flt. To 14 OTU.
X3566	From 1474Flt. To 26 OTU.
Z1047	From 1474Flt. To 11 OTU.
AD590	From 1474Flt. To 26 OTU.
HE226	From 1474Flt. To 12 OTU.
HE227	From 1474Flt. To 11 OTU.
HE228 DT-C	From 1474Flt. FTR from Special Duties operation to Düsseldorf 25/26.5.43.
HE229	From 1474Flt. To 12 OTU.
HE230	From 1474Flt. FTR from special duties operation in the Bay of Biscay 16.8.43.
HE231	From 1474Flt. Crashed in Huntingdonshire soon after take-off for an air-test 25.1.43.
HE232	From 1474Flt. To 83 OTU.
HE233	From 1474Flt. To 11 OTU.
HE380	From 1474Flt. To 20 OTU.
HE438	To 11 OTU.
HE439	To 22 OTU.
HE472	From BDU. To 11 AGS.
HE498	To 24 OTU.
HE826	To 2 AGS.
HE852	To 17 OTU.
HE857	To 22 OTU.
HF454	Crashed on landing at Feltwell after air-test 2.7.43.
HF837	From 1474Flt. To 3 OTU.
HZ412 DT-U	FTR from Special Duties sortie off the Dutch coast 24.6.43.
HZ415	From 6 OTU. To 24 OTU and back.
LN172	To 11 OTU.
LN349 DT-X	Ditched in the Bay of Biscay during special duties operation 5/6.8.43.
LN398	Crash-landed in Norfolk 4.7.44.
LN402	To 424 Sqn.
LN556	To 22 OTU.
LN673	To 24 OTU.
LN716	FTR RCM sortie to North France 19/20.3.44.
LN879	To 21 OTU.
LP156	To 21 OTU.
LP345	Crashed on landing at Foulsham 16.8.44.
NA724	To 21 OTU.
NC706	To 29 OTU.
Halifax	From August 1943.
DK244 DT-Q	Crashed at Feltwell after recall from Ludwigshaven 18.11.43.
DK246	To 431 Sqn.
DT735	From 1474Flt. To 1475Flt.
DT737	From 1474Flt. To 1473Flt.
LK780	To 296 Sqn.
LK781	To 1658CU.
LK782	To 171 Sqn.
LK874	To 171 Sqn.
LL132	To 1659CU.

Mosquito	From January 1943.
W4071	From 105 Sqn via 1655MTU. SOC 4.45.
DK292	From 105 Sqn via 1655MTU and 13 OTU. FTR from bomber support sortie 27.4.44.
DK327	From 139 Sqn. Crash-landed at Freiston 28.6.44.
DK333	From 109 Sqn.
DZ375 DT-L	From 1474Flt. FTR from special duties sortie to Bay of Biscay 11.8.43.
DZ376	
DZ377	To 1473Flt and back. Destroyed in accident after landing at Foulsham 28.4.44.
DZ405	From 521 Sqn. FTR from special duties sortie to Stendal 27.8.44.
DZ410	From TFU.
DZ483	To 105 Sqn.
DZ491	From 139 Sqn. Crashed on landing at Foulsham 3.3.45.
DZ535	From 618 Sqn. Force-landed in Norfolk 23.9.44.
DZ590	From A&AEE.
DZ617	From 139 Sqn.
HJ671	To Defford.
NS776	To 1409Met Flt.
NS784	
NS797	
NS799	
NS816	To 1409Met Flt.
PF572	From 109 Sqn. Returned to 109 Sqn.

195 SQUADRON

Motto: Velocitate fortis (Strong by speed)   Code A4, JE

When 195 Squadron was formed on the 16th of November 1942 it was intended as a fighter/bomber unit. Typhoons arrived, but no operations had been carried out when the squadron was disbanded in February 1944. It was reborn from C Flight of 115 Squadron on the 1st of October to fly Lancasters. It operated as a 3 Group frontline unit for the remainder of the war.

STATIONS

Witchford	01.10.44 to 13.11.44
Wratting Common	13.11.44 to 14.08.45

COMMANDING OFFICERS

Wing Commander D H Burnside DFC*	01.10.44 to 10.04.45
Squadron Leader B R W Forster	10.04.45 to 17.04.45
Wing Commander D H Burnside DFC*	17.04.45 to 25.04.45
Wing Commander A E Cairnes	25.04.45 to 14.08.45

AIRCRAFT

Lancaster I/III	01.10.44 to 14.08.45

OPERATIONAL RECORD

Operations	Sorties	Aircraft Losses	% Losses
87	1,384	14	1.0

Category of Operations
All bombing

TABLE OF STATISTICS

Out of 59 Lancaster squadrons

45th highest number of overall Lancaster operations in Bomber Command.
42nd highest number of Lancaster sorties in Bomber Command.
47th highest number of Lancaster operational losses in Bomber Command.

Out of 28 squadrons in 3 Group

21st highest number of overall operations in 3 Group.
12th highest number of sorties in 3 Group.
20th highest number of operational losses in 3 Group.

Out of 11 Lancaster squadrons in 3 Group

10th highest number of overall Lancaster operations in 3 Group.
9th highest number of Lancaster sorties in 3 Group.
8th highest number of Lancaster operational losses in 3 Group.

AIRCRAFT HISTORIES

Lancaster	From October 1944.
HK613	From 186 Sqn. To 38MU.
HK658 A4-C	FTR Solingen 4.11.44.
HK660	
HK663	Crash-landed in Allied Holland on return from Homburg 2.11.44.
HK679	
HK681	To 38MU.
HK683 A4-M	FTR Gelsenkirchen 23.11.44.
HK684	From 186 Sqn.
HK686	FTR Saarbrücken 13.1.45.
HK687	
HK689 A4-B	FTR Solingen 4.11.44.
HK690	
HK697 A4-C	From 75 Sqn. FTR Witten 12.12.44.
HK701	
HK759	From 186 Sqn.
HK764	
HK771	
HK794	From 186 Sqn.
HK796	From 186 Sqn. To 550 Sqn.
HK797	To 625 Sqn.
HK800	To 550 Sqn.
HK801	To 106 Sqn.
HK802	From 186 Sqn. To 100 Sqn.
HK804	To TFU 4.45.
JB475	From 15 Sqn. To 186 Sqn.

LM543	From 207 Sqn. To 186 Sqn.
LM743 A4-R	From 115 Sqn. FTR Homburg 2.11.44.
LM744	From 115 Sqn. To GH Flt.
LM753	From 115 Sqn.
NF995	
NG162	From 115 Sqn.
NG166	
NG181	From 617 Sqn. Returned to 617 Sqn.
NG186 A4-O	FTR Dessau 7/8.3.45.
NG187	
NG188	
NG219 JE-T	FTR Solingen 4.11.44.
NG236	To 514 Sqn.
NG305 JE-C	Force-landed near Ghent on return from Hamm 5.12.44.
NG351 JE-E	FTR Witten 12.12.44.
NG388	From 149 Sqn.
NG450	To 218 Sqn.
NG452	
NN740	
NN755	From 115 Sqn.
PB112 JE-H	From 15 Sqn. FTR Witten 12.12.44.
PB139	From 15 Sqn.
PB196 JE-D	From 90 Sqn. FTR Witten 12.12.44.
PB703	From 625 Sqn.
PB760	
PB790	To 186 Sqn.
PB794	
PB818	From 115 Sqn. To 44 Sqn.
PB837	From 218 Sqn.
PB856	
PB858	To 186 Sqn.
PB877	
PB896	To 186 Sqn.
PD395	
PD399	
PD426	From 218 Sqn.
PP665	
PP667	
PP671	

196 SQUADRON

Motto: Sic fidem servamus (Thus we keep faith)   Codes ZO, 7T

First formed at Driffield as a 4 Group Wellington unit, 196 Squadron was posted to 3 Group in July 1943 and converted to Stirlings. Bombing operations began in August, but the squadron was transferred to 38 Group for transport duties in November.

From 4 Group   19.07.43

STATIONS

Witchford   19.07.43 to 18.11.43

COMMANDING OFFICERS

Wing Commander N Alexander   26.06.43 to 08.44

AIRCRAFT

Stirling III	07.43 to 02.44
To 38 Group	18.11.43

OPERATIONAL RECORD

Operations	Sorties	Aircraft Losses	% Losses
30	166	8	6.6

Category of Operations

Bombing	Mining
12	18

TABLE OF STATISTICS

Out of 28 squadrons in 3 Group

27th number of overall operations in 3 Group.
26th highest number of sorties in 3 Group.
22nd highest number of aircraft operational losses in 3 Group.

Out of 12 Stirling squadrons in 3 Group

Lowest number of Stirling overall operations in 3 Group.
11th highest number of Stirling sorties in 3 Group.
10th highest number of Stirling operational losses in 3 Group.

AIRCRAFT HISTORIES

Stirling	From July 1943 to February 1944.
BF520	From 149 Sqn. To 1665CU.
BF529	From 90 Sqn. To 513 Sqn.
BK663 ZO-K	From 214 Sqn. Crashed on approach to Witchford on return from Hanover 28.9.43.
BK771	From 214 Sqn. To transport duties with the Sqn.
EE874	From 214 Sqn. To 1665CU.
EE957	To 199 Sqn.
EE964 ZO-F	FTR Mannheim 5/6.9.43.
EE972	To 1665CU.
EE973 ZO-U	Crash-landed at Witchford on return from Mannheim 6.9.43.
EE975	To 1660CU.
EF114 ZO-H	FTR Modane 16/17.9.43.
EF116	To 513 Sqn and back. To 1665CU.
EF146	To 513 Sqn.
EF160	To 1665CU.
EF178	To 1665CU.
EF190	To 1665CU.
EF210	To 1665CU.
EF464 ZO-P	Crashed near Witchford following early return from Kassel 3.10.43.

EF467	To 1665CU.
EF468	To transport duties with the Squadron.
EF469	To Transport duties with the Squadron.
EF488	To 1653CU.
EF492	To 1665CU.
EF494 ZO-C	Ditched off Norfolk coast following early return from Bremen 9.10.43.
EF516	To 1665CU.
EH899	From 214 Sqn. To 1665CU.
EH932	To 1665CU.
EH950	To 299 Sqn.
EH952	FTR from sea-search 24.8.43.
EH954	To 1665CU.
EH960 ZO-X	Crashed into The wash during an air-test 17.10.43.
EH961 ZO-D	FTR Berlin 31.8/1.9.43.
EH981	To 1665CU.
EJ110	To transport duties with the Squadron.
LK403	From 622. To 1665CU.

199 SQUADRON

Motto: Let Tyrants Tremble   Code EX

No. 199 Squadron was first formed in June 1917 to train pilots for night bomber squadrons operating in France. The squadron was disbanded in June 1919, and remained on the shelf until its re-formation as a 4 Group Wellington unit in November 1942. In June 1943 the squadron was posted to 3 Group to convert to Stirlings, and resumed operations at the end of July. At the beginning of May 1944 the squadron joined 100 Group for RCM duties, and remained in this role until the war's end.

From 1 Group   21.06.43

STATIONS

Lakenheath   20.06.43 to 01.05.44

COMMANDING OFFICERS

Wing Commander L W Howard DFC   20.03.43 to 06.10.43
Wing Commander N A N Bray DFC   06.10.43 to 08.44

AIRCRAFT

Stirling III   06.43 to 03.45

To 100 Group   01.05.44

OPERATIONAL RECORD

Operations	Sorties	Aircraft Losses	% Losses
332	2,863	32	1.1

Category of Operations				
Bombing	Mining	SOE	RCM	Other
65	75	16	175	1

Stirling

Operations	Sorties	Aircraft Losses	% Losses
237	2,059	18	0.9

Category of Operations

Bombing	Mining	SOE	RCM	Other
30	52	16	138	1

TABLE OF STATISTICS

Out of 28 squadrons in 3 Group

17th highest number of overall operations in 3 Group.
20th highest number of sorties in 3 Group.
21st equal (with 195 Sqn) highest number of operational losses in 3 Group.

Out of 12 Stirling squadrons in 3 Group

8th highest number of Stirling overall operations in 3 Group.
8th highest number of Stirling sorties in 3 Group.
9th highest number of Stirling operational losses in 3 Group.

AIRCRAFT HISTORIES

Stirling	From July 1943 to March 1945.
BF473	From 75 Sqn. To 1651CU.
BF481	From 214 Sqn. To 1654CU.
BK695	From 75 Sqn. To 1653CU.
BK762 EX-C	From 214 Sqn.
BK772 EX-A	From 149 Sqn. To 1657CU.
BK806 EX-S	From 149 Sqn. FTR Nuremberg 27/28.8.43.
BK816	From 622 Sqn. To 90 Sqn.
EE910 EX-Q	From 15 Sqn. Crashed on landing at St Athen during transit following an SOE sortie 22.4.44.
EE911 EX-G	FTR from mining sortie 2/3.9.43.
EE913 EX-F	From 15 Sqn. FTR Nuremberg 27/28.8.43.
EE917 EX-L	FTR Mönchengladbach 30/31.8.43.
EE940	To 15 Sqn.
EE941	From 218 Sqn. To 1332CU.
EE943 EX-X	From 218 Sqn. To 1657CU.
EE946 EX-P	FTR Berlin 31.8/1.9.43.
EE947 EX-D	Crashed on approach to Lakenheath following early return from mining sortie 24.9.43.
EE948 EX-Q	To 1332CU.
EE953 EX-E	To 149 Sqn.
EE954	To 15 Sqn.
EE957 EX-Q	From 196 Sqn. FTR from SOE sortie 3/4.3.44.
EF118 EX-O	FTR Hanover 27/28.9.43.
EF138 EX-Y	Crashed on approach to Lakenheath on return from SOE sortie 10.4.44.
EF153 EX-D	From 622 Sqn. Crashed soon after take-off from Lakenheath when bound for SOE sortie 10.2.44.
EF154 EX-V	From 622 Sqn. FTR from mining sortie 1/2.12.43.
EF161	From 15 Sqn. To 149 Sqn.
EF192 EX-J	To 149 Sqn.
EF262	From 149 Sqn. Returned to 149 Sqn.

EF271 EX-F	From 214 Sqn. FTR from SOE sortie 15/16.2.44.
EF300	To 1653CU.
EF301	To 1653CU.
EF304	To 1653CU.
EF450 EX-N	Crashed on landing at Lakenheath after early return from Mannheim 18.11.43.
EF453 EX-F	FTR from mining sortie 4/5.11.43.
EF455 EX-B	To 1651CU.
EF459 EX-X	From 90 Sqn. To 1653CU.
EF460	To 15 Sqn.
EF505 EX-K/R	FTR from mining sortie 28/29.1.44.
EF508 EX-G	To 1653CU.
EF514	From 75 Sqn. To 1651CU.
EH909 EX-Z	From 149 Sqn. Crashed while trying to land at Lakenheath after early return from Kassel 3.10.43.
EH926 EX-T	From 218 Sqn. To 1654CU.
EH927 EX-E	From 149 Sqn. FTR Berlin 23/24.8.43.
EH930 EX-N	From 15 Sqn. To 1651CU.
EH934 EX-K	From 149 Sqn. FTR Berlin 23/24.8.43.
EH995 EX-H/L	To 1657CU.
EJ111 EX-P	Destroyed by fire at Lakenheath 23.11.43.
EJ115 EX-H	To 90 Sqn.
LJ480 EX-S	From 214 Sqn. FTR from mining sortie 11/12.3.44.
LJ501	From 214 Sqn. To 140 Sqn.
LJ510 EX-A	
LJ513 EX-E	To 171 Sqn.
LJ514 EX-B	
LJ516 EX-H	From TFU.
LJ518 EX-K	Crashed in Norfolk on return from RCM sortie 25.9.44.
LJ520 EX-Z	
LJ525 EX-R	
LJ531 EX-N	FTR from RCM sortie 17.6.44.
LJ536 EX-P	FTR from RCM sortie 16.9.44.
LJ538 EX-T	Became ground instruction machine.
LJ541 EX-K	To 171 Sqn and back.
LJ542 EX-G	
LJ543 EX-J	
LJ544 EX-D	To 171 Sqn.
LJ557 EX-Y	To 196 Sqn.
LJ559 EX-Q	To 171 Sqn and back. Damaged on return from RCM sortie 6.12.44.
LJ560 EX-H	Crashed on take-off from North Creake when bound for RCM sortie 29.8.44.
LJ562 EX-V	To 171 Sqn.
LJ565 EX-Q	To 171 Sqn and back.
LJ567 EX-Y	To 171 Sqn and back. Belly-landed at Woodbridge on return from RCM sortie 5.12.44.
LJ568 EX-L	From 149 Sqn. To 171 Sqn and back.
LJ569 EX-C	
LJ578 EX-S	Crashed on take-off from North Creake when bound for RCM sortie 10.9.44.
LJ580 EX-X	From 149 Sqn.
LJ582 EX-L	From 149 Sqn. To 171 Sqn.
LJ595 EX-N	From TFU.

LJ611	To 171 Sqn and back.
LJ614	From TFU.
LJ617	To 171sqn and back. Shot down by US flak during RCM sortie over France 5.3.45.
LJ649	From TFU. To 171 Sqn and back.
LJ651	From TFU. To 171 Sqn and back.
LJ670	To 171 Sqn.
LK381 EX-Z	To 1657CU.
LK385	To 149 Sqn.
LK387	From 623 Sqn. Returned to 623 Sqn.
LK397	To 149 Sqn.
PW256	To 171 Sqn and back.
PW258	To 171 Sqn.
PW259EX-V	To 171 Sqn and back.

214 (Federated Malay States) SQUADRON

Motto: Ultor In Umbris (Avenging in the shadows)   Codes BU, PX

The formation of 214 Squadron coincided with that of the Royal Air Force, and took place on the 1st of April 1918. Stationed in France, it spent the remaining few months of the Great War as a bomber unit, operating against enemy bases and ports in Belgium and France. Following a spell in Egypt, the squadron was disbanded on the 1st of February 1920, and remained on the shelf until its re-formation from B Flight of 9 Squadron on the 16th of September 1935. The squadron became the eighth in Bomber Command to equip with Wellingtons, when the first three examples were taken on charge on the 26th of May 1939. The squadron began the Second World War as a reserve squadron engaged in aircrew training for 3 Group, and it was not until June 1940 that it began operations. Conversion to Stirlings took place in April 1942, and operations continued until January 1944, when the squadron was posted to 100 Group for RCM duties with Fortresses.

STATIONS

Methwold	03.09.39 to 12.02.40
Stradishall	12.02.40 to 05.01.42
Honington	05.01.42 to 12.01.42
Stradishall	12.01.42 to 01.10.42
Chedburgh	01.10.42 to 10.12.43
Downham Market	10.12.43 to 16.01.44

COMMANDING OFFICERS

Wing Commander W Sanderson AFC	11.38 to 02.40
Wing Commander F E Nuttall	02.40 to 10.40
Wing Commander G H Loughnan	10.40 to 03.41
Wing Commander R B Jordan DFC	03.41 to 08.41
Wing Commander G L Cruikshanks DFC	08.41 to 07.09.41
Wing Commander R D B Macfadden DFC	09.41 to 12.02.42
Wing Commander E J P Davy	02.42 to 04.42
Wing Commander K D Knocker	04.42 to 02.07.42
Wing Commander A H Smythe DFC AFC	15.07.42 to 03.43
Wing Commander M V M Clube	03.43 to 07.43
Wing Commander D J Mcglinn	07.43 to 08.44

AIRCRAFT

Wellington I/Ia/Ic	05.39. To 04.42
Wellington II	06.41. To 01.42
Stirling I/III	04.42. To 01.44
To 100 Group	16.01.44

OPERATIONAL RECORD

Operations	Sorties	Aircraft Losses	% Losses
407	2,964	99	3.3

Category of Operations

Bombing	Mining	Leaflet
315	89	3

Wellingtons

Operations	Sorties	Aircraft Losses	% Losses
185	1,532	45	2.9

Category of Operations

Bombing	Mining
184	1

Stirlings

Operations	Sorties	Aircraft Losses	% Losses
222	1,432	54	3.8

Category of Operations

Bombing	Mining	Leaflet
131	88	3

TABLE OF STATISTICS

15th highest number of overall operations in Bomber Command

Out of 42 Wellington squadrons

10th highest number of Wellington overall operations in Bomber Command.
8th highest number of Wellington sorties in Bomber Command.
9th highest number of Wellington operational losses in Bomber Command.

Out of 28 squadrons in 3 Group

6th highest number of overall operations in 3 Group.
9th highest number of sorties in 3 Group.
6th highest number of aircraft operational losses in 3 Group.

Out of 18 Wellington squadrons in 3 Group

6th highest number of Wellington overall operations in 3 Group.
6th highest number of Wellington sorties in 3 Group.
5th highest number of Wellington operational losses in 3 Group.

Out of 12 Stirling squadrons in 3 Group

4th highest number of Stirling overall operations in 3 Group.
6th highest number of Stirling sorties in 3 Group.
6th highest number of Stirling operational losses in 3 Group.

AIRCRAFT HISTORIES

Wellington	To January 1942.
L4222	From 99 Sqn. To 215 Sqn.
L4224	From 99 Sqn. To 215 Sqn.
L4229	From 149 Sqn. To 10BAT Flt.
L4261	From 9 Sqn. To 9BAT Flt.
L4269	From 9 Sqn. To 20 OTU.
L4306	From 115 Sqn. To 20 OTU.
L4326	From 37 Sqn. To 15 OTU.
L4327	From 37 Sqn. Became ground instruction machine.
L4332	From 37 Sqn. To 311 Sqn.
L4337	From 37 Sqn. To 15 OTU.
L4338	From 37 Sqn. To 311 Sqn.
L4341	To 5BAT Flt.
L4342	To 1 OTU.
L4343	To 40 Sqn via 418 Sqn and 15 OTU.
L4344	To 10BAT Flt.
L4345 BU-L	Crashed while landing at Methwold during training 6.11.39.
L4346	To RAE.
L4354	To RAE.
L4356	To 419 Sqn.
L4357	To 20 OTU.
L4358	To 9 Sqn.
L4359	To 11 OTU.
L4361	To RAE.
L4362	To 11 OTU.
L4363	To 9 Sqn.
L4364	To 9 Sqn and back. To 15 OTU.
L4365	To 15 OTU.
L4369	From 75 Sqn. Returned to 75 Sqn.
L7773	To 15 OTU.
L7774	To 115 Sqn and back. To CGS.
L7783	From 37 Sqn. To 99 Sqn.
L7815	To 3 Gp TF.
L7840	Crashed on take-off from Stradishall while training 11.10.40.
L7843	FTR Mannheim 27/28.9.40.
L7847	To 75 Sqn.
L7849	Crashed off Norfolk coast on return from Le Havre 28.12.40.
L7851	To 99 Sqn via 5BAT Flt.
L7853	To 5BAT Flt.
L7856	To RAE.
L7859	Crashed on approach to Stradishall on return from Düsseldorf 25.2.41.
L7863	To 3 Group TF.
L7869	From 305 Sqn. To 101 Sqn.
N2746	FTR Hamburg 13/14.3.41.
N2747	From 75 Sqn. To 11 OTU.
N2776	Crashed on landing at Stradishall on return from Boulogne 6.2.41.
N2778 BU-R	To 3 Group TF.

N2800	To 21 OTU.
N2802 BU-N	Crashed in Berkshire on return from Brest 14.9.41.
N2867	From 149 Sqn. Returned to 149 Sqn.
N2871	To 9 Sqn.
N2878	To 115 Sqn.
N2903	From 37 Sqn. To 11 OTU.
N2906	From 38 Sqn. To RAE.
N2993	From 37 Sqn. Crashed in Cambridgeshire during training 6.6.40.
N2994	From 37 Sqn. To 15 OTU.
N3005	From 99 Sqn. To 11 OTU.
N3007	To 311 Sqn.
N3010	To 311 Sqn.
N3011	To Swinderby.
P2519	To 305 Sqn via 15 OTU.
P2525	From 37 Sqn. To 311 Sqn.
P2529	To 15 OTU.
P2530	Crashed on landing at Stradishall on return from Berlin 31.8.40.
P2531	To 305 Sqn.
P2532	To 12 OTU.
P9213	To 37 Sqn.
P9214	To 301 Sqn via 15 OTU.
P9215	To 37 Sqn.
P9216	To 37 Sqn.
P9217	To 37 Sqn.
P9218	To 149 Sqn.
P9222	From 99 Sqn via 20 OTU. To 3 Group TF.
P9233	From 99 Sqn. To RAE.
P9239	From 9 Sqn. To 22 OTU.
R1032	To 21 OTU.
R1046	To 311 Sqn.
R1136	To 27 OTU.
R1223	To 23 OTU.
R1226 BU-L	FTR Hamburg 8/9.5.41.
R1239	To 40 Sqn.
R1321	To 3 Group TF.
R1328	From 218 Sqn. To 40 Sqn.
R1342	To 23 OTU.
R1376	To 18 OTU.
R1380	FTR Kiel 7/8.4.41.
R1402	To 20 OTU.
R1403	To 15 OTU.
R1447	FTR Mannheim 9/10.5.41.
R1462	From 57 Sqn. FTR Hamburg 11/12.5.41.
R1465	To 22 OTU.
R1505	From 101 Sqn. To 22 OTU.
R1604	FTR Mannheim 29/30.8.41.
R1609	FTR Emden 24/25.6.41.
R1611 BU-X	Crashed in Cambridgeshire during training 4.6.41.
R1613 BU-G	FTR Bremen 14/15.7.41.
R1614 BU-H	FTR Bremen 14/15.7.41.
R1621	To 22 OTU.
R1623	To 7 OTU.

R1712	From RAE. Crash-landed at Manston on return from Berlin 20/21.9.41.
R1717	FTR Frankfurt 2/3.9.41.
R1759	FTR Hamburg 15/16.1.42.
R1784	From RAE. FTR Berlin 7/8.9.41.
R1789	FTR Hanau 1/2.4.42.
R2699	Crashed on approach to Methwold during training 13.12.39.
R3171	To 75 Sqn.
R3178	To 11 OTU.
R3208	FTR Hamburg 8/9.5.41.
R3209	FTR Düsseldorf 7/8.12.40.
R3217	To 99 Sqn.
R3232	From 115 Sqn. To 3 Group TF.
R3233	To 1503BAT Flt.
T2469	From 311 Sqn. To 3 Group TF.
T2470	Crashed near Stradishall on return from Hamburg 5.11.40.
T2471	FTR Berlin 23/24.11.40.
T2476	FTR Düsseldorf 8.11.40.
T2542	FTR Kiel 8/9.4.41.
T2559	FTR Berlin 30/31.8.40.
T2562	To FPP.
T2612	To 3 Group TF.
T2708	To 99 Sqn and back. To 23 OTU.
T2709	To 21 OTU.
T2738	To 3 Group TF.
T2802	To 3 Group TF.
T2819	Burnt out on the ground at Stradishall 22.7.41.
T2827	To 70 Sqn.
T2828	To 70 Sqn.
T2841 BU-K	rashed on take-off from Stradishall bound for Wilhelmshaven 30.1.41.
T2850	From 99 Sqn. To 16 OTU.
T2877	To Wellington Flt.
T2893	Crashed in Warwickshire during operation to Germany 30.11.40.
T2918	From 15 Sqn. To 30 MU.
T2956	Crashed in Suffolk during an air-test 8.1.41.
T2992	FTR Cologne 7/8.7.41.
W5442 BU-V	To 12 Sqn.
W5450	Crashed in Suffolk on return from Berlin 2/3.6.41.
W5452 BU-U	Crashed while trying to land at Manston on return from Berlin 21.9.41.
W5627	To 304 Sqn.
W5713	To 7 OTU.
X3206	From 101 Sqn. FTR Berlin 7/8.11.41.
X3390	From 419 Sqn. Returned to 419 Sqn.
X9660	From 9 Sqn. To 29 OTU.
X9744	To 57 Sqn.
X9750	To 9 Sqn.
X9752	Crashed near Oakington during transit 29.11.41.
X9758	From 149 Sqn. To 16 OTU.
X9762	From 9 Sqn. FTR Nuremberg 12/13.10.41.
X9785	From 9 Sqn. To 40 Sqn.

X9817	From 149 Sqn. To 22 OTU.
X9884	FTR Stettin 29/30.9.41.
X9890	From 149 Sqn. FTR Münster 28/29.1.42.
X9939	Crash-landed at Stradishall on return from Kiel 26.2.42.
X9974	To 40 Sqn.
X9979	FTR Hanau 1/2.4.42.
Z1052	From 156 Sqn. FTR Hanau 1/2.4.42.
Z1068 BU-T	From 156 Sqn. To 1429 Flt.
Z1081	From 101 Sqn. FTR from shipping strike (Channel Dash) 12.2.42.
Z1094	To 22 OTU.
Z1095	From 419 Sqn. To 22 OTU.
Z1114	From 156 Sqn. To 22 OTU.
Z1139	To 11 OTU.
Z1143	From 99 Sqn. FTR Essen 26/27.3.42.
Z1148	From 101 Sqn. FTR Dortmund 14/15.4.42.
Z1156	From 99 Sqn. FTR Hanau 1/2.4.42.
Z1158	To 26 OTU.
Z1169 BU-W	To 1483Flt.
Z8373	From 101 Sqn. To 9 Sqn and back. FTR Emden 26/27.11.41.
Z8409	To 12 Sqn.
Z8411	To 104 Sqn.
Z8490	To 158 Sqn.
Z8805	From 311 Sqn. FTR Hanau 1/2.4 42.
Z8842	From 101 Sqn. FTR Hanau 1/2.4.42.
Z8858 BU-B	From 75 Sqn. Crash-landed in Cambridgeshire on return from Kiel 26.2.42.
Z8891	From 101 Sqn. To 99 Sqn.
Z8894	From 99 Sqn. To 15 OTU.
Z8900	From 9 Sqn. Damaged beyond repair during operation to Emden 15/16.11.41.
Z8943	To 9 Sqn and back. To 23 Sqn.
Z8949	To 27 OTU.
Z8951	From 57 Sqn. FTR Dortmund 15/16.4.42.
Z8953	To 9 Sqn and back. FTR Hamburg 30.11/1.12.41.
Z8962	To 18 OTU.
Z8965	From 218 Sqn. To 20 OTU.
Z8970	From 218 Sqn. To 11 OTU.
Z8979	FTR Hanau 1/2.4.42.
Z8982	From 218 Sqn. To 22 OTU.
DV509	From 419 Sqn. To 16 OTU.
DV518	To 156 Sqn and back. To 16 OTU.
DV672	To 1505Flt.
DV696	To 1505Flt.
DV730	To 16 OTU.
DV734	To 16 OTU.
DV735	To 304 Sqn via 16 OTU.
DV738	To 311 Sqn.
DV768	FTR Kiel 28/29.4.42.
DV775	To 16 OTU.
DV776	To 156 Sqn.
HF852	To 16 OTU.
HF853	To 1429 Flt.
HF856	FTR Essen 10/11.4.42.

Stirling	From April 1942.
N3646	From 15 Sqn. To 214CF. Crashed on take-off from Waterbeach 25.4.42.
N3674	From 15 Sqn. Conversion flight only. To 1651CU.
N3678	From A&AEE. Conversion flight only. To 1651CU.
N3729 BU-P/R	Crashed on landing at Stradishall following early return from Duisburg 7.8.42.
N3751 BU-P	Crashed on landing at Stradishall on return Bremen 28.6.42.
N3756	To 15 Sqn.
N3761 BU-E	FTR Emden 6/7.6.42.
N3762 BU-C	FTR Emden 19/20.6.42.
N3764	From 15 Sqn. To 7 Sqn.
N3766	From 149 Sqn. To 1651CU.
N3767	To 1657CU.
N3768 BU-E	Crashed on take-off from Stradishall when bound for St Nazaire 17.6.42.
N3769 BU-B	To 1651CU via 214CF.
N6036	From 7 Sqn. Conversion flight only.
N6092	From 15 Sqn. Crashed on take-off from Stradishall during training 5.5.42.
N6125	From 149 Sqn via 149CF. To 1651CU via 214CF.
R9141 BU-G	To 1651CU.
R9145 BU-K	FTR Berlin 1/2.3.43.
R9146 BU-S	FTR Cologne 15/16.10.42.
R9148 BU-J	To 1651CU.
R9152 BU-C	To 1651CU.
R9155 BU-Q	FTR Kassel 27/28.8.42.
R9163 BU-C	From 149 Sqn. Abandoned over Hampshire on return from mining sortie 18.2.43.
R9165 BU-W/Y	Crashed on landing at Chedburgh on return from Turin 21.11.42.
R9166 BU-H	FTR Bremen 13/14.9.42.
R9186 BU-F	To 1651CU.
R9191 BU-O	To 1651CU.
R9194 BU-N	FTR Turin 28/29.11.42.
R9197 BU-V	FTR Hamburg 3/4.2.43.
R9198 BU-M	To 90 Sqn.
R9200	To 149 Sqn.
R9203 BU-X	From 218 Sqn. To 1651CU.
R9242 BU-O	From 149 Sqn. FTR Bochum 13/14.5.43.
R9254	From A&AEE. To 1653CU.
R9257 BU-V	From 1657CU. Crashed on take-off at Chedburgh when bound for Turin 12.8.43.
R9258 BU-W	From 7 Sqn. FTR Hanover 22/23.9.43.
R9269	From NTU. To 1657CU.
R9277	From NTU. To BDU.
R9282 BU-Q	FTR Hamburg 3/4.2.43.
R9283	From 7 Sqn. To 1657.
R9284	From 7 Sqn. To 1651CU.
R9285 BU-J	To 1665CU.
R9288 BU-Q	From 7 Sqn. Damaged at Chedburgh during take-off for Boulogne 8.9.43.
R9289	From 7 Sqn. Crashed on take-off from Tempsford when bound for SOE sortie 10.12.43.

R9303	From 15 Sqn. To 101CF via 214CF.
R9316	To 75 Sqn.
R9317 BU-U	Crashed while landing at Stradishall following return from Bremen 4.6.42.
R9319 BU-S	From 15 Sqn. Crashed on landing at Stradishall after early return from Emden 20.6.42.
R9322 BU-C	Destroyed by fire on the ground at Stradishall 3.6.42.
R9323 BU-C/D/R	To 1665CU.
R9325 BU-F	Crashed on landing at Stradishall on return from Cologne 31.5.42.
R9326 BU-G	FTR from mining sortie 12.6.42.
R9328	To 7 Sqn.
R9329	To 149 Sqn.
R9350 BU-T	FTR Essen 16/17.9.42.
R9355 BU-O	Crash-landed at Manston on return from Frankfurt 9.9.42.
R9356 BU-U	FTR Munich 19/20.9.42.
R9358 BU-E/A	Crashed soon after take-off from Chedburgh when bound for Munich 9.3.43.
W7449	From 7 Sqn. To 218CF via 214CF.
W7455	From 15 Sqn. To 1657CU.
W7459	From 218 Sqn via 1651CU. To 1651CU via 214CF.
W7465 BU-W	From 149 Sqn. To 620 Sqn.
W7526 BU-M	From 149 Sqn. Returned to 149 Sqn.
W7527 BU-B/O	To 1665CU.
W7532	To 1651CU.
W7534 BU-E	FTR Cologne 30/31.5.42.
W7537 BU-H	FTR Bremen 3/4.6.42.
W7538 BU-T	Crash-landed at Coltishall on return from Bremen 26.6.42.
W7539	To 7 Sqn.
W7560 BU-C	FTR Hamburg 26/27.7.42.
W7567 BU-S	From 149 Sqn. FTR Duisburg 23/24.7.42.
W7575	From 218 Sqn. To 90 Sqn.
W7577 BU-P	To 1651CU.
W7584 BU-D	Abandoned over Stradishall on return from Turin 21.11.42.
W7586	To 1657CU.
W7610 BU-A	To 1665CU.
W7621 BU-G	FTR Kiel 4/5.4.43.
W7626 BU-J	Crashed near Chedburgh when bound for Aachen 5.10.42.
W7627	To 90 Sqn.
W7631 BU-G	Crash-landed on approach to Chedburgh on return from Genoa 24.10.42.
W7637 BU-W	FTR Lorient 15/16.1.43.
BF313 BU-T	FTR Bremen 2/3.7.42.
BF314 BU-W	To 1651CU via 214CF.
BF318	To 1665CU.
BF324	To 90 Sqn.
BF326 BU-X	Crashed on landing at Chedburgh after aborting sortie to Stuttgart 14.4.43.
BF330 BU-H	FTR Osnabrück 17/18.8.42.
BF337 BU-B	FTR Bremen 4/5.9.42.
BF341	To 1665CU.
BF344	To 1657CU.

BF357 BU-Q	From 149 Sqn. Crashed on take-off from Chedburgh when bound for Munich 9.3.43.
BF373	To 1651CU.
BF374	To 1651CU via 214CF.
BF375	From 218 Sqn. To 1651CU.
BF377	To CRD.
BF381 BU-J/P2	FTR Duisburg 12/13.5.43.
BF382 BU-Q	To CRD.
BF404	From 90 Sqn. To 1657CU.
BF441 BU-N	Crashed on take-off from Exeter for ferry flight 18.2.43.
BF444 BU-N	To 1665CU.
BF445 BU-H	Crashed in Hertfordshire while trying to land on return from Nuremberg 26.2.43.
BF453 BU-L	FTR Berlin 27/28.3.43.
BF466 BU-B	From 90 Sqn. To 620 Sqn.
BF467	From 75 Sqn. Returned to 75 Sqn.
BF469 BU-M	From 15 Sqn. FTR Stuttgart 11/12.3.43.
BF478 BU-G	FTR Dortmund 23/24.5.43.
BF481 BU-M	To 199 Sqn.
BF511 BU-V	To 620 Sqn.
BF516 PX-E	From 75 Sqn. Ditched in Pevensey Bay on return from Nuremberg 10/11.8.43.
BF525 BU-A	To 620 Sqn.
BF528 BU-L/L2	FTR Dortmund 23/24.5.43.
BF562 BU-Q	To 622 Sqn.
BF563 BU-J	Crashed on landing at Chedburgh while training 18.6.43.
BF565	To 218 Sqn.
BF568	From 623 Sqn. To 1651CU.
BF574	To 90 Sqn.
BK592	To 7 Sqn.
BK593 BU-L	Crashed soon after take-off from Chedburgh when bound for Turin 28.11.42.
BK599 BU-R	FTR Kiel 13/14.10.42.
BK600	To 1651CU.
BK601	To 149 Sqn.
BK612 BU-Z	From 149 Sqn. FTR from mining sortie 12.4.43.
BK613	To 1657CU.
BK621	From 7 Sqn. To 1651CU.
BK653 BU-A	FTR Mannheim 16/17.4.43.
BK659 BU-N	FTR Düsseldorf 25/26.5.43.
BK662 BU-K/C	FTR Essen 5/6.3.43.
BK663	To 196 Sqn.
BK686 BU-C	FTR Essen 25/26.7.43.
BK689 BU-E	To 218 Sqn.
BK690 BU-U	To 620 Sqn.
BK693	From 90 Sqn. Returned to 90 Sqn.
BK707 BU-P	To 15 Sqn.
BK717 BU-U	FTR Cologne 3/4.7.43.
BK720 BU-Y	To 620 Sqn.
BK724	From 7 Sqn. To 620 Sqn.
BK727	From 623 Sqn. To 1651CU.
BK762	To 199 Sqn.
BK763 BU-F	To 1653CU.
BK767 BU-L	FTR Gelsenkirchen 25/26.6.43.

BK771 BU-L	To 196 Sqn.
BK800 BU-Z	To 620 Sqn.
BK801	To 620 Sqn.
BK802	To 620 Sqn.
BK808 BU-Q	Crashed on landing at Chedburgh after a training flight 19.5.43.
DJ973 BU-A	Crashed near Stradishall after early return from Bremen 25.6.42.
DJ975	To 1651CU.
EE871	To 90 Sqn.
EE874	To 196 Sqn.
EE876 BU-N	To 623 Sqn.
EE882 BU-J	FTR from mining sortie 4.7.43.
EE883 BU-T	FTR Wuppertal 24/25.6.43.
EE899 BU-O	To 623 Sqn.
EE901 BU-L	To 90 Sqn.
EE902 BU-P	FTR Hamburg 24/25.7.43.
EE906	To 620 Sqn.
EE914	To 1654CU.
EE950	To 1660CU.
EE956	To 1661CU.
EE959 BU-E	FTR Berlin 31.8/1.9.43.
EE960	To 1651CU.
EE961	To 1653CU.
EE965	To 1660CU.
EE967	To 1660CU.
EE970 BU-B	FTR Berlin 31.8/1.9.43.
EF115	To 1660CU.
EF120	To 1660CU.
EF121	To 620 Sqn.
EF125	To 1660CU.
EF199	From 623 Sqn. To 1651CU.
EF215	To 75 Sqn.
EF233	To 75 Sqn.
EF245	From 161 Sqn. To 1653CU.
EF262	To 149 Sqn.
EF271	To 199 Sqn.
EF291	To 218 Sqn.
EF329 BU-C	FTR Hamburg 3/4.3.43.
EF331 BU-H	FTR Stuttgart 14/15.4.43.
EF332	To 149 Sqn.
EF335	To 149 Sqn.
EF350	To 1665CU.
EF358 BU-Q	To 1651CU.
EF362 BU-N	Collided with BK663 (214 Sqn) over Suffolk following early return from Berlin 29.3.43.
EF363	From 7 Sqn. To 1653CU.
EF368	From 7 Sqn. To 1653CU.
EF385	To 1651CU.
EF388	From 7 Sqn. To 1651CU.
EF390 BU-A	From 7 Sqn. FTR Turin 12/13.8.43.
EF393 BU-R	From 7 Sqn. FTR Hanover 22/23.9.43.
EF394	To 620 Sqn.
EF401 BU-Y	From NTU. FTR Berlin 31.8/1.9.43.

EF402 BU-E	From 7 Sqn. FTR Hanover 27/28.9.43.
EF403	From BDU. To 1660CU.
EF404	From NTU. To 1657CU.
EF405 BU-R	From BDU. To 1660CU.
EF406	From 7 Sqn. To 1660CU.
EF407 BU-A	FTR Hamburg 29/30.7.43.
EF409 BU-V	FTR Hamburg 2/3.8.43.
EF429	To 620 Sqn.
EF433	To 620 Sqn.
EF444	To 1660CU.
EF445 BU-J	Ditched in North Sea on return from Berlin 22/23.11.43.
EF447	To 1660CU.
EF463	To 1660CU.
EF493	From 623 Sqn. To 1657CU.
EF498	To 1660CU.
EH882 BU-O	FTR Mülheim 22/23.6.43.
EH886	To 620 Sqn.
EH891	To 620 Sqn.
EH895 BU-M	FTR Berlin 23/24.8.43.
EH899 BU-D/X	To 196 Sqn.
EH921 BU-J	To 622 Sqn.
EH933	To 1660CU.
EH951	To 1660CU.
EH953	To 1653CU.
EH959	To 1660CU.
EH977	To 1660CU.
EH978	To 1660CU.
EJ123	From 623 Sqn. To 1657CU.
EJ124	From 623 Sqn. To 149 Sqn.
LJ477	From 623 Sqn. To 90 Sqn.
LJ480	To 199 Sqn.
LJ501	To 199 Sqn.
LJ509	From 623 Sqn. To 90 Sqn.
LJ517	To 218 Sqn.
LJ521	From 623 Sqn. To 218 Sqn.
LK445	To 149 Sqn.
MZ261 BU-T	FTR Dortmund 23/24.5.43.

218 (GOLD COAST) SQUADRON

Motto: In Time   Codes HA, XH

No. 218 Squadron was formed in April 1918 as a light bomber unit and moved to France in the following month. The squadron returned to the UK in February 1919 and was disbanded in June. In March 1936 the squadron was reborn from A Flight of 57 Squadron, and traded in its Hinds for battles in January 1938. The squadron moved to France on the outbreak of war as part of the Advanced Air Striking Force, but was involved in little action until the German advance into the Low Counties in may 1940. No. 218 Squadron was knocked out of the fight in a matter of days as its out-performed battles were hacked out of the sky, and the remnant returned to the UK in June 1940 to join 2 Group as a Blenheim unit. In November 1940 the squadron was posted to 3 Group, where it would remain until war's end, operating successively Wellingtons, Stirlings and Lancasters.

THE SQUADRONS 285

STATIONS

Mildenhall	13.06.40 to 18.07.40
Oakington	18.07.40 to 25.11.40
Marham	25.11.40 to 07.07.42
Downham Market	07.07.42 to 07.03.44
Woolfox Lodge	07.03.44 to 04.08.44
Methwold	04.08.44 to 05.12.44
Chedburgh	05.12.44 to 10.08.45

COMMANDING OFFICERS

Wing Commander L B Duggan	01.06.39 to 28.06.40
Wing Commander A R Combe	13.07.40 to 02.02.41
Wing Commander G N Amison	02.02.41 to 22.04.41
Wing Commander H J Kirkpatrick	22.04.41 to 31.12.41
Wing Commander P D Holder DFC	01.01.42 to 30.09.42
Wing Commander M F B Read	01.09.42 To 02.10.42
Wing Commander O A Morris	05.10.42 to 28.03.43
Wing Commander D T Saville DSO DFC	28.03.43 to 24.07.43
Wing Commander W G Oldbury DFC	27.07.43 to 09.03.44
Wing Commander R M Fenwick-Wilson AFC	09.03.44 to 21.10.44
Wing Commander W J Smith	21.10.44 to 10.08.45

AIRCRAFT

Wellington Ic	11.40 to 02.42
Wellington II	03.41 to 12.41
Stirling I	01.42 to 04.43
Stirling III	04.43 to 08.44
Lancaster I/III	08.44 to 08.45

OPERATIONAL RECORD

Operations	Sorties	Aircraft Losses	% Losses
610	5,302	130	2.5

Category of Operations

Bombing	Mining	Others
447	153	10

Wellingtons

Operations	Sorties	Aircraft Losses	% Losses
115	854	21	2.5

(All Bombing)

Stirlings

Operations	Sorties	Aircraft Losses	% Losses
340	2,600	91	3.5

Category of Operations

Bombing	Mining	Leaflet	Window
183	153	3	1

Lancasters

Operations	Sorties	Aircraft Losses	% Losses
127	1,726	16	0.9

(All Bombing)

TABLE OF STATISTICS

(Heavy squadrons.)

10th highest number of overall operations in Bomber Command.
21st highest number of sorties in Bomber Command.
22nd highest number of bombing raids in Bomber Command.
2nd highest number of mining operations in Bomber Command.
28th highest number of operational losses in Bomber Command.

Out of 42 Wellington squadrons

17th highest number of overall Wellington operations in Bomber Command.
17th highest number of Wellington sorties in Bomber Command.
23rd highest number of Wellington operational losses in Bomber Command.

Out of 59 Lancaster squadrons

38th equal(with 419 Sqn) highest number of overall Lancaster operations in Bomber Command.
38th highest number of Lancaster sorties in Bomber Command.
44th equal (with 189 and 227 Sqns) highest Lancaster operational losses in Bomber Command.

Out of 28 squadrons in 3 Group

5th highest number of overall operations in 3 Group.
5th highest number of sorties in 3 Group.
5th highest number of aircraft operational losses in 3 Group.

Out of 18 Wellington squadrons in 3 Group

10th highest number of overall Wellington operations in 3 Group.
11th highest number of Wellington sorties in 3 Group.
12th highest number of Wellington operational losses in 3 Group.

Out of 12 Stirling bomber squadrons in 3 Group

3rd highest number of overall Stirling operations in 3 Group.
2nd highest number of Stirling sorties in 3 Group.
Equal highest (with XV Sqn) number of Stirling operational losses in 3 Group.

Out of 11 Lancaster squadrons in 3 Group

7th highest number of overall Lancaster operations in 3 Group.
7th highest number of Lancaster sorties in 3 Group.
7th highest number of Lancaster operational losses in 3 Group.

AIRCRAFT HISTORIES

Wellington	From November 1940.
L4234	From 38 Sqn via 20 OTU. Became ground instruction machine 10.41.
L4293	From 148 Sqn via 15 OTU. To 1505Flt.
L7797 HA-F	From XV Sqn. To 20 OTU.
L7798 HA-S	From 115 Sqn. FTR Brest 22/23.4.41.
N2844 HA-M	FTR Duisburg 18/19.8.41.
N2937	From 75 Sqn. SOC 1.5.41.
P9207	From 115 Sqn. Crashed in Norfolk during training 13.1.41.
P9291	From 115 Sqn. To 2METS.
P9296	From 115 Sqn. To 11 OTU.

P9299 HA-R	From 115 Sqn. To Czech OTU.
R1008 HA-A	FTR Hanover 14/15.8.41.
R1009 HA-L	Crash-landed in Norfolk on return from Düsseldorf 25.2.41.
R1025 HA-B/J	To 16 OTU.
R1135 HA-S/N	FTR Kiel 15/16.11.41.
R1183	To 18 OTU.
R1210 HA-C/D	Abandoned over Westmoreland on return from Bremen 12.2.41.
R1326 HA-G	FTR Bremen 12/13.3.41.
R1328	From 12 OTU.
R1339 HA-J	From 149 Sqn. FTR Kiel 20/21.6.41.
R1346 HA-B	To 16 OTU.
R1368 HA-F	Abandoned over Norfolk on return from Brest 23.4.41.
R1400 HA-L	To 22 OTU.
R1401	To 27 OTU.
R1436 HA-M	From XV Sqn. To 20 OTU.
R1442 HA-D	FTR Brest 10/11.4.41.
R1448 HA-L/S/N	To 20 OTU.
R1496 HA-O/R	Fate uncertain. SOC 19.11.44.
R1497	To 311 Sqn.
R1507 HA-V	FTR Kiel 25/26.4.41.
R1511 HA-L	FTR Bordeaux 10/11.10.41.
R1524 HA-S	To 149 Sqn.
R1536 HA-G	FTR Duisburg 15/16.7.41.
R1594	To 311 Sqn.
R1596	From XV Sqn. SOC 1.7.44.
R1597	To 23 OTU.
R1601	To 1505BAT Flt.
R1713 HA-V	From 115 Sqn. FTR Kiel 20/21.6.41.
R1719	From 11 OTU. To 22 OTU.
R1726 HA-O	FTR Brest 24.7.41.
R3153	From 115 Sqn. Destroyed by fire on the ground at Marham 16.9.41.
T2739	From 99 Sqn. To 311 Sqn.
T2801 HA-E	To 15 OTU.
T2806 HA-T	From XV Sqn. FTR Bremen 29/30.6.41.
T2885 HA-D	Force-landed in Gloucestershire on return from Bremen 12.2.41.
T2887 HA-W	From 115 Sqn. To 22 OTU.
T2958 HA-T	Crashed in Norfolk while trying to land at Marham on return from Kiel 25.4.41.
W5400	To 99 Sqn.
W5434	To 57 Sqn.
W5445	To 9 Sqn.
W5447 HA-C	To 305 Sqn.
W5448 HA-Z	Crashed in Norfolk while training 18.5.41.
W5449 HA-Y	From XV Sqn. Crash-landed in Norfolk on return from Berlin 8.9.41.
W5457 HA-Z	FTR Duisburg 18/19.8.41.
W5526	From 115 Sqn. To 305 Sqn.
W5727 HA-V	From 40 Sqn. Crash-landed in Wiltshire after early return from Brest 11/12.12.41. Became ground instruction machine.
X3217	To 18 OTU.
X9663	To 115 Sqn and back via 149 Sqn. To 16 OTU.

X9670 HA-N	FTR Frankfurt 12/13.9.41.
X9672	To 115 Sqn.
X9674 HA-H	To 99 Sqn.
X9677 HA-V	From 115 Sqn. Ditched in Channel on return from Bordeaux 11.10.41.
X9678 HA-F	To 22 OTU.
X9679 HA-D	From 149 Sqn. To 99 Sqn.
X9745	From 57 Sqn. To 311 Sqn.
X9747 HA-E	Abandoned over Norfolk when bound for Hanover 3.8.41.
X9751	From 115 Sqn. To 304 Sqn.
X9753 HA-G	FTR Hanover 14/15.8.41.
X9755	From 115 Sqn. To 25 OTU.
X9757	From 419 Sqn. To 20 OTU.
X9785 HA-X/O	From 40 Sqn. Crash-landed in Dorset on return from Brest 15/16.12.41.
X9787 HA-S	To 99 Sqn.
X9788	To 25 OTU.
X9810 HA-K	FTR Ostend 2/3.9.41.
X9833 HA-A	Force-landed in Norfolk while training 29.10.41.
X9871	To 115 Sqn.
X9875	From 115 Sqn. Returned to 115 Sqn.
Z1069 HA-J	From 115 Sqn. FTR Berlin 7/8.11.41.
Z1070	From 115 Sqn. To 311 Sqn.
Z1101	To A&AEE.
Z1103 HA-A	Ditched off Norfolk coast on return from Emden 26/27.11.41.
Z8375 HA-Z	From 115 Sqn. To 405 Sqn.
Z8399	To 305 Sqn.
Z8431 HA-J	To 405 Sqn.
Z8437 HA-X	To 405 Sqn.
Z8781 HA-S	FTR Hanover 3/4.8.41.
Z8853 HA-H	From 115 Sqn. Force-landed in Yorkshire on return from Kiel 15/16.11.41.
Z8865 HA-O	Crashed on approach to Marham following early return from Nuremberg 15.10.41.
Z8894	From 40 Sqn. To 99 Sqn.
Z8910 HA-F	Damaged beyond repair on landing at Marham on return from Nuremberg 13.10.41.
Z8957 HA-L	Abandoned over Norfolk after early return from Duisburg 16/17.10.41.
Z8965 HA-L	From 57 Sqn. To 214 Sqn.
Z8970	To 214 Sqn.
Z8982	To 214 Sqn.
Stirling	From January 1942.
N3700 HA-O	From 7 Sqn. To 1657CU via 218CF.
N3706	To 7 Sqn.
N3708	To 7 Sqn.
N3709	To 7 Sqn.
N3710	To 7 Sqn.
N3712 HA-Y	Destroyed by exploding bomb on landing at Marham on return from Billancourt 3.3.42.
N3713	Crashed on landing at Lakenheath while training 13.2.42.
N3714 HA-Q	FTR Saarbrücken 1/2.9.42.

N3715	Crashed on landing at Marham while training 27.2.42.
N3717 HA-S	Collided with parked aircraft on landing at Marham on return from Nuremberg 29.8.42.
N3718 HA-C	FTR Bremen 2/3.7.42.
N3720 HA-B	From 7 Sqn. To 1651CU.
N3721 HA-C/S/P	To 1651CU.
N3722 HA-E	To 1657CU via 218CF.
N3725 HA-D	Crashed in Norfolk on return from Wilhelmshaven 15.9.42.
N3753 HA-U	Crash-landed at Marham after early return from Essen 2.6.42.
N3763 HA-Q	FTR Lübeck 1/2.10.42.
N6049	From 26CF. To 1651CU.
N6070 HA-A	FTR Pilsen 4/5.5.42.
N6071 HA-G	FTR from mining sortie 17/18.5.42.
N6072 HA-F/J/P	FTR Duisburg 6/7.8.42.
N6076	To XV Sqn.
N6077 HA-V	FTR from mining sortie 27/28.1.43.
N6078 HA-P	FTR Emden 22/23.6.42.
N6089 HA-L	From 26CF. To 1657CU.
N6104	From 1651CU. To 1657CU via 218CF.
N6126	To 149 Sqn.
N6127 HA-T	To 149 Sqn.
N6128 HA-T	From 26CF. To 1427CU via 218CF.
N6129 HA-X	From 7 Sqn. To 218CF. FTR Hamburg 28/29.7.42.
R9159	To 1651CU.
R9160 HA-G	FTR Kassel 27/28.8.42.
R9184 HA-U	FTR Genoa 23/24.10.42
R9185 HA-Y	FTR from mining sortie 6/7.11.42.
R9187 HA-A	FTR Vegesack 23/24.9.42.
R9189 HA-K	Crashed on take-off from Downham Market when bound for St Nazaire 28.2.43.
R9190 HA-E	FTR from mining sortie 11/12.10.42.
R9196 HA-G	To 1651CU.
R9203 HA-D	From 149 Sqn. To 214 Sqn.
R9241 HA-L	From 7 Sqn CF. Broke-up over Suffolk and crashed when bound for Milan 24.10.42.
R9244 HA-W	To 1651CU.
R9287	From 149 Sqn. To 1651CU.
R9297	To 7 Sqn.
R9298	To 7 Sqn.
R9303	From 101CF. Conversion Flt only.
R9311 HA-L	From XV Sqn. Belly-landed at Marham on return from Cologne 31.5.42.
R9313 HA-Q	From XV Sqn. Victim of friendly fire, crashed in Sussex on return from leafleting sortie to Laon 5.5.42.
R9332 HA-G	To 218CF. Crashed at Marham 31.7.42.
R9333 HA-Y	FTR Essen 5/6.3.43.
R9349	To 90 Sqn.
R9354 HA-N	Crashed on landing at Downham Market on return from Hamburg 27.7.42.
R9357 HA-E	To 218CF. FTR Düsseldorf 10/11.9.42.
W7449	From 214 Sqn via 214CF. To 1657CU.
W7451	From 7CF. Conversion Flt only. To 1657CU.
W7454	From 26CF. To 1657CU via 218CF.

W7459	From 26CF. To 214 Sqn via 1651.
W7464 HA-Z	From 15 Sqn. To 218CF. FTR Hamburg 28/29.7.42.
W7466	To 7 Sqn.
W7467	To 7 Sqn.
W7468	To 7 Sqn.
W7469 HA-M	To 149 Sqn.
W7473 HA-F	Crashed in Norfolk when bound for Rostock 23.4.42.
W7474 HA-K	FTR Bremen 3/4.6.42.
W7475 HA-H	FTR Hamburg 9/10.11.42.
W7502 HA-N	FTR Cologne 30/31.5.42.
W7503 HA-B/R	FTR Bremen 25/26.6.42.
W7506 HA-K	FTR Pilsen 25/26.4.42.
W7507 HA-P	Damaged beyond repair during operation to Lübeck 28.3.42.
W7521 HA-U	Crash-landed in Norfolk on return from Stuttgart 5.5.42.
W7530 HA-Q	From 149 Sqn. FTR Emden 20/21.6.42.
W7535 HA-C	FTR Gennevilliers 29/30.5.42.
W7562 HA-R	FTR Frankfurt 24/25.8.42.
W7568 HA-D	Crashed in Suffolk when bound for Mainz 11.8.42.
W7571	From 1427Flt. Conversion Flt only. To 1427Flt.
W7573 HA-U	FTR from mining sortie 20/21.8.42.
W7575	To 214 Sqn.
W7612 HA-T	Crashed while trying to land at Tangmere on return from a leafleting sortie to France 9.11.42.
W7613 HA-N	FTR Lübeck 1/2.10.42.
W7614 HA-J	FTR Fallersleben 17/18.12.42.
W7615 HA-M	FTR from mining sortie 20/21.8.42.
W7618 HA-V	FTR Flensburg 18/19.8.42.
W7622 HA-B	To 1657CU.
W7636 HA-L	Crashed on take-off from Downham Market when bound for Krefeld 2.10.42.
BF309 HA-M	FTR Hamburg 28/29.7.42.
BF315 HA-F	FTR Kassel 27/28.8.42.
BF319 HA-C	FTR from mining sortie 20/21.8.42.
BF322 HA-F	Crashed in Suffolk when bound for Aachen 5.10.42.
BF338 HA-Q	FTR from mining sortie 20/21.8.42.
BF343 HA-M	FTR Stuttgart 11/12.3.43.
BF346 HA-S	To 90 Sqn.
BF349	From 149 Sqn. To 1651CU.
BF351 HA-C	FTR Düsseldorf 10/11.9.42.
BF375 HA-O	To 214 Sqn.
BF385	To 1651CU.
BF395 HA-Z	To 1651CU.
BF401 HA-N	Crashed on landing at Downham Market on return from Frankfurt 2.12.42.
BF403 HA-R	FTR Fallersleben 17/18.12.42.
BF404	To 90 Sqn.
BF405 HA-U	FTR from mining sortie 27/28.5.43.
BF406 HA-Q/E	FTR Hamburg 3/4.2.43.
BF408 HA-T	FTR Hamburg 3/4.2.43.
BF413 HA-H	To 1651CU.
BF416 HA-T	From 149 Sqn. To 1651CU.
BF440 HA-U/T	Crash-landed at Downham Market on return from Remscheid 31.7.43.
BF446 HA-B/H	To 1665CU.

BF447 HA-F	FTR from mining sortie 28/29.4.43.
BF450 HA-X	FTR Nuremberg 25/26.2.43.
BF452 HA-V	To 1657CU.
BF468 HA-K	To 1657CU.
BF472 HA-D	FTR Hanover 27/28.9.43.
BF473	To 90 Sqn.
BF480 HA-I	Crashed on landing at Downham Market on return from Bochum 14.5.43.
BF501 HA-N	From 7 Sqn. FTR Wuppertal 24/25.6.43.
BF502 HA-P	FTR Duisburg 8/9.4.43.
BF505 HA-Z	FTR Dortmund 4/5.5.43.
BF514 HA-X	FTR Mannheim 16/17.4.43.
BF515 HA-N	FTR from mining sortie 28/29.4.43.
BF519 HA-E	FTR Remscheid 30/31.7.43.
BF522 HA-N	FTR Berlin 23/24.8.43.
BF565 HA-H	From 214 Sqn. FTR Wuppertal 29/30.5.43.
BF567 HA-P	FTR Hamburg 24/25.7.43.
BF568 HA-B	To 623 Sqn.
BF572 HA-K	FTR Mülheim 22/23.6.43.
BF578 HA-A	FTR Hamburg 29/30.7.43.
BK596 HA-B	FTR Rostock 20/21.4.43.
BK597	From 149 Sqn. To 1651CU.
BK606 HA-N	Crashed in Cambridgeshire on return from Genoa 8.11.42.
BK607HA-X	Crashed on landing at Downham Market after early return from Turin 29.11.42.
BK650HA-L/T	FTR Mönchengladbach 30/31.8.43.
BK666HA-Q	Crashed in Norfolk on return from Berlin 2.3.43.
BK687HA-R	FTR Bremen 8/9.10.43.
BK688HA-A	FTR Wuppertal 29/30.5.43.
BK689	From 214 Sqn. To 1657CU.
BK700HA-W/L	FTR Hanover 22/23.9.43.
BK702HA-O	FTR Berlin 29/30.3.43.
BK705HA-K	FTR Duisburg 12/13.5.43.
BK706HA-Y	FTR Dortmund 23/24.5.43.
BK712HA-D	FTR Krefeld 21/22.6.43.
BK716HA-J	FTR Berlin 29/30.3.43.
BK722HA-G	FTR Krefeld 21/22.6.43.
BK727	To 623 Sqn.
BK761	From 7 Sqn. To 1661CU.
BK803	To 623 Sqn.
DJ974 HA-T	FTR Bremen 27/28.6.42.
DJ976 HA-A	To 1657CU.
DJ977 HA-F	FTR Mannheim 19/20.5.42.
EE884 HA-X/B	FTR Mannheim/Ludwigshafen 18/19.11.43.
EE885 HA-G	FTR Nuremberg 10/11.8.43.
EE888 HA-H/K	FTR from mining sortie 16/17.12.43.
EE895 HA-S	FTR Hamburg 29/30.7.43.
EE903 HA-Q	FTR Mönchengladbach 30/31.8.43.
EE909 HA-H	To 623 Sqn.
EE937 HA-S/A	FTR Hanover 27/28.9.43.
EE941	To 199 Sqn.
EE943	To 199 Sqn.
EE944 HA-O/H	Crashed while trying to land at Tempsford on return from SOE sortie 5.3.44.

EE949	To 623 Sqn.
EE966	To 623 Sqn.
EF124	To 149 Sqn.
EF133 HA-A	From 15 Sqn. To 149 Sqn.
EF139 HA-B	From 623 Sqn. FTR Hanover 22/23.9.43.
EF141 HA-H/N	To 1654CU.
EF180 HA-D	FTR Berlin 22/23.11.43.
EF181 HA-J	From 75 Sqn. Crashed on take-off from Woolfox Lodge when bound for mining sortie 12.6.44.
EF184 HA-L/V/I	Crash-landed at Woodbridge on return from Chambly 2.5.44.
EF185 HA-L	To 149 Sqn.
EF207 HA-F	From 75 Sqn. To 149 Sqn.
EF233	From 75 Sqn. To 149 Sqn.
EF249 HA-H	Crashed on landing at Woolfox Lodge on return from mining sortie 9.5.44.
EF259 HA-G	FTR Chambly 1/2.5.44.
EF291 HA-C	From 214 Sqn. To 1653CU.
EF299 HA-Z	From 1657CU. Crashed on landing at Woolfox Lodge on return from mining sortie 13.6.44.
EF340	To 149 Sqn.
EF346	To 90 Sqn.
EF349	To 90 Sqn.
EF352 HA-Q	To 1657CU.
EF353 HA-O	To 1657CU.
EF356 HA-O	FTR from mining sortie 28/29.4.43.
EF365 HA-G/U	Crash-landed in Norfolk during air-test 31.5.43.
EF367 HA-G	Crashed at Chedburgh on return from Bochum 13/14.5.43.
EF410 HA-Z	To 1653CU.
EF413	To 1654CU.
EF425 HA-C	Crashed on take-off from Downham Market when bound for air-test 15.9.43.
EF430 HA-W	FTR Gelsenkirchen 25/26.6.43.
EF448 HA-P	FTR Nuremberg 27/28.8.43.
EF449 HA-J/D	To 1660CU.
EF452 HA-V/O	Crash-landed in Algeria after being shot-up by another Stirling during Turin operation 13.8.43. Posthumous VC awarded to F/S Aaron.
EF462	From 75 Sqn. To 1653CU.
EF489	To 623 Sqn.
EF504 HA-P	FTR Chambly 1/2.5.44.
EH878 HA-I	To 623 Sqn.
EH884 HA-X	FTR Turin 16/17.8.43.
EH887 HA-Z	FTR Düsseldorf 25/26.5.43.
EH892 HA-U	FTR Wuppertal 24/25.6.43.
EH898 HA-G	FTR Gelsenkirchen 25/26.6.43.
EH923 HA-W/E	To 1654CU.
EH925	3.7.43. To 623 Sqn.
EH926	To 199 Sqn.
EH940	From 15 Sqn. To 1661CU.
EH942 HA-M	FTR Laon 22/23.4.44.
EH982	From 90 Sqn. To 149 Sqn.
EH984 HA-C	FTR Kassel 3/4.10.43.
EH986 HA-X	FTR Berlin 23/24.8.43.

EH988	To 1661CU.
EJ104 HA-G	FTR Mannheim 23/24.9.43.
EJ105 HA-N	Crashed in Suffolk on return from Hanover 22/23.9.43.
EJ112 HA-Q	To 1651CU.
EJ125 HA-J	FTR from mining sortie 21/22.2.44.
LJ446	To 1653CU.
LJ447 HA-F	To 149 Sqn.
LJ448 HA-D	FTR Chambly 20/21.4.44.
LJ449 HA-E	To 149 Sqn.
LJ452 HA-S	To 1651CU.
LJ472 HA-K	To 149 Sqn.
LJ481 HA-B	To 149 Sqn.
LJ506	From 90 Sqn. To 1657CU.
LJ517 HA-U	From 214 Sqn. To 1657CU.
LJ521 HA-W	From 214 Sqn. To 1657CU.
LJ522 HA-N	To 149 Sqn.
LJ568	To 149 Sqn.
LJ625	From 90 Sqn. To 149 Sqn.
LJ632	To 149 Sqn.
LK396 HA-M	From 75 Sqn. To 149 Sqn.
LK401 HA-I	To 149 Sqn.
LK568 HA-O	From 90 Sqn. To 149 Sqn.
MZ263HA-B	Crash-landed at St Eval on return from mining sortie 17.12.43.

Lancaster	From August 1944.
LM187 XH-H	From 90 Sqn. Crashed in Belgium while returning from Neuss 7.1.45.
LM257 HA-P	
LM258	From 514 Sqn. FTR Vincly 25.8.44.
LM281 HA-F/T/E	FTR Cologne 28.1.45.
LM282 XH-C	From 622 Sqn. To 138 Sqn.
LM577 HA-Q	From 622 Sqn.
LM753 XH-B	From 195 Sqn.
ME303 XH-K	From 622 Sqn.
ME350 HA-L	To 138 Sqn
ME352	To 149 Sqn.
ME428	To 550 Sqn.
ME438 HA-H/XH-H	
ME545 XH-L	
ME842 HA-G/R	From 514 Sqn.
ME860 XH-G	From 90 Sqn.
NF906 HA-B	FTR Frankfurt 12/13.9.44.
NF911 HA-F	FTR Frankfurt 12/13.9.44.
NF916	To XV Sqn.
NF926 HA-X	FTR Vohwinkel 31.12.44.
NF934	FTR Witten 12.12.44.
NF955 HA-H	Crashed on take-off from Chedburgh when bound for Bad Oldesloe 24.4.45.
NF956 HA-E	
NF994 HA-N	Crashed while trying to land at Chedburgh following early return from Bremen 22.4.45.
NG187 HA-J	From 195 Sqn. To 138 Sqn.
NG330 HA-M	FTR Vohwinkel 31.12.44.

NG335	To 149 Sqn
NG362	To 149 Sqn.
NG450 XH-B/HA-B	From 195 Sqn. FTR Gelsenkirchen 22.2.45.
NG462 HA-B	
NG463 HA-F/XH-F	
NN704 HA-S	From XV Sqn. To 514 Sqn.
NN706 HA-A	To 115 Sqn.
NN716 XH-A/Y	
PB259 HA-A	From 514 Sqn. To XV Sqn.
PB291 HA-O/C	From 514 Sqn.
PB352	From 460 Sqn.
PB674 HA-Q	From XV Sqn. FTR Witten 12.12.44.
PB721	To 115 Sqn.
PB766 XH-C	Ditched off Felixstowe on return from Witten 12.12.44.
PB768 XH-B	FTR Vohwinkel. Shot down by US flak 2.1.45.
PB837	To 195 Sqn.
PD223 HA-U	
PD229 XH-D	From 622 Sqn.
PD234	To XV Sqn.
PD252 HA-D	FTR Rüsselsheim 12/13.8.44.
PD256 HA-B/J/X	To 514 Sqn.
PD262 HA-G	FTR Frankfurt 12/13.9.44.
PD277 HA-A	To 115 Sqn.
PD278 HA-V	FTR Dessau 7/8.3.45.
PD279 HA-W	
PD288 HA-H/XH-F	To 514 Sqn.
PD296 HA-B	FTR Cologne 28.1.45.
PD323 HA-K	
PD364 HA-R/T	To 149 Sqn.
PD374 HA-C	FTR Homburg 8.11.44.
PD426	To 195 Sqn.
PD439 XH-J	To 514 Sqn.
PD440	To 90 Sqn.
RA522 HA-V	From 186 Sqn.
RA532 HA-L/XH-L	Emergency landing at Brussels-Evere on return from Gelsenkirchen 19.3.45. Damaged beyond repair.
RF133 HA-M	
SW269HA-R	

311 SQUADRON

Motto: Na mnozstui nehledte (Never regard their numbers)   Code KX, PP

No. 311 Squadron was formed as a bomber unit at the end of July 1940 and manned by Czechoslovak personnel. For the first year a British advisor was appointed to work alongside the Czech commanding officer to help with RAF procedures and administration. The squadron served with 3 Group until being posted to Coastal Command in April 1942.

STATIONS

Honington	29.07.40 to 16.09.40
East Wretham	16.09.40 to 28.04.42

COMMANDING OFFICERS

Wing Commander P C Pickard (British Adviser)   29.07.40 to 05.41
Wing Commander K Toman-Mares   29.07.40 to 19.03.41
Wing Commander J Schejbal   19.03.41 to 03.07.41
Wing Commander K S Batchelor (British Adviser)   05.41 to 28.07.41
Wing Commander J Ocelka   03.07.41 to 20.04.42

AIRCRAFT

Wellington Ia/Ic   08.40 to 07.43

To Coastal Command   28.04.42

OPERATIONAL RECORD

Operations	Sorties	Aircraft Losses	% Losses
152	1,029	19	1.8
	(All bombing)		

TABLE OF STATISTICS

Out of 42 Wellington squadrons

14th highest number of overall Wellington operations.
16th highest number of Wellington sorties.
25th highest number of Wellington operational losses.

Out of 28 squadrons in 3 Group

14th highest number of overall operations in 3 Group.
16th highest number of sorties in 3 Group.
18th highest number of aircraft operational losses in 3 Group.

Out of 18 Wellington squadrons in 3 Group

8th highest number of overall Wellington operations in 3 Group.
10th highest number of Wellington sorties in 3 Group.
13th highest number of Wellington operational losses in 3 Group.

AIRCRAFT HISTORIES

Wellington	From July 1940.
L4332	From 214 Sqn. To 11 OTU.
L4338	From 214 Sqn. To 11 OTU.
L4343	From 15 Sqn. To 20 OTU.
L7776	To CGS.
L7778	From 9 Sqn. To 15 OTU.
L7785	From 9 Sqn. To CGS.
L7786	From 9 Sqn. Crashed in Suffolk during training 17.10.40.
L7788	From 9 Sqn. FTR Berlin 23/24.9.40.
L7806	From 149 Sqn. To 18 OTU.
L7841	To Czech TU and back via 1429Flt. Crashed on landing at East Wretham 24.2.42.
L7842 KX-T	FTR Boulogne 6/7.2.41.
L7844	FTR Kiel 16/17.10.40.
L7847	From 99 Sqn. To ATA.

L7852	To 9 Sqn.
L7895	To 115 Sqn.
N2752	From 15 Sqn. Returned to 15 Sqn.
N2771	Iced up and crashed in Middlesex when bound for Kiel 16.10.40.
N2772	To 21 OTU.
N2773	Abandoned over Nottinghamshire on return from Kiel 17.10.40.
N2775	From 149 Sqn. To 1429Flt.
N2880	From 38 Sqn. To CLE.
N2885	From 115 Sqn. To 20 OTU.
N2938	From 57 Sqn. To 12 OTU.
N3000	From 40 Sqn. To 12 OTU.
N3007	From 214 Sqn. To 20 OTU.
N3010 KX-L	From 214 Sqn. Crashed soon after take-off from Langham during training 25.5.41.
P2525	From 214 Sqn. To 15 OTU.
P9209	From 75 Sqn. To 57 Sqn.
P9212	From New Zealand Flt. Crashed near Honington during training 16.4.41.
P9224	From 115 Sqn. To Czech TU.
P9226	From 115 Sqn. To 12 OTU.
P9230	From 115 Sqn. To CGS.
P9235	From 115 Sqn. To RAE.
R1015 KX-L	FTR Hamburg 15/16.9.41.
R1021	To 7 OTU.
R1022	To 11 OTU.
R1034	To 115 Sqn.
R1036	To 22 OTU.
R1046 KX-L	From 214 Sqn. FTR Bremen 20/21.10.41.
R1137	To SFP.
R1161	From 75 Sqn. To 105 OTU.
R1225	To 9 Sqn.
R1228	From 305 Sqn. To 21 OTU.
R1371 KX-F	FTR Hanover 19/20.7.41.
R1378 KX-K	Crashed while landing at East Wretham on return from Bremen 18.3.41.
R1410	To 12 OTU.
R1441	To 57 Sqn.
R1451	To 18 OTU.
R1466	To 75 Sqn.
R1497	From 218 Sqn. Became a ground instruction machine.
R1516 KX-U	Shot down by friendly fighter over Somerset during operation to Cherbourg 1/2.7.41.
R1523	From 3PRU. To 20 OTU.
R1532	To 27 OTU.
R1594	From 218 Sqn. Destroyed by fire 27.6.41. Details uncertain.
R1598	To 3 OTU.
R1599 KX-J	FTR Berlin 17/18.4.41.
R1600	From 11 OTU. To 232 Sqn after conversion.
R1718 KX-N	FTR Hamburg 16/17.7.41.
R1771	From 75 Sqn. To 1429Flt and back. To 1429Flt.
R1777	To 21 OTU.
R1802 KX-P	From 149 Sqn. FTR Kiel 12/13.3.42.

R1804	Crashed on take-off from East Wretham for air test 19.7.41.
R3166	From 75 Sqn. To 21 OTU.
R3177	Lost 28.10.40. Details uncertain.
R3206	From 149 Sqn. To 1429Flt.
R3218	From 75 Sqn. To 1429Flt.
R3230	To 9 Sqn.
R3234	To 1429Flt.
R3277	To 75 Sqn.
T2467	To 27 OTU.
T2468	From 40 Sqn. To 1429Flt.
T2469	To 214 Sqn.
T2519 KX-Y	FTR Wilhelmshaven 16/17.1.41.
T2553 KX-B	FTR Wilhelmshaven 28/29.12.41.
T2561	To 20 OTU.
T2564	To 9 Sqn. Returned to 311 Sqn via 11 OTU and 140 Sqn. Crashed near Northolt 18.10.42.
T2577	Crashed soon after take-off from East Wretham when bound for Mannheim 16.12.40.
T2578	To 9 Sqn.
T2613	To 115 Sqn.
T2624	From 15 Sqn via Czech TU. Ditched in Irish Sea during training 23.10.41.
T2716	To 40 Sqn.
T2739	From 218 Sqn. To 21 Sqn.
T2962	From 57 Sqn. To 21 OTU.
T2971 KX-J	FTR Bremen 17/18.1.42.
T2972	To ATA.
T2990 KX-T	FTR Bremen 22/23.6.41.
W5668	From 304 Sqn. To 1420Flt.
W5682 KX-Y	Crash-landed in Devon on return from Brest 9/10.1.42.
W5711	To 105 OTU.
X3178	From 21 OTU. SOC 1.11.44.
X3221	To 57 Sqn.
X3281	From 9 Sqn. Returned to 9 Sqn.
X9664	From 304 Sqn. To 21 OTU.
X9733	From 149 Sqn. To 105 OTU.
X9741	To 1505Flt.
X9742	To 75 Sqn.
X9745	From 218 Sqn. To 303FTU.
X9760	From 57 Sqn. SOC 1.6.44.
X9787	From 156 Sqn. FTR Essen 1/2.6.42.
X9803	From 11 OTU. To 1473Flt.
X9806	From 75 Sqn. To 1429Flt.
X9827	From 304 Sqn. To 303FTU.
X9871	From 150 Sqn. To 23 OTU.
X9877	From 149 Sqn. To 7 OTU.
X9880	From 156 Sqn. To 21 OTU.
X9888	To 115 Sqn.
Z1070 KX-Y	From 218 Sqn. FTR Billancourt Renault Factory in Paris 3/4.3.42.
Z1090	From 156 Sqn. Posted with squadron to Coastal Command in April 1942.
Z1098 KX-U	FTR Dortmund 14/15.4.42.

Z1105	Posted with squadron to Coastal Command in April 1942.
Z1110	To 101 Sqn.
Z1111	To 7 OTU.
Z1147	From 57 Sqn. Posted with squadron to Coastal Command in April 1942.
Z1155	Posted with squadron to Coastal Command in April 1942.
Z1167 KX-A	FTR Emden 3/4.3.42.
Z8784	To 21 OTU.
Z8805	To 214 Sqn.
Z8832	From 18 OTU. To 304 Sqn.
Z8837	From 156 Sqn. To 25 OTU.
Z8838 KX-Z	From 149 Sqn. FTR Essen 10/11.4.42.
Z8845	To 9 Sqn.
Z8853	To 9 Sqn.
Z8966 KX-E	Ditched in Irish Sea on return from Kiel 15/16.11.41.
DV474	From 22 OTU. To 104 OTU.
DV507	From 156 Sqn via 15 OTU.
DV515 KX-D	FTR Bremen 21/22.1.42.
DV516	To 6 OTU.
DV664	To 7 OTU.
DV665	Posted with squadron to Coastal Command in April 1942.
DV716	Posted with squadron to Coastal Command in April 1942.
DV738	From 214 Sqn. To 232 Sqn after conversion.
DV757	To 18 OTU.
DV779	Posted with squadron to Coastal Command in April 1942.
DV886	To 7 OTU.
DV922	To 304 Sqn.

419 (MOOSE) SQUADRON

Motto: Moosa Aswayita (Beware of the moose)   Code VR

No. 419 Squadron Royal Canadian Air Force was born out of Article XV of the British Commonwealth Air Training Plan (BCATP) Agreement, which was signed on the 7th of January 1941, and called for the formation of twenty-five Canadian squadrons by May 1942. All such units were to be numbered in the 400 series, and 419 Squadron was the third to be formed in Bomber Command after 405 and 408 Squadrons. The former found its first home in 4 Group, and the latter in 5 Group, while 419 Squadron became the first from Canada to enter 3 Group. Equipped with Wellingtons the squadron served in the front line until being posted to 4 Group in August 1942. It became a founder member of the Canadian 6 Group on New Year's Day 1943, and took part in the main offensive until war's end.

STATIONS

Mildenhall   15.12.41 to 12.08.42

COMMANDING OFFICERS

Wing Commander J Fulton DSO DFC AFC	21.12.41 to 29.07.42
Squadron Leader Wolfe (Temp)	29.07.42 to 05.08.42
Wing Commander Ap Walsh DFC AFC	05.08.42 to 03.09.42

AIRCRAFT

Wellington Ic	01.42 to 11.42
Wellington III	02.42 to 11.42
Posted to 4 Group	12.08.42

OPERATIONAL RECORD

Operations	Sorties	Aircraft Losses	% Losses
88	648	24	3.7

Category of Operations

Bombing	Mining	Other
67	18	3

Eleven of the above Wellington operations were flown under 4 Group following the departure from 3 Group on 12.8.42. The number of 4 Group sorties is not known, but nine Wellingtons were lost as a result of operations, and three others were written off in non-operational incidents.

TABLE OF STATISTICS

Out of 42 Wellington squadrons

22nd equal (with 37 Sqn) highest number of Wellington overall operations in Bomber Command.
24th highest number of Wellington sorties in Bomber Command.
22nd highest number of Wellington operational losses in Bomber Command.

Out of 28 squadrons in 3 Group

22nd highest number of overall operations in 3 Group.
21st highest number of sorties in 3 Group.
18th equal (with 37 Sqn) highest number of aircraft operational losses in 3 Group.

Out of 18 Wellington squadrons in 3 Group

14th equal highest number of Wellington overall operations in 3 Group.
14th highest number of Wellington sorties in 3 Group.
12th equal (with 37 Sqn) highest number of Wellington operational losses in 3 Group.

AIRCRAFT HISTORIES

Wellington	From January 1942.
L4356	From 214 Sqn. To GRU.
R1801	From 101 Sqn. To 12 OTU.
X3201	From 149 Sqn. To 22 OTU.
X3277 VR-F	From 9 Sqn. To 101 Sqn.
X3308 VR-O	Ditched off Suffolk coast on return from Bremen 14.9.42.
X3344	From 115 Sqn. To 17 OTU.
X3357 VR-T	To 196 Sqn.
X3359 VR-N	From 75 Sqn. FTR Essen 16/17.6.42.
X3360 VR-R	FTR Essen 5/6.8.42.
X3390	From 75 Sqn. To 214 Sqn and back. To 57 Sqn and back. To 427 Sqn.
X3404	To 16 OTU.
X3416 VR-J	From 115 Sqn. FTR Duisburg 13/14.7.42.
X3420	From 75 Sqn. To 426 Sqn.

X3451	From 150 Sqn. To 75 Sqn.
X3467 VR-N	FTR Hamburg 8/9.4.42.
X3470 VR-E	From 9 Sqn. To 23 OTU.
X3477 VR-G	From 75 Sqn. FTR Lübeck 28/29.3.42.
X3480	From 429 Sqn. FTR Warnemünde 8/9.5.42.
X3481	To 25 OTU.
X3483 VR-S	To 23 OTU.
X3484 VR-O	FTR Dortmund 14/15.4.42.
X3486 VR-U	FTR Essen 5/6.6.42.
X3488 VR-H	From 75 Sqn. FTR Hamburg 28/29.7.42.
X3541	To 101 Sqn.
X3556 VR-L	Crashed in Huntingdonshire while training 6.7.42.
X3562	To 427 Sqn.
X3563 VR-T	To 427 Sqn.
X3592 VR-E	From 115 Sqn. To 23 OTU.
X3659 VR-B	To 427 Sqn.
X3699 VR-V	To 426 Sqn.
X3703 VR-Q	FTR Warnemünde 8/9.5.42.
X3711 VR-R	FTR Karlsruhe 2/3.9.42.
X3712 VR-D	FTR Saarbrücken 29/30.7.42.
X3715 VR-G	FTR Gennevilliers 29/30.5.42.
X3717 VR-C	FTR Stuttgart 6/7.5.42.
X3723 VR-H	FTR Essen 16/17.6.42.
X3726	To 57 Sqn.
X3727	To 27 OTU.
X3752	To 427 Sqn.
X3796 VR-C	Crashed in Lincolnshire during air-test 15.9.42.
X3840 VR-J	FTR Warnemünde 8/9.5.42.
X3873	To 427 Sqn.
X9748	From 57 Sqn. To 23 OTU.
X9757	From 75 Sqn. To 218 Sqn.
X9819	From 101 Sqn. To 18 OTU.
X9874	From 57 Sqn. To 12 OTU.
X9920	From 101 Sqn. To 1474Flt.
X9975	From 20 OTU. Returned to 20 OTU.
Z1053 VR-F	From 57 Sqn. To 23 OTU.
Z1067 VR-C	From 57 Sqn. To 23 OTU.
Z1077 VR-P	From 75 Sqn. Crashed on landing at Mildenhall on return from Essen 10.3.42.
Z1083 VR-O	From 75 Sqn. To 23 OTU.
Z1091 VR-A	From 57 Sqn. FTR from shipping strike (Channel Dash) 12.2.42.
Z1095 VR-Q	From 101 Sqn. To 214 Sqn.
Z1145 VR-A	From 57 Sqn. Ditched off Spurn Head on return from Hamburg 15/16.1.42.
Z1146 VR-E	From 101 Sqn. FTR from shipping strike (Channel Dash) 12.2.42.
Z1562 VR-N	From Tempsford. FTR from mining sortie 17/18.5.42.
Z1572 VR-Q	From 75 Sqn. To 427 Sqn.
Z1597 VR-T	Crashed in Wiltshire on return from mining sortie 6/7.7.42.
Z1599	To 426 Sqn.
Z1604	To 427 Sqn.
Z1623 VR-V	FTR Aachen 5/6.10.42.
Z1626 VR-G	To 427 Sqn.

Z1676	To 427 Sqn.
Z1680	From 29 OTU. To 426 Sqn.
Z1727	To 156 Sqn.
Z8800	From 57 Sqn. To 12 OTU.
Z8899	From 99 Sqn. To 22 OTU.
Z8964	From 99 Sqn. To 20 OTU.
Z8967 VR-E	From 99 Sqn. To 21 OTU.
Z8980	From 99 Sqn. To 20 OTU.
Z8981 VR-H	From 57 Sqn. To 20 OTU.
Z9757 VR-N	
Z9894 VR-G	
Z9920 VR-Z	
BJ602 VR-J	FTR Bremen 4/5.9.42.
BJ604 VR-A	To 427 Sqn.
BJ643	To 156 Sqn.
BJ668 VR-X	To 427 Sqn.
BJ729 VR-R	FTR Aachen 5/6.10.42.
BJ778	To 427 Sqn.
BJ886	To 427 Sqn.
BJ887 VR-H	Destroyed at Topcliffe when struck by 405 Sqn Halifax BB212 returning from Düsseldorf 11.9.42.
BJ919	To 426 Sqn.
BK268	To 427 Sqn.
BK269 VR-C	FTR Krefeld 2/3.10.42.
BK270	FTR Cologne 15/16.10.42.
BK276	To 427 Sqn.
BK335 VR-Y	Crashed on approach to Croft while training 10.10.42.
BK343	To 427 Sqn.
BK364	To 427 Sqn.
BK389	To 427 Sqn.
DF664 VR-E	FTR Kiel 13/14.10.42.
DF665 VR-Q	FTR Saarbrücken 28/29.8.42.
DV509 VR-S	From 101 Sqn. To 214 Sqn.

514 SQUADRON

Motto: Nil obstare potest (Nothing can withstand)　　　　　Codes JI, A2

Formed on the 1st of September 1943, 514 Squadron was equipped initially with Mk II Lancasters and later Mk I/III. The squadron took part in 3 Group operations until the end of hostilities.

STATIONS

Foulsham	01.09.43 to 23.11.43
Waterbeach	23.11.43 to 22.08.45

COMMANDING OFFICERS

Wing Commander A J Sampson DFC	01.09.43 to 15.05.44
Squadron Leader E G B Reid (Temp)	15.05.44 to 24.05.44
Wing Commander M Wyatt DFC	24.05.44 to 01.45
Wing Commander P I B Morgan	01.45 to 22.08.45

AIRCRAFT

Lancaster II   09.43 to 06.44
Lancaster I/III   06.44 to 08.45

OPERATIONAL RECORD

Operations	Sorties	Aircraft Losses	% Losses
222	3,675	66	1.8

Category of Operations

Bombing	Mining
218	4

TABLE OF STATISTICS

Out of 59 Lancaster squadrons

24th highest number of Lancaster overall operations in Bomber Command.
19th highest number of Lancaster sorties in Bomber Command.
23rd highest number of Lancaster operational losses in Bomber Command.

Out of 28 squadrons in 3 Group

11th highest number of overall operations in 3 Group.
7th highest number of sorties in 3 Group.
8th equal (with 9 Sqn) highest number of aircraft operational losses in 3 Group.

Out of 11 Lancaster squadrons in 3 Group

4th highest number of overall Lancaster operations in 3 Group.
3rd highest number of Lancaster sorties in 3 Group.
2nd highest number of Lancaster operational losses in 3 Group.

AIRCRAFT HISTORIES

Lancaster	From September 1943.
DS633 JI-B	FTR Duisburg 21/22.5.44.
DS669 JI-C	From 115 Sqn. FTR Düsseldorf 22/23.4.44.
DS682 JI-N	From 115 Sqn. FTR Düsseldorf 22/23.4.44.
DS706 JI-G	FTR Berlin 30/31.1.44.
DS735 JI-A	FTR Berlin 30/31.1.44.
DS736 JI-D	FTR Leipzig 19/20.2.44.
DS738 JI-J	FTR Berlin 2/3.12.43.
DS781 JI-R	From 115 Sqn. FTR Duisburg 21/22.5.44.
DS783	To 5MU.
DS784 JI-C	From 115 Sqn. FTR Mannheim 18/19.11.43.
DS785 JI-D	FTR Schweinfurt 24/25.2.44.
DS786	To 1668CU.
DS787 JI-G	FTR Kamen 11.9.44.
DS795	From 115 Sqn. Returned to 115 Sqn.
DS796	To 115 Sqn.
DS813 JI-N	FTR Stuttgart 28/29.7.44.
DS814 JI-M	FTR Berlin 26/27.11.43.

DS815 JI-N	FTR Frankfurt 22/23.3.44.
DS816 JI-O	FTR Valenciennes 15/16.6.44.
DS817 JI-P	FTR Frankfurt 20/21.12.43.
DS818 JI-Q	FTR Gelsenkirchen 12/13.6.44.
DS820 JI-R	Crashed on landing at Martlesham Heath while training 17.3.44.
DS821 JI-S	Ditched on return from Berlin 29/30.12.43.
DS822 JI-T	FTR Massy-Palaiseau 7/8.6.44.
DS823 JI-M	FTR Leipzig 19/20.2.44.
DS824 JI-K	FTR Magdeburg 21/22.1.44.
DS825	No operations. To 115 Sqn.
DS826	No operations. To 1678CU and back. To 1668CU.
DS828 JI-D	To 1678CU and back. FTR Düsseldorf 22/23.4.44.
DS834	To 115 Sqn.
DS836 JI-L	From 115 Sqn. FTR Nuremberg 30/31.3.44.
DS842	To 1668CU.
HK570 JI-P	FTR Homburg 20/21.7.44.
HK571 JI-L	FTR Homburg 20/21.7.44.
JB228	From 156 Sqn. To 1668CU.
JB475	From 7 Sqn. To 15 Sqn.
LL620 JI-T	FTR Villers Bocage 30.6.44.
LL624 JI-B	From 115 Sqn. Damaged beyond repair during an after fourth crash and SOC 28.9.44.
LL625 JI-C	FTR Berlin 24/25.3.44.
LL627 JI-U	FTR Magdeburg 21/22.1.44.
LL635	From A&AEE. Damaged beyond repair during an operation to Vincly 25.8.44.
LL639 JI-R	From 115 Sqn. FTR Aachen 11/12.4.44.
LL641 JI-K	Crashed in Cambridgeshire on return from Le Mans 20.5.44.
LL644	To 115 Sqn.
LL645 A2-R	Crashed while trying to land at Waterbeach on return from Nuremberg 31.3.44.
LL650	To 115 Sqn.
LL652 JI-C	From 115 Sqn. FTR Aachen 27/28.5.44.
LL653 JI-E	FTR Stuttgart 15/16.3.44.
LL666	From 115 Sqn. To 1668CU.
LL667	To 115 Sqn.
LL668	To 115 Sqn.
LL669 JI-S	From 115 Sqn. Crash-landed after overshooting Woodbridge during training 17.3.44.
LL670	From 115 Sqn. To 1668CU.
LL671 A2-B	FTR Berlin 23/24.12.43.
LL672 JI-C	FTR Magdeburg 21/22.1.44.
LL674 A2-D	Crashed on landing at Waterbeach following early return from Berlin 27.1.44.
LL677 JI-E	Damaged beyond repair during an operation to Le Havre 8.9.44.
LL678 JI-L	From 115 Sqn. FTR Gelsenkirchen 12/13.6.44.
LL679 JI-J	FTR Brunswick 14/15.1.44.
LL680 JI-H	From 115 Sqn. FTR Magdeburg 21/22.1.44.
LL681 JI-J	From 115 Sqn. FTR Leipzig 19/20.2.44.
LL683 JI-P	Force-landed in Hertfordshire on return from Nuremberg 31.3.44.

LL684 JI-B	FTR Frankfurt 22/23.3.44.
LL685 JI-G	From 115 Sqn. FTR Brunswick 14/15.1.44.
LL690 JI-J	FTR Valenciennes 15/16.6.44.
LL691 A2-D	From 115 Sqn. Crashed off Dover while training 1.5.44.
LL692 JI-C	From 115 Sqn. FTR Stuttgart 28/29.7.44.
LL695 JI-A	FTR Duisburg 21/22.5.44.
LL696 JI-A	FTR Nuremberg 30/31.3.44.
LL697 A2-B	Damaged beyond repair during an operation to Lens 11.8.44.
LL698 JI-J	FTR Nuremberg 30/31.3.44.
LL703 JI-L	Crash-landed at Graveley on return from Le Mans 20.5.44.
LL716 JI-G	From 115 Sqn. FTR Bois de Cassan 3.8.44.
LL726	From 115 Sqn. To 1668CU.
LL727 JI-C	FTR Maissy-Palaiseau 7/8.6.44.
LL728 JI-L	FTR Kiel 26/27.8.44.
LL730	To 115 Sqn.
LL731 JI-U	FTR Frankfurt 12/13.9.44.
LL732 JI-H	FTR Chambly 1/2.5.44.
LL733 JI-S	FTR Caen 30.7.44.
LL734	From 115 Sqn. To 1668CU.
LL738 JI-D	FTR Nuremberg 30/31.3.44.
LL739 JI-M	FTR Louvain 11/12.5.44.
LM180 JI-G	FTR Rüsselsheim 12/13.8.44.
LM181 JI-E	FTR Homburg 20/21.7.44.
LM206 JI-C	FTR Stuttgart 28/29.7.44.
LM258	To 218 Sqn.
LM265 JI-E	From 75 Sqn. FTR Rüsselsheim 12/13.8.44.
LM275	To 138 Sqn.
LM277 JI-F	FTR Calais 20.9.44.
LM285 JI-A	Crash-landed safely in Allied Holland on return from Bremen 22.4.45.
LM286 JI-F	FTR Homburg 20.11.44.
LM288	To BCIS 3.45.
LM627	To 1668CU.
LM684 JI-C	FTR Homburg 21.11.44.
LM685 JI-B	FTR Dortmund 3/4.2.45.
LM717	To GH Flt. at Feltwell.
LM719	To 1653CU.
LM724	To 1661CU.
LM727	To 103 Sqn.
LM728	To 75 Sqn.
LM733	To 75 Sqn.
LM734	To 115 Sqn.
LM735 JI-G	FTR Emmerich 7.10.44.
ME336	To 106 Sqn.
ME351/G	
ME354/G	To 83 Sqn.
ME355	
ME358/G	To 83 Sqn.
ME359	
ME363	To 83 Sqn.
ME364/G	To 83 Sqn.
ME365 JI-T	FTR Salzbergen 6.3.45.

ME367	To 35 Sqn.
ME380	
ME387/G	
ME422/G	
ME425/G	
ME482	
ME523 A2-G	Force-landed near Topcliffe Yorkshire while training 23.4.45.
ME529	
ME530/G	
ME535	
ME841	To 3LFS.
ME842	To 218 Sqn.
ME858 JI-J	FTR Homburg 20/21.7.44.
NE181	From 75 Sqn.
NF966	To 138 Sqn.
NF968	To 1668CU.
NG118	
NG121 JI-H	FTR Homburg 21.11.44.
NG141	Destroyed when PD325 blew up at Waterbeach 29.12.44.
NG142	
NG203	
NG236	From 195 Sqn.
NG298	
NG350 JI-C	FTR Osterfeld 11.12.44.
NN717	
NN718	From 12 Sqn. To 300 Sqn.
NN772 JI-C	FTR Wiesbaden 2/3.2.45.
NN773	To 75 Sqn.
NN775 JI-F	FTR Gelsenkirchen 5.3.45.
NN776	
NN781	
NN782	
PA186	To 149 Sqn.
PB142	
PB143 JI-B	FTR Stettin 29/30.8.44.
PB178 JI-P	Collided with ME695 of XV Sqn over Sussex on return from Villers-Bocage 30.6.44.
PB185 JI-F	FTR Stuttgart 24/25.7.44.
PB259	From SIU. To 218 Sqn.
PB291	To 218 Sqn.
PB419	
PB423	
PB426	
PB482	To 1653CU.
PB767	From 75 Sqn. To 115 Sqn.
PB789	To 115 Sqn.
PB798	To 115 Sqn.
PB902	To 149 Sqn.
PB906 JI-B	FTR Wanne-Eickel 16/17.1.45.
PD256	From 218 Sqn.
PD265 JI-G	FTR Homburg 21.11.44.
PD288	From 218 Sqn.
PD324	To 429 Sqn.

PD325 JI-L	Blew up at Waterbeach 29.12.44.
PD333	
PD334	
PD389	
PD439	From 218 Sqn.
RA541	From 75 Sqn.
RA599	
RA600	
RA601	
RA602	
RE116	
RE117	
RE120	
RE123	
RE137	
RE140	
RE158	
RE159	
RF230	Crashed in France while attempting an emergency return to Juvincourt during Operation Exodus 9.5.45.
RF231	
RF272	

620 SQUADRON

Motto: Dona ferentes adsumus (We are bringing gifts)   Codes QS, D4

No. 620 Squadron began life on the 17th of June 1943 as a 3 Group frontline bomber squadron equipped with Stirlings. Operations began almost immediately, and continued until the squadron was transferred to 38 Group for transport duties in November.

STATIONS

Chedburgh   17.06.43 to 23.11.43

COMMANDING OFFICERS

Wing Commander D H Lee DFC   17.06.43

AIRCRAFT

Stirling I	17.06.43 to 08.43
Stirling III	08.43 to 02.44
To 38 Group	23.11.43.

OPERATIONAL RECORD

Operations	Sorties	Aircraft Losses	% Losses
61	339	17	5.0

Category of Operations

Bombing	Mining
32	29

TABLE OF STATISTICS

Out of 28 squadrons in 3 Group

24th highest number of overall operations in 3 Group.
25th highest number of sorties in 3 Group.
19th highest number of aircraft operational losses in 3 Group.

Out of 12 Stirling squadrons in 3 Group

9th highest number of Stirling overall operations in 3 Group.
9th highest number of Stirling sorties in 3 Group.
8th highest number of Stirling operational losses in 3 Group.

AIRCRAFT HISTORIES

Stirling	From June 1943.
W7465	From 214 Sqn. To 1657CU.
BF466	From 214 Sqn. Crashed while landing at Chedburgh following an air-test 31.7.43.
BF503	From 90 Sqn. To 1665CU.
BF511 QS-A	From 214 Sqn. FTR Essen 25/26.7.43.
BF525	From 214 Sqn. To 1653CU.
BF573	From 149 Sqn. To 1653CU.
BF576 QS-F	From 149 Sqn. FTR Nuremberg 27/28.8.43.
BF580	From 149 Sqn.
BK690 QS-G	From 214Sq. FTR from mining sortie 6/7.8.43.
BK713 QS-E	From 149 Sqn. FTR Turin 12/13.8.43.
BK720 QS-Y	From 214 Sqn. Crashed on landing at Chedburgh on return from Wuppertal 25.6.43.
BK724 QS-Y	From 214 Sqn. Crashed in Suffolk after a collision with EF394 of 620 Sqn during a fighter affiliation exercise 2.7.43.
BK800 QS-Z	From 214 Sqn. FTR Wuppertal 24/25.6.43.
BK801 QS-X	From 214 Sqn. FTR Berlin 23/24.8.43.
BK802 QS-Z	From 214 Sqn. Abandoned over Berkshire during a cross-country exercise 20.10.43.
EE875 QS-A	From 149 Sqn. FTR Mülheim 22/23.6.43.
EE905 QS-S	FTR Remscheid 30/31.7.43.
EE906 QS-C	From 214 Sqn. FTR Essen 25/26.7.43.
EE942 QS-R	FTR Nuremberg 27/28.8.43.
EE945	From 7 Sqn. To 1665CU.
EE971	To 1665CU.
EF117	To 1665CU.
EF121	From 214 Sqn. To 1665CU.
EF134	To 1665CU.
EF136	Crashed on take-off from Chedburgh when bound for Boulogne 8.9.43.
EF143	To 1653CU.
EF149 QS-X	Crashed on take-off from Chedburgh while training 15.10.43.
EF159	To 90 Sqn.
EF189	To 1653CU.
EF197	To 1665CU.
EF203	To 1654CU.
EF336 QS-D	From 149 Sqn. Crashed on take-off at Chedburgh while training 29.7.43.

EF338	From 149 Sqn. To 1657CU.
EF394	From 214 Sqn. Collided with BK724 of 620 Sqn over Suffolk during a fighter affiliation exercise and crashed 2.7.43.
EF429	From 214 Sqn. To 196 Sqn.
EF433	From 214 Sqn. To 1665CU.
EF440	From 75 Sqn. To 1653CU.
EF442	From BDU. To 1653CU.
EF451 QS-D	FTR Nuremberg 27/28.8.43.
EF456	From 75 Sqn. To 1665CU.
EF457 QS-A	FTR Peenemünde 17/18.8.43.
EF470	To 295 Sqn.
EH886	From 214 Sqn. Force-landed at Chedburgh after an air-test 5.7.43.
EH891	From 214 Sqn. To 1665CU.
EH894	To 1665CU.
EH896 QS-P	FTR Remscheid 30/31.7.43.
EH924 QS-B	FTR Essen 25/26.7.43.
EH931 QS-O	FTR Mannheim 5/6.9.43.
EH945 QS-H	From 1657CU. FTR Hanover 27/28.9.43.
EH946 QS-P	From 75 Sqn. FTR Berlin 31.8/1.9.43.
EH983	To 1665CU.
LJ440	To 196 Sqn via 1665CU.
LJ445	To 1653CU.
LJ456	To 1665CU.
LJ459	To 1665CU.
LJ463	To 1665CU.
LK391	To 1665CU.
LK395	FTR from SOE sortie to France 5.2.44.
LK432	
LK433	From 190 Sqn.

622 SQUADRON

Motto: Bellamus Noctu (We make war by night)   Code GI

Formed on the 10th of August 1943 from C Flight of XV Squadron, 622 Squadron took part in Bomber Command's offences until the end of the war operating Lancasters throughout.

STATIONS

Mildenhall   10.08.43 to 15.08.45

COMMANDING OFFICERS

Squadron Leader J Martin	10.08.43 to 20.08.43
Wing Commander G H N Gibson DFC	20.08.43 to 01.02.44
Wing Commander I C K Swales DFC DFM	01.02.44 to 19.10.44
Wing Commander G K Buckingham	19.10.44 to 15.08.45

AIRCRAFT

Stirling III	10.08.43 to 12.43
Lancaster I/III	12.43 to 15.08.45

OPERATIONAL RECORD

Operations	Sorties	Aircraft Losses	% Losses
268	3,000	51	1.7

Category of Operations

Bombing	Mining
231	37

Stirling

Operations	Sorties	Aircraft Losses	% Losses
41	195	7	3.6

Category of Operations

Bombing	Mining
21	20

Lancaster

Operations	Sorties	Aircraft Losses	% Losses
210	2,805	44	1.6

Category of Operations

Bombing	Mining
210	17

TABLE OF STATISTICS

Out of 59 Lancaster squadrons

22nd highest number of Lancaster overall operations in Bomber Command.
27th highest number of Lancaster sorties in Bomber Command.
32nd highest number of Lancaster operational losses in Bomber Command.

Out of 28 Squadrons in 3 Group

9th highest number of overall operations in 3 Group.
8th highest number of sorties in 3 Group.
11th highest number of aircraft operational losses in 3 Group.

Out of 12 Stirling squadrons in 3 Group

10th equal (with 623 Sqn) highest number of Stirling overall operations in 3 Group.
10th highest number of Stirling sorties in 3 Group.
Lowest number of Stirling operational losses in 3 Group.

Out of 11 Lancaster squadrons in 3 Group

2nd highest number of Lancaster overall operations in 3 Group.
5th highest number of Lancaster sorties in 3 Group.
5th highest number of Lancaster operational losses in 3 Group.

AIRCRAFT HISTORIES

Stirling	From August 1943.
BF521 GI-H	From 15 Sqn. FTR Berlin 23/24.8.43.
BF533 LS-H	From 15 Sqn. Returned to 15 Sqn.
BF562 GI-H	From 214 Sqn. To 1661CU.
BK652 GI-E	From 15 Sqn. To 1665CU.
BK766 GI-T/G	From 15 Sqn. To 1661CU.
BK816 GI-X/B	From 15 Sqn. To 199 Sqn.

EE908 LS-V	From 15 Sqn. Returned to 15 Sqn.
EE954 LS-J/F	From 15 Sqn. Returned to 15 Sqn.
EF119 GI-Q	FTR Berlin 31.8/1.9.43.
EF122 GI-M	To 1661CU.
EF123 GI-A	Crashed in Cambridgeshire on return from Leverkusen 19.11.43.
EF126 GI-F/Q	Crashed on take-off from Mildenhall when bound for mining sortie 21.9.43.
EF127 GI-N	To 1661CU.
EF128 GI-D	FTR Mannheim 18/19.11.43.
EF132 GI-Q	To 1654CU.
EF144 GI-R	To 1654CU.
EF145 GI-D	To 1653CU.
EF150 GI-E	FTR Berlin 22/23.11.43.
EF151	To 1661CU.
EF153	To 199 Sqn.
EF154	To 199 Sqn.
EF161 GI-Z	To 15 Sqn.
EF177	To 15 Sqn.
EF186	To 15 Sqn.
EF208	To 1661CU.
EF217	To 75 Sqn.
EF351 GI-I	From 15 Sqn. To 1665CU.
EF391 GI-M	From 15 Sqn. To 1665CU.
EF460	From 15 Sqn. To 1653CU.
EF461 GI-C	From 15 Sqn. To 1661CU.
EF490 GI-F	From 15 Sqn. To 1651CU.
EH897 GI-Z	From 15 Sqn. To 570 Sqn.
EH921 GI-D	From 214 Sqn. To 1661CU.
EH956 GI-F	To 1653CU.
EH991 GI-P	FTR Hanover 27/28.9.43.
EH992 GI-O	To 1661CU.
EJ113 GI-Q	FTR Mannheim 18/19.11.43.
EJ114 GI-R	To 1654CU.
LJ444 GI-A	To 1653CU.
LJ451	From 15 Sqn. To 1653CU.
LJ455 GI-E	To 1653CU.
LK396	To 75 Sqn.
LK403	To 196 Sqn.
MZ264 GI-A	From 15 Sqn. FTR Berlin 31.8/1.9.43.
Lancaster	From December 1943.
L7576 GI-L/M/K	From 1660CU. FTR Stuttgart 28/29.7.44.
R5483 GI-D	From 1654CU. FTR Berlin 20/21.1.44.
R5490	From 1654CU. To 15 Sqn.
R5514 GI-O/T	From 1654CU. To 3LFS.
R5625 GI-B	From 83 Sqn. FTR Lisieux 9.7.44.
R5739	From 15 Sqn. Returned to 15 Sqn.
R5846	From 15 Sqn. To 75 Sqn.
R5906	From 15 Sqn. To 3LFS.
R5915 GI-P	From 9 Sqn via 1660CU. FTR Berlin 20/21.1.44.
W4158GI-U	From 9 Sqn. To 3LFS.
W4163GI-A	From 50 Sqn via 1667CU. Crash-landed at Mildenhall on return from Brunswick 14.1.44.

W4174	From 15 Sqn. Returned to 15 Sqn.
W4248GI-H/T	From 460 Sqn via 1667CU. To 3LFS.
W4268GI-A	From 44 Sqn via 1654CU. FTR Berlin 15/16.2.44.
W4272GI-C	From 15 Sqn. FTR Berlin 15/16.2.44.
W4885GI-N	From 1662CU. To 15 Sqn.
W4980	From 1656CU. To 15 Sqn.
ED364 GI-Q	From 207 Sqn via 1654CU. FTR Berlin 30/31.1.44.
ED383	From 1656CU. To 15 Sqn.
ED425 GI-F	From 97 Sqn via 1660 and 1654CU. To 75 Sqn.
ED430 GI-A	From 50 Sqn. To 3LFS.
ED437 GI-D	From 617 Sqn via 1661CU. To 3LFS.
ED474 GI-L/S	From 15 Sqn via NTU and 1667CU. To 3LFS.
ED610	From 1656 and 1662CU. To 15 Sqn.
ED619 GI-M/T	From A.V.Roe. FTR Nuremberg 30/31.3.44.
ED624 GI-G	From 1660CU. FTR Berlin 27/28.1.44.
ED631 GI-B	From 1662CU. To 617 Sqn.
ED727	From 15 Sqn. To 5LFS.
ED808 GI-O/R/U	From 15 Sqn. FTR Laon 10/11.4.44.
HK545	To 115 Sqn.
HK614GI-R	From 15 Sqn. To 46MU.
HK615GI-Z	From 15 Sqn. To 138 Sqn.
HK616GI-W	From 15 Sqn. To 44 Sqn.
HK617GI-Q	From 15 Sqn. FTR Mönchengladbach 1.2.45.
HK621GI-P/O	FTR Koblenz (crash-landed in France) 5/6.11.44.
HK623GI-F	
HK626	To 15 Sqn.
HK628GI-X	
HK644GI-D	FTR Koblenz 6/7.11.44.
HK646GI-M	
HK651GI-B	
HK700GI-Y	
HK769GI-D	FTR Cologne 2.3.45.
HK770GI-T	FTR Bremen 22.4.45.
HK787GI-F	
HK805GI-H	
JA876 GI-E	From 106 Sqn. To 1661CU.
LL782 GI-H	FTR Trappes 31.5/1.6.44.
LL793 GI-Q	FTR Duisburg 21/22.5.44.
LL802 GI-M	Collided with LM167(622 Sqn) over Essex while training 20.9.44.
LL803 GI-G/M/S	FTR Homberg 2.11.44.
LL812 GI-C/Z	FTR Gelsenkirchen 12/13.6.44.
LL828 GI-J	FTR Stuttgart 15/16.3.44.
LL859 GI-N/U/Q	FTR Homberg 20/21.7.44.
LL885 GI-J	Completed 113 operations.
LM108GI-N	FTR Angers 28/29.5.44.
LM138GI-N	FTR L'Hey 23/24.6.44.
LM167GI-N	From 15 Sqn. Collided with LL802 (622 Sqn) over Essex while training 20.9.44.
LM235GI-B/G	
LM241GI-Q	FTR Rüsselsheim 25/26.8.44.
LM282 To 218 Sqn.	
LM283GI-O	FTR Stuttgart 19/20.10.44.
LM291GI-F	FTR Frankfurt 12/13.9.44.

LM442GI-P	FTR Schweinfurt 24/25.2.44.
LM443GI-T/G	To 1653CU.
LM466GI-P	FTR Rüsselsheim 12/13.8.44.
LM477GI-L	FTR Stuttgart 24/25.7.44.
LM491GI-C/E	FTR Massy-Palaiseau 7/8.6.44.
LM511GI-E/C	FTR from mining sortie 11/12.9.44.
LM577GI-E	To 218 Sqn.
LM593	From 75 Sqn. Returned to 75 Sqn.
LM595GI-D/O	FTR Homberg 20/21.7.44.
ME383	
ME693GI-F	FTR Karlsruhe 24/25.4.44.
ME736GI-J	To 103 Sqn.
ND765 GI-M/O/C	FTR Massy-Palaiseau 7/8.6.44.
ND767 GI-D	FTR Nuremberg 30/31.3.44.
ND781 GI-R	FTR Friedrichshafen 27/28.4.44.
ND926 GI-D	FTR Trappes 31.5/1.6.44.
NE146 GI-F	FTR Stuttgart 24/25.7.44.
NF915 GI-U	FTR Bonn (Hangelar airfield) 24/25.12.44.
NF939 GI-D	FTR from mining sortie 6/7.1.45.
NF964 GI-L	FTR Dortmund 3.1.45.
NF965 GI-S	FTR Frankfurt 12/13.9.44.
NG299GI-O	To 149 Sqn.
NG300GI-T	
NG301	
NG447GI-U	FTR Kiel 9/10.4.45.
NN709 GI-H	
PA164 GI-P	
PA218 GI-K/L	
PA285 GI-O	FTR Regensburg 20.4.45.
PB795 GI-V	
PB802	To 15 Sqn.
PB819	
PD219 GI-L	To 1654CU.
PD225 GI-G	
PD228 GI-A	
PD229 GI-K	To 218 Sqn.
PD285	From 15 Sqn.
PD332 GI-N	
PD366 GI-E	

623 SQUADRON

No Motto: Code IC

No. 623 Squadron was formed on the 10th of August 1943 with a nucleus provided
by 218 Squadron, and began operations that very night. A decision to increase
the complement of conversion units led to a demand on Stirlings, and the squadron
was disbanded on the 6th of December 1943.

STATIONS

Downham Market   10.08.43 to 06.12.43

COMMANDING OFFICERS

Wing Commander E J Little DFC	10.08.43 to 01.09.43
Wing Commander G T Wynne-Powell	01.09.43 to 28.11.43
Wing Commander F M Milligan AFC	29.11.43 to 06.12.43

AIRCRAFT

Stirling III	10.08.43 to 06.12.43
Disbanded	06.12.43

OPERATIONAL STATISTICS

Operations	Sorties	Aircraft Losses	% Losses
41	150	10	6.7

Category of Operations

Bombing	Mining
19	22

TABLE OF STATISTICS

Out of 28 squadrons in 3 Group

26th highest number of overall operations in 3 Group.
27th highest number of sorties in 3 Group.
24th highest number of aircraft operational losses in 3 Group.

Out of 12 Stirling squadrons in 3 Group

10th equal (with 622 Sqn) highest number of Stirling overall operations in 3 Group.
Lowest number of Stirling sorties in 3 Group.
11th highest number of Stirling operational losses in 3 Group.

AIRCRAFT HISTORIES

Stirling	From August 1943.
BF568	From 218 Sqn. To 214 Sqn.
BK727	From 218 Sqn. To 214 Sqn.
BK803	From 218 Sqn. To 1654CU.
EE876	From 214 Sqn. To 1654CU.
EE899	From 214 Sqn. To 1654CU.
EE909 IC-H	From 218 Sqn. FTR Nuremberg 27/28.8.43.
EE949 IC-G	From 218 Sqn. FTR Berlin 31.8/1.9.43.
EE966	From 218 Sqn. To 299 Sqn.
EF139	To 218 Sqn.
EF155 IC-O	FTR Mannheim 18/19.11.43.
EF156 IC-E	FTR from mining sortie 7/8.11.43.
EF157	To 1654CU.
EF158 IC-S	FTR Kassel 3/4.10.43.
EF194	To 1654CU.
EF199	To 214 Sqn.
EF204	To 1654CU.
EF252	To 1657CU.
EF489	From 218 Sqn. To 1654CU.

EF493	To 214 Sqn.
EF499 IC-K	Crashed on landing at Downham Market after early return from mining sortie 25.9.43.
EH878 IC-I	From 218 Sqn. FTR Mannheim 5/6.9.43.
EH925 IC-C	From 218 Sqn. FTR Berlin 23/24.8.43.
EH957	To 1654CU.
EH979	To 1654CU.
EH994 IC-P	FTR Kassel 3/4.10.43.
EJ121	To 1654CU.
EJ123	To 214 Sqn.
EJ124	To 214 Sqn.
LJ443	To 1654CU.
LJ450	To 1654CU.
LJ454 IC-E	FTR Mannheim 18/19.11.43.
LJ477	To 214 Sqn.
LJ482	To 1651CU.
LJ509	To 214 Sqn.
LJ521	To 214 Sqn.
LK387 IC-P	To 199 Sqn and back. FTR from mining sortie 4/5.12.43.

Key to Abbreviations

A&AEE	Aeroplane and Armaments Experimental Establishment.
AA	Anti-Aircraft fire.
AACU	Anti-Aircraft Cooperation Unit.
AAS	Air Armament School.
AASF	Advance Air Striking Force.
AAU	Aircraft Assembly Unit.
ACM	Air Chief Marshal.
ACSEA	Air Command South-East Asia.
AFDU	Air Fighting Development Unit.
AFEE	Airborne Forces Experimental Unit.
AFTDU	Airborne Forces Tactical Development Unit.
AGS	Air Gunners School.
AMDP	Air Members for Development and Production.
AOC	Air Officer Commanding.
AOS	Air Observers School.
ASRTU	Air-Sea Rescue Training Unit.
ATTDU	Air Transport Tactical Development Unit.
AVM	Air Vice-Marshal.
BAT	Beam Approach Training.
BCBS	Bomber Command Bombing School.
BCDU	Bomber Command Development Unit.
BCFU	Bomber Command Film Unit.
BCIS	Bomber Command Instructors School.
BDU	Bombing Development Unit.
BSTU	Bomber Support Training Unit.
CF	Conversion Flight.
CFS	Central Flying School.
CGS	Central Gunnery School.
C-in-C	Commander in Chief.
CNS	Central Navigation School.
CO	Commanding Officer.
CRD	Controller of Research and Development.
CU	Conversion Unit.
DGRD	Director General for Research and Development.
EAAS	Empire Air Armament School.
EANS	Empire Air Navigation School.
ECDU	Electronic Countermeasures Development Unit.
ECFS	Empire Central Flying School.
ETPS	Empire Test Pilots School.
F/L	Flight Lieutenant.
Flt	Flight.
F/O	Flying Officer.
FPP	Ferry Pilots School.
F/S	Flight Sergeant.
FTR	Failed to Return.

FTU	Ferry Training Unit.
G/C	Group Captain.
Gp	Group.
HCU	Heavy Conversion Unit.
HGCU	Heavy Glider Conversion Unit.
LFS	Lancaster Finishing School.
MAC	Mediterranean Air Command.
MTU	Mosquito Training Unit.
MU	Maintenance Unit.
NTU	Navigation Training Unit.
OADU	Overseas Aircraft Delivery Unit.
OAPU	Overseas Aircraft Preparation Unit.
OTU	Operational Training Unit.
P/O	Pilot Officer.
PTS	Parachute Training School.
RAE	Royal Aircraft Establishment.
SGR	School of General Reconnaissance.
Sgt	Sergeant.
SHAEF	Supreme Headquarters Allied Expeditionary Force.
SIU	Signals Intelligence Unit.
S/L	Squadron Leader.
SOC	Struck off Charge.
SOE	Special Operations Executive.
Sqn	Squadron.
TF	Training Flight.
TFU	Telecommunications Flying Unit.
W/C	Wing Commander.
Wg	Wing.
WIDU	Wireless Intelligence Development Unit.
W/O	Warrant Officer.

Bibliography

Air War over France. Robert Jackson. Ian Allan.
Als Deutschlands Dämme Brachen. Helmut Euler. Motor Buch Verlag.
At First Sight. Alan B Webb.
Avenging in the shadows. Ron James. Abington Books.
Avro Lancaster. The definitive record. Harry Holmes. Airlife.
Avro Manchester. Robert Kirby. Midland Counties Publications.
Battle-Axe Blenheims. Stuart R Scott. Budding Books.
Battle Under the Moon. Jack Currie. Air Data.
Beam Bombers. Michael Cumming. Sutton Publishing.
Beware of the Dog at War. John Ward.
Black Swan. Sid Finn. Newton.
Bomber Command. Max Hastings. Pan.
Bomber Command War Diaries. Martin Middlebrook/Chris Everett. Viking.
Bomber Group at War. Chaz Bowyer. Book Club Associates.
Bomber Harris. Dudley Saward. Cassel.
Bomber Harris. Charles Messenger. Arms and Armour Press.
Bomber Intelligence. W E Jones. Midland Counties Publications.
Bomber Squadron at War. Andrew Brookes. Ian Allan.
Bomber Squadrons at War. Geoff D Copeman. Sutton Publishing.
Bombers over Berlin. Alan W Cooper. Patrick Stephens Ltd.
Bombing Colours 1937–1973. Michael J F Bowyer. Patrick Stephens Ltd.
Confounding the Reich. Martin W Bowman/Tom Cushing. Patrick Stephens Ltd.
De Havilland Mosquito Crash Log. David J Smith. Midland Counties Publications.
Despite the Elements. 115 Squadron History. Private.
Diary of RAF Pocklington. M Usherwood. Compaid Graphics.
Each Tenacious. A G Edgerley. Square One Publications.
Feuersturm über Hamburg. Hans Brunswig. Motor Buch Verlag.
Forever Strong. Norman Franks. Random Century.
From Hull, Hell and Halifax. Chris Blanchett. Midland Counties Publications.
Gordon's Tour with Shiney 10. J Gordon Shirt. Compaid Graphics.
Great Raids. Vols 1 and 2. Air Commodore John Searby DSO DFC. Nutshell Press.
Halifax at War. Brian J Rapier. Ian Allan.
Hamish. The story of a Pathfinder. Group Captain T G Mahaddie. Ian Allan.
Heavenly Days. Group Captain James Pelly-Fry DSO. Crecy Books.
In Brave Company. W R Chorley. P A Chorley.
Joe. The Autobiography of a Trenchard Brat. Wing Commander J Northrop DSO
    DFC AFC. Square One Publications.
Lancaster at War. Vols 1, 2, 3. Mike Garbett/Brian Goulding. Ian Allan.
Lancaster. The Story of a Famous Bomber. Bruce Robertson. Harleyford Publications
    Ltd.
Lancaster to Berlin. Walter Thompson DFC*. Goodall Publications.
Low Attack. John de L Wooldridge. Crecy.
Massacre over the Marne. Oliver Clutton-Brock. Patrick Stephens Ltd.
Master Airman. Alan Bramson. Airlife.
Melbourne Ten. Brian J Rapier. Air Museum Publications (York) Ltd.

Mission Completed. Sir Basil Embry. Four Square Books.

Mosquito. C Martin Sharp and Michael J F Bowyer. Crecy.

Night Fighter. C F Rawnsley/Robert Wright. Collins.

Night Flyer. Squadron Leader Lewis Brandon DSO DFC. Goodall Publications.

Night Intruder. Jeremy Howard-Williams. Purnell Book Services.

No Moon Tonight. Don Charlwood. Goodall Publications.

On The Wings Of The Morning. RAF Bottesford 1941-45. Vincent Holyoak.

On Wings of War. A history of 166 Squadron. Jim Wright.

Only Owls And Bloody Fools Fly At Night. Group Captain Tom Sawyer DFC. Goodall Publications.

Pathfinder. AVM D C T Bennett. Goodall Publications.

Pathfinder Force. Gordon Musgrove. MacDonald and Janes.

Reap the Whirlwind. Dunmore and Carter. Crecy.

Royal Air Force Aircraft Serial Numbers. All Volumes. Air-Britain.

Royal Air Force Bomber Command Losses. Vols 1, 2, 3, 4, 5, 6. W R Chorley. Midland Counties Publications.

Silksheen. Geoff D Copeman. Midland Counties Publications.

Snaith Days. K S Ford. Compaid Graphics.

Start im Morgengrauen. Werner Girbig. Motor Buch Verlag.

Stirling Wings. Jonathon Falconer. Alan Sutton Publications.

Strike Hard. A bomber airfield at war. John B Hilling. Alan Sutton Publishing.

Sweeping the Skies. David Gunby. Pentland Press.

The Avro Lancaster. Francis K Mason. Aston Publications.

The Berlin Raids. Martin Middlebrook. Viking Press.

The Dambusters Raid. John Sweetman. Arms and Armour Press.

The Halifax File. Air-Britain.

The Hampden File. Harry Moyle. Air-Britain.

The Handley Page Halifax. K A Merrick. Aston Press.

The Hornets' Nest. History of 100 Squadron RAF 1917–1994. Arthur White. Square One Publications.

The Lancaster File. J J Halley. Air-Britain.

The Other Battle. Peter Hinchliffe. Airlife.

The Pedulum and the Scythe. Ken Marshall. Air Research Publications.

The Starkey Sacrifice. Michael Cumming. Sutton Publishing Ltd.

The Stirling Bomber. Michael J F Bowyer. Faber.

The Stirling File. Bryce Gomersall. Air-Britain.

The Wellington Bomber. Chaz Bowyer. William Kimber.

The Whitley File. R N Roberts. Air-Britain.

The Squadrons of the Royal Air Force. James J Halley. Air-Britain.

They Led the Way. Michael P Wadsworth. Highgate.

To See The Dawn Breaking. W R Chorley.

Valiant Wings. Norman Franks. Crecy.

Wellington. The Geodetic Giant. Martin Bowman. Airlife.

White Rose Base. Brian J Rapier. Aero Litho Company (Lincoln) Ltd.

Wings of Night. Alexander Hamilton. Crecy.

2 Group RAF. A Complete History. Michael J F Bowyer. Crecy.

101 Squadron. Special Operations. Richard Alexander.

207 Squadron RAF Langar 1942–43. Barry Goodwin/Raymond Glynne-Owen. Quacks Books.

408 Squadron History. The Hangar Bookshelf. Canada.

Other *Titles* by this Author

RAF Bomber Command Squadron Profile Series

Squadron Numbers
7, 9, 10, 12, XV, 35, 40, 44, 49, 50, 51, 57, 61, 75 (NZ), 77, 78, 83, 90, 97, 100, 101, 102, 103, 105, 106, 115, 138, 139, 144, 149, 150, 153, 156, 189, 207, 214, 218, 405, 408, 415, 419, 420, 424, 425, 426, 427, 428, 429, 431, 432, 433, 434, 460, 467, 550, 578, 617, 619, 622, 625, 626, 627, 630

Mosquito Squadrons of the Pathfinder Force

Operational Statistics of Bomber Command and its Squadrons

Dambusters

Dambuster Crash Sites

5 Group Bomber Command